English Writing and India, 1600–1920

This book explores the formations and configurations of British colonial discourse on India through a reading of prose narratives of the 1600–1920 period.

Arguing that colonial discourse often relied on aesthetic devices in order to describe and assert a degree of narrative control over Indian landscape, Pramod Nayar demonstrates how aesthetics furnished both a vocabulary and representational modes for the British to construct particular images of India. Aesthetics helped not only to describe the landscape, but also to discursively 'prepare' it for colonial projects and intervention. Aesthetics was thus a crucial anterior moment in the rhetoric of colonial India – it narrated, and it colonized.

Looking specifically at the aesthetic modes of the marvellous, the monstrous, the sublime, the picturesque and the luxuriant, Nayar marks the shift in the rhetoric – from the exploration narratives in the proto-colonial age of mercantile exploration to that of the 'shikar' memoirs of the late nineteenth and early twentieth century's extreme exotic. *English Writing and India* provides an important new study of colonial aesthetics, even as it extends current scholarship on the modes of early British representations of new lands and cultures.

Pramod K. Nayar teaches at the University of Hyderabad, India. His recent publications in literary and cultural studies include *The Great Uprising: India, 1857* (2007), *The Penguin 1857 Reader* (2007), *Reading Culture: Theory, Praxis, Politics* (2006) and *Virtual Worlds: Culture and Politics in the Age of Cybertechnology* (2004).

Postcolonial Literatures

Edited in collaboration with the Centre for Colonial and Postcolonial Studies, University of Kent at Canterbury, this series presents a wide range of research into postcolonial literatures by specialists in the field. Volumes will concentrate on writers and writing originating in previously (or presently) colonized areas, and will include material from non-anglophone as well as anglophone colonies and literatures. The series will also include collections of important essays from older journals, and re-issues of classic texts on postcolonial subjects. Routledge is pleased to invite proposals for new books in the series. Interested authors should contact Lyn Innes or Rod Edmond at the Centre for Colonial and Postcolonial Studies, University of Kent at Canterbury, or Routledge's Commissioning Editor for Literature.

The series comprises three strands.

Routledge Research in Postcolonial Literatures is a forum for innovative new research intended for a specialist readership. Published in hardback, titles include:

1. *Magical Realism in West African Fiction: Seeing with a Third Eye* by Brenda Cooper
2. *The Postcolonial Jane Austen* edited by You-Me Park and Rajeswari Sunder Rajan
3. *Contemporary Caribbean Women's Poetry: Making Style* by Denise deCaires Narain
4. *African Literature, Animism and Politics* by Caroline Rooney
5. *Caribbean-English Passages: Intertextuality in a Postcolonial Tradition* by Tobias Döring
6. *Islands in History and Representation* edited by Rod Edmond and Vanessa Smith
7. *Civility and Empire: Literature and Culture in British India, 1822–1922* by Anindyo Roy
8. *Women Writing the West Indies, 1804–1939: 'A Hot Place, Belonging To Us'* by Evelyn O'Callaghan
9. *Postcolonial Pacific Writing: Representations of the body* by Michelle Keown
10. *Writing Woman, Writing Place: Contemporary Australian and South African Fiction* by Sue Kossew
11. *Literary Radicalism in India: Gender, Nation and the Transition to Independence* by Priyamvada Gopal
12. *Postcolonial Conrad: Paradoxes of Empire* by Terry Collits
13. *American Pacificism: Oceania in the U.S. Imagination* by Paul Lyons

Postcolonial Literatures makes available in paperback important work in the field. Hardback editions of these titles are also available, some published earlier in the *Routledge Research* strand of the series. Titles in paperback include:

Readings in Postcolonial Literatures offers collections of important essays from journals or classic texts in the field. Titles include:

English Writing and India, 1600–1920

Colonizing aesthetics

Pramod K. Nayar

Routledge
Taylor & Francis Group

LONDON AND NEW YORK

First published 2008
by Routledge
2 Park Square, Milton Park, Abingdon, Oxon OX14 4RN

Simultaneously published in the USA and Canada
by Routledge
270 Madison Ave, New York, NY 10016

Routledge is an imprint of the Taylor & Francis Group, an informa business

© 2008 Pramod K. Nayar

Typeset in Baskerville by
Book Now Ltd, London
Printed and bound in Great Britain by
Biddles Ltd, King's Lynn, Norfolk

British Library Cataloguing in Publication Data
A catalogue record for this book is available from the British Library

Library of Congress Cataloging in Publication Data
Nayar, Pramod K.
English writing and India, 1600–1920: colonizing aesthetics / Pramod K. Nayar.
    p. cm. – (Postcolonial literatures; 18)
Includes bibliographical references and index.
1. English literature–History and criticism. 2. India–In literature.
3. Authors, English–Aesthetics. 4. National characteristics, English, in literature. 5. Imperialism in literature. 6. Colonies in literature.
7. Exoticism in literature. 8. Narration (Rhetoric) I. Title.

PR149.I6N39 2007
820.9–dc22   2007011778

ISBN10: 0–415–40919–5 (hbk)
ISBN10: 0–203–93100–9 (ebk)

ISBN13: 978–0–415–40919–3 (hbk)
ISBN13: 978–0–203–93100–4 (ebk)

Contents

Acknowledgements

This book has sailed in and out of years and spaces. It has benefited hugely from advice, suggestions, references from many people, spread over many universities and geographical sites. It is a privilege to be able to say: 'here, it's done', and thank them while saying so. However, a project of thanking everybody who has contributed to this work runs the unavoidable risk of drowning at least a few in the anonymity of the alphabet: several, perhaps, may have been missed out here, and my sincere apologies for the same.

In the United Kingdom: Kate Teltscher defined the field for me with her work. Her comments on early versions contributed greatly to the eventual shape of the book. Nigel Leask (who generously shared his 'imperial picturesque' chapter with me in its incipient form), Chris Bayly (who put me on to Arthur Young and the Board of Agriculture documents), Anthony Hopkins and Gordon Johnson at Cambridge University offered suggestions and comments. At Canterbury, Lyn Innes' special affection – and those coffee breaks – made such a huge difference to the months there. Also at Canterbury, Malcolm Andrews, Rod Edmond and Martin Scofield deserve special mention for their time. At Nottingham, Tim Youngs, whose probing questions at my seminar proved extremely productive in thinking through the question of aesthetics and colonialism. Elleke Boehmer, for her invitation to speak at Nottingham Trent, and her interest in my work over the years. Patrick and Jen Williams were gracious hosts on my trip to Nottingham. Indira Ghose, from our first meeting at her Oxford lectures, has been a valuable friend over the years, even as her own work in colonial travel writing in India has proved to be inspirational.

In the United States: Laura Brown at Cornell, for her infectious enthusiasm for the eighteenth century and her own fascinating work on 'cultural fables'. Jonathan Culler, for smoothing the process of affiliation and stay.

I am grateful to the Smuts Memorial Fund and the Charles Wallace Trust, which secured my stay in the United Kingdom, and the Fulbright Senior Fellowship that facilitated the months at Cornell. The University of Hyderabad granted me a year's leave to avail myself of the Fulbright, and thus gave me the time to finish this work, for which I am very grateful.

In Hyderabad figures most closely associated with this project (frequently without their knowledge) include the following. Mohan Ramanan introduced me to English colonial writing. Sudhakar Marathe, with characteristic generosity, gave time, material and ideas. Narayana Chandran has, by speaking of (among other things) the 'social life of English in India', provoked me to rethink colonialism and its rhetorics. He also deserves special mention for his detailed comments on my published 'imperial sublime' essay. Sachidananda Mohanty invited me for my first travel writing conference. Probal Dasgupta has for a long time remained an inspiring conversationalist and fellow-punster in arms. Anindita Mukhopadhyay's stimulating conversations in the more recent past have helped tremendously.

This work could not have been possible without the kind efficiency of the people in many libraries. It is a pleasure to mention, in particular:

The staff of the excellent Cambridge University Library (particularly its Rare Books Room) and the South Asia Studies Centre, and the phenomenal British Library, London (and its India Office section) for their efficiency.

The staff of the Elmer Bobst library, New York University, for helping a confused library user find material (and resolve the intricacies of the photocopying machine, which seemed to develop into an alien intelligence each time I wanted something in a hurry).

Soma Ghosh and Dinesh at the Salar Jung Museum Library (Hyderabad); the staff of the Nehru Memorial Museum Library (New Delhi); the National Archives of India (New Delhi); the Andhra Pradesh State Archives (Hyderabad); and that space which has continued to remain for many of us, despite its various metamorphoses, the 'ASRC' (Hyderabad).

I would like to thank the editors and referees of the journals in which parts of this book first appeared: *Journal for Early Modern Cultural Studies*, *Journal of British Studies*, *Studies in Travel Writing* and *Prose Studies*.

Audiences at my talks in various places have queried, commented and advised. All this has greatly enriched my work (the flaws and deficiencies I acquired on my own): audiences at Nottingham Trent (UK), University of Kent at Canterbury (UK), Roanoke College (Virginia, USA), South Asia Institute (Columbia University, NY), the conference on Aesthetic Encounters (2001, University of Kuwait), Santa Clara University (US), University of Houston Downtown (US), University of Texas at El Paso (US), South Asia Programme (Cornell University, US).

I gratefully acknowledge the editorial board of the Routledge Studies in Postcolonial Literature, Lyn Innes, Rod Edmond and Caroline Rooney, for their interest in the project. The referees of the proposal, who offered valuable suggestions and comments, deserve special mention – this book is richer because of their advice. At Routledge, my thanks to Liz Thompson, Polly Dodson and Gabrielle Orcutt. Thanks also to Christine Firth for her copy-editing the work with precision and care.

Friendships over these many years and locations have contributed in great measure to my work. I would like to thank: Mawuna Quayson and Camena

Guneratne for their friendship during the stay in Cambridge; Walter Perera for his unrelenting jollity (even in the Ithaca winter) at Cornell; Kakoli-Bharat and Divya-Anish at Cornell for their friendship and Kavita whose visits made the Cornell stay even more unforgetable; Ajeet and Panikkar, who remain friends despite my schedule.

Anna Kurian – for her critical comments, friendship, unstinting affection and comradeship, no number of 'thank yous' suffice for honouring me thus.

My parents, the often bewildered witnesses to my crazy schedules: for their support, prayers and love beyond belief – can I even begin to thank you?

It is, as always, a pleasure to acknowledge the enduring affection of Sri Anil and Smt Neelima Khadakkar, especially for indulging me thoroughly during my vacations. To Neeraj and Claire, ever-reliable suppliers of books, and affection: a very big thank you. Nandini and Pranav, first victims of my work schedule: I am grateful for your monumental patience, steely support and unalloyed affection. Let us hope the next book will have an easier schedule!

Some of the chapters have appeared previously in different versions. Chapter 1 appeared as 'Marvelous excesses: English travel writing and India, 1608–1727', in *Journal of British Studies* 44.2 (2005): 213–38 and 'The "discourse of difficulty": English travel writing and India, 1600–1720', in *Prose Studies* 26.3 (2003): 357–94. Chapter 3 appeared as 'The imperial sublime: English travel writing and India, 1750–1820', in *Journal for Early Modern Cultural Studies* 2.2 (2002): 57–99. I am grateful to the University of Chicago Press for allowing me to reprint sections of the article from *Journal of British Studies*, Taylor and Francis (www.tandf.co.uk) for the article from *Prose Studies* and Indiana University Press for the article from *Journal for Early Modern Cultural Studies*.

Introduction
Aesthetic negotiations

This book is on the aesthetics of colonial discourse, with specific reference to English writings on India. It moves across non-fictional genres as diverse as official reports, travel accounts, memoirs and letters from the early moments of England's 'encounter' with India in the seventeenth century to the 1920s. Aesthetics, this book argues, furnishes a descriptive vocabulary that enables the English traveller to cast India in ways that call for particular kinds of colonial or imperial responses.

If discourse, in Hayden White's (1978: 2) terms, 'constitutes the objects that it pretends only to describe realistically and to analyze objectively', colonial discourse constructs subjects in order to dominate. Colonial discourse is, in Peter Hulme's (1992: 2) succinct formulation, 'an ensemble of linguistically based practices unified by their common deployment in the management of colonial relationships'. Colonial discourse is not simply a set of linguistic devices. On the contrary, they 'actually do much of the crucially important work of colonialism' (Greenblatt 1993: xvi). *Colonizing Aesthetics* explores how different aesthetic approaches in colonial discourse construct particular images of India as a preliminary to English 'interpretation', governance and alteration. The informing assumption therefore is that aesthetic modes and their narrative structures act as contexts for and narrative methods of colonial 'action', often suggesting a rhetorical-textual control over India.

Travel in foreign and alien spaces was often accompanied by writing that explained and documented the new. In fact, as Mary Fuller (1995: 2–7) has shown, travel and writing have always gone together. The vast corpus of English writings on India is an archive of travel, documentation and assorted colonial ideologies. This book is interested in the languages of description, particularly of Indian landscape, in English writings, and demonstrates how these languages adapted aesthetic and literary conventions of the time. Representations of the landscape have always encoded political interests and power relations (Barrell 1985; Bermingham 1986; Helgerson 1986; Fulford 1996, among others). In the case of European travellers in Asia and Africa, as Mary Pratt's (1992) work has shown, the rhetoric of landscape description and mapping was clearly of imperial intent. This book argues that colonial narrative and its concomitant ideology were mediated by and facilitated through aesthetics.

Early modern travel literature has been variously seen as attempts to define

England (and Europe's) sense of nationhood, the problems of the body politic and the identity of an emergent bourgeois (Helgerson 1992; Hadfield 1998; Lim 1998; Linton 1998; Scanlan 1999). The exploration and trading voyages might have been driven primarily by the needs of capital investment rather than political aims during a time of cultural and national xenophobia (Canny 1998; Harris 1998, 2004). Thus the early encounters with the Orient and India may not have been overtly colonial in nature. However, critics have argued for the existence of a colonial and Orientalist imaginary in early modern Europe (Raman 2002; Barbour 2003). There is, in Jyotsna Singh's (1996) terms, a 'colonizing imagination' through which the stage is set for empire later in the eighteenth century (Singh 1996: 2–3, 28). This book aligns itself with such an interpretation: seventeenth-century England, I believe, was informed by colonial or imperial fantasies. The troping of India in certain ways seem to suggest a proto-colonial imaginary, where texts by Edward Terry or John Ovington encode the desire for empire and function as 'allegories of desire' (Scanlan 1999).

India was always central to European 'fantasy' and imagining of the other or new worlds. By the end of the seventeenth century, sixteen major separate accounts appeared on the Mughal empire. Ten more reported extensively on it and other parts of Asia (see Lach and Van Kley 1990). English newspapers regularly carried advertisements for voyages or travelogues, globes, and maps of 'new' areas being 'discovered', suggesting an avid readership for travel news and writing.[1] The English 'encounter' with India starting from the last decades of the sixteenth century generated a massive imperial archive: Richmond Barbour (2003: 8) informs us that in the British Library's India Office, East India Company material occupies nine miles of shelving (see also Richards 1993).

The many genres of English writings on India that this book deals with create a vast 'network of intertextual relations', as Kate Teltscher (1997: 3) in her field-defining work puts it. Faced with radical difference and the incomprehensible, the English traveller sought a degree of assurance through rhetorical control. Teltscher (1997: 14–15) thus discerns an 'editorial struggle' in early English writings about India, a struggle that suggests anxiety, vulnerability and uncertainty (see also Leask 2002: 16). While Teltscher (1997) is correct in pointing to the search for narrative control, she pays less attention to one particular device used to attain this control: aesthetics. Indeed, except for a few select studies, the aesthetics of pre-colonial and colonial India has not been scrutinized with any degree of rigour.[2]

Gerhard Stilz (2002: 85) has persuasively demonstrated that aesthetics 'informed colonial travellers overseas with the perceptions and discursive strategies of coping with alien realities'. Aesthetics and rhetoric invent paradigms for viewing the world and serve serious epistemological purposes. Travel narratives themselves are a literary phenomenon, as K.K. Dyson (1978: 2) has argued, and employ aesthetic devices in the narrative. In the colonial travel narrative the descriptive vocabulary not only facilitated an *immediate* rhetorical control over Indian space, but also functioned as a ground-clearing device for an avowedly colonial discourse of the *later* years of British occupation of India. Aesthetics is here a colonial 'project'. It is 'a socially transformative endeavour that is localized, politicized and partial, yet also engendered by longer historical developments and ways of narrating them', but also with an interest in creating something new (Thomas 1994: 105). Further, aesthetics understood as 'projects' are 'willed' by the English 'agent', even though it may not be apparent to them. 'Projects' presuppose a 'particular imagination of the social situation . . . and a diagnosis of what is lacking, that can be rectified by intervention' (Thomas 1994: 106). Aesthetics thus had an interventionary and transformative role in the colonial narrative of travel. It permeated discursive formations of the Other, subjects, spaces and the empire in English colonial writings on India. It was, in other words, a colonizing aesthetics.

My purpose in this book is to show how particular aesthetic modes trope India in specific ways in order to demonstrate English control and power over it. The various tropings of India were *transformative* in nature, proposing particular roles for the English in India. In the early, mercantile age it helps English rhetorical or narrative control over Indian variety and vastness. The later aesthetics of the picturesque and the sublime map a colonial shift from a primitive, poor and desolate India to an altered and 'improved', 'Englished' one.

Aesthetics provided the English traveller with the vocabulary to describe varied phenomena and events. Monsoons and agriculture, people, architecture, religious beliefs, processions and gatherings, marketplaces, literature and history – all these and more could be captured within images that drew upon the age's dominant aesthetic conventions and vocabulary. What is intriguing is that the languages of description were extraordinarily homogenizing. Thomas Metcalf (2005: 173–74) argues, correctly, that the colonial aesthetic distanced the British from India, ordering Indian elements in new ways 'with scant regard for the contexts in which they were rooted'. It is indeed startling to see cities as diverse as Calcutta and Madras being inscribed within a descriptive vocabulary that uses the same tropes for all of them. This 'ordering', where the descriptive vocabulary of the English homogenized India, is what I call a colonizing aesthetics.

As the obverse of such a colonizing aesthetics, it is fascinating to see travellers of different class or social backgrounds appropriate similar rhetorical strategies to describe India. Thus chaplain Terry and physician John Fryer, traveller-spy George Forster and mercenary George Thomas all seem to borrow from a ready database of tropes and aesthetic devices. Part of the explanation of such a commonality of devices might be attributed to a common readership and review system. Instructions were issued to travellers – on what to see, what to record and how to record them. Albertus Meierius' *Certain Briefe and Speciall Instructions for Gentlemen, Merchants, Students, Souldiers, Marriners* appeared in 1589. Francis Bacon's 'Of Travel' appeared in 1625. Robert, Earl of Essex, Philip Sidney and William Davidson published *Profitable Instructions* in 1633. The *Philosophical Transactions* of the Royal Society issued 'inquiries' for travellers in 1666–67. Josiah Tucker's instructions for travellers were published in 1757. Further, the numerous writings on the Grand Tour and their vocabulary, landscape descriptions and aesthetic perspectives may have provided models for English people seeking to write travel narratives about India. There was a huge amount of informed interest in the travelogue in general and the 'Eastern' travelogue in particular, as evidenced by the dozens of reviews in *Monthly Review*, *Critical Review*, *Gentleman's Magazine*, the *Philosophical Transactions* and other periodicals.[3] All of these factors put together may have determined the form, language and ideology of the travel account. India was therefore narrated in ways that would appeal to and obtain the approval of informed readers back in England.

The intention is not to posit a lineage of aesthetics in the colonial encounter, or to draw a one-to-one correspondence of British aesthetic negotiations with India and the European history of ideas. Aesthetic and rhetorical constructions of India demonstrate 'attachments' to the English conceptual systems, but are not necessarily confined to them.[4] The 'moments' or 'moves' I identify in a narrative are not always clear cut, sequential or deriving from one another, even though, admittedly, the book's organization suggests a fixed schema of aesthetic categories. Narratives are as fractured as the experiences, and every travel account uses multiple forms – autobiography, history-writing, chorography – within the same narrative. However, it is possible to locate dominant aesthetic modes within a narrative, and the modes themselves within specific socio-political contexts. Thus, for instance, the sublime becomes a dominant mode during the period of transition – 1750–1820 – when the East India Company was transforming itself from a trading company into a political power. The picturesque, similarly, furnished the colonial missionary with a usable aesthetic device to map the anterior moments of conversion and evangelical colonialism in the 1790–1850 period. While it would be foolhardy to draw exact contextual 'sources' of these modes, the evidence of tropes circulating across genres and narratives suggests a widely prevalent 'system'.

I have drawn upon varied and multiple sources in order to explore and identify a particular aesthetic mode as 'dominant'. I have used travel literature – a problematic and amorphous genre that includes and adapts the conventions from autobiographies, guidebooks and memoirs – along with government administrative reports, historical accounts, letters and discursive writings from British India.[5] I have also used a vast amount of periodical literature, with the assumption that commentaries and reviews best reflect the circulation of these tropes of India in the public domain and the reception of the colonial travel narrative in England. The aim here is to explore the aesthetics of colonial discourse as it cuts across and permeates multiple genres, and to see the intertextual nature of colonial tropes in the languages of description. For this purpose I have quoted extensively – more to prove than to illustrate.

This study moves across the 1600–1920 period. It maps the aesthetic conventions and their attendant languages in English writings from very different historical and political contexts, starting with the early traders and factors to the period of high imperialism and evangelical colonialism. It explores five principal aesthetic modes from this period: the marvellous, the monstrous, the sublime, the picturesque and the luxuriant. In the case of the last two modes, I have focused on specific genres: the missionary narrative and the sporting memoir as best illustrating the specific aesthetic mode.

The early encounters with India revealed to English people a landscape of vastness, plenty and prosperity. Seeking trading privileges and negotiating with the natives to set up 'factories' and places of residence, the English also faced the task of comprehending variety, quantity, difference and vastness. The marvellous aesthetic, explored in Chapter 1, enables the early English people to negotiate with such a landscape. The key 'project' in this first moment is the exploration and explanation of Indian difference through specific strategies of description and narration. Narratives during this period posit and describe a land of variety, novelty and difficulty – before demonstrating how the English could obtain a degree of control over this material. The 'project' of the marvellous aesthetic renders India 'difficult' in order to highlight the English people's triumph. Using versions of the marvellous such as the theological-moral and the scientific, the English transform an India of enviable plenty into a landscape of wicked excesses, an India of vast, ungovernable variety into a catalogue.

Even as the marvellous generates its rhetoric of plenty and excess preliminary to an iconoclastic rejection of the same, the first century of English travellers encountered the Indian monstrous. The monstrous, as Chapter 2 demonstrates, is a category that folds into the grotesque to domesticate the frightening as or into the ludic. Taking recourse to corporeal, moral and theological discourses, the monstrous aesthetic with its 'fashion monsters', the 'aesthetic' of idleness and 'erotic beasts' shifts the grotesque from individual instances to the larger community and contexts. The monstrous was a part of the project to dehumanize Indian space, to locate Indian culture as radically different and flawed. With these two proto-colonial aesthetic modes the English mapped India as different, inhuman, chaotic, varied and dark. As anterior moments of the colonial phase (1750 and after), these two aesthetic modes of the marvellous and the monstrous play crucial roles in setting up the grounds for intervention and transformation.

With the East India Company assuming political power after the 1750s, a different aesthetic 'project' becomes visible, as I argue in Chapter 3. The sublime aesthetic mode of the 1750–1820 period, driven by a newly acquired confidence, mapped an India of borderless, desolate and wasted lands. Within this 'negative sublime' of emptiness, the aesthetic of the sublime locates English and colonial spaces of amenity. The aesthetics of the sublime is the first clearly imperial aesthetic, where the 'improvement' of desolate Indian lands has been achieved under the aegis of English rule. The 'imperial sublime', as I have termed it, reveals the full transformative power of the aesthetic 'project' within colonialism.

Missionary writings on India in the 1790–1850 period, as Chapter 4 demonstrates, employed its own brand of aesthetics. The colonial evangelical 'project' of 'improvement' and 'cultivation' of Christian natives is admirably served by the aesthetics of the picturesque. Locating paganism within the beauty of the Indian landscape, the missionary picturesque treats India as a site of Christian georgic labour by the missionary. The 'aesthetics of poverty' leads into a transformative aesthetic that proposes a unification of Indian variety into a garden of Christian faith, a *Concordia discors*, a movement transformation from the primitive pictur-esque to a Christian one.

In the latter half of the nineteenth century the Indian landscape was well mapped and documented. Searching for a truly adventurous space, which I term the 'extreme exotic' in Chapter 5, the English sportsman (and, in at least a few cases, sportswoman) sought the jungles. The hunting expedition narrates the Indian wilds through the aesthetic of the luxuriant, an aesthetic that combines beauty with danger. Moving from a passive picturesque through the encounter with wild animals – narrated through an aesthetics of risk – the English *shikari* transforms the landscape into a triumphal space. In the wake of the turbulent events of 1857, the luxuriant enables a colonial 'project' of empowerment, trium-phal conquest and control. The sporting luxuriant also, like the earlier aesthetic modes, transforms India and colonizes it.

These are not mutually exclusive moments in the aesthetics of colonial writing. Aesthetic 'projects' in the English–India encounter overlap and fold into each other. Versions of the sublime are visible in the seventeenth-century writings of John Ovington and others. The picturesque stretches from the last decades of the eighteenth century till the later decades of the nineteenth. The sense of an Indian luxuriant can be detected in the military memoirs of the 1750–1850 period. What I have tried to do is to locate a dominant aesthetic mode in any given 'age' via a reading of the descriptive vocabulary of the colonial narrative.

My intention is not to draw a genealogy for any particular aesthetic mode, but rather to show how any aesthetic, in the context of English writings on India, served proto-colonial and colonial purposes of knowledge-gathering, categorizing, transformation and rhetorical control. More often than not, aesthetics enables a self-portrait of the English in control, with a full sense of intention and purpose. The colonial discursive construction of India that grants particular roles for colo-nial governance and power is, I believe, served well by aesthetic modes. How it is done is what this book sets out to demonstrate.

1 Marvellous difficulty, 1600–1720

Thomas Herbert's 1634 travelogue, *A Relation of Some Years Travel into Afrique, Asia, Indies*, declares:

> This journal was taken in danger, which admits of no curiosity, and craves but the same favourable light for approbation, it was drawn by. Many storms it has endured for company, but more hot days, which have sun-burnt my lines, as well as my face. And though I am on shore, yet I fear, the sea is not yet calm, for each book, sent into the world, is like a bark put to sea, and is as liable to censures as the bark is to foul weather.
>
> (Herbert 1634: unpaginated Preface)

Immediately afterwards, opening his main narrative, Herbert writes:

> But I was on my way to many countries, and travellers have enough to do with variety, in men and manners, which make up a library to themselves, besides the situations and present beings of cities and territories, seeming better than to labour in uncertain stories, which not only perplex the hearers, but beget incredulity, often times amongst the credulous.
>
> (Herbert 1634: 2)

The two Herbert passages present a catalogue of the rhetorical devices and tropes used to describe India and Asia in the 1600–1720 period: difficulty, variety, wonder and the need to organize the new sights.

Merchants, 'factors', ambassadors, chaplains and surgeons travelled out to India seeking employment and profits. In some cases they were entrusted with tasks by the English government (Sir Thomas Roe, for instance, was the ambassador from James I to Jahangir, the Mughal emperor). East India Company (EIC) travellers of this period were not, in the strict sense of the term, 'colonial', but they do exhibit a 'colonizing imagination' (Singh 1996: 2–3, 2b).[1] The early English travellers confronted a radically different topography, climate, fauna and flora, diseases, cultures and belief systems. Their travelogues, cast as exploration narratives, often take recourse to a trope of 'discovery' in order to deal with the absolutely new (Singh 1996). This 'discovery' narrative also embodies a rhetoric of similarity and difference, comparing and contrasting the new (India) with familiar England or Europe (Teltscher 1997: 18–19, 20, 25–28; Metcalf 1998: 41). In addition to the narrative's oscillation between the twin poles of similarity and difference, the travelogue engaged in an 'editorial struggle', seeking a degree of textual ordering over the new sights and experiences (Teltscher 1997: 14–15).

New worlds required new cognitive techniques and new rhetorical strategies. Jonathan Sell has argued that English traveller-writers from the sixteenth century could have written rhetorically only because rhetoric had been established as the best system of organizing experiences and ideas, making them intelligible and communicating them (Sell 2006: 13). Sell's argument proposes the existence of narrative models to be adhered to by traveller-writers. The demand for accurate, factual and organized accounts of their 'discoveries' and travels cast the traveller as a responsible observer, one who pursued knowledge for its own sake, as opposed to an 'irresponsible' viewer who pursued pleasure (Stafford 1993; Gilbert 1999).[2] Such a traveller also had to guard against being enchanted by exotic India.[3] The responsible traveller was not only to explore or observe but also to order the new into suitable categories and narratives so that readers in England could find both pleasure and knowledge in the travelogue. Francis Bacon listed in his essay, 'Of Travel' (1625) – like Robert Boyle was to do a few years later – the things a traveller must note when in new and strange lands:

> The things to be seen and observed are, the courts of princes, especially when they give audience to ambassadors, the courts of justice . . . the churches and monasteries . . . the walls and fortifications of cities and towns . . . antiquities and ruins; libraries, colleges, disputations, and lectures . . . shipping and navies; houses and gardens of state and pleasure, near great cities; armouries; arsenals, magazine; exchanges; burses; warehouses; exercises of horsemanship, fencing, training of soldiers, and the like; comedies . . . treasuries of jewels and robes, cabinets and rarities; and, to conclude, whatsoever is memorable in the places where they go.
>
> (Bacon 1860 [1625], 12: 138)

Philip Sidney and his secretary William Davison provided a similar framework in their *Profitable Instructions* (1633: 2–7). Prospective travellers were also aware of other models like Edward Leigh's *The Gentleman's Guide* for travel through advertisements (*London Mercury* 23–27 June 1682).[4] The Royal Society published Boyle's suggestions for a 'natural history' and a list of 'inquiries' for Surat in the East Indies in *Philosophical Transactions* (*PT* 1. 11 [1665–66]: 186–89; 2. 23 [1666–67]: 415–19).[5] Such lists and inquiries took into account everything, from the manners of the people to the soil's fertility. The numerous natural histories compiled during this period also provided narrative models for these travelogues. These histories, like maps, categorized an otherwise unknown or unknowable, wild land into something more orderly and comprehensible.[6] Thus William Allingham in his *A Short Account of the Nature and Use of Maps* argues that with the help of maps 'the divine, merchant, soldier and traveller may . . . take a particular view of those vast and pleasant countries, they have occasion to visit' (Allingham 1698: unpaginated Preface). The several physic and botanic gardens – Padua, 1545; Leiden, 1587; Oxford, 1621; Paris, 1626 – collected and reported about plant species from exotic places.[7]

The narrative ordering of India in the seventeenth-century travelogue is greatly facilitated and informed by a particular aesthetic – that of the marvellous – that tropes India in particular ways preliminary to demonstrating rhetorical control and transformation. The descriptive vocabulary of these early travel narratives reveals extensive use of two key components of the marvellous aesthetic: *variety* and *otherness* (Platt 1997: 41; Daston and Park 1998: 33). Together, variety and otherness construct a strange and wondrous India, simultaneously frightening and fascinating, invoking feelings of awe and revulsion, and demanding investigation and interpretation. Troping India as a wondrous, if 'difficult', space enables English travellers to carve out a definite role for themselves because the marvellous, like wonder, demands investigation, inquiry and interpretation.[8] The marvellous was an *explanatory* and *exploratory* aesthetic that enables the traveller to wonder at, organize, define and ultimately explain (away) India's newness.[9]

This marvellous narrative consists of three prominent, interpenetrating thematic strands: profusion, difficult excesses and demystification. Travelogues of the period invariably construct a prosperous Indian landscape, as images of wealth map a landscape of profusion (a feature that persists from the marvellous travel narrative of the medieval age: Daston and Park 1998: 33). Eventually, this same discourse of plenty modulates into a second strand where the traveller tropes India as a space of 'difficulty'. Troping India as difficult excess demanded from English travellers acts of rhetorical control and narrative order. This marks the third thematic strand of the marvellous narrative where 'difficulty' is overcome through specific rhetorical modes that demystify Indian excesses. The third strand of the marvellous narrative *interprets* and *explains* Indian landscape's excesses in both 'rational' and moral terms.

This third thematic strand in the discourse of the marvellous is crucial for two reasons. On the one hand, it enables a shift from the discourse of a wondrous India to an explanation of the same. The marvellous in the English encounter marks a proto-colonial 'wonder shift' – from the *effects* of the marvellous to its *causes*, a shift that helps the English traveller attain a degree of certitude in the face of difference.[10] On the other hand, it anticipates the later, active *colonial* ideology and intervention. Effectively, this is an anterior moment to late-eighteenth-century 'repopulation' of Indian landscape with British icons such as memorials, edifices, boundaries and buildings.

The early marvellous was thus a method of inquiry and interpretation. The traveller's marvellous attempts, at one level, to capture a varied, strange, vast and 'difficult' India within an ordered narrative, deriving its model from natural histories, and cast as a 'scientific' explanation or exploration of the new. At another level, the explanations frequently swerve into the theological, a direct result of the travellers' own lack of training in the sciences, as Michael Adas (1990: 26–27) has argued. The marvellous was thus a schismatic aesthetic, divided along the drive for a scientific and rational account of the new, and the traveller's own fascination for the supernatural and the exotic.

The marvellous aesthetic was applied equally to varied topographical terrain in India. That is, aesthetics helped 'level' all cities and towns, deserts and rivers within the same descriptive vocabulary in a sort of 'colonial topography', where differences and historical/architectural/cultural specificities between, say, the Deccan and northern India are erased through the same set of tropes and descriptive vocabulary. The marvellous was therefore a project of categorizing and homogenization that cast the traveller as a proto-colonial.

Pleasurable profusion

In his *History of the World* (1614) Sir Walter Ralegh writes:

> Paradise was a place created by God . . . in which climate the most excellent wines, fruits, oil, grain of all sorts are to this day found in abundance. And there is nothing that better proves the excellence of this said soil and temper, than the abundant growing of palm-trees, without the care and labour of man.
>
> (Ralegh 1971 [1614]: 133)[11]

Ralegh's description echoes several themes of the seventeenth-century travel narrative. To the English traveller the Indian landscape presented a similar 'completeness' in its fertility, thick woods, massive harvests, and commodity-filled markets.[12] Ralegh's rhetoric of intensification and incomparability becomes a standard feature of English narratives about India. Here is the EIC chaplain, Edward Terry (1655), in his first topographical descriptions:

> This most spacious and fertile land (called by the inhabitants Indostan) so much abounds in all necessaries for the use and service of man, to feed, and cloathe and enrich him, as that it is able to subsist and flourish of itself, without any help from any neighbour prince or nation . . .
>
> When the ground there hath been destitute of rain nine months together, and looks all of it like the barren sands in the deserts of Arabia, where there is not one spire of green grass to be found, within a few days after those *fat enriching showers* begin to fall, the face of the earth there (as it were by a *new Resurrection*) is *so revived*, and throughout *so renewed*, as that it is presently *covered all over* with a pure green mantle . . . amongst the many hundred acres of corn of diverse kinds I have there beheld, I never saw any but what was *very rich and good, standing as thick on the ground as the land could well bear it*.
>
> (Terry 1655: 92, 100, emphasis added)

Terry presents an Indian marvel of fertile soils, plentiful harvests and lush vegetation, treating the variety, uniqueness and plenty as magical, even as his rhetoric of intensification reveals the sense of wonder and pleasure at the sight of the rich Indian landscape. This is the first strand of the Indian marvellous.

Every English traveller marvels at the Indian soil's fecundity, the fields with their load of crops, the dense woods, and markets with a variety of fruits and vegetables. Thomas Bowrey in his *A Geographical Account of Countries Round the Bay of Bengal 1669 to 1679* notes Bengal's abundance (Bowrey 1997 [1905]: 133–34, 165–68). William Bruton's narrative is full of descriptions of Bengal's fertility, populousness, and the wealth of the court (Bruton 1638: 6, 9, 22–23, 32). Food, Terry (1655: 92) notes, the Mughal empire produces 'in abundance'. Herbert (1634: 184) claims: 'these negroes . . . have no famine of nature's gifts and blessings'. John Fryer (1698: 179) employs a biblical turn of phrase to describe India's profusion: 'and to give the soil its due praise, it obeys in all things the first commandment, increase and multiply'. Fryer (1698: 178–83) states that India's two harvests are 'most natural and uncompelled'. Alexander Hamilton (1997 [1727], 2: 21) declares: 'To mention all the particular species of goods that this rich country produces, is far beyond my skill'. The English traveller invariably proceeds to itemize and enumerate Indian plenty – noting the variety of fruits, trees and crops (Herbert 1634: 182–83; Terry 1655: 95–97, 102; Fryer 1698: 56, 76. 134–35, 178–83, 186, 188, 411–12; Hippon in Purchas 1905 [1625], 3: 83; Best 1934: 230–34; Hamilton 1997 [1727], 1: 160–61).[13] A sense of wonder is unmistakable in these descriptions, which are, it must be noted, couched in terms of praise in this, the first strand of the marvellous narrative.

Each of the above descriptions of profusion carefully omits descriptions of farming labour. The apparently 'magical' flowering of harvests – suggested by Terry's 'Resurrection', Herbert's 'gifts and blessings' and Fryer's 'natural and uncompelled' – suggests a land or field that was ripe and fertile without any human effort. The traveller then appropriates the trope of easy fertility and productivity of Indian soil to describe childbirth and Indian femininity. This careful observation of both, the fertility of the soil and of the women, was something the traveller was instructed to do, for instance by Robert Boyle in 'General Heads for a Natural History of a Country, Great or Small' (*PT* 1. 11 [1665–66]: 188).

Fryer (1698: 94, 198) notes that Indian women were 'quick in labour' – Fryer's comment resonates in his French contemporary Gabriel Dellon (1698: 106) – and Terry (1655: 305) comments that Indian women have an 'easy bringing forth of children into the world'. Nearly a century later the image of easy farming and easy childbirth persisted. The historian Robert Orme, writing in 1782, claims authoritatively that Indian women were 'extremely' fertile and that Indian babies were 'brought into the world with a facility unknown to the labours of European women' (Orme 1974 [1782]: 262, 300). And, like Terry and Fryer before him, Orme (1974: 262, also 303) notes that 'productions peculiar to the soil of India exceedingly contribute to the ease of various labours'. The traveller suggests a link between economies of labour: the fertility and productivity of Indian soil and the fecundity and easy childbirth in Indian women. The female body and the land come together in a circulation of maternal, sexual and financial images that suggest the wondrous in the marvellous narratives on India.[14]

Raymond Williams (1973) has argued in the context of seventeenth-century English country-house poems that the erasure of the presence of working-class results in the creation of a magical paradise, a marvellous, wonder-inducing landscape (Williams 1973: 30–34, 120–26).[15] This erasure serves three purposes. First, the emphasis on a naturally fertile Indian land rather than on actual conditions of production becomes the inaugural moment of the colonial theme of native ineptitude and indolence (I shall return to this point later). The wealth of the Indians was thus undeserved because they did not toil for it, and India was a paradise for no perceivable reason. Second, the emphasis on the *intrinsic* goodness of the land aestheticizes it, empties it of people and their activities, and distances native or human threat from the English traveller who is free to perceive the land clearly and fearlessly. In an allied strategy, these travellers or narratives appear more comfortable viewing or describing India's mineralogical, botanical and zoological marvels rather than its anthropological ones (on this theme of the European preference for mineralogical-botanical marvels, see Mary Baine Campbell 1988: 69–71). Indeed, the anthropological scene in these travelogues is invariably marked by a description of 'monstrous', abhuman forms such as *fakirs* or crowds (see Chapter 2).[16] Third, the absence of toilers becomes, for the English traveller, symbolic of an oppressive system. It enables the traveller to suggest (as Terry, Fryer and Herbert do repeatedly: see Chapter 2 for an analysis of this theme) that the absence of private property in India was a sign of Oriental despotism.

The traveller is frequently amazed at the profusion and variety of birds and animals. Terry writes of the 'sweet music' of the birds in the woods, the 'wild apes and monkeys and baboons', the birds which 'please the eye with their curious colours, and the ears with their variety of pleasant notes', and the excellent horses and elephants of the Mughal rulers (Terry 1655: 102–03, 107–09, 139–41, 141–45). Ovington and Fryer catalogue the animals, fruits and spices, and expressed amazement at the Indian's control over crocodiles and alligators (Ovington 1696: 224–26, 303–04; Fryer 1698: 34–37).

In addition to such botanical and zoological plenty, India also possessed other, more material, forms of wealth. Descriptions of Indian wealth or prosperity often took the form of accumulated detail as the traveller's eye moves across various items to capture the plenty. A rhetoric of accumulation is central to the marvellous narrative of India, and enables the traveller to map a landscape of plenty. As early as the 1580s, the merchant Ralph Fitch had described the town of Belgaum entirely in terms of its minerals and precious commodities: 'a great market of diamonds, rubies, sapphires, and many other soft stones' (Locke 1997 [1930]: 99–100).[17] William Hawkins, a merchant with the EIC, attempts to compute the annual income of the Mughal empire (Purchas 1905, 3: 30–33, 34–35, 41–42). Hawkins describes the Mughal emperor thus:

> He is exceeding rich in diamonds, and all other precious stones, and usually wears every day a fair diamond of great price . . . He also wears a chain of pearl, very faire and great, and another chain of emeralds, and . . . rubies.
>
> (Purchas 1905, 3: 42)

Sir Thomas Roe confesses: 'I had thought all India a China Shop' (Roe 1990 [1926]: 116). Terry (1655: 158–59) describes the Mughal emperor as the owner of 'unknown treasure'. Herbert (1634: 42, 187–88) describes Cambay's 'great wealth' and drew attention to women's jewellery. Fryer (1698: 196) describes the 'noble pomp' of the native merchants, their apparel, train of followers and caparisoned horses before declaring that this phenomenon was 'not encountered abroad'. He thus underlines the uniqueness (and therefore, marvellousness) of the event. Ovington describes Surat as 'the most fam'd emporium of the Indian empire', speculates on the value of the Emperor's crown, and comments on the excess jewellery worn by the women (1696: 178, 196, 218–19, 319–21).

One mode of underscoring the marvellous profusion of India was through the use of the rhetoric of intensification and incomparability. Terry's *first* description of India goes like this: 'the *most spacious* monarchy under the subjection of the Great Mogol divides itself into thirty and seven *several and large* provinces' (1655: 78, emphasis added). Terry's descriptions are full of superlatives when elaborating India's astounding fertility, harvest, flora and zoological marvels (1655: 92, 95–97, 100–102, 102, 109–10). Like Terry, Fryer uses superlatives to describe India's magnitude (1698: 55–56, 64, 73, 84, 104–05, 143, 178). He sees 'trees, corns, and herbs grac[ing] the world [India] with infinite variety of delightful forms, and pleasant colours' after the monsoons (Fryer 1698: 138). The melons in India, Ovington (1696: 305) declares, possess a 'flavour and taste superior to any of that kind in the world'.

The use of superlatives suggests hyperbole, which, as Chloe Chard (1999: 48–63) points out, is integral to the intensificatory mode in travel writing. In Terry's description, India itself seems impossibly large: it is excessive in itself. In order to render this already infinite expanse even more incomprehensible and illimitable, Terry and the others move beyond the Indian geographical borders to include the whole world. This serves as a metaphor of expanse and difficulty – there are no standards, boundaries or measures to compare India with – that is apparently immeasurable and insurmountable. This hyperbole of incomparability, in which India's landscape, extent and produce are far better and superior to those found anywhere in the world, informs every travelogue of this period.

This incomparability of India's nature is visible in other aspects too. Terry describes the Mughal emperor in these terms: '[He is] the greatest, and richest master of precious stones that inhabits the *whole earth*'. He cannot believe that 'there is [any] monarch in the *whole world* that is daily adorned with so many jewels' (Terry 1655: 392, emphasis added). Likewise, Ovington states: 'the riches and extent of Asia surpass the other quarters of the world', and markets such as Surat's exhibit an 'abundance of pearls . . . and other stones of splendour and esteem, which are vended here in great quantities'. He sees India's wealth as emblematized in women's jewellery, and writes that 'the meanest woman in Surat is not destitute of ornaments upon her body' (Ovington 1696: 166, 218–19, 320–21).

The rhetoric of intensification renders the Mughal emperor, markets, Indian agriculture and produce, fauna and flora the wealthiest and the best in the entire world. The traveller's sweep of study and observation extends beyond the immediate geographical location. This discourse of intensified admiration for India is crucial, for it is an originary moment of a persistent theme in colonial writing. Fryer's or Ovington's descriptions of India's natural and material wealth anticipate statements from Warren Hastings and others in the 1780s. By the last decades of the eighteenth century, with the EIC in power, this rhetoric of incomparable wealth and prosperity is well entrenched in English writing on India. Only this time, the wealth and prosperity are the effects of a benevolent English rule.[18]

The first strand of the discourse of the marvellous in these travelogues thus presents an India of plenty – of fertility, natural produce, mineral wealth, animal and plant life, and material possessions. The very *scale* of plenty, unique in itself, is a source of wonder in these travellers (Adas 1990: 43). The traveller's attention to the variety and sheer uniqueness (where the latter is constantly emphasized through a rhetoric of incomparability) that constituted this plenty inscribed India firmly within an aesthetic of the marvellous. Diversity, novelty, unfamiliarity and expanse become sources of awe, pleasure and delight. The marvellous aesthetic first embodies the traveller's praise, envy and wonder at India. Later, these very sites of agrarian, botanical-mineral and material marvels become the sites at which the traveller begins to effect the rhetorical transformation of India. Pleasure now modulates into anxiety demanding alleviation.

Marvellous excesses

Sara Suleri (1992) in her perceptive reading of Edmund Burke's (1987) Indian sublime points to the 'discourse of difficulty' that permeates his imperialist idiom. Suleri (1992: 39) argues that, in Burke, difficulty often 'strips' into 'secrecy'. This 'discourse of difficulty' that Suleri locates in Burke is prefigured and anticipated in the rhetoric of numerous proto-colonial travelogues of the seventeenth century.

In the proto-colonial marvellous narrative of India, 'difficulty' eventually leads to interpretation and knowledge, for, as Angus Fletcher in his study of the allegory has argued, 'difficulty' implies a calculated obscurity, one that elicits an *interpretive* response in the reader (Fletcher 1975: 234–35). The 'discourse of difficulty' is central to the English traveller's epistemological conquest of India. It enables travellers to project themselves as the 'knowing' English person, a construction of the Self that was necessitated and facilitated by the encounter with the Other.[19]

Difficult magnitude

The seventeenth-century English traveller to India was struck by the sheer expanse of the country, and the travelogues of the period are full of descriptions that attempt to capture this expanse. In the previous section I demonstrated how the rhetoric of intensification enables the English traveller to convey a sense of Indian magnificence and plenty. This rhetoric of intensification, however, also achieves another effect: it transforms pleasurable profusion into difficult excess. Thus William Bruton's *News from the East-Indies* notes India's 'variations of climates and situations, with the *diversities* of dispositions, of tongues, religions, habits, manners,

laws, and customs of sundry nations' (Bruton 1638: 1). Such diversity is not necessarily a positive feature. Ovington (1696: 185), therefore, suggests that the Indian
territory is 'so large' that it is necessary for the Mughal emperor to employ a
numerous Army to 'awe his infinite multitude of people, and keep them in an
absolute subjection'. Diversity is thus imaged as a problem that requires oppressive action. This intensificatory rhetoric is also used to capture the zoological
diversity and populousness of India. Ovington (1696: 143–45) describes Indian
fauna as overgrown. Terry (1655: 122), describing the terrors of India's animals,
notes that even the snakes seem 'overgrown'. Size, number, extent are all here
emphasized in terms of their excess, even as expanse is now transformed into
uncontrollable vastness.[20]

Difficult magnitude in the marvellous travelogue consists of corporeal, numerical, zoological and botanical excesses. Corporeal excess generates a proto-
colonial grotesque – to which I return in a subsequent chapter, and which need
not therefore detain us here – in seventeenth-century writings on India. Difficult
magnitude is also an arithmetical excess in early English writings on India.
Travellers such as Sir Thomas Roe describe the zoological and botanical population of India in terms of frighteningly large numbers. Travelling to Bhadwar, Roe
(1990: 67) notes the cattle population: 'I met in one day 10,000 bullocks in one
troop laden with corn, and most days others, but less; which shows plenty'. Even
Indian rains are described in terms of superlatives: 'This day and the night past,
fell a storm of rain . . . usual at going out of the rains, but for the greatness very
extraordinary . . . the water was so grown that it break over in one place' (1990:
217).[21] Describing the Mughal army's march, Terry's tone reveals a certain
anxiety at the large numbers of people. Terry uses the terms 'numerous', 'great'
and their cognates to refer to the army's strength. These descriptives appear four-
teen times in sixteen paragraphs (Terry 1655: 419–20). Terry also uses a similar
rhetoric of inflation to capture the zoological danger of India:

> [There are] *many* harmful beasts of prey, as lions, tigers, wolves, jackals, with
> others; those jackals seem to be wild dogs, who in *great companies* run up and
> down in the silent night, much disquieting the peace thereof; by their *most*
> hideous noise. Those *most ravenous* creatures will not suffer a man to rest quietly
> in his grave . . . in their rivers are *many crocodiles* . . . on the land, not a few *over-*
> *grown* snakes.
>
> (Terry 1655: 122, emphasis added)

The iteration of superlatives suggests uncontrollable excess.

The presence of crowds threatened English travellers in their journey through
India. India's populousness – praised at an early stage by Terry, as we have
already seen – now evokes a sense of threat, as, for instance, in an incident when
angry natives surrounded the English residence (Terry 1655: 173). He refers to
'mountains of prey and tabernacles of robbers' infesting the woods. These 'wild'
men, writes Terry (1655: 182), shout 'kill, kill, kill . . . as loud as they can'. The
threat of being overwhelmed by numbers is very real here. Later, travelling with

the Mughal emperor's army, Terry again experiences a sense of unease. He describes the camping site of the army:

> Which indeed is very glorious, as all must confess, who have seen the infinite number of tents, or pavilions there pitched together, which in a plain make a show equal to a most spacious and glorious city. These tents I say, when they are altogether, cover such a great quantity of ground, that I believe it is five English miles at the least . . . very beautiful to behold from some hill, where they may be all seen at once.
>
> (Terry 1655: 419)[22]

Later, Terry, adopting the device of accumulative description, emphasizes the numerical excess of the army repeatedly in a particular paragraph. The extraordinary passage is worth quoting in full:

> Now to make it appear that the number of people of all sorts is *so exceeding great*, which here get, and keep together in the Mogol's leskar [lashkar], or Camp Royal; first there are *one hundred thousand soldiers*, which always wait about that king (as before observed) and all his Grandees have a *great train* of followers and servants to attend them there, and so have all other men according to their several qualities, and all these carry their wives and children, and *whole families* with them, which must needs amount to *a very exceeding great number*. And further to demonstrate this, when that King removes from one place to another, for the space of twelve hours, a broad passage is *continually fill'd* with passengers, and elephants, and horses, and asses, and oxen, (on which the manner sort of men and women with their little children, ride), *so full* as they may well pass one by the other. Now in such a broad passage, and in such a long time, *a very great number of people*, the company continually moving on forward, may pass.
>
> (Terry 1655: 420, emphasis added)

Having already described the vast expanse of the army, Terry's admission that it looks beautiful from a *distant*, panoptical point suggests a sense of insecurity when faced with the might of an entire native army. Terry's description clearly embodies an anxiety at this accumulation of natives.

The topography and climate – first described as magical and providential, as we have seen in Terry, Herbert and Fryer – are now transformed into hazards. The fertility of the soil is transformed into excess, when the English traveller shifts focus onto the wild and the overgrown. Terry's Preface opens with this description: '[the] large territories, a numerous court, most populous, pleasant and rich provinces' (unpaginated). Later this same image of the populous and large territory of the Indian empire acquired a negative valence when Terry expresses his unease at the crowds. After describing India's 'great variety of trees' Terry blunts the symbolic valence (and marvel) of this variety: 'but I never saw any there of those kinds of trees which England affords' (1655: 418, 419, 103). Later, Terry transforms his description of an ideal or Edenic Indian garden with this statement: '[as] the Garden of Hesperides . . . was guarded by a serpent, so there are stings here, as well as fruits'. His description of 'the annoyances of these countries' concludes with a declarative statement: 'that hot sulphurous air . . . there were no living in that Torrid Zone for us English . . . the air in that place is so hot to us English that we should be everyday stewed in our own moisture' (1655: 121–25). Having first described the Indian monsoon as effecting a 'resurrection', he subsequently deflates the iconic value of the same: 'These showers at their beginning [of the monsoon] season most extremely violent are ushered in, and usually take their leave with the most fearful tempests of thunder . . . [and] Lightning, more terrible than I can express' (1655: 99). Fryer also refers to the 'violence of the monsoons' that seems to prophecy a 'general deluge' (1698: 46, 76–77).

Terry, after noting an abundance of deer, transforms the image of plenty into an excess of disorder: 'Their deer are no where imparked, the whole empire being (as it were) a forest for them . . . But because they are everymans Game that will make them so, they do not multiply to do them much hurt' (1655: 93–94). Here Terry is referring to the English practice of enclosed parks as reserved places for gentlemen to hunt, while transforming the plenitude of Indian wildlife to suggest an excess of disorder (lack of parks) and depletion (the deer do not breed). The description is also paradoxical since it mentions an excess of freedom and the imminent death of unenclosed wildlife. Later, describing the woods in the town of Mandu, Terry writes: 'in those vast and far extended woods, there are lions, tigers, and other beasts of prey, and many wild elephants'. In the exact centre of the above passage, immediately *preceding* his description of the dangerous beasts, Terry comments: 'there is much delight in beholding them [the woods] either from the bottom or top of that hill' (1655: 193–94). Woods and wilderness are pleasant only when viewed from a distance, and not when the traveller is enclosed within them.

Terry also describes the lizards, rats, flies and mosquitoes, imaging them, through accumulative description, as excesses: 'abundance of flies . . . their numberless number . . . cover our meat as soon as it was placed on the table'. Describing the demographic distribution of flies and mosquitoes, he writes: 'there was such an abundance of large hungry rats, that some of us were bitten in the night as we lay in our beds' (Terry 1655: 123–24). Fryer first writes admiringly of the beauty of the Indian nights: 'the splendour of the moon', where the hillside appears 'all marble'. Then, this description of beauty quickly swerves into a rhetoric of intense difficulty and horror:

> [The hill] from whence is beheld the world all furled with clouds, the Caerulean ocean terminating the horizon, the adjacent islands bordering on the main, the mountains fenced with horrible gulfs, till strange vertigos prejudicate fancy, not daring longer to be made spectator: the bandying echo still persecutes with terrible repeated sounds.
>
> (Fryer 1698: 129)

The narrative constructs an India of wild, overgrown woods rather than cleanly organized gardens. The images of a wild Indian vegetation set up a dialectic of landscape description, as georgic England contrasts with Indian wilderness (wilderness, during this period, was treated as the truly 'Other': Murdoch 1990: 188–89; Helsinger 1997: 16–17). Incidentally, Nathaniel Hardy in his 1658 sermon to travellers leaving for the East Indies concludes with an image of England as a fenced in, organized and safe *hortus conclusus*.[23] Hardy prays on behalf of all England:

> Not only may come to your [the travellers'] native country in peace, but, that, when you come again, you may find it in peace, the breaches of Church, and State healed, everyone enjoying the rights in quiet, sitting under his own fig-tree, and eating the fruit of his labours with joy and thankfulness.
>
> (Hardy 1658: 52)

Thus England becomes the safe landscape for the traveller to return to after a sojourn in the wilds. In the absence of enclosed gardens in India, the *hortus conclusus* of safety and refuge (which, apparently, was the georgic English country), the English traveller felt threatened.

After noting that 'the woods are everywhere', Fryer announces that wild beasts ('the fiercest tigers in the world') and strange men inhabit the woods. Fryer treats these as dangerous spots: 'a gravelly forest with tall benty grass offers . . . wild boars, tigers and wild elephants, which are dreaded by travellers . . . the like terror is conceived by the crashing noise among the woods made by the wild bulls'.[24] He then describes how, in order to escape 'the noise of these buzzing hornets', they fled towards Surat. Excesses of sound disturb them: 'deafened by the roarings of tigers, cries of jackals, and yellings of baloos, or over-grown wolves . . . the croaking [of] frogs making so hideous a noise' (Fryer 1698: 56, 135, 141–42; see also 178–79, 189–90).

The troping of overgrown bodies, botanical, zoological or numerical excess is also achieved through the rhetoric of intensification as excess crowds, wild storms and dangers threaten the English traveller. Incomparable magnitude, thus, is not just one of positive wonder at Indian plenty: it almost always masks an anxiety about excess and extravagance. Magnitude here frequently represents a danger, where Indian expanse and variety cannot be captured within the English traveller's narrative. Thus the rhetoric works to a dual effect: awe at India's plenty and expanse, and the terror of the multiple and the vast. It is the latter (terror) that essentially constitutes the 'discourse of difficulty'. English travellers' efforts direct them to categorize, codify and, in general, provide an epistemological-hermeneutic 'understanding' of India. Such a rhetoric is also a colonizing mode of homogenization, where the terms are catachrestically applied to all things Indian, linking and reducing all to the same set of (ascribed) grotesque, obscene and repulsive 'qualities'. The rhetoric of intensification is complicated further when it suggests a narrative control – through homogenization – even as it seeks to present the unpresentable Indian vastness and diversity. Terry and other seventeenth-century travellers present an Indian excess that is dangerous, and anticipate the ways in which George Forster, William Hickey and several others in the eighteenth century use an inflationary rhetoric of excess to present a desolate India. In these descriptions India occupies the blurred space between the natural and the unnatural, thus defying classification and understanding. In short, it is rendered a difficult space.

Difficult darkness

Central to the construction of India as a 'difficult' space demanding observation and interpretation is a set of interrelated tropes of visibility, obscurity and darkness. In the seventeenth century marvellous narrative darkness is both literal and metaphoric, and facilitates a movement to the second, interpretive stage in the reading of India.

The imagery of close observation, the trustworthiness of the senses and the significance of personal eye-witnessing by the curious inquirer frames the rhetoric of darkness and obscurity in the seventeenth-century travelogue (Singh 1996: 21). Rooted, in part, in the visualist ideology of the early modern period and in the invention of optical instruments such as the microscope, every travelogue of the period begins with an emphasis on personal 'observation' and the significance of eye-witnessing.[25] Personal experience and oral report were modes of verification in the narrative of wonder, especially in the absence of divine revelation (Daston and Park 1998: 24, 63). The responsible viewer pursued knowledge for its own sake. Emphasizing that their observations could serve the dual purposes of 'instruction and use' as well as 'relation and novelty' (Terry: unpaginated Preface), these travellers projected themselves as 'responsible' observers (Stafford 1993). Such a responsible viewing was, of course, informed by assumptions of knowing and possessing.[26]

Terry (1655) states in his dedicatory note: 'For my self I was an eye-witness of much here related, living more than two years at the court of that mighty monarch the great Mughal' (unpaginated Preface). In his address to the reader he states that his attempt is to 'so contrive it [his narrative] for every one who shall please to read it through that it may be like a *well formed picture*, that seems to look steadfastly upon every beholder, who so looks upon it' (Terry 1655: unpaginated Preface, emphasis added; I shall have reason to return to this particular image later). Edward Waterhouse's prefatory poem to Terry's travelogue declares: 'a man's not born to see and to observe for one's self alone' (unpaginated Preface). Terry agrees with this assumption, underlining such a responsibility of the observer when he writes later in his work:

Yet he is the best observer, who *strictly and impartially* so looks about him, that he may see through himself. That as the beams of the sun put forth their virtue, and do good by their reflection: so in this case the only way for a man to receive good, is by reflecting things upon himself.

(Terry 1655: 453, emphasis added)

Another prefatory poem to Terry's work, by Henry Ashwood, states:

> To please and profit both thy virtuous mind
> He shows what reason finds in her dim night
> By groping after God with nature's light.
> > (Terry 1655: unpaginated Preface)

Thomas Herbert writes in his dedicatory note to the Earl of Pembroke:

> My desire to see, took away my sight, as it fares with those who are suddenly
> taken with a killing beauty, or gaze upon the sun. Yet some glimmerings I
> have observed, like an ill-sighted man, who sees with spectacles or perspec-
> tives.
> > (Herbert 1634: unpaginated Preface)[27]

John Ovington defends the publication of his travelogue by declaring that he has
described things that have 'escaped the observation of other travellers' (1696:
unpaginated Preface). N[ahum?] Tate in his poem preface to Ovington's work
describes the 'curious eye' that looks at 'each pregnant page' of 'the vast book the
world' (1696: unpaginated Preface). John Fryer, in a similar vein, defends the
publication of his work thus: 'Considering those travellers before me had few of
them been in those parts I had been, or at least not dwelt so long there, I venture
to offer some novelties, either passed over by them, or else not so thoroughly
observed' (Fryer 1698: unpaginated Preface). The prefaces construct the 'observer'
role for travellers themselves, people of experience setting out in pursuit of knowledge of unknown India. Each of the above images lays emphasis on personal experience. Herbert's (1634) description of 'perspectives' and 'spectacles', like Robert
Hooke's hagiography of optical instruments such as the microscope (in
Micrographia, 1665, a text to which I shall return), imbricates notions of scientific
observation, the emphasis on personal viewing or seeing, and curiosity.

The word 'curious', recurrent in all the travelogues, suggests a certain attitude.
A 'curious' person was one with many interests, who pursued knowledge for its
own sake, and who retained a lively scepticism about the knowledge attained
through the sensate body (Peter Burke 1999: 124–37).[28] Astonishment and wonder,
associated in the sixteenth century with the ignorant, was a characteristic of the
connoisseur (Daston and Park 1998: 321). When travellers declare their account to
be a true, 'eye-witness' description of India generated from their 'curiosity' to
know, they present themselves as responsible observers who observe, assimilate
and record details for the common good of the English back home. The dual ideologies of 'curiosity' and visualism that frame the English viewing of India in this
period has more to do with intensive study than imagination, to adapt Stephen
Bann's (1999: 9–17, 103) formulation. Both therefore emphasize the quest for
knowledge, understanding and epistemological ordering. The curious and obser-
vant traveller seeks out new areas for the expansion of knowledge, records what is
seen (and here the word 'observe' flourishes in both its senses of 'seeing' and

'following an established programme') and frames it in a narrative. With this, the troping of India as dark, veiled and mysterious appears almost as a logical follow-up to the visualism since it facilitates a concomitant ideology and practice of exploration, knowledge-seeking and analysis. The 'discourse of difficulty' begins, as seen above, with an intensification of things Indian. Later, darkness, obscurity and menacing secrecy become central to the 'discourse of difficulty'.

Edward Terry, as already noted, describes India's botanical and zoological population in substantial detail. He now asserts, in an image that achieves an unusual effect in terms of the 'discourse of difficulty': 'In our houses we often see lizards, shaped like unto crocodiles, of a sad green colour, and but little creatures, the fear of whom presents itself most to the eye' (Terry 1655: 109–10, 122). If darkness prevents clear vision, what observation reveals is danger. Indeed, in India, danger is (what is) first revealed to the eye. The danger of darkness and the dangers of clear vision are peculiarly connected to the discourse of difficulty in a kind of Moebius twist in Terry's narrative. Terry has already stated (in his Preface) for the reader's benefit, that everything he narrates is an eye-witness account, which he promises will be a 'well-formed picture'. Later, Terry states the dark danger of India more explicitly. Muslim places of worship are, he writes, 'made up close like a firm wall, and so are both ends, in which there are no lights'. He then proceeds to declare that 'heathens, . . . have neither light nor guide . . . and to live in darkness has not so much wonder in it' (Terry 1655: 265, 345; see also 460).

Terry's *modus operandi* is fairly simple. He first projects and presents himself as a curious, committed and clear-sighted observer seeking to deliver India to his English readers through careful observation and narration. He then proceeds to image India as dark and difficult. However, despite such difficulty, as a 'responsible' traveller he has observed all this with great clarity. That is, he penetrates the darkness of India in order to come to certain conclusions. It is this Englishman's clear(-sighted) prose that transparently reveals the dangers of India to the (English) reader. It becomes necessary to trope India as dark and difficult in order to imply his own clarity of vision. In a sense, the Indian darkness is central to the powers of observation – and, subsequently, interpretation – that this English traveller has ascribed to himself. The darkness resists – and this is the central 'difficulty' – the Englishman's vision and overwhelming desire to make a correct observation. This is a crucial move, for it sets up the Englishman in a position of authority, the solver of mystery and the India-cataloguer. What this rhetorical ploy does is to convey a sense of Indian danger to the reader. The English reader is supposed to trust Terry's descriptions because they are eye-witness accounts. The picture that the narrative forms has been reordered to deliver this realist image, but *without* the threat of danger that Terry himself experienced when he 'saw' it in India. This distancing of the reader from the danger that is India becomes the preliminary to the resolution of 'difficulty' itself. That is, the traveller presents his 'questing' narrative as a product of his curiosity. Such a narrative had to be accurate and realistic enough to capture the dangers of India. Yet, it also had to be a 'safe' consumption of India: as a 'well formed *picture*'. The eye-witnessing supposedly makes the narration authentic, and the 'decoding' of events renders them non-threatening when the traveller resolves the darkness and mystery of India. Such a resolution, I shall demonstrate, often took the form of a theologically determined interpretation of India's excesses.

John Fryer (1698: 39) creates an air of mystery and backwardness around Indian religion when he describes Hindu temples thus: 'The work is inimitably durable, the biggest closed up with arches continually shut . . . admitting neither light nor air'.

Soon after, Fryer describes a town, Palapatnam, as 'overgrown with the weeds of Mahomedanism, the Moors planting themselves here'. A similar description of the dark Hindu temple occurs later (Fryer 1698: 56, 159). Fryer's description and metaphors fit smoothly into the rhetoric of intensification. Here is Fryer describing in similar terms another Indian setting:

> These plants set in a row, make a grove that might delude the fanatic multitude into an opinion of their being sacred; and were not the mouth of that grand impostor hermetically sealed up. Where Christianity is spread, these would still continue . . . and may still be labouratories of fallacious oracles.
>
> (Fryer 1698: 40)

Fanaticism and blind belief are both linked to the darkness of Indian buildings. What is crucial here is the binary being set up – the in-visibility of Indian temples/mosques/houses and the general darkness of India's culture as opposed to the highly visible Englishman who is always in the public eye.

This image of being in the open and visible is central to the seventeenth-century travelogue. Sir Thomas Roe describes numerous occasions when he wished to be placed next to the emperor at Durbar, so that he may be 'seen' by all members of the audience (Roe 1990: 71, 87, 91, 95, 108–09, 133).[29] At one point Fryer makes an explicit comparison between the Indian and English attitudes towards light and darkness. He is describing the travelling coaches:

> The coach where the women were, was covered with cheeks, a sort of hanging curtain . . . Ours was open, and guarded by such a troop as went to apprehend our saviour, dressed after the same manner we find them on old landscapes, and led by the same fanatic lights we see there painted.
>
> (Fryer 1698: 83)

Terry and Fryer both mention the spectators who stared at the English wherever they travelled in India (Terry 1655: 218; Fryer 1698: 52). This emphasis on public appearance and visibility extends into the eighteenth century, as a directive in the Bengal Public Consultations of 1 September 1714 emphasizes: 'It is absolutely necessary that we appear in a more public manner than it's possible to do at present; that we may have the greater respect from the government' (*Early Annals of the English in Bengal* 2.2: 2). This visibility of the English person is in sharp contrast with the hidden, dark and secretive condition of the Indian houses, religion and life itself.

At one point in his narrative, Fryer mentions the trading rights granted to the East India Company, and the company's responsibility to the English crown. Describing this event Fryer (1698: 87) writes: 'This [trading privilege] was granted presently after the happy restoration of our gracious sovereign, when order began to dawn, and disperse the dark chaos of popular community'. Having isolated one component of the metaphor's binary – England-as-bright-and-sunny – Fryer proceeds with the second one. This second component in the rhetoric of difficult darkness, is the image of Indian mystery. Fryer combines the sense of obscurity with the air of mystery when he describes a Hindu temple: 'Then setting upon the gates of the pagod, they received all the unsanctified crew, and shut them in: where how they conclude their rites, is not to be divulged, ignorance with them being the mother of devotion'. Later, examining ancient Indian texts, Fryer describes the libraries containing them thus: 'their libraries being old manuscripts of their own cabalas, or mysteries understood only by the Brahmins' (Fryer 1698: 44, 161). Such descriptions of the 'darkness' and 'mystery' of Hinduism in partic-ular, and India in general, in Fryer and Terry sets in motion a discourse of dark-ness that persists well into the eighteenth century in the works of George Forster, Jemima Kindersley, Alexander Dow and dozens of other travellers, as I shall demonstrate later (see Chapter 3). Darkness becomes, in these texts, a symbol of general Indian depravity. The 'hiddenness' of things in India troubles the English gaze, and the Indian tendency to conceal is mourned by almost every English traveller in this period. Thus John Ovington mentions that 'all women of fashion in India are close penned in by their jealous husbands, who forbid them the very sight of strangers'. Immediately following his comment on the concealed Indian woman, he describes Indian houses (Ovington 1696: 210, 216). Ovington empha-sizes the visibility element clearly in his description of Indian mercantile transac-tions:

> They preserve [cash] as close and private as they can, lest the Moghul's exchequer should be made their treasury. This curbs them in their expenses, and awes them to great secrecy in their commerce, especially in their receiving, or payments of money, for which they either make use of the dark-ness of the night, or of the obscurity of the morning.
>
> (Ovington 1696: 317–18)

Ovington's theme is a persistent one in other writers as well (Terry 1655: 191–92; Bowrey 1997: 63–64, 127).

Interestingly, the imagery of darkness is used to describe other areas as well. Like Fryer, Ovington (1696: 248) refers to Sanskrit as the language where the 'mysteries of their theology' are written. Terry (1655: 239) refers to the 'Mohammedan who lives in the dark'. Thomas Herbert (1634: 38, 42) refers to Hindu religion as 'rare and wonderful, beyond apprehension', and the priests of Cambay as 'veiled and obscure in their best aspect'. Of the people of the Coromandel coast, Herbert (1634: 191) writes: 'their belief is beyond their own expression and others apprehensions'. As late as 1713, the image of a dark and mysterious Hindu religion figures prominently in the English imaginary. A letter in the newspaper, *The Englishman*, for instance, writes: 'Gloomy terrors, abstracted solitudes, painful penances, and bodily mortifications, are the dreadful acts by which the AntiChristian world is deluded' (29–31 October 1713, n.p.). Darkness is clearly integral to English descriptions of India.

With the rhetoric of intensification seventeenth-century English travellers have achieved several effects. They have portrayed India as a land of profusion – in terms of variety, numbers and extent. They have also provided evidence that most of what appears to be profusion is actually a negative excess, overgrown and unsafe. Further, they suggest that India is an area of darkness and mystery. Having allocated themselves the task of providing true and reliable information about India for readers back home, the travellers suggest that the mystery and darkness of India must be entered, conquered and explicated. The rhetoric of intensification and incomparability becomes a necessary first moment in this act because it constitutes a 'discourse of difficulty' and constructs an English traveller as an unselfish inquirer who braves these dangers in search of knowledge.

Thus the marvellous plenty of India, approximating to an earthly paradise teeming with plant and animal life, is now imaged as a dangerous wilderness in the second moment. The English traveller now locates a landscape of disease, death and deprivation in the same features once imaged as pleasurable profusion. However, this does not complete the representation of India. Travellers conflate physical and moral topographies when they read climatic conditions, landscape features, town planning and disease as symptomatic of moral conditions. Further, they began to evacuate the landscape of Indian icons by rejecting, altering or explaining away their valence and value to the natives.

Demystification and the marvellous

In the third strand of the marvellous narrative of English travellers' encounters with the Indian landscape, they adopt a two-pronged aesthetic of the marvellous, appropriating moral-theological and the scientific-rational (or what I call the 'categorical marvellous') modes for their purpose.

The marvellous narratives on India drew upon contemporary rhetorical conventions that linked, at least metaphorically, empire, knowledge and epistemological effort on the part of the English scientist. Francis Bacon used metaphors of travel, journey, light, fountains as symbols for truth and the process of knowledge-gathering. Bacon also takes recourse to images of the labyrinth, cloudiness and darkness (Vickers 1968: 174–201). Robert Hooke in his *Micrographia* (1665) deploys a whole range of metaphors that conflate travel, seeing or observation, knowledge-gathering *and* empire-building. In his letter to the monarch of England Hooke suggests that the microscope will 'offer some of the least of all visible things, to that mighty King, that has established an empire over the best of all invisible things of this world, the minds of men' and facilitate an 'enlargement of the dominion of the senses'. He then adds:

By means of the telescope, there is nothing so far distant but may be represented to our view; and by the help of the microscope, there is nothing so small, as to escape our inquiry; hence there is a new visible world discovered to understanding. By this the earth itself, which lies so near us, under our feet, shows quite a new thing to us, and in every little particle of its matter, we now behold almost as great a variety of creatures, as we were able before to reckon up in the whole universe itself.

(Hooke 1665: unpaginated Preface)

Francis Bacon in *The New Atlantis* (1627) states the case more bluntly: 'The end of our foundation is the knowledge of causes, and secret motions of things; and the enlarging of the bounds of human empire, to the effecting of all things possible' (http://etext.lib.virginia.edu/etcbin). Travel is thus treated as a means of discovery, knowledge-gathering and as a method of access to new cultures and lands.[30] Travellers into new regions brought back knowledge, which, in turn, fuelled greater travel.

The *Philosophical Transactions* illustrates this attitude when it describes the usefulness of a volume of travels:

The present collection reaching to the most distant parts of the Southern and Northern regions of the globe, and being performed by skilful navigators, and faithful observers, must needs contain many uncommon and useful things upon most of the heads of natural and mathematical sciences, as well as trade and other profitable knowledge, which contribute to the enlarging of the mind and empire of man.

(*PT* 18. 211 [1694]: 166–67)

A later issue praises John Fryer's India travelogue on similar grounds: for having 'the curiosity to travel' and 'record' his information in 'writing' and thus increase the knowledge of the English about the other 'habitable and inhabited' countries of the world (*PT* 20. 244 [1698]: 338).

The process of travel-as-knowledge-acquisition was clearly driven by the 'disinterested' curiosity of the gentleman-traveller, where disinterested curiosity ensures both, a selfless quest for knowledge and reliable narration.[31] Every traveller of the age, in his prefatory remarks, offers either of two justifications for publishing his work. One, as in the case of Terry, he has been *asked* to do so by publishers and friends who had realized the immense value of his observations (unpaginated Preface). This mode, as Jonathan Sell (2006: 71) points out, an extension of the 'modesty topos', is a commonplace in early modern narratives. Two, as in the case of Fryer (unpaginated Preface) and Ovington (unpaginated Preface), he had observed things that no one else had, and thereby was in possession of something unique and potentially interesting for others. The traveller collects knowledge with no intention of publishing it for personal gain. The person who stays at home explores distant worlds through the microscope or the telescope. The person who actually travels also speaks of the right 'perspective' in which to view India (as noted of Herbert's Preface). For this to happen, travel and knowledge needed to follow a planned, systematic itinerary of journey, exploration and narration. The information had to be provided in the right format, catalogued, explained and organized for both pleasure and knowledge. Such formats for organization were readily available to the travellers in the form of 'instructions for travellers', the so-called apodemic manuals (secular versions of the manuals for pilgrims) and influential travelogues such as the *Itinerario* of Jan Huygen van Linschoten (English translation, 1598).

Reviews of travelogues in the *Philosophical Transactions* used such instructions as criteria for evaluating the travelogues (Batten 1978: 91). Categories – ranging from the fertility of the soil to native architecture – were meant to increase the knowledge of that new place, an expansion of the empire of knowledge. Information from these travelogues also disseminates into English culture through their widespread popularity.[32] While these acquisitions were informed by the need for accurate information about possible mercantile trading routes, markets and resources, travel knowledge also rendered the new and strange place familiar. The rhetoric of demystification presents an India that was explicated, organized and therefore less dangerous. Demystification was therefore an act of interpretation.

The marvellous often embodies two strands: the moral-theological and the 'categorical marvellous'. To take the second mode first, the 'categorical marvellous' enables the traveller to negotiate the strangeness of Indian landscape through rational explanations and categorizations. It demystifies the Indian landscape, behaviour, religion and, with its spirit of enquiry, effected a transformation of wonder itself. This not only reduced the Other into something knowable, but also enabled travellers to retain their epistemological or cultural integrity in the face of the Other's excesses.

English travellers to India during this period demonstrate a tension between scientific rationality and the belief in the supernatural. Michael Adas (1990) points out that even the better educated European traveller and those best informed about Asian sciences were concerned primarily with religion and not with science. Noting the emphasis on prayers and such 'non-scientific' sights among the travellers, Adas (1990: 31) argues that virtually all travellers 'believed that supernatural forces could, and regularly did, influence the workings of the natural order'. John Ovington, the EIC chaplain, for instance, locates the hand of Providence in disseminating India's diseases and cures. Having described the Surat plague, Ovington proceeds to enumerate the suffering among the Indians. His final comment is as follows:

> But that which creates the greatest admiration in the Moors, and not a little joy in the English, is our escaping all this while the direful influence of this mortal disease, so that not one English man was ever yet affected by it. This makes the heathens cry out, that God is among us, whilst they observe whole families of their own swept away, without the least infection touching any one of our nation.

> (Ovington 1696: 348–49)

John Fryer ends his narrative with the description of a spectacular marvel of his times: the sighting of a comet in India. Having first termed it a 'wonderful sign', he proceeds to claim that Indians did not see it as ominous. He concluded with a prayer: that 'it may not affect our Europe kingdoms', since all comets are 'grievous to mankind' (Fryer 1698: 418–19, 446). Thomas Mun in his tract on the East India trade describes the very discovery of navigation to India in terms of miracles and destinies: 'But by the very Providence of almighty God, the discovery of that navigation, to the East-Indies . . . it has also brought a further happiness to Christendom in general, and to the realm of England in particular' (Mun 1621: 9).

Iconoclasm and the moral marvellous

Marvellous narratives about India adopted at least one of the conventions of the pilgrimage-narrative: the moral 'reading' of new spaces. John Fryer's Preface declares that one of his intentions in publishing his account is 'the reclaiming of atheists, by leading them first to behold the beauty, order, and admirable disposition of the universe' (unpaginated Preface). The iconoclastic moral marvellous looks, primarily, at indolence, waste and immoderation, native beliefs, and such 'moral' states. Jyotsna Singh, adapting the work of John Gillies (1994), has argued that early travellers to India drew 'moral boundaries' between the Christian Europeans and the pagan Indians (Singh 1996: 23). What is fascinating is that such distinctions and boundaries are drawn using a rhetoric almost entirely derived from the aesthetics of the marvellous. In addition, the third strand of the discourse of the marvellous is characterized by an attention to ruins – which, to the traveller, are iconic of a general degradation of Indian civilization itself – and native aesthetics.

William Finch travelling in 1610 describes a series of fires that severely damaged Agra town, before passing a moral judgment on the event. Finch writes:

> The town was much vexed with fires night and day, flaming in one part or other, whereby many thousands of houses were consumed, besides men, women, children, and cattle, that we feared the judgement of Sodom and Gomorrah upon the place.
>
> (Purchas 1905, 4: 39)

Edward Terry (1655: 203, 403–06) reports on jugglers, witches, and the strange – preternatural, a constituent of the marvellous – antics of an ape. In order to explain this marvel, Terry adopts a strategy that Daston and Park (1998: 323) isolate as characteristic of seventeenth-century travelogues: expressing wonder at objects in order to praise God. After the description, which, one notes, is only *reported* to Terry, of the marvel of the ape, Terry embarks upon a disquisition on God's wonders:

> This I am sure of that Almighty God, who can do what he will do (for all things are so far from being impossible to him, that nothing is hard) can do

wonderful things by the weakest of means, that the weaker the instruments are, the more glory may be ascribed unto him while he acts by them.

(Terry 1655: 405–06, emphasis in original)

Here Terry has explained away India's events, which are clearly 'magical', inexplicable and therefore 'difficult', by suggesting divine causes. In the absence of scientific explanations of these 'phenomena' the traveller has provided a theological cause–effect schema. This schema is arranged along the axes of belief/non-belief, miraculous/natural. The descriptions and explanations often dwell self-reflexively on the incredulous nature of these narrative. William Bruton (1638: 52) refers to the 'incredulous' nature of his narrative. Thomas Bowrey (1997: 209–10) mentions that, even before coming out to India, he had heard several 'incredible reports' about the river Ganga. Terry (1655: 446) explains these marvels of elephantiasis-afflicted, misshapen men by attributing their misfortune to a sinful life, where the disability is God's retribution, and disease becomes a marker of the (unchanging, essential) difference in cultures itself, between the Christian world and the pagan East.[33]

John Fryer (1698: 102–03) spends a great deal of time describing the *'fakirs'* of India and their penances, and admits that the sight of these grotesque forms would 'make a man disbelieve his own eyes'. Similar accounts occur elsewhere in Fryer's narrative (1698: 95–97, 192, 196). They are thus, technically, marvels. Fryer then significantly alters the appeal of the Indian *fakir*'s bodily penances by describing them with a series of pejoratives: 'traitors . . . the most dissolute, licentious, and profane persons in the world . . . curs[ing] God and Mahomet' (1698: 196). Fryer and the other travellers reinscribe the actions of the *fakirs* within a religious-moral narrative of degradation and superstition (Bruton 1638: 27; Terry 1655: 282–83; Ovington 1696: 364–67).[34] Here is Fryer describing the great water tanks built by Indian rulers:

The great tanks or ponds of rain-water, where it wants the other benefits, with deep wells, of extraordinary costs and charges; some purely for pomp, and to transmit their names to posterity; others for the good of travellers, but most for the sake of religion, in which they are extravagantly profuse.

(Fryer 1698: 188)

Benevolent wealth is transformed into immoderate, and therefore immoral, expense. Later Fryer writes: 'The plain country is rich in all things necessary . . . cocoas grow all along the sea-side round India . . . and betel-nut is in great request'. Then, to dim this picture of plenty, Fryer (1698: 188) describes the betel-nut: 'it exhilarates and makes a kind of pleasant drunkenness'. Fryer has effectually effaced the value of the natural product by pointing to its negative qualities.

The moral marvellous functioned in precisely this manner – by diminishing the significance of the event/place/condition by rendering it ordinary, or by denigrating it as morally questionable. For instance, the traveller explained away the enormous wealth of the native kings by suggesting that this wealth was obtained through the unremitting oppression of the artisan and the ordinary working class. Note, as an illustration, Fryer's comments:

> There is another thing above all the rest of an unpardonable offence; for banyan or rich broker to grow wealthy without protection of some great person; for it is so mighty a disquiet to the governor that he can never be at ease till he have seen the bottom of this mischief; which is always cured by transfusion of treasure out of the banyans into the governor's coffers.
>
> (Fryer 1698: 97–98)

The marvel of the emperor's wealth is thus diminished to the not-very-surprising, and finally to the repulsive. This slippage from profusion to excess and finally to lack (of knowledge, kindness, rights and freedom) is one of the central patterns in early English writing.

In other cases, the wealth of the natives was presented as grotesque exhibitionism. Terry describes the Mughal emperor as 'blind' and wealthy, and suggests that the English king has 'more cause to pity, than to envy his greatness' (unpaginated Preface). In the case of Thomas Herbert, John Ovington and John Fryer, icons of wealth – such as jewellery on Indian women, are first admired as marvels, catalogued and then transformed into a 'social monstrous', erasing the value of the jewels by taking recourse to the moral (see Chapter 2). In such cases the traveller desacralizes signs of India's prosperity by pointing to the negative effects – real or perceived – of this wealth.

English vulnerability is also imaged in terms of the moral marvellous. Terry (1655: 219) writes: 'the consideration of this might shame and make us to blush at it . . . shame I say and condemn too, the lightness, and wantonness, the want of sobermindedness, and inconstancy of our people here'. He points out the ill-effects of the English consumption of native liquor, and illustrates his arguments by discussing the behaviour of a drunken cook (1655: 173–74). Thomas Herbert (1634: 184) mentions the generous hospitality of the natives, which proceeds, he believes, from the plenitude of resources they possess. John Fryer (1698: 63, 69) refers to intemperance as the primary cause of ill-health among the English in India. The suggestion here is of a land where things are *dangerously* plenty, a site of temptation where the vulnerable Englishman may easily 'fall'. Terry's (1655: 297) reference to India as a 'fleshly paradise' is a comment on the moral threat that India poses.

The moral marvellous transforms the rich vegetation into an allegory of blindness and ignorance, of the impenetrable darkness of the native minds. Here is Fryer on the theme. He first describes the groves as 'labouratories of . . . fallacious oracles' where the 'blinded' natives get 'deluded'. He continues: 'Six miles up stands Palapatam, of building base, it is overgrown with the weeds of Mahommedanism, the Moors planting themselves here' (1698: 40, 56). Later Fryer launches a major attack on Brahmins and priests, comparing them to vermin and parasites. Here Fryer maps the moral character of the human onto the demography of other life forms. This is a common mode of shifting the condition of profusion into that of excess in Fryer. Islam becomes an 'infection' and the Maratha King Shivaji becomes a 'diseased limb of Deccan'(1698: 82, 53, 170–71).

The rejection of man-made idols is a particularly relevant example of the iconoclastic moral marvellous. Fryer writes: 'Their [temples] outside show workmanship and cost enough, wrought round with monstrous effigies, . . . *pains and cost to no purpose*' (1698: 39, emphasis added). The criticism of the aesthetic is in terms of a moral condition. Fryer's specific reference to the wastage involved also becomes iconoclastic in its rejection of native efforts. Terry, after describing the gardens of pleasure as filled with 'vineyards that afford marvailous fair and sweet grapes', transforms the idyllic setting into a dangerous excess. He notes that for entertainment the natives hire jugglers and mountebanks, who 'keep venomous snakes in their baskets'. These jugglers were, he admits, 'the cunningest that I have ever seen' (Terry 1655: 99–101). When Fryer actually finds a pleasant Indian garden, he transforms this Edenic site into a scene of martial excesses:

> This garden of Eden, or place of terrestrial happiness . . . are now open to the sun, and loaded with hardy cannon: the bowers dedicated to rest and ease, are turned into bold ramparts for watchful sentinels to look out for, every tree that the airy choristers made their charming choir, trembles, and is extirpated at the rebounding echo of the alarming drum, and those slender fences only designed to oppose the sylvan herd, are thrown down to erect others of a more war-like force.
>
> (Fryer 1698: 63–64)

Fryer also mentions that the English had a 'neat' garden, but 'Shivaji's coming destroyed it'. Fryer notes that instead of gardens, India has 'many . . . wilderness, overspread with trees'. His description of a flourishing Indian garden illustrates how the moral marvellous functioned as iconoclasm. He writes: 'Though these people delight much in gardens, yet they are but rude, compared to ours of Europe . . . Roses would grow here if they would but cultivate them' (Fryer 1698: 84, 104–05). Referring to the banyan tree Fryer writes: 'however, it is possible to be so contrived, if it be looked after, to make a wood alone of itself'. Referring to the tides in the river, he comments: 'the river; it glides by the town in swift tides, and at Spring Tides (which it would always do, were they industrious enough to keep it in its banks)' (Fryer 1698: 105, 106). Alexander Hamilton (1997, 1: 178), in a similar move, links trade, topography and morality of natives in his description of Bassein: 'It is a place of small trade, because most of its riches lie dead and buried in their churches, or in the hands of indolent lazy country gentlemen who loiter away their days in ease, luxury and pride'.

Fryer and Hamilton gesture at native indolence in an iconoclastic critique that suggests a moral decline of the native. Here the lack of cultivation is also attributed to a certain moral condition. Fryer suggests that the excessive or disorderly growth, or neglected lands in India is a direct reflection of the laziness encoded in their religions. This discourse of native laziness and the resultant wasted landscape in Fryer and others launched a theme that persists in several eighteenth-century writers.[35]

The ruin, iconic of a general decline in civilization or cultivation, came in for some special attention in these travellers. The rhetoric of accumulation that enables ruin descriptions renders the Indian landscape into an excess emptiness of decay and devastation. The word 'ruin' and its cognates occur at least once in every paragraph in William Finch's narrative (Purchas 1905, 4: 42–45, 48–49). Old mosques falling to ruins attracted Terry's attention (1655: 82). Fryer (1698: 183) speaks of how Shivaji's tyranny left arable land 'unmanured' and ruined. Seen in contrast with Britain's old and 'fixed' villages that suggests permanence, these ruins testify to India's decay.[36]

The iconoclastic moral marvellous rejects native faith. Terry (1655: 283–84) believes that the penances undertaken by the Indian priests are 'all to no purpose', and thereby dismisses native rituals and belief systems. Fryer's (1698: 95–96, 103, 192) comments on the *fakirs* and *jogis* (*fakirs* and *jogis* are wandering mendicants) are of the same tenor. William Bruton (1638: 27) and Alexander Hamilton (1997, 1: 155–56) also describe the *jogis* in similar tones of revulsion and distaste. When Fryer, for instance, dismisses them as vagabonds and outlaws, he effectively reduces a native icon to the morally corrupt. With this everything of the Indian marvellous – from soil fertility through climate to its religious icons – has been desacralized.

Terry's description of the Mughal prince is particularly illustrative of the iconoclastic moral marvellous. Consider this passage:

> Where first, for their numerous armies, it will appear to be no strange thing, if we consider the Great Mogul to be what he is, an overgrown Prince in the vast extent of his territories, being like a huge Pike in a great pond, that preys upon all his neighbours.
>
> (Terry 1655: 158)

Here the description of grotesque excesses of unsightly bulk ('overgrown') and of avarice ('prey') convert a wealthy native king into a devouring monster, and highlights the moral 'flaws' of this person. The image of great wealth and power at the service of a monster is a moral topography. Later Terry also transforms the image of strength (numerical superiority) into one of excessive weakness when he writes: 'a man of resolution will beat one of these [native soldiers] out of all his weapons, with a small stick or cane . . . the natives being most strong and valiant in their base lusts and not otherwise' (1655: 162–63). The threat of the *numerically* large Mughal army is neutralized rhetorically with this image of a *morally* weak army. Years later, Robert Orme, the historian, makes similar observations. In a section leadingly titled 'Effeminacy of the inhabitants of Indostan', he writes:

> The sailor no sooner lands on the coast, than nature dictates to him the full result of this comparison; he brandishes his stick in sport, and puts fifty

Indians to flight in a moment . . . it is well if he recollects that the poor Indian
is still a man. Two English sawyers have performed in one day the work of
thirty-two Indians.

(Orme 1974 [1782]: 299)

Likewise, the great talents of the native artists, which Terry himself has praised
earlier, are subsequently reduced in intensity. Terry now suggests that the native
artist's greatest talent is for imitation: 'the natives of that monarchy are the best
apes for imitation in the world, so full of ingenuity that they will make any new
thing by pattern'. He adds: 'it is *no marvel* if the Natives there make Shoes, and
Boots, and Clothes, and Linen, and Bands and Cuffs of our English fashion' (Terry
1655: 134–36, emphasis added). Ovington (1696: 279–80) makes a similar
comment: 'The Indians are in many things of matchless ingenuity in their several
employments, and admirable mimics of whatever they affect to copy after'.

Even the open air is not left untouched by such iconoclastic moral transformations. Here is Terry's description of the terraces of Indian houses:

These broad terraces, or flat roofs, some of them lofty, are places where many
people may stand (and so they often do) early in the morning, and in the
evening late . . . to draw and drink in fresh air; and they are made after this
fashion, for prospect as well as pleasure.

(Terry 1655: 189)

Terry admits that the terraced house enables the resident to be out in the fresh air.
However, Terry also suggests that such an arrangement of the houses encourages
voyeurism and moral depravity. As an example he cites the story of David and
Bathsheba, and suggests that it was David's sighting of Bathsheba from the roof of
his house that led to the problems. Terry (1655: 189–90) thus links the physical
topography with a moral one and iconoclastically deflates the value of native
architecture.

John Fryer's attention is drawn to the prevalence of elephantiasis in the St
Thomas Mount area of Madras city. He offers a remarkable explanation for this
condition:

About this Mount lives a caste of people, one of whose legs are as big as an
elephant's; which gives occasion for the divulging it to be a judgement on
them, as the generation of the assassins and murderers of the Blessed Apostle
St Thomas.

(Fryer 1698: 43)

An endemic disease is taken as an external symptom of a deeper *moral*
malaise of the inhabitants.[37] Ovington conflates moral and physical topography when he suggests that the illnesses of the English were partly the results
of their own intemperance and vulnerability to the Indian climate.[38] The
rhetoric of inflation and accumulation is very clear in Ovington's description:

But there seldom happens any great defect in the natural world, without some preceding in the moral . . . I cannot without horror mention to what a pitch all vicious enormities were grown in this place, . . . these fatal infelicities which are not wholly imputable to an impure contagion of the air, or the gross infection of the elements. Their principles of action, and the consequent evil practices of the English forwarded their miseries, and contributed to fill the air with those pestilential vapours that seized their vitals . . . luxury, immodesty, and a prostitute dissolution of manners.

(Ovington 1696: 143)

Elaborating, Ovington (1696: 144–45) writes: 'The prodigious growth of vermin and of venomous creatures . . . do abundantly likewise demonstrate the malignant corruption of the air'. Ovington links three issues: the climate, cultural habits (food and its consumption) and morality of the Indians. However, Ovington is also careful to represent the natives as equally, if not more, dissolute and depraved as the English, as in this passage:

Because of the heat, they eat at eight or nine in the morning, then at four or five in the afternoon. Then, often at midnight, after their nocturnal embraces, they recover their spirits by some nourishing food, to excite them again to fresh amours.

(Ovington 1696: 313)[39]

The moral marvellous effects a rhetorical transformation of India, from a place of plenty to one of uncontrolled excess. It maps the strange topography of India onto a moral topography and vice versa. The iconoclasm of this moment transforms valuable native achievements or icons into everyday objects, or attributes negative values to them. The iconoclastic moral marvellous empties the Indian landscape of all value, and thus effectively prepares the ground for a repopulating with *English* icons (memorials, constructions, towns) in the late eighteenth century. The third strand in the discourse of the marvellous is important for a very intricate manoeuvre executed by these narratives. It set up India as a site of testing: of the moral fibre, vulnerability and strength of English character. The numerous references to diseases, deprivation and danger in these catalogues dovetails neatly into the *moral topography* of both Indians and English. A critique of Indian icons – achieved through the moral marvellous – simultaneously set up, by implication, the superior character of the English traveller.

The categorical marvellous

I have already indicated how one of the 'constituents' of India's 'difficulty' for the seventeenth-century English traveller was its variegated vastness. Mary Baine Campbell (1999) and Karl Guthke (1990) have argued that multiplicity – a central concern of the early modern age, as manifest in the debates over plural worlds – was often handled through compartmentalization. Ordering the vast and the numerous, and bringing the 'light' of reason to bear on the darkness, were crucial narrative moves in these travellers. Adopting a scientific-rational mode the English traveller in India rejected the natives' icons and events as irrational. They consigned these to the realm of superstition and blind belief, even as they found them morally degenerate. In other cases the categorical marvellous translated icons of great symbolic value to the native into mundane things, thereby depreciating their significance. It also meant 'translating' Indian profusion and wealth into ready categories and tables, thereby rendering them into numbers. The use of the word 'account' in the above document and in the titles of many of the travelogues is perhaps not entirely innocent. (One of the meanings of the word 'account', the *OED* informs us, signifies maintaining of details of *commercial* transactions.) The detailed tabulated lists of products and crops, castes, seasons, prices, currency and distances in these early travel accounts is an enumeration and evaluation of the plenty of India in a form that the merchant or investor would understand.[40]

The rhetoric of the marvellous' aesthetic when describing the profusion of India uses two principal modes to achieve compartmentalization: enumeration and accumulation. Enumeration, allied with the 'scientific' cataloguing characteristic of early modern Europe and the post-Renaissance episteme, itemizes India's plenty. Enumeration, as Eilean Hooper-Greenhill (1992: 140) has argued, meant the cataloguing of objects and detailed accounts in the form of lists, and ties into the context of the publication of specific schemes for writing.[41] Several schemes, such as Robert Boyle's suggestions for 'a natural history' of a country (*PT* 1. 11 [1665–66]: 186–89), or his 'inquiries for Surat' (*PT* 2. 23 [1666–67]: 15–19) recommend a compartmentalization of topics, places, events and peoples. It orders difficult excesses into something more manageable through a narrative that is organized into sections, with headings and subheadings, place names, geographical locations and details – in short, an enumerative format (Teltscher 1997: 14–15). Kate Teltscher and Thomas Metcalf have independently pointed out that the travelogues of this period adopt a rhetoric of similarity and difference, treating Indian objects or events as either similar to or different from the English ones (Teltscher 1997: 24–25; Metcalf 1998: 3–5). However, in many cases – as seen in the English traveller's rhetoric of intensification where the overgrown and the gigantic populate descriptions – this is a difference in *degree* rather than in kind, and the difficulty that the traveller encounters is the sheer expanse or magnitude of Indian things.

The English traveller's enumerative task was an imperative from the company itself, even *before* his arrival in India. The bond executed by the pursers when joining the ship (1607–08) reads:

And according to the charge he is now employed as Pursar do keep a true and perfect account accompanied by inventory of all such provisions tackle munitions furniture victuals and other necessaries which are or shall be during the said voyage brought aboard the said ship or provided for those of the same. And also an inventory of all the goods, wares and merchandise as shall be brought into or carried of the said ship.

(Birdwood 1965: 221–22)

Enumeration, a basic rhetorical strategy of medieval travelogues as Mary Baine Campbell (1999: 69) has demonstrated, essentially meant an inventory of India's fauna and flora, seasons, castes, prices, currency, distances, minerals, agricultural and commercial products. The lists thus become testimonials to India's bewildering and wondrous variety, while simultaneously marking a narrative control over this diversity. Accumulation is the descriptive rendering of excellence and abundance, and is rooted in the rise of descriptive geography in the middle and late seventeenth century in England (Cormack 1997). Employing devices of enumeration and accumulation, the English traveller transforms India into an understandable space. The terms 'survey', 'description' and 'chorography', common to most seventeenth-century travelogues, are 'related' in that they order and particularize space. Such attempts in Terry and others anticipate similar but assuredly more colonial efforts in eighteenth-century writings on India. The narratives of Alexander Dirom, Richard Owen Cambridge, James Bristow and others from the 1750–1820 period contain detailed surveys, maps, toponymy and extensive descriptions of geographical and topographical features and distances. The catalogue is a categorical imperative that captures the marvellous, awe-inspiring vastness, variety and multiplicity of India, while simultaneously seeking to confine them within tables, maps and descriptions.

Thomas Bowrey (1997: 1) states his intention in the opening paragraph of *A Geographical Account of Countries Round the Bay of Bengal 1669 to 1679*: to 'particularize' things of the 'present state, religion, commerce, laws etc.' of the various countries. Bowrey's particularization is an enargheiac cataloguing of India, and is a common feature of the seventeenth-century travelogue.[42] Enargheiac cataloguing, marked by richness of detail, was concerned with the perceptual and pictorial reconstruction of India and its objects in minute detail. This rhetorical form, clearly visible in the instructions of the Royal Society, Francis Bacon and the travelogues supplies an illuminating picture of India. The 'well-formed picture', in these cases, took the shape of an ordered, detailed and compartmentalized, demystified India. The categorical marvellous is this very mode of compartmentalization that, paradoxically, reveals only the illimitable, a picture that constantly disrupts the frame.

The enargheiac categorizing is thus an attempt to provide the reader with a scale. Thus descriptions of size and shape are common to all catalogues in these travelogues. Terry comments that the Indian wheat is '*more* full and *more* white than ours', and that the Indian musk melon is 'very much *better*' (1655: 92, 95, emphasis in original). Commenting on the climate, Terry (1655: 125) declares that 'the coldest day in the whole year at noon . . . is hotter there than the hottest day in England'. Measurement and order – two central features of the seventeenth-century episteme – are both visible in the enargheic mode. Essentially, what the traveller did was an 'informatization' of India, readily available for consumption as an 'India catalogue'.[43]

William Hawkins devotes the last sections of his travelogue to lists and catalogues. He first *lists* the various ranks of the Mughal hierarchy, before moving on to the Mughal emperor's jewellery and 'treasures', and the number of elephants and horses in the army (Purchas 1905, 3: 29–30, 31–33, 33–34). Edward Terry (1655: 111–17, 118) provides *lists* of woods and trees, textiles and minerals.

Thomas Herbert (1634: 184) mentions that but for the boredom it may have entailed for the reader, he would have put in a longer list of fruits into his 'catalogue'. Fryer, Herbert and Bowrey catalogue the animals, trees, coins and currency, units of measurement and fruits in considerable detail (Herbert 1634: 182–83; Fryer 1698: 34–35, 37, 178–79, 182, 205–16; Bowrey 1997 114–16). Paralleling this enumerative cataloguing and narrativization of India was the *Philosophical Transactions'* detailed listing of India 'curiosities': it regularly published accounts of the plants imported by or gifted to the Royal Society for scientific study, as noted above.[44] The linkage between curiosity-knowledge and narrative emerges in works such as these. The demand for curiosities from the East enabled the *Philosophical Transactions* to publish extracts from the travelogues. The form of the travelogue therefore had to be one that provided a speedy access to India. Hence the stress on lists and descriptions. The intensity, expanse and difficulty could be summarized, formalized and ordered into these lists to provide an at-a-glance picture. The lists literally contracted Indian 'difficulty' into something more manageable.

In a different realm, the English traveller paid attention to the religious and symbolic significance of these natural events for the natives. The English traveller desacralizes native icons not only through the rhetoric of the moral marvellous but also by suggesting everyday uses for the objects sacred to the native. Fryer, for instance, expressed his disbelief at Hindu interpretations of icons. He visited mountain burrows believed by the natives to have been built by Alexander, and noted that 'this place by the Gentiles is much adored'. Immediately after this Fryer comments: 'but this is contradictory to the story delivered of Alexander'. He then concludes: '[it is] more probabl[y] . . . heathen Fane, or idolatrous Pagod, from the superstitious opinion they still hold of its sacredness'. Later Fryer, bringing his scientific training (he was a surgeon with the EIC) tries to offer an explanation for the revered *fakir*'s feats of bodily asceticism.[45] He repeats this rationalizing exercise in the case of 'holy' caves and 'fireflies' (Fryer 1698: 73, 103, 138, 141). Native interpretations of the miraculous or divine nature of these events or places were rejected in favour of rational explanations. The marvellous – which reduced the heightened status of the miraculous, as Stephen Greenblatt (1991: 20) has argued – thus also gestured at the irrational, and therefore suspect, native beliefs. Terry notes the several old mosques in the Mughal empire. His description of the scene is worth detailing:

> [Mandu] not much inhabited before we came thither, having more ruins by far about it, than standing houses. But amongst the piles of building that had held up their heads above ruin, there were not a few unfrequented Mosques or Mahomedan churches; yet I observed, that though the people who attended the King there, were marvellously straitened for room, wherein they might dispose of very great numbers of most excellent horses, which were now at that place, they would not make stables of any of those churches, though before that time, they had been forsaken, and out of use.
>
> (Terry 1655: 195)[46]

Terry thus converts a sacred native site and religious icon into an ordinary object. John Ovington desacralizes the Hindu chants that accompany rituals by offering a scientific explanation and linking it to the climate:

> The warmth of the air, which is apt to stupefy the spirits, and render them unwieldy and dull, was as likely a reason for introducing this melodious diversion, which is apt to keep them active and awake at their work.
>
> (Ovington 1696: 292)

In each of these cases, the traveller has offered a quotidian explanation while rejecting native beliefs.

Travel, toponymy and chorography become central to this project of categorization and demystification. The map had by the end of the sixteenth century become an instrument of rule and national surveys – an extension of the map – became obligatory towards the end of the eighteenth (Biggs 1999). More importantly maps enabled European claims to 'new' territories in Africa, Asia and America – land that was not acknowledged as anyone else's property (Helsinger 1997). English newspapers of the time advertised travelogues, maps and globes with astonishing regularity in the early decades of the eighteenth century.[47] Maps and 'faithful' descriptions of the area, these instances suggest, were probably much in demand. The descriptions and maps were clearly 'forward-looking', intended as a knowledge-base for future use, as several of the advertisements state explicitly. Thus in its 8–11 May 1701 advertisement *The Postman* mentions that the Preface to the Hakluyt-Purchas volumes will list the 'great advantages the public receives from the faithful relations of able and inquisitive travellers, with some directions for such as shall go on far voyages for the *future*' (n.p., emphasis added). Another advertised a 'new and correct map of the whole world', with the intention of making it 'useful both by land and sea' (*Evening Post* 29–31 January 1719).

It is in this context of increased demand for and wide-ranging publicity of India information that we need to locate the cartographic and chorographic efforts of these travellers. I have already described how every traveller refers to the vast expanse of India and the Mughal empire. Correcting maps, accurate naming and recording of place names and detailed descriptions, if possible in comparison with English towns and cities, mark the work of these travelogues. Thus Thomas Roe (1990: 104) corrects and updates the map in his letter to the Archbishop of Canterbury. At one point Roe gifts Mercator's maps to the Jahangir stating: 'to a great King I offered the world, in which he had so great and rich a part'. The last section of Roe's journal is devoted to a listing of various cities (Roe 1990: 380, 489–96). Terry's opening reference (in his Preface) to the 'vast compass of that huge monarchy' (quoted above) is not simply a description of expanse, it serves as a symbol for the purpose of the work that follows: mapping India. Terry states that he has recorded the 'true names', which he has procured 'out of the Mughal's own records', and that he would be taking 'notice' of 'some particulars in them which are most remarkable'. Soon after, like Roe, Terry (1655: 78, 90) points out the errors of the geographical maps of India, China and other places. And immediately after, he writes: 'their ground is not enclosed, unless some small quantity near towns and villages, which stand scattered up and down this vast empire very thick, though, *for want of the true names, not inserted in the map*' (Terry 1655: 101, emphasis added). The necessity of recording 'true names' was a tradition of the chorographic narrative, because chorography was seen primarily as a repository of proper names. It enabled them to distinguish between places, since the marking of difference was their main justification for writing the narrative in the first instance (Helgerson 1986: 490–96). For Terry, the absence of proper names for the towns and villages meant that Indian magnitude remains uncontrolled and unknowable. Terry's map, therefore, is one that has not categorized, identified and 'framed' India effectively into a picture. The places were not placed on the map because, without the right name and the location, they would not present a 'well formed picture'. Terry is in fact mourning the impossibility of ordering India and the sense of irresolvable mystery that attaches to the place.

In addition to the obvious one of the Enclosure Acts and ordering of England's landscape during the period, the symbolic significance of enclosed land is crucial to the categorical enarghiea of Terry and others. Cultivated landscapes, gardens and orchards symbolized culture, the spirit of scientific inquiry and Christian faith, a discourse clearly visible in Abraham Cowley's poem to the Royal Society (Sprat 1667: unpaginated; see also Murdoch 1990). Nathaniel Hardy's sermon of 1658, already quoted, ends with an image of England as a *hortus conclusus*.

In such a context of the valorization of the enclosed garden, forests, overgrown spaces or barren plains were perceived as negative topographies. They also become symbolic of something else – the dangers of India's over-fertile nature, the laziness of the natives, the unruliness of India itself which, with its breaking boundaries, refused to be tamed or bounded. References to forests and such unorganized lands abound in seventeenth-century travelogues. The wilderness, mostly represented as 'woods' or forested spaces in seventeenth-century India travelogues, stood for ignorance, primitiveness, lack of culture and heathenism. The landscape becomes iconic of larger (or deeper) moral and ethical conditions of the Indians themselves. This theme looks forward to comments by later, eighteenth-century travellers such as Jemima Kindersley, Moorcroft and Trebeck and others, writing well into the times of 'British India', all of whom mourned Indian laziness in not cultivating gardens.[48] The observations of Fryer and Bowrey thus look forward to the clearly colonial writing of the eighteenth century.

The English traveller thus successfully negotiates and explains the Indian landscape through moral and scientific explanations that were, in the first place, necessitated by their extravagant descriptions of India. The negotiation had its tensions, such as the one between a moral-theologically inflected reading and an empiricist, rational explanation of Indian difficulty that I have outlined above. The 'discourse of difficulty', I suggest, is essentially about overcoming mystery and danger in the act of narration and interpretation. The aesthetic of the marvellous first constructs a landscape of great vastness and near-magical profusion. Later, threatened by this same profusion, the marvellous tropes a landscape of excess through its 'discourse of difficulty'. Such a discourse, I have argued, is simultaneously a discourse of interpretation and control. Moving from a troping of India as possessing incomparable magnitude, dangerous excess and difficult darkness, it seeks to 'frame' the vastness of India, penetrate its many mysteries and to organize the variety into manageable categories and groups. The careful rationalization and categorization of India, or its theologically determined condemnation, after a recognition of its vastness and mystery, is an attempt to alleviate the difficulty, at least within rhetoric. By paying attention to ruined buildings, the depravity of the natives, the unhealthy climate of India and the excessive threat of (native) disease, the traveller was articulating a very complex discourse of the Indian landscape. These texts are layered with descriptions of English vulnerability, their adaptability, native immunity and the native (as) disease. The description of Indian excess, working along with the tirade against luxury, articulated a discourse of Western morality versus Eastern temptation and depravity.[49]

Thus marvellous 'difficulty' becomes a necessary anterior moment to the interpretive one. At the conclusion of the travelogue, even if India has not been controlled, it has been cast into a 'well-formed picture' with each element carefully located, labelled and framed, but one that threatens to burst its frames. Difficulty thus 'strips' into a dynamic of moral-theological or scientific-rational desacralization, quantification and interpretation.

The rhetorical devices through which the seventeenth-century travelogue suggests control over India anticipates the efforts at aesthetic and rhetorical control over post-Baksar India – when the East India Company established itself as a political power – where the aesthetics of the sublime operated on the axis of desolation and improvement. This two-stage process of the 1750–1820 period relied on the 'emptying' of the Indian landscape by focusing on sublime destruction and ruin *before* proposing an imperial programme of improvement. This mode, visible in the works of George Forster, William Hodges and several other writers of the last decades of the eighteenth century, has as its anterior moment, the intensification-demystification modes of Edward Terry and others. The aesthetic of the marvellous was therefore a project of ordering, cataloguing and space-clearing. It demonstrated the English traveller's authority to describe and inscribe India's plenty. A reading of the seventeenth-century travelogue for this dual rhetoric enables us to see how a proto-colonial move of understanding, controlling or emptying the landscape looks forward to more avowedly colonial actions in the late eighteenth century. The 'discourse of difficulty', as I see it, is a preliminary move in the larger discourse of 'framing' an India amenable to, suitable for and profitable to England in the eighteenth century.

2 The social monstrous, 1600–1720

> Where first, for their numerous armies, it will appear to be no strange thing, if we consider the Great Mogol to be what he is, an overgrown Prince in the vast extent of his territories, being like a huge Pike in a great pond, that preys upon all his neighbours.
>
> (Terry 1655: 158)

This is Edward Terry's description of one of the richest emperors of the early modern world. Terry's description, with its images of predatory actions, greed, excessive bodily growth and excessive consumption, is aligned with other, similar ones in early English writing on India.

The English traveller paid close attention to temples, art forms, individual bodies and events in India, and found them hideous, horrific and 'monstrous', as Partha Mitter's (1977) excellent study has shown. My interest lies in another dimension of this encounter with the Indian monstrous: that with Indian bodies and spectacles rather than with art. Encountering static temple icons and art was, I believe, a very different experience from encountering the semi-naked '*fakir*' or the snake charmer 'in the flesh'.

Troping the king as a creature of vast dimensions and appetites, as Terry does, is a component of the aesthetic that informs many India travelogues of the period. This aesthetic is, however, not restricted to descriptions of monarchs alone. Towards the end of his massive travelogue, for instance, Edward Terry has a section titled 'corrollarie, and conclusion'. Meditating on the various cultures, religions and people he has encountered in India, Terry (1655: 500) dismisses the 'Gentiles' in India as 'wild, neglected, unnatural'. Taken together, the image of the overgrown Mughal prince and the three terms in Terry's description of Gentiles sum up the entire schema of tropes employed in the early English travelogue on India, tropes that render India a site where the terrifying and the ludicrous coexist. The Terry passage relies on two key aspects of the discourse of monstrosity: form and function. The native ruler is morally deformed and functions as a predator. (The *OED* informs us that 'deformity' was also used in this period to suggest moral corruption.) The conjunction of the trope of corporeal deformity with that of a 'deformed' function generates a discourse where Indian hierarchy, social structures and political economy are all imaged as 'monstrous'. The monster's body – or the monstrous body – is, in Jeffrey Cohen's (1996: 4) terms, a 'cultural body', a *construction* and projection. The aesthetic project of the social monstrous enables the English traveller to dehumanize the native, dismiss native beliefs and critique Indian political economy and principles of governance.

The troping of India, and the Indian body in particular, takes recourse to the monstrous and the grotesque – the two are often used as synonyms, though there exist significant distinctions (Dorrian 2000) – using particular images and rhetorical modes. The monstrous, an integral part of the early modern imagination across Europe, had corporeal, aesthetic and moral dimensions (Crawford 2005: 3–18). It was related not only to the 'strange', 'unnatural' and 'obscene' but also to the 'disruptive and "uncivil" ways that an object was put to use' (Bailey 2001: 253). That is, the discourse of monstrosity paid attention to the *functions* to which an object was put. The 'traditional' early modern monstrous was a category used to describe anything that lay outside the perceived natural order.[1] Thomas Browne (1970 [1642]: 30), therefore, famously declared in *Religio Medici* that 'there are no grotesques in nature'. It was a common mode of portraying the alien where the monstrous often overlapped with the category of 'foreign' (Campbell 1988, 1996; Burnett 2002: 2–3). They evoked, according to Daston and Park (1998: 176), at least three 'complexes of interpretations and associated emotions': horror, pleasure and repugnance. They were seen as portents of disaster (Brammall 1996). Browne (1970: 35) goes on to qualify his statement (quoted above): 'Nature so ingeniously contriving the irregular parts, as they become sometimes more remarkable than the principall fabrick'. In the case of the grotesque there was often a suggestion of *artifice*, bordering on the ludicrous, where the monstrous could be *contained* in art, or was artifice itself.[2] Browne here is emphasizing the *constructed* nature of the monstrous, a move that shifts away from the 'divine portent' theory of monsters of the late medieval period. By the 1570s there occurs a shift in ideas of monstrosity. John Knox and others expanded the definition of monstrous beyond that of mere physical deformity and deviance and monstrosity was not about appearance alone, but also about behaviour. Tyranny, heresy, pride, treason were all described as 'monstrous'. Concomitantly, as Kathryn Brammall (1996) has demonstrated, the 'rhetoric of monstrosity' became more comprehensive. The monstrous itself, despite its overwhelming affect of horror, could generate gossip, amusement and delight, and provide the sources for satirists, as Daston and Park (1998: 196–200) have demonstrated in the case of early modern Europe teratology. There is evidently considerable overlap between the monstrous and the grotesque in the early modern worldview. What is consistent in these interpretations is that monsters were deemed to violate the norms of regularity not only in nature, but also in society and the arts. It is also crucial to note that the monstrous was often treated as an icon or portent of social decay where order and the correct or balanced correlation between form and function had collapsed. It was this interpretation that gives rise to the dominant response to monsters in the seventeenth century: repugnance (Daston and Park 1998: 202). The early modern grotesque also relied heavily on Oriental settings and themes.

Inigo Jones designed William D'Avenant's *The Temple of Love*, produced in London in 1634, with an Indian motif. On the side pillars there appeared 'Indian trophees': elephants, *fakirs*, camels, a figure representing Tigris. Thomas Herbert used the term 'grotesque' to describe Persian wall carvings. Jacques Callot introduced the grotesque in the form of Balli (dancers), Gobbi (hunchbacks) and beggars in 1622 (Barasch 1971: 59, 70, 81–82).

In the case of English writings on India, the rhetoric of monstrosity served several purposes, as this chapter demonstrates. The monstrous, in the case of English writings on India, might be treated as a natural and logical outcome of the aesthetic of the marvellous because of the latter's reliance on excess (and in this I differ from Greenblatt's (1991: 76) argument that the marvellous did not swerve into the monstrous).

Troping the Indian body or the Indian religious procession as strange and/or deformed, the English traveller often folds or shades the monstrous into the grotesque. The latter – and this is my main argument – located deformity as a *social* phenomenon.[3] It orders Indian people, monarchy, bodies and events into the category of the unnatural to create what I term the 'social monstrous'.[4] The 'monstrosities' perceived in Indian bodies, the narratives suggest, were portents of the imminent decay of Indian culture and civilization. That is, the aesthetics of the monstrous shifts focus from isolated and individual instances of deformity, excessive consumption or ugliness to their *contexts* of production and reception so that an overarching comment on India as a whole is made possible. The narrative makes the singular 'monstrosity' iconic of a larger social monstrosity, thereby dismissing the culture in its entirety.

In the rest of this chapter I shall isolate some of the more dominant modes of troping an Indian monstrous in the writings of Edward Terry, John Ovington and other seventeenth-century travellers.

Monstrous consumption

Edward Terry's (1655: 435) description of the Mughal emperor as an 'overgrown pike' – which he repeats later – that opens this chapter is one of a series of images that appropriates the metaphor of ingestion and monstrous consumption in the early English travelogue on India. John Fryer's inaugural description of the king of Golkonda details the monarch's expenses and armies, before concluding with this interesting comment: 'All that he consumes is on his voluptuousness, with which he is swallowed up' (Fryer 1698: 29). Later Fryer describes Indian political economy through an analogy that echoes verbatim Terry's description. 'The great fish prey on the little', writes Fryer (1698: 147). These descriptions of overgrown Indian rulers constitute a dominant trope that occurs with astonishing regularity in early English writings on India. Deploying the aesthetics of the monstrous and the grotesque, the English traveller in India presents not merely a landscape of excess (see Chapter 1), but an excess of gross misproportion, combination, bestiality and social deformity (for Terry (1655: 524–26), in fact, moral corruption is almost always 'deformity'; in his discourse against moral corruption, he uses the image of deformed bodies extensively, referring to ulcerous, decaying, misshapen bodies).

Central to the proto-colonial monstrous was the *rhetoric of consumption.* 'Consumption' here serves as a dual motif: of ingestion or incorporation and that of excessive use.[5] These two semantic possibilities are fully utilized in seventeenth-century writings on India.[6] What is fascinating about this narrative of consumption is that both the jewelled, elaborately costumed aristocrat and the under-dressed, under-fed *fakir* are coded as 'monstrous'. Excessive consumption and minimal consumption are both, apparently, 'unnatural'. Both Terry and Ovington warn the English traveller against succumbing to the 'consumptive' mode because of the plenitude of India. Terry (1655: 462, 498–99, 507) launches a tirade against excessive consumption and covetousness in English people too. 'Monstrous consumption' is as much a failing of Indians as it might be a threat to the European in India. The image of snares and monstrous entanglements, especially in terms of excessive luxury and material wealth, is common in the travelogue and other writings of the period. As late as 1708, William Anderson, preaching in Fort William, Bengal, speaks of how the ancient Jews had to destroy their neighbours because 'their idolatrous worship, and the strange and monstrous dissolution of their manners was sure to be a snare to a people' (Anderson 1708: 2–3). Clearly there is a link between wealth, entanglement and the monstrous. I will return to this trope of entanglement a little later.

The English traveller often portrays the Indian king and aristocracy as a grotesque creature prone to excessive greed and gluttony. Two related tropes figure here: ingestion and appropriation. If the first relies on images of eating and consumption, the second presents a more insidious and indirect mode of incorporation: the exploitative greed of the aristocratic class that takes away the wealth of the lower classes. As Maggie Kilgour (1990: 103) in her exemplary reading of Ben Jonson suggests, both food and money are 'objects of corporeal and economic consumption'. Excessive consumption was also a trait of the monstrous (McAvoy and Walters 2002).[7] It is therefore significant that gluttony, greed, desire, hoarding – all images of excessive consumption – are seen as *social* rather than individual traits in the English travelogue. In their ethnographic portraits of Indian society, the English travellers often pointed to caste, class or regional traits in terms of their consumption patterns. Here is Thomas Herbert's detailed description of the bania caste:

> The bannyas . . . make many well minded simple men lose themselves, when by a heedless stupid admiration of their sincere hypocrisie they entangle themselves by crediting their sugrd words in way of trade or complement, baits pleasingly swallowed when we contemplate their temperance.
>
> (Herbert 1634: 28)

The trope of ingestion here is tied into the social contexts of exploitation, vulnerability and deception. Ovington (1696: 235) 'documents' how Indians *in general* (i.e. as a race) ate excessively, especially spicy food that inflamed their senses and

rendered their behaviour monstrous. In a detailed description he mentions that
Muslims, though prohibited by their religion from drinking, often become 'intoxicated to madness'. Indians are given to substance abuse, with people 'running a
muck' under the influence of drugs and alcohol. Ovington's detailed narrative is
couched entirely in the rhetoric of consumption: picturing the Indian as drunk,
immoderate and intemperate. The temper, he writes, 'continues with him in the
highest pitch'. Alcoholic spirits are consumed in 'large dose[s]', inducing 'gay
humours', 'strange actions' and 'mad frenzy'. Even Europeans in India, he
complains, partake of these in 'immoderate draughts' (Ovington 1696: 236–40).
The narrative here showcases Indian consumption and its negative effects.
Ovington describes drunken Indians running amok, killing their family members
before committing suicide. It creates an image of a culture prone to frenzy as a
consequence of excessive consumption. Even snakes and locusts in India, he
suggests, feed indiscriminately, and thereby destroy entire harvests. What is fascinating is Ovington's mode of concluding this argument about Indian gluttony and
immoderate pleasures of the table. Describing a feast arranged by an Englishman,
he claims that the Muslims he met in India ate pork and drank alcohol. He writes:
'swines-flesh is under a dis-repute . . . an abomination. Yet the Grandees will taste
of this' (Ovington 1696: 130–32, 240).

> When they had tasted, applauded the delicacy of the meat, ate it with abun-
> dance of delight, and boasted that they had never seen any such plump kids,
> whose relish outdid anything they had ever tasted; and heartily wisht for the
> opportunity of such other repast, and the liberty of banqueting frequently
> upon such dishes. They admired the Christian indulgence in such noble
> liquor, and such exquisite fare, and believed that the unconfined luxury in
> eating was equal to the pleasure of their desirable variety of women; and that
> the carnal excesses approv'd by Mahomet do not outvie the unconstrained
> liberty which the Christians take in sumptuous repasts, and such kind of luxu-
> rious sensuality.
>
> (Ovington 1696: 240–42)

Ovington's strategy is insidious here. He first 'proves' how the Muslims do not
adhere to their religious principles when it comes to the pleasures of the dining
table. Then, he is also able to demonstrate how they even envy the Englishman his
pleasures of consumption. Ovington, who in his 1699 tract, *An Essay upon the Nature
and Qualities of Tea*, would be critical of the Japanese for using 'a multitude of
servants and a stately furniture of instruments' just to prepare and consume tea
(1699: 8–9), here suggests that the Indians wait for opportunities to indulge themselves. The rhetoric of consumption here effects a grotesque with its images of gluttony, feasting and indulgence. Ovington also makes it clear that the Indians'
gluttony is a transgressive act, since the eating of pork is prohibited by their religion. Rendering the act of consumption as transgressive enables Ovington to posit
a culture that breaks laws and boundaries of appropriate and inappropriate
behaviour.

The quote from Terry that opens this chapter places corporeal and moral deformities side by side. He goes on to portray the Mughal emperor, whom he has already described as a preying fish, thus: 'The Mogol feeds and feasts himself with this conceit; that he is the conqueror of the world' (Terry 1655: 367). The Mughal's avarice is also mapped as excessive:

> although the Mogol had such infinite treasures, yet he could finde room to store up more still, the desires of a covetous heart being so unsatiable, as that it never knows when it hath enough, being like a bottomless purse that can never be fill'd, for the more it hath, the more still it covets.
>
> (Terry 1655: 398; also 400, 412, 422)

Ovington, like Terry, argues that the Mughal emperor's 'desires' are not 'abated by his accessions'. In fact, once again taking recourse to the trope of excessive growth or deformity and monstrous consumption, such 'accessions' 'stretch and swell the more'. Later, he comments that Indian business transactions are conducted under the cover of darkness in order to avoid attracting the attention of the greedy Mughal (Ovington 1696: 202, 316–18). Thomas Bowrey (1997: 127) makes a similar observation about the native subjects who, he believes, bury their wealth so as to not attract attention from the predator-kings. Avarice and tyranny become hallmarks of the subversion of monarchical functions. Instead of protecting the commercial profits and processes of the subjects, the Mughal, suggest the English travellers, feeds off them.

In each of these accounts we have images of gluttony, feasting and excessive consumption that mark a profligate, dissipated, unruly social condition.[8] Appetite, as Nicholas Watson (2002: 18–19) argues, is as much about power as it is about desire, taste or need. In the case of the Indian emperor, therefore, the excessive consumption imaged in this rhetoric is about the power of the tyrant to exploit and consume the wealth of his citizens. The image of devouring monarchs, exploited citizens and suffering will return repeatedly in these narratives. This conjunction creates the effect of monstrosity because it links form and function. It signifies the collapse of India's social order for the English traveller.

The rhetoric of consumption also enables the English person to posit an Indian *ensnared* within material desires, wealth and luxuries. Rooted in a discourse against luxurious apparel and excessive 'style', incidentally described as 'monstrous' in at least one document from the period (*England's Vanity* written by a 'Compassionate Conformist', 1683),[9] the English traveller expressed outrage at the amount of jewellery on the bodies of the Indian aristocrats and women. Seeing these as signs of moral degradation and temptation, the rhetoric against luxurious clothes and accessories often generates a 'fashion monster', a human whose excessive use of fashion – apparel, jewellery – produces a hideous and morally corrupt being.[10] Tropes of snares and monstrous entanglements, especially in terms of luxury and material wealth, are common in the travelogue and other writings of the period. John Bulwer, therefore, had described the practice of wearing heavy jewellery in the ears as 'monstrous' because they lacerate the soft flesh (quoted in M.B.

Campbell 1999: 243). If frugality was Christian, as some documents of the period suggest, then luxury and material possessions were clearly consigned to the realm of the devil.[11] Monstrous consumption here is mainly imaged in terms of jewellery. This evidence of wealth is rendered ludicrous by a narrative that emphasizes the grotesque distortions of the body *produced* by the jewels.

Indian women, notes Thomas Herbert (1634), wear a lot of jewels, what he calls in a telling term, 'fetters'. He writes: 'their ears are extended and dilacerated very much' because of the 'great and ponderous' jewels, and adds: 'the women dilacerate their ears to a monstrous proportion, for by the ponderousness of their eare jewels they teare their eares to that capacity: that I have easily put my arme through their eareholes' (Herbert 1634: 28, 38, 188). John Fryer echoes Herbert when he writes: 'Their women are manacled with chains of silver (or fetters rather) and hung with ear-rings of gold and jewels, their noses stretched with weighty jewels'. He repeats this image of the 'manacled' Indian woman burdened with jewels later (Fryer 1698: 31, 110, 133, 156). Thomas Bowrey (1997: 35, 208) also refers to the 'shackles' on the bodies of women. Ovington (1696: 319) criticizes the Indian women who, he complains, 'ambitiously affect a gayety in their dress and cloathing'. He then spends three pages describing their jewellery (1696: 319–21). Like Fryer and Herbert, Ovington also uses the image of the snare to describe the Indian woman when he says: 'their toes are adorned with rings, and their legs with shackles of gold'. He also provides an anecdote about the emperor Aurangezebe in which the Mughal 'stripped' the *fakirs* of their wealth and jewels (Ovington 1696: 320, 202–05). Terry (1655: 214–18) has an extended critique of the pursuit of fashion by his fellow countrymen in England, arguing that fashion is essentially evil and an index of moral depravity, especially when practiced by the lower classes.

The trope of ensnarement and entanglement contributes in a major way to the grotesque in early English narratives on India. It is significant that the Indian woman is described as being 'fettered' and 'manacled'. Entanglement of human bodies with vegetation was a characteristic of the medieval grotesque (Farnham 1971: 11). If vegetation suggests a 'natural' grotesque, the same motif is transformed into a social or civic setting in the case of India. Here it is artifice and social manners that create a context for women to be so 'entangled'.[12] Man-made jewellery entangles the Indian woman in a grotesque that is clearly social. In other cases it is the sexuality of the Indian woman that 'insnares' the man (both the Indian and the European), but especially the wealthy one. The 'rich spectator', writes Ovington (1696: 257–58), is 'enchanted' into parting with his wealth. Terry (1655: 207–16) provides a detailed criticism of fashion – in England and in India. He berates people who give in to this craze for fashion, arguing that by doing so 'they have so *deformd* that simple fashion, in which he [God] first created them' (1655: 210, emphasis added).

In each of these cases the Englishmen tropes Indians as 'fashion monsters' with excesses of jewels and material wealth.[13] Material wealth translates as an index of greed and consumption in many texts during this period.[14] The fashion monster, now more accurately a 'fashion grotesque' because of the ludic dimension, becomes a mode of dismissing the very obvious Indian wealth, while remaining fascinated by the same. Like the traditional grotesque that both fascinates and repulses, the early English travellers were both impressed and repulsed by Indian wealth and material prosperity, while losing no opportunity to treat such wealth as the result of greed or exploitation. Fryer (1698: 39) therefore refers to the 'Mammon of Unrighteousness' among the Indians. The disparaging reference to the medieval deity of riches who was coded as a devil renders Indian wealth as evil. Later, describing a ceremony, Fryer returns to the same image. The event is a harvest festival, when the Indians are, in Fryer's words, 'expecting a plentiful crop', that is, more material prosperity. The procession, writes Fryer, included Hindu 'Gods in State, garnished with the riches of the Orient'. Having empha-sized the material wealth, this description quickly swerves into the fashion grotesque. Fryer writes: 'they [the idols] were cut in horrid shape . . . deformities'. Finally, in a remarkable shift of emphasis, Fryer turns his attention to the revelry and spectacle:

> Their dancing wenches . . . with ephods of silk and gold upon their breasts; with these in a ring hand in hand, were the dancing boys, all naked but a clout about their privities, like the Bacchanalian youths that used to revel it with Flora's strumpets through the streets of Rome.
>
> (Fryer 1698: 44)

Several things occur in this description. Fryer links the Indian revelry with the despised Roman ones. Ovington (1696: 203) also compares the Indian spectacle of the *fakirs* to Romish mendicants. (British commentators on India used such comparisons as late as 1811. See, for instance, the *Edinburgh Review*'s comments on Indian and ancient Greek gods, 17 [1811]: 317). It moves from a focus on the signs of wealth (silk and gold) to semi-clad youth. By reducing the festivities to grotesque ludicrousness, Fryer ensures that Indian wealth and celebrations of prosperity are imaged as despicable, a fashion grotesque that relegates wealth to the realm of the hideous and the morally reprehensible. Such a rendering ludicrous was part of the seventeenth-century grotesque's condemnation as immoral, indecorous and inharmonious, as Barasch (1971: 56) has argued. Fryer's emphasis on the indeco-rous costume of the native inscribed the religious procession firmly within the domain of the grotesque to be condemned. The music is inharmonious, the costumes inappropriate and the gestures lewd. The fashion grotesque recodes signs and evidence of Indian wealth and celebrations as *deformity*, emphasizing, for instance, the nakedness of the Indian boys. The celebratory spectacle is now read as an exercise in deformity, moral depravity and the ludicrous. This is a general tendency in Fryer's narrative, where he moves from wealth to poverty, from signs of prosperity to icons of exploitation and suffering.[15]

Culture, coded as fashions or manners and customs, in the writings of the seventeenth century, was often associated with barbarians (Campbell 1999: 245). In the case of the Indians, the English traveller was able to translate signs of wealth into a 'fashion monster' and reject the culture as a whole. Further, by coding jewellery as 'shackles' or 'fetters', the traveller's rhetoric transformed fashion into 'snares'. The rhetoric of monstrous consumption relying upon the trope of ensnarement and shackling in the above descriptions approximates to a 'mannerist grotesque' (Semler 1996: 69–82). In the mannerist grotesque there exist 'artificial patterns of transformation and entanglement', and 'disorder is order' (Semler 1996: 73).[16] Fashion, manners and culture in general seem to stand in synechdochically for each other in these narratives. It is significant that icons of wealth become grotesque. The English traveller proposes that Indian society is so barbaric that it shackles its women, even if it does so with jewels. Travellers create the image of Indian society, as they 'see' it in the cities of Agra, Surat, Bombay or Delhi, where people are grotesque because they seem to be obsessed with bodily harm, distortion and self-mutilation in the guise of fashion. Artificially induced distortion and mutilation, the traveller suggests, is grotesque.

Consumption also takes a slightly different form in this rhetoric when the traveller describes how the Indians hoard wealth. The Mughal emperor and his officers, writes Ovington (1696: 105, 216), are avaricious, 'with an innate ambition for empire and command'. Hence, the inhabitants are 'always anxious to conceal their riches'. The general populace also, writes Ovington, is 'addicted to . . . the amassing of treasure'. Indians are all the time 'thinking thoughts of increasing their wealth', and some actually go on to accumulate a 'prodigious treasure'. Later, he emphasizes the Mughal's greed in exploiting his subjects, which forces them to hoard wealth 'close and private', even conducting their commerce in the night to avoid the unwanted attention of the Mughal (Ovington 1696: 277–78, 317, 318). Greed for wealth and hoarding, suggests Ovington, is a central trait of the Moors, banias and the general Indian populace. Consumption is also the excessive wealth spent on wedding and funeral feasts. He claims that such extravagance often 'drains their fortunes' (Ovington 1696: 330, 318–19, 332).

Having described the mourning Moharram procession – he calls them 'anticks' – John Fryer (1698: 109) comments: 'then returning, repeat with veneration their names, and after this they trim their beards, wash and shift their cloaths, (all this while worn negligently, as mourners) and return to their more beastly vomit of luxury'.[17] Here Fryer (1698: 108) begins by describing the procession as 'furies', clearly a source of threat and unease. When he concludes, he has shifted focus on to the end of the Moharram period. The reference to 'beastly' ways and the trope of the 'vomit of luxury' combine two central features of the India grotesque: the species confusion of rendering the native in animal terms, and the aesthetics of consumption. More importantly, by calling the religious event 'anticks', Fryer has transformed them into the ludic grotesque, deserving no more than ridicule and dismissal. 'Anticks', Frances Barasch informs us, were treated as part of the grotesque and rejected on moral grounds by early modern writers like George Herbert in works like *A Priest to the Temple* (1634). These 'anticks' were considered frivolous and therefore immoral (Barasch 1971: 60–64). Fryer's recourse to the very term situates the Indian grotesque firmly within the early modern tradition. Rendering wealth as deformity – moral, physiognomic and corporeal – enables the English traveller to negotiate India's evident prosperity as morally empty, manageable and even ludicrous.

Fryer also marks the native celebrations as frightening before rendering them ludicrous (the image of vomit returns later in Fryer's narrative, when he describes a *fakir* as going back to his vomit, 1698: 127). Vomit, related closely to metaphors of ingestion and excessive consumption, here functions as an analogy for 'immoral' rituals.

Beastly bodies

Tropes of ingestion, consumption and entanglement, as seen above, generate a 'fashion monster' and render India a ludic grotesque. However, the representation of the Indian monstrosity did not end with this. The focus on Indian bodies took recourse to different rhetorical moves to achieve a grotesque 'effect'.

The human animal

A significant element in the grotesquification of the Indian body is the troping of the Indian in animal terms. Thomas Roe, describing his encounter with a local governor, Zulfikar Khan, writes:

> [The Governor] going rudely like a horse forward got before me, which thinking he did on purpose, I crossed the way and was at the stair's foot before him; and so telling him I would lead him in, a servant of his pulled me and said I might not go before the Governor.
>
> (Roe 1990: 42–43)

Christopher Farewell (1633: 18) describes the populous streets of Surat town thus: 'and so along the many streets (humming like bees in swarmes), with multitudes of people'. Thomas Bowrey (1997: 33) describes the Brahmins as 'chattering with a lowd voice'. Fryer (1698: 72) describes the 'mole-like industry' of natives. In an extended passage Fryer describes 'two kinds of vermin' in India: the 'fleas and the banyans', elaborating on the latter as 'horse-leeches', and warning other Englishmen of these 'spawn' of Jews (1698: 82–83). Fryer, having described the natives as vermin, then proceeds to warn his countrymen that these banias are 'expert in all the studied art of thriving and insinuation' and how they always manage to make a profit (1698: 83) – traits that are distinctly unanimal like!

What this achieves is a classical grotesque move of species confusion where the native Indian is moved beyond the pale of the human without abandoning the 'essence' of the racial other. Fryer's portrait of the Indian caste conflates animal and human traits into a racial grotesque. The dehumanization of the Indian body or caste into animal-like, beastly and inhuman beings is central to the early English narratives on India. This kind of objectification, which is a recurrent feature of human grotesquification, confounds categories because a human cannot, by definition, be made into an animal (Cassuto 1997: 12–15). The racial grotesque here is the inhuman Indian/nature. This process of grotesquification, however, does not end with such a dehumanization or animalization.

English descriptions of Indian bodies invariably focused, in addition to the Indian fashion of jewels, on the clothing used, the state of hygiene and physical form. Thus John Fryer's very *first* description of Indian bodies makes a reference to disease and personal hygiene of Indians. He comments how 'long hair not cleanly kept' causes 'Plica Polonica' (a disease of the scalp which entangles hair, and may be accompanied by infestation of lice), to which, he adds, Indians are 'incident'. Later he returns to his concern with lice and other such creatures when describing Surat city's inhabitants (Fryer 1698: 26, 92). Descriptions of threatening physiognomies, unhealthy bodies and deformity abound in the English narratives about India. In other cases, the state of weaponry, the capabilities to fight or even a threatening appearance are rendered grotesque in the Englishman's narrative. Thus Fryer encounters a regiment of soldiers on one of his travels. His description of the meeting is fascinating.

> I made him not tarry along, following the messenger, who brought me into the middle of a ragged regiment, distinguishable from the Mogul's on that score, but more peculiarly by their hair appearing on both ears under their puckeries [Fryer obviously means pugries or turbans]; their weapons are much alike, though to me they give more cause of laughter, than terror (considering the awkwardness of their wearing them) notwithstanding they are instruments of death.
>
> (Fryer 1698: 127)

Here Fryer is at pains to underscore the ludicrousness of the Indian regiments. His attention to the hirsute soldiers and the weaponry conceals an anxiety at being in the 'middle' of a regiment of armed natives. Fryer transforms the threat into something laughable, though his passing reference to potential or real terror should not escape our attention.

The grotesque is about bodies, both animal and human, that are 'exaggerated', either in terms of proportion or combination (Dorrian 2000). Parts have grown to excess or features from assorted species seem to have merged in them. Fryer calls Shivaji a 'diseased limb of the Deccan', who has 'swoln too big for the body', driven by 'extravagant desires'. He also provides a detailed description of the grotesquely swollen limbs of elephantiasis victims in Madras city (1698: 170, 43). Edward Terry (1655: 446) also describes the 'misshapen' legs of elephantiasis victims. We have already noted Terry's description of the overgrown and preying Mughal prince, compared to 'a huge Pike in a great pond'.[18] He also refers to India's humanity as corrupt in terms that are consistent with the rhetoric of dehumanization and grotesquification, speaking of 'that mass of corruption, which hath infected the whole world' and has 'sowred the whole lumps of mankind' (Terry 1655: 158, 488). Christopher Farewell (1633: 59–60, 63) mentions 'trees covered with over-grown apes and monkies' and 'corpulent' natives. Fryer, describing the animals and birds in the Indian forests, writes of creatures '[with] heads like an owl, bodied like a monkey, without tails; only the first finger of the right hand was armed with a claw like a birds, otherwise they had hands . . . they were coloured like a fox'. The 'bats and wasps' are 'overgrown and desperately revengeful', as are the wolves (Fryer 1698: 88–89, 135, 141–42, 178–79, 189–90). John Ovington notes: 'I cannot without horror mention to what a pitch all vicious enormities were grown in this place'. He notes that spiders and 'venomous creatures', all grow larger than normal. He also claims that wounds – essentially damage to bodily 'form' – do not heal quickly in India (1696: 143, 144–45, 145). Ovington renders the tyrannical (but unnamed) Indian king in corporeal terms when he writes:

> If his martial arms be proportionably as extensive as his natural, they will certainly reach very far, and stretch his authority farther than any potentates in the East; for they are so long, that as he stands, his hands reach down below his knees.
>
> (Ovington 1696: 188)

Terry's description of the 'overgrown' native king has already been noted.

Such images of malformed bodies construct India as a place of grotesque corporeality. Animals, fruits, humans all seem to possess odd forms and mannerisms. Their growth is awkward and their behaviour does not fit in with their species (humans). The descriptions clearly indicate a confusion and conflation of categories. Thus, descriptions of Indian bodies or people as 'swarms' (Farewell), 'chattering' (Bowrey) or monstrous (Ovington) merge categories of humans and animals. In the case of the latter, they are excessive in size and malformed. The tyrannical king possesses an unusually formed body, which seems to be out of proportion, large and therefore grotesque. The gigantic, as Susan Stewart (1984: 86) has demonstrated, reflects the 'order and disorder of historical forces'. In the case of India, disorder reigns in the form of an overgrown monarch. The body and the behaviour reflect each other in the descriptions of Terry and Ovington.[19]

Beasts of passion

Integral to the troping of Indian society as grotesque was a rhetoric in which the image of malformed bodies was concomitant with descriptions of the Indian's behaviour. Tales of non-European barbarism and cruel behaviour appeared in the newspapers of the time, and frame the reception of the India narratives. Here is a news report from *The English Post*: 'The Betty-Frigot is arrived at Barbados from the East Indies, and that about 40 Negroes who were on Board, got out of the Hold, and fell upon the Ships Crew, killing several of them' (4–6 March 1702).

Such news reports immediately created images of the savage non-European, whose behaviour approximates to the beastly. The English travel narrative of the seventeenth century pays a great deal of attention to Indian mannerisms, customs and behaviour. Using an aesthetic of the grotesque, the traveller often created a picture of India where the humans were not always human and the Indian's behaviour often intersected with that of the non-human. The traveller images Indians as lascivious, intoxicated, uncontrollable – all of which contributed to the image of the beast-like Indian living in a condition of the social monstrous. Fertility and idolatry – closely linked with each other from the time of the Renaissance, as Marie-Hélène Huet (1993: 29) points out – come in for special attention in these narratives. Description of the Indian woman's sexuality, the lascivious *fakir* or the horrid idol in almost every single narrative of this period seems to propose a society where there is a direct link between sexuality and the monstrous. The monstrous imagination of the seventeenth-century English narrative on India maps devilish rituals, fertility rites and hypersexuality.

Ovington believes that Muslims were 'privately licentious' with 'inflamed', 'vital heats' being often 'intoxicated to madness'. He describes Indians as 'running a muck' under the influence of drugs and alcohol (1696: 235, 236, 236–40). Ovington writes in a passage that again takes recourse to tropes suggesting animal appetites: 'Often at midnight, after their nocturnal embraces, they recover their spirits by some nourishing food, to excite them to fresh amours'. He then declares: 'they seldom go to sleep without a wench in their arms' (Ovington 1696: 313).

The beast-like hypersexuality of the native is a central theme in English writings on India. The descriptions render the Indians 'erotic beasts', endowed with certain animal sexuality.[20] Thomas Herbert believes they have a 'variety of carnal objects' that indicates 'distruction'. He describes the Indian girls being made to lose their chastity to 'devilish idols', paying particular attention to the blood and pain she suffers in the process (Herbert 1634: 186, 40). Thomas Bowrey (1997: 24) echoes Herbert when he claims that the 'insatiable idolatrous priests' exploit the young, virginal girls who come to them. Edward Terry (1655: 297) describes India as a 'fleshly paradise' and believes the Muslims 'walk so much after the flesh', in an image that combines sexuality with consumption of meat.[21] Terry has an extended attack on 'incontinence' and 'intemperance' where he uses the term 'filthy' to describe promiscuity, thus linking sexuality with the abject. He is appalled that Islam sanctions four wives to each man, a condition he terms 'filthy liberty' once again rendering an aspect of Indian life monstrous. In another instance, he attributes animal qualities to Indians, when he describes the prostitutes as 'pretend[ing] to love, as monkies and apes do their little ones' (Terry 1655: 303, 305, 462, 304). Fryer comments that the women of aristocratic Muslims in India were kept under close surveillance ('debar[red] the sight of anything male'), which proves, he says, they are 'incontinent in their desires' (Fryer 1698: 133). Herbert reports that strangers are not invited into houses in Surat because the men are jealous of their wives and daughters, who are 'venerous and lustful'. Priests, however, are allowed to mingle with the women and even 'use (I might say abuse) them' (Herbert 1634: 42, 187). Terry (1655: 303) is amused at the stress on sexual fidelity among the Muslims. Fryer claims that he saw a *fakir* with a 'gold ring fastned into his virile member' as a 'check to incontinency'. Later, he presents idolatry as animal sexuality, where native women 'receive the pleasure of copulation' from 'jougis', one of whom 'lay with two and twenty'. He uses an interesting set of terms to describe the situation: 'delusions of the devil', 'captivated by his will', 'spirit of fascination', 'shame of incantations and charms' (Fryer 1698: 160, 179). Herbert describes girls who 'prostitute themselves to the libidinous heat of wicked men' in order to 'enrich their pagod, or adored devil'. Sati, he declares, evolved because of the excessive libido of their women. The women have 'abused liberty', 'grown audaciously impudent', and 'nothing but the harmless lives of their too much loving husbands would satiate their lustfull boldness'. This libido itself, Herbert believes, has been 'procured by poison' (1634: 192, 191–92, 192). Ovington claims that hospitality in India often includes offering the wife to the guest (1696: 212–13; see also Herbert 1634: 40–41). Ovington argues that there are no public houses in India because Indian men are afraid that these would offer their 'wives and daughters' 'temptations'. Even the king worries about his women. Ovington also claims that sati was introduced because 'the libidinous disposition of the women, who thro' their inordinate lust would often poison their present husbands, to make way for a new lover' (Ovington 1696: 312, 343, 209–10, 343). Ovington, a little later in his narrative, talks of child-marriages in India, arguing that the 'tender passions' are 'blow[n] up into a lively flame' right from childhood. The image of traps is used once more when Ovington describes them as 'insensibly captivated by each others snares'. On another occasion he describes a man 'insnar'd' into parting with his wealth by dancing women. Terms like 'lively flame', 'volatile affections', 'souls' that are 'pliant' like 'melted wax' suggest a sexuality that is not in control of itself (Ovington 1696: 322, 257–58, 322–23, 324). Bowrey (1997: 63–64), like all others, also refers to the guarding of Indian women.[22] The connection of the Indian woman with the *fakir* and the idol is eroticized in Herbert, Ovington, Fryer and others. The imaging of an erotic monstrous here may perhaps be linked to the worries over the influence of the maternal imagination in the production of monsters during this period (Huet 1993: 11–13; Crawford 2005: 18–20).

Herbert and Fryer's erotic grotesque is predicated on the treatment of Indian bodies as driven by forces that are not human or physiological. This, I believe, enables a shift of focus from Indian bodies to something beyond. The threats of sexualized bodies, and signs or sights of sexuality, are negotiated by proposing a magical state, which renders them grotesque. The aggressive sexuality of the Indian body is thus attributed to a state of emotional and spiritual 'possession', clearly locating it within the realm of the grotesque (for magicality is a component of the grotesque: McElroy 1989: 4). Very bodily and human activity is recast as 'devilish', that is, something beyond the human. Fryer thus rejects the bodily here in favour of something more metaphysical (such as 'possession', a term he uses, 1698: 179). Conflating the human with the 'spiritual' and the animal in a way that it becomes impossible to distinguish among them, Fryer translates Indian sexualized bodies as a 'species of confusion' (Harpham 1982: xv). It is surely no coincidence that Fryer's description of sexual rites is followed by an extended discussion of religious beliefs, metaphysics and godheads (1698: 180–82). Is sexuality a bodily need or act or is it 'spiritual' and the result of 'delusion'? The emphasis on magicality, delusion and the non-physical within the physical or corporeal transform eroticism and sexuality into the grotesque.

Sexuality is not the only realm in which the English traveller posits an inhuman Indian. By the end of the sixteenth century a misguided opinion, aberrant thought or behaviour were taken as proof of monstrosity (Brammall 1996: 15–16). In the

English narrative the Indian is frequently troped as possessed, and under the control of ungovernable forces. Ovington describes the Indian emperors – in the plural, thereby making a generic comment – as 'incontrollable in what they say, as well as in their actions'. This leads, he argues, to a situation where the emperor's 'flatterers' agree with even the most absurd statements of the king (Ovington 1696: 182). Terry (1655: 267–70, 427) refers to the misplaced 'zeal' of the Muslims.

In each of these cases the Indian is troped as prey to excessive, inhuman emotions and behaviour, which aligns her/him more with beasts than the rest of the species. Exploring the 'borders of the human' enables the English traveller to construct an India full of intoxicated, zealous and tyrannical people (Healy 1999: 51–73). The kings exploit, the Brahmins deceive, the men are drunk and lascivious and the women are hypersexual. The references to drunken states and uncontrollable passions – a central aspect of medical books from the second half of the sixteenth century (Healy 1999: 54) – constitute a rhetoric of the grotesque because ungovernable passions suggest a beast rather than a human being. By encoding the human as a beast the narratives of early English travellers locate Indians at the boundary of species, and thus generates a racial grotesque.

The aesthetics of idleness

Another mode of dehumanizing the Indian body in the English narrative about India is to focus on idling bodies. While idle bodies have been deemed monstrous right from medieval times, productive bodies were valued because they contributed to the economy of the community (Healy 1999: 56; Jordan 2001: 62–79; Youngquist 2003: xvi–xix).

What the English narrative does is to map the idleness of the native. Having mapped in considerable detail the non-labouring bodies of the natives, the English traveller is ready to make a judgement about India's civilization as a whole. Terry (1655: 171) complains about people who 'eat up the bread of the poor', and 'having able limbs to carry them that they may beg from house to house, and hands to receive alms, but none to labour; both these being the very vermin of the commonwealth' (the other 'vermin' he identifies are, incidentally, robbers). Here Terry tropes the human vagabond as an animal, in a process of making him monstrous, for the reason that he does not *labour*. He also associates idleness with sin, arguing that David's affair with Bathsheba could be attributed to his idling on the terrace. He argues that the Muslims in India thrive on the labours of the Hindus, and remain idle most of the time (Terry 1655: 252). Even the emperor, Aurangazebe, does not appear to be industrious (Ovington 1696: 189–90, 252, 169).[23]

John Fryer (1698: 55–56), comparing English and native seafarers, complains that while the former works with 'horrid oaths and hideous cursing', the natives 'never let their hands do any labour'. Here the odious oaths and swearing among English sailors is excusable because these are 'performed' within the context of labour. The natives of India, on the other hand, are unpardonable because they do not labour at all. If the former is horrific for his language, the latter is grotesque due to his idleness. Later, in an extended section on Indian mendicants, Fryer deploys the aesthetics of idleness to its fullest potential. He describes in considerable detail the bodily contortions of the *fakirs*, with their 'lyons, tygres, or leopard skins' and their incomprehensible chants (Fryer 1698: 95–96). Linking these two detailed passages is Fryer's evaluation of the *fakirs*.

> Most of these are vagabonds, and are the pest of the nation they live in . . . they profess poverty, but make all things their own where they come: all the heat of the day they idle it under some shady tree.
>
> (Fryer 1698: 95)

John Ovington's first and primary objection to the *fakirs* is that they 'assum'd a liberty of taking that by violence, which they find is denied their civil requests'. That is, rather than work to earn, they grab what is not rightfully theirs. They are 'imperious' because of their numbers (Ovington 1696: 361).

Ovington and Fryer's revulsion at the *fakirs* is rooted in two discourses: that of appearance, and that of the Protestant work ethic. The idling body, in this case worsened in appearance with the bodily regimen of self-torture, is grotesque and Fryer's final, categorizing term for them indicates the (Englishman's) legal and social rejection of such a body. He terms them 'outlaws'. The grotesque idling body is beyond law and society. In order to emphasize this Fryer (1698: 96) follows up his description of the idle *fakirs* with a passage on the toiling labourers, who, he claims, are under 'severer restraints'. John Ovington claims Indians, especially those of the bania caste, spend the 'heat of the day' in 'rest and sleeping'. But this 'rest', interestingly, is not to recover from hard labour, but from sexual efforts. Ovington has just finished describing how the Indians engage in 'nocturnal embraces', eat and drink at midnight, and return to 'fresh amours'. Thus the days are spent in bed 'to refresh their exhausted strength' (Ovington 1696: 313). The description suggests a culture given to the pleasures of the flesh and idleness. The *fakir* 'tak[es] by violence' (as Ovington puts it), which appears to him to subvert the function of the holy man or mendicant.

Idleness is the absence of any functional or productive use of bodies, and generates the monstrous in English writings on India. Once more the English traveller draws attention to the problematic relationship between form and function in Indian society. Terry, for instance, underscores the fact that despite possessing arms and hands, the 'vagabonds' use them only to beg (quoted above). The form of the body, therefore, does not serve its designated and appropriate or 'natural' function. Instead it is used for unnaturally contortions and antisocial deeds. The aesthetics of idleness emphasizes this monstrous dissonance.

The social monstrous

The deformed body of the toiling labourer, the manacled woman and the devouring tyrant-king constitute the anterior moments of the English travelogue's overarching aim: the creation of a social or civic monstrous in India. In this mode the traveller, having surveyed numerous instances of the monstrous and the grotesque, negotiates the threat of the excess by rendering it as artifice, the *creation of a monstrosity by social systems.* These instances of monstrosity are beyond the pale of nature.

That is, the *individual* body of the *fakir*, labourer or beggar is transformed into an icon of a larger social monstrous that is India. The observer in the case of the English narratives on India makes two significant moves. In many cases the English traveller sees the grotesque Indian body as the *product* of a set of dehumanizing conditions. Then, the narrative also explores the *responses* to such grotesque spectacles. In both cases the aesthetics of the monstrous-grotesque enables the English traveller to depict a morally depraved India: an exploitative, unjust social order that dehumanizes the labourer-body, or a superstition-ridden society that glorifies vagabonds and idlers as great men (for the Puritans, the grotesque meant superstitions too: Barasch 1971: 86). What we have is a social grotesque of an entire civilization or culture, which is now 'deformed'. This social monstrous becomes an overarching element of the English description of India.

It is important to note that Terry, Ovington and others move between the Indian and English or European monstrosities. As Geoffrey Harpham (1982: 5) has pointed out, 'things' are grotesque not because they are hideous but because there is something we recognize as corrupted familiarity within the monstrous. Every single English travel narrative locates Indian monstrosities alongside ancient Roman ones. Terry (1655) uses his observations of Indian 'fashion' to reflect on the English taste for fashion. Thus there is a sense of recognition and identification when dealing with the Indian monstrous.

The social monstrous is best instantiated in the Englishman's description of the Indian labouring bodies and the *fakir*. Multiple elements of the grotesque and the abject come into play in these descriptions, where the narrative seems to see the *fakir*, his acceptance by Indians and his iconology as symptomatic of a general depravity in Indian (especially Hindu) culture. These abject bodies of deformity and dirt mark the border between a civilized society and chaos, between culture and the jungle. The description of the *fakir*'s body with its long, matted hair, uncut nails, dirt and general filth is the coding of the native, non-European body as 'abject'.[24] What is significant about the *fakir*'s body for the English traveller is that it crosses the line from clean to unclean, from proper to improper. The overgrown nails, hair, dirt all suggest an animal, something primal that exists prior to and outside human society.

John Fryer's description of the hierarchy of the society in Malabar details the labouring body of poorer Indians:

> When a bad year fills not the publick granaries; drubbing the poor hinds till their bones rattle in their skins, they being forced often to sell their children for rice, which is the best here on this coast of any place else in the whole world.
>
> (Fryer 1698: 52–53)

Fryer negates the value of the 'best' rice in the world when he describes the pathos of people being forced to sell children for the same. In another context Fryer (1698: 125) writes that Shivaji 'commonly reaps the harvest', and 'hardly leaves the tillers as will keep body and soul together'. Here the descriptions of the poor, unhealthy bodies of the Indians, an instance of the corporeal grotesque, are located within a larger set of themes about India's political economy. Fryer situates this description of the starving poor immediately *after* this comment:

> the artizans and tillers of the earth . . . they reap the least benefit; their vassals are commonly employed in that service, they being drudges to both their masters and prince, who here as in all India, is sole proprietor of lands; allowing the occupiers no more than a bare subsistence.
>
> (Fryer 1698: 52)

On another occasion he mentions that labourers were 'famished almost to death . . . racked and tortured most inhumanly', before elaborating the tortures. Then, having described the tortured bodies of the enslaved Indian farmer, he examines the social and economic contexts: Shivaji's (mis)rule, the King of Bijapur's taxation system and social injustices. The coolies 'are the dregs of the people', horribly 'abject' (Fryer 1698: 146–47, 194). John Ovington also underscores the Mughal emperor's absolute ownership of the lands, minerals and all forms of wealth, and groups the emperors of Ottoman empire and India under one category: 'inhumane' (Ovington 1696: 197–99, 202–03, 171). The Indian ruler, Aurangezebe, had come to power through the use of what Ovington calls 'unnatural methods'. He had earlier referred to the Eastern kings' 'slaughter' of their 'brethren' to get the throne, and he comments that the people are deliberately kept poor by the Mughal in order to 'break their spirits and fortunes' (Ovington 1696: 175, 105, 331). Terry also mentions the Mughal emperor's absolute ownership of property. He hints at sodomy on the part of the cruel Indian kings (Terry 1655: 367, 370, 403–05, 407).

The deformed, starved bodies are, the English narratives imply, the direct effect of the skewed land ownership systems of India. That is, the grotesquely deformed bodies (the beggar's body was, in any case, a grotesque sight during the seventeenth century: Barasch 1971: 81–82) that Fryer sees, for instance, are a consequence of the Indian political economy and social systems. The corporeal suffering of the labourer and the general citizenry is the effect of the moral corruption of the rulers, even as the trope of the honest working man suffering bodily injury generates pathos (Davis 2002).

The descriptions of native kings as excessive consumers and preying monsters outlined in the first section must be read in conjunction with the images of poor, starved bodies of the labourer. The fact that the Indian kings are invariably described as predatorial not only blurs the boundaries between animal and human – a feature of the monstrous – but also reflects the conditions in which such a monstrosity can flourish: a social monstrous. The king is monstrous because he consumes far too much, at the cost of the artisan, the farmer and the labourer. Consumption (of various kinds) thus becomes a differentiating mechanism in this rhetoric of the Indian monstrous. Early modern discourse frequently aligned the tyrant with the beast, situating them at the borders of the human (Brammall 1996: 13; Healy 1999: 51). And this is precisely what we see in these narratives. Ovington's terms for the ruler – unnatural, inhumane – and the standard description of the exploited, crushed poor citizen's body ('inhumanly', in Fryer's terms, quoted above) in the narratives tropes India's social monstrosity. It is also interesting to see how the elaborately dressed aristocrat and the under-dressed *fakir* both become 'monstrous' in the English narrative.

Christopher Farewell (1633: 27), seeing the *fakirs*, is appalled at the bodily mutilation, and the native worship of such grotesques. Ovington (1696: 362–70) says they 'gather a constant supply of dust and filth'; he spends a great deal of time explaining the *fakir*'s body. Terry (1655: 281–87, 293–94) also describes the bodily self-tortures of the *fakirs*. Thomas Bowrey (1997: 20–23) terms them 'vultures' because, according to him, they cause 'many injuries' to the 'poor inhabitants' of the country, who are 'devoted' to them. Fryer attacks the monarchy in India, which seems to favour the idler *fakir* over the hard working labourer. The governor, he states, cannot 'correct their insolencies'. Later, he would return to the grotesque *fakir* body, describing one as a 'walking skeleton', while another has 'filthy running ulcers' (Fryer 1698: 95, 102, 103). Fryer is appalled that these men are given 'divine honours'. They begin to occupy the position of 'heroes or Demi-Gods in their superstitious kalender' (Fryer 1698: 103). In another incident Fryer visits Gokarna and witnesses a religious procession. He once again focuses on the *fakirs* at the local temple and their bodily deformities. Later, eyeing the procession Fryer describes devotees who 'ran cudgelling themselves', some who 'belaboured themselves till they could not stand' (Fryer 1698: 160–61). Fryer attributes these bodily grotesques as the effect of 'blind and heated' 'zeal'. Later, on the same page he locates the exact reasons for their behaviour: 'whether religion makes these people morose; or it be attributed to the virtue of their manners'. He reduces the *fakir* to an animal, describing them as leading a 'beastly' life. These are the 'most dissolute, licentious, prophane persons in the world' (Fryer 1698: 161, 191, 196). Terry suggests that Islam itself is full of 'monstrous fables', and that Mohammed the prophet is a 'monstrous seducer'. Here Terry links monstrosity with religious belief systems, like Fryer seems to do. This shifts the focus from the acts of the individual Muslim to a context. In fact, Terry's travelogue explicitly links monstrous acts in human history to their religious contexts (Terry 1655: 261, 284–85, 288–90, 297–305, 536–45). In another case he describes the 'wild devotion' of the Indians, their 'wild conceivings', 'wild and mad fancy' (Terry 1655: 291, 328, 336, 340, 345).

The religious procession – especially Jagannath's rath yatra – comes in for sustained attention in many of these travelogues. William Bruton (1638: 27) is appalled at the enthusiasm of the crowds in its procession, where people watch others being crushed. Herbert (1634: 192) describes religious processions where 'poore wretched bodies [are] miserably crusht in pieces' by the 'ponderousness of the idoll'. Ovington, having described a native king metaphorically as malformed (quoted above), then proceeds to speculate on the Indians' responses to such monstrous form: 'And may be the Indians, who upon this account [of his malformed body] are apt to harbour superstitious thoughts concerning him, may be the easier won to his alliance and designs' (Ovington 1696: 188).

Thomas Bowrey (1997: 7, 17–18) mentions the procession, and the crowd's responses to it – including hurling themselves under the chariot wheels – in some detail in his narrative. A related instance would be that of sati. Bowrey, having described a sati he purportedly witnessed, describes another in which '27 [of a man's] wifes and concubines were burned'. In the course of these descriptions, he pays attention to the crowd's responses to the horrific act: 'To make the ceremonie seeme more pleasant, they at that instant tuned up severall sorts of musicke, vizt. Pipes, drums, trumpets, accompanied with shouting in such measure, that not one screech of the woman in torment could be heard'. Finally, he locates the sati in 'parts of India where the countrey is governed by the gentue naiques' (Bowrey 1997: 38–39), thereby suggesting that the conditions under which the act takes place, and the rulers who allow it, are the true monstrous. The monstrous here serves as a mode of describing an Other religion.

In the narrative both the act and the people's response to the act constitute the monstrous. The inhumanity of Indian human beings is coded as monstrous because they encourage and cheer such monstrous acts. The enjoyment of the spectacle of the dying woman is, for the English traveller, unacceptable. It is therefore the *response* of the people to what the English perceive as a monstrous effigy/idol/act that marks the 'moral monstrous'. The monstrous and the grotesque are primarily about affect, and the moral monster is one who enjoys another's suffering. That is, monstrosity resides in the emotional *response* to the cruel act and makes the observer a 'moral monster' (Steintrager 2004: 5–12). To the English, the enthusiastic response reflects Indian society's general degradation. The idols and the processions are themselves, no doubt, hideous and horrific. But the enthusiasm demonstrated by the crowds is unpardonable to the English eye. And it is this that constitutes the moral monstrous, for the people actually respond positively to fellow human beings dying, crushed under the wheels of the chariot.

Bodily regimen, public spectacles and mannerisms are all therefore treated as the *consequence* of social conditions. The collapse of *form* – of the body and of civil hierarchy, especially because of the monarch's immorality – and *function* (once again seen as reflected in the 'inhumane' acts of native kings) marks the disruption of social order. The English traveller thus shifts focus from the grotesque body of the *fakir*, the monstrosity of *sati* and the horror of the Jagannath yatra to the social *contexts* and *reception* of these bodies. The displacement from the material-corporeal deformity to a moral context (responses to *fakirs*, delusion of religion) means that the so-called heinous acts of the *fakir* become a code for the moral depravity of his devotees. In this case the abject is not just the condition of the body but the condition of the context in which the body is located. It is not enough to identify the body of the labourer or *fakir* as abject but to see how the abject is received or constructed by specific social, economic or cultural contexts. And this is precisely what the travel narrative sets out to do.

Thus the starved body of the labourer that attracts Fryer's attention is iconic of the consequence of the appalling socio-economic conditions in which the body 'lives'. In other cases the English traveller sees the grotesque body in terms of the response it generates among the natives. The Indian populace accepts the grotesque spectacles of the *fakirs* (like swallowing a chain) because they are 'deluded' (Fryer 1698: 192). They 'acquire constant homage' from the people, in which they are similar to Indian monarchs, who demand absolute servility (Ovington 1696: 362, 151). The Indian religion, writes Herbert (1634: 192), 'shadow[s] all deformities'. In the case of the *fakir*, the bodily regimen is also described as an 'indulgence' by Ovington, connecting to his earlier description of the 'profligate' use of their bodies by Indians (see note). Men and women lose their 'coyness' when speaking with these naked men when they ought to be 'startled at such an immodest spectacle' (Ovington 1696: 362–63). The absence of shame – shame being an integral part of the 'correct' social structure – is an example of how decadent the society has become.

It is also important to note that the description of the *fakir* – which has strong parallels with the images of the 'wild man' in medieval and early modern texts – reorganizes Indian society itself.[25] The wild man here is not 'outside' in the jungle,[26] but well *within* civilization, roaming the streets of the town. In fact the wilds have intruded into the city. In effect, then, the English narrative marks the breakdown of barriers between savage (outside) and civilized (inside), jungle and city. The 'licentious' (the term Fryer uses, as noted above) *fakir* is like the wild man who, in Hayden White's (1972: 21) terms, is 'desire incarnate, possessing the strength, wit, and cunning to give full expression to all his lusts'. The *fakir* is the ultimate transgressive body in the English travel narrative because it breaks all the barriers of civilized society: it becomes beast-like. Further, if the monstrous was a portent of coming misfortune – as the French surgeon Ambroise Paré put it in his 1573 text, *On Monsters and Marvels* (Paré 1982: 3) – the circulation of the *fakir* could very well be seen as the signs of a decaying society. When English travellers place the toiling body of the labourer, the tortured body of the *fakir*, the tyrannical king and the deluded masses of India on a continuum, they are inscribing a condition of imminent decay.

Religion itself, therefore, becomes an example of the social monstrous that *folds* into a ridiculous grotesque. Ovington complains that the hold of religion is so pervasive in India that even the coronation ceremony is transformed into ritual. He writes: 'they had converted the civil into a religious observation of that day'. About the *fakirs* Ovington says: 'by these distortions of their bodies they gain the repute of men of perfect hearts and of upright minds' (1696: 178, 367). Interestingly, Ovington emphasizes that Aurangzebe himself once pretended to be a *fakir*, a role reversal that is *unnatural* for a king (173–74). Terry says that the Indians call such madmen 'prophets' (1655: 264). If, as J.B. Friedman argues, monstrous races are associated with sin, heresy and evil in medieval times, the reception of the monstrous body of the *fakir* or the idol by 'normal' bodies symbolizes a monstrous culture (Friedman 2000: 103). The *fakir* is lascivious (Herbert), deceitful and preys upon the gullibility of the Indians (Fryer, Ovington, Bowrey).

They commit heinous acts against their own bodies (Ovington). When the Indians accept and legitimize these corporeal and moral deformities, they generate the social monstrous. The social monstrous is one where 'fear and distress, poverty and famine' make 'the universal air and genius of those unquiet abodes' (Ovington 1696: 187), where the people are 'wild, neglected, unnatural' (Terry 1655: 500). The two images taken together propose monstrous events and acts that could be attributed to a decaying society's 'air'.

The social monstrous in English writings on India is clearly predicated on the idea of a normal function served by extraordinary means – a feature of the seventeenth century monstrous (Daston and Park 1998: 204) – and the subversion of the 'correct' function. *Fakirs* make people worship god by and through their own malformed bodies. When the crowds draw towards the undernourished, dirty and repulsive bodies of the *fakir*, the English commentator suggests, the function of worship or praise of the almighty is served through unnatural processes. The princes' ascension to the throne – a 'natural' process – is in the Indian context achieved through inhumane means (as Ovington points out). More significantly, natural functions of kings such as care of the subjects or protection are subverted, where the king uses a large army to keep his subjects under control rather than for their protection. The army, notes Ovington (1696: 185), is used to 'awe his [the Mughal emperor's] infinite multitude of people, and keep them in an absolute subjection'. The rhetoric of monstrosity in the English travelogues on India relies on expanding the scope of the monstrous to include 'deviant' behaviour, the disjunction between form (here coded as hierarchy, power, wealth) and function.

The English traveller by moving from the singular deformity of the beggar's or *fakir*'s body to the *production* and *reception* of these bodies has made a comment about the society that encourages, admires and thus produces such deformity. The English traveller has mapped a moral monstrous here. Thus when Fryer describes the enthusiastic response of the Indians to what he deems to be obscenities and barbaric rituals he cleverly moves from the spectacle to the spectator. In each case he describes the natives as responding to such 'inhuman' sights with great fervour, and thereby creates the social monstrous.

With the rhetoric of the monstrosity the English traveller images an India that is decaying. Images of consumption, ensnarement, idleness and bodily mutilation or deprivation, all studied obsessively by the English traveller, create a social monstrous. This monstrous folds into a mannerist grotesque where the king is alienated from his subjects, the subjects prey on (consume?) each other and unnatural acts such as that of the *fakirs* are revered.[27] Form and function are in dissonance: able bodies do not labour, kingly bodies devour their subjects' wealth instead of protecting it, and holy men are sacrilegiously unhygienic and lascivious. Bodies and behaviour, all out of proportion, reflect the disorder of India. The overgrown king and the emaciated *fakir* or peasant are both 'malformed' icons of the imminent collapse of India.

In India the social structure thrives on exploitation, suffering and false beliefs. The Indian monstrous is artifice, outside the pale of nature, and on the same level as ancient Rome's. When English travellers locate the 'pedigree', so to speak, of the Indian monstrous they also generate a narrative of comprehension.[28] The monstrous is about revelation, and here English travellers reveal the 'truth' about India. Having explored various kinds of monstrosities – excessive consumption, beastly bodies and idleness – they discern a dominant principle that organizes all of them. This dominant principle is that of the social monstrous folding into the grotesque of disorder, ridiculousness and decay. I have pointed out how the narratives move between isolated instances of the monstrous to larger racial, social and cultural 'traits', which are now identifiable as grotesque. The social monstrous is the context in which individual instances of idleness or deformity may be located. Thus, the social monstrous enables the English traveller to undertake a project of classification and categorization of the entire visible Indian culture through individual examples. The English traveller penetrates the sign to locate the signified: the social monstrous that is India.

3 The imperial sublime, 1750–1820

The period 1757–1820 was one of both crisis and profit for the English in India. The several wars, charges of corruption and mismanagement, infighting at the East India House (London), mounting debts, the parliamentary investigations of the 1780s, and the trial of Warren Hastings (beginning in 1788), followed by the appointment and disputed recall of Governor-General Arthur Wellesley, all eroded the East India Company's standing.[1] Meanwhile, numerous English soldiers died in battles or suffered imprisonment across India, even as the company built up a huge standing army, especially after the war against Tipu. Numerous contemporary periodicals noted the crisis (see Bibliography for abbreviations). Indian affairs were described as 'embarrassed' (*CR* 35 [1773]: 1) and India itself as a 'precarious possession' (*The Times*, 25 February 1785: 3). The expression echoes decades later in a review that draws attention to the 'very precariousness of that possession [India]' (*ER* 20 [1812]: 39). One terms India a 'distant and magnificent appendage to the British empire' (*QR* 29 [1823]: 383), while another expresses anxiety about the 'insecurity' of British possessions (*TE* 6 [1839]: 84). However, India's importance to England continued to grow amidst these problems. Soon after Plassey a commentator writes glowingly of 'the whole trade of the vast peninsula of India, from the Ganges to the Indies, the most extensive and profitable sphere in the world' (*AR* 7 [1761]: 56. Also 9 [1766]: 20; *AR* 10 [1767]: 41). The EIC, writes another commentator, has acquired 'such superiority of power' that its possessions were 'secure' (*AR* 11 [1768]: 66). The *Monthly Review* took note of the fortunes made by EIC servants, and how the East remained a career for Englishmen (*MR* 42 [1770]: 322–24; 78 [1788]: 396). 'British ascendancy' and 'British existence in India', writes the *Eclectic Review*, 'comes nearly to the same thing' (*EcR* 7 [1811]: 477). William Thomson (1788, 1: 305) states: 'the preservation of India . . . [is] . . . the only means of saving us from a general bankruptcy'. By 1793 India was making a direct contribution of 500,000 pounds annually to the English exchequer (Bayly 1989: 120). Commercial interests inspired the government to involve itself deeper in Indian affairs, especially after the Pitts India Act of 1784. The *Plan of an Asiatic Register* terms India a 'valuable possession' (1799: 1), and the accounts compiled by the Select Committee of the Court of Directors (*First, Second and Third Reports of the Select Committee of the Court of Directors of the East India Company*, 1793) demonstrates the exact volume of this value. In another comment on the value of India to England, the *Edinburgh Review* lists the 'parties' whose 'interests are involved in the questions of Indian trade and government'. The list reads, in that order: 'the East-India Company; the British nation; and the people of India' (*ER* 20 [1812]: 472–73). A letter from the Court of Directors dated 21 November 1766 expresses concern about 'Company . . . servants . . . guilty of frauds, oppression and extortion' (Long 1973: 625). The *Ninth Report of the Select Committee* of the House of Commons (1783) appointed to enquire into the administration of Bengal states that in the early years of Britain's connection with India, 'the English Company flourished . . . the Nation considerably benefited . . . and the Dividends of the Proprietors were often high', but that after 1765 things had become worse in terms of trade. As evidence it cites 'an intelligent person concerned in trade' who reports that by 1779 'there was little or no trade remaining' in Madras (House of Commons 1783: 54–56). Reviewing Alexander Dow's *The History of Hindostan* (1768), the *Monthly Review* deplored the 'morality that hath . . . already produced many iniquitous events' (*MR* 40 [1769]: 510). As late as the 1830s there was criticism of the company's policies, and administrators like John Malcolm were quoted as saying: 'India is as quiet as gunpowder' (*The Athenæum* 30 September 1829: 654). In other cases, the English at 'home' saw their countrymen's life in India as luxurious, easy and satisfying (see, for instance, Captain Medwin's 'A Bengal Yarn', *AM* 2 [1842]: 57–63). There was also, however, an anxiety that imports from India were damaging English industries. *The Times*, for instance, reported that 'English Cotton Manufactories suffer much by the importations from India' (10 January 1791: 2). *The Times* titled one of its reports from this period 'instability of power in India', and noted with anxiety the tensions caused by Hyder Ally (18 March 1792: 3). But by 1818, after the various annexations, 'British dominion in India became the British dominion of India', in Percival Spear's (1961: 225) pithy phrase.

Control over land, revenue, trade, and military superiority emerged as the prime concerns for the EIC, as the several letters between Fort William (Calcutta) and India House illustrate. Extensive descriptions of the Indian landscape also mark travelogues of this period of economic and military crises and the changing nature of the EIC. I focus in this chapter on the manner in which aesthetics and colonial ideology imbricate in the descriptive vocabulary of this period. Aesthetics frequently helped camouflage colonial ideology at a time when English superiority in India was not fully established (though it was growing after the battle of Baksar in 1764). My focus is the rhetorical transformation of the Indian landscape from a site of desolation and danger to potential improvement in the 1750–1820 period. I shall demonstrate how the mid- and late-eighteenth-century travelogue's aesthetics of the sublime, with its emphasis on emptiness and waste, effectively prepares the ground for colonial representations and practices of a georgic Indian landscape of renewal.

The aesthetics of the sublime, circulating in England around the mid-eighteenth century, suggested an aesthetic framework for the travellers.[2] An aesthetics of terror and vastness, darkness and obscurity, danger and challenge furnished a set of tropes which, I shall demonstrate, was applied equally to varied topographical terrain in India. That is, the descriptive vocabulary of aesthetics helped 'level' all cities and towns, deserts and rivers with the same mode of description. This in itself becomes a colonial topography and a colonizing aesthetics where differences and historical/architectural/cultural specificities between, say, Madras and Calcutta are ignored when the travellers employ the same set of images and metaphors to describe both places. Further, the sublime seems to function as a regulating framework in different kinds of travellers – from Lord Valentia to botanical enthusiasts like William Moorcroft, mercenaries like George Thomas to intrepid explorer-spies like George Forster. The recourse to the sublime, I believe, helps unify the discourses of and about India, even though the attitudes, class origins and professional training of the travellers show considerable variations.[3]

The Indian landscape of desolation, characterized by emptiness, vastness, ruins, and excessive natural phenomena, is one that threatens. The English traveller's negotiation of this threatening, sublime desolation is organized into three 'moments'. The first is the moment of self-preservation in the face of a threat from the landscape. The second is the moment of affirmation, when the traveller tries to inscribe some meaning into the excessive emptiness or desolation of the landscape in a bid to alleviate the threat. Finally, through acts of self-affirmation, the traveller moves from solitude to society, from the threatened to the safe, in a moment of 'appreciation', when an equivalence is restored between the traveller and the landscape.[4] The narrative concludes with the traveller in a state of relative safety, or what may be termed, following the work of Malcolm Andrews, a *locus amoenus* – the landscape of amenity (Andrews 1999: 53–75). Each of these moments meshes aesthetics with colonial ideology, and the ideology becomes more pronounced in the second and third moments when the traveller suggests affirmative action (itself a colonial, masculinist trope in the colonial text) for the transformation of the landscape is suggested. The three moments of the travelogue also adopt specific aesthetic approaches and rhetorical strategies in their representations of the Indian sublime or landscape. In the first stage, where the traveller is frightened or uncertain, the aesthetic may be characterized as one of the negative sublime. In the negative sublime there is an excess of signifiers but no signified, signs but no clear meanings. Here the landscape is empty, devoid of markers or directions. The desolation frightens because there is no *discernible* meaning. In the second moment, the traveller seeks to attribute meaning to this emptiness. This hermeneutic sublime, where an allegory, metaphor or the attribution of meaning alleviate the threat of the emptiness is also the assertion of individual agency (Weiskel 1986: 26–29). The meanings attributed to the land become justifications for affirmative action suggested in the third moment. Therefore, the desolation itself is treated as a source or site for 'improvement' in the second and third moments of the sublime. It is in this shift that colonial ideology permeates landscape descriptions.

Several descriptions of desolate sublime landscapes circulated in England by the eighteenth century, well before Burke framed his famous theory. Thomas Gray's description of the Grand Chartreuse (1935, 1: 74) and of the Scottish Highlands (1935, 2: 899), John Brown's 1753 description of Keswick (Bicknell 1981: x), Horace Walpole's 1739 description of Savoy (Walpole 1948), John

Dennis's (1693) description of the Alps, and Samuel Johnson's 1774 description of Hawkestone (S. Johnson 1995) are examples of such sublime topographical scenes in eighteenth-century writing.[5] A set of images and tropes for landscape description was already in circulation, and thus available for adaptation to 'new' areas.

Reviews of such India travelogues acknowledged the descriptions in them to be sublime. Thus the *Edinburgh Review* refers to the 'wild scenes' in a travelogue as something that would appeal to the 'fancy of Salvator Rosa' – the iconic artist of the sublime (*ER* 60 [1835]: 409). In other cases, the news from India itself seems to burst boundaries. The *Calcutta Monthly Register* writes, in a rhetoric that becomes common to the imperial sublime: 'The retrospective view of the occurrences in India . . . have encroached so largely on the prescribed limits of this number, that other matter hath been unavoidably omitted' (1 [1790]: 3). Another declares: 'Even the broad line of the Indus no longer limits our dominion, and the natural boundaries of empire have been swept away before the onward course of our standards' (*NBR* 16 [1851]: 230). India and the empire, it appears, can be imaged and imagined only in sublime terms.

The topography of desolation

Landscape, cultivation, agricultural imagery, and labour were central images for this period.[6] Dr Francis Buchanan, for example, had clear instructions on what he was supposed to observe and record during his travels (*ER* 13 [1808]: 84–85). Landscape, in particular, was the focus of observation for the eighteenth-century traveller, as demonstrated by John Lettsom's *The Naturalist's and Traveller's Companion* (1772). Josiah Tucker, whose *Instructions for Travellers* (1757) was an influential text of this period, wrote about the responsibilities of the traveller:

> During his travels he should constantly bear in mind the grand Maxim, That the Face of Every Country through which he passes, the Looks, Numbers, and Behaviour of the People, their general Cloathing, Food, and Dwelling, their Attainments in Agriculture, Manufactures, Arts and Sciences, are the Effects and Consequences of some certain Causes; which Causes he was particularly sent out to investigate and discover.
>
> (Tucker 1757: 10)

Historical accounts, especially of the East India Company, a review of John Bruce's *Annals of the Honourable East India Company* (1810) suggests, must be 'disposed in a clear, natural, and instructive order' (*EcR* 4 [1811]: 4). Formats for travelogues were thus evidently in circulation.

In the travelogues of the eighteenth century, sublime and beautiful landscapes are suggested by a set of oppositions: barren/cultivated, uninhabited/populated, uncontrolled/regulated, poverty-stricken/prosperous, unsafe/safe. These oppositions are also temporally categorized, where the sublime features of barrenness and emptiness are associated with an Indian past. Safety and prosperity are associated with English activities in the present, while being directed toward the future.

George Forster opens his *A Journey from Bengal to England* (1798) thus:

> The English should no longer account themselves sojourners in this country;
> they are now, virtually, its lords paramount, and their policy should not be
> that of a day; but, considering the opulence and wealth of the subject as
> closely tending to enrich the common state, they should, at large support his
> wants, and encourage his labours.
>
> (Forster 1798, 1: 3)[7]

This is a 'framing' comment – which incidentally echoes an earlier text, Henry
Watson's unpublished work from 1764–77, where Watson declares the EIC to be
'Lords paramount of these three large provinces' (Mss. Euro D 759: unpaginated)
– for what is to follow. Forster proceeds to elaborate what he believes is the role of
the English in India: 'As the welfare of the British dominion in India ultimately
depends on the prosperity of Bengal, no labour should be thought irksome, no
rational plan left untried, which may improve its revenue, or encourage its trade'
(Forster 1798, 1: 8). Several themes common to the travelogues of the period are
summarized and anticipated by Forster's comments. First, the English traveller
has begun to describe India as a 'possession'. Second, with the opposition of
'sojourners'/'lords paramount', Forster is suggesting a shift in the nature of
English presence in India. From the early temporary residents, they are now a
permanent presence. Third, the agenda of improvement (here interlinking the
improvement of both India and England), even if an act of 'retribution' (as Forster
terms it), can be implemented only when land is controlled. Forster's comments
therefore assume (imperial) significance. Fourth, as I shall demonstrate, Forster's
emphasis on 'labour' in the above quotations becomes a rhetorical device for the
traveller-as-individual to negotiate India's vastness. Forster's narrative, like several
others of this period, therefore suggests a movement from a temporary, threatened
presence in India – of both individuals and England – to a confident, empowered
one. (However, it wasn't that the company's monopoly was undisputed or its
sovereignty beyond question. In fact, it was quite the contrary, with furious
debates raging about it, as a commentator notes, *ER* 20 [1812]: 473. Similarly,
there was widespread public concern about the abuse of East India patronage
right from the 1760s and continuing well into the nineteenth century. *AR* 7 [1764]:
147; *The Times*, 6 and 30 March 1809, 12 April 1809; *CaR* 7 [1847]: 228.)

Eighteenth-century English travellers were exposed to several instances and
types of the Indian sublime. In the first moment of the traveller's negotiation of
India's 'limitless' desolation, the encounter is with a natural sublime. The traveller
begins his/her narrative by *describing* the threatening, overflowing/barren/empty/
vast landscape. The description of the Indian sublime generally adopts a rhetoric
of *inflation*, where the rhetoric enables him/her to suggest a terrifying spillage.
There are no lists or tables of information (characteristic features of seventeenth-
century travelogues). On the contrary, the travelogues describe situations where
lists *cannot* be drawn up or boundaries marked. The central images therefore are of
boundaries that dissolve, numbers that are incomputable, markers and meanings

that are obscured, and, most significantly, limits that are exceeded. The traveller's 'project' is to transform this chaos into a *locus amoenus* by suggesting or demarcating in contrast to this boundarilessness, a certainty of number, well-defined boundaries and clear markers on the landscape. The binary opposites of overflowing/ regulated, unmarked/marked, boundariless/bounded constitute two related (colonialist) rhetorical forms in these travelogues. The *rhetoric of improvement*, which I argue informs all travelogues of the 1750–1820 period, hinges upon the *rhetoric of inflation* that *first* characterizes Indian landscape as a potential *locus amoenus* even in its present desolate state.

Forster begins by mentioning that Europeans in Bengal enjoy 'even the luxuries of life' (1798, 1: 12–13). It is this luxurious *locus amoenus* that he leaves behind when he sets out on his journey, and his entire journey may then be seen as the quest for a similar *locus amoenus*. On his first stop Forster notes the ruined state of the town. Forster (1798, 1: 13) writes: 'It would be difficult to discover, that this place [Raj Mahal] had been, so lately, the principal city of a powerful and opulent chief'. This echoes, almost verbatim, an image from William Petrie's evidence before the Secret Committee: '[Tanjore] one of the most flourishing, best cultivated, populous districts in Hindostan . . . but its decline has been so rapid . . . it would now be difficult to trace the remains of its former opulence' (*Fourth Report of the Committee of Secrecy*: House of Commons 1782b: 705). Maria Graham visiting Calicut 'finds no trace of its former grandeur and beauty', a review reports (*QR* 8 [1812]: 416). Yet another reviewer comments about India's past glories: 'we are yet to trace the shadowy outline of her earlier fortunes' (*QR* 48 [1832]: 1). Forster and the anonymous reviewers, across four decades, have all supplemented desolation with obscurity: not only is India's grandeur well in the past, but also this past itself is beyond retrieval. There is no way of determining with any degree of certainty that it was once a great city. From this point Forster's travelogue maps a landscape of desolation, troping it in inflationary terms. At Jungherah, he notes the ruins of a well and conjectures that 'it must have pertained to some village, bordering on the Ganges; now destroyed by the *encroachment of its flood*' (1798, 1: 15, emphasis added). At Bidgi-ghar, Forster encounters a truly Burkean sublime that is at once frightening and attractive. Climbing the hill-fort Forster describes the view:

> The prospect around is diversified and picturesque, but when you throw the eye on the deep and rugged precipice beneath, the view is infinitely grand, though not divested of that horror, which naturally affects the mind in contemplating objects from so abrupt a height.
>
> (Forster 1798, 1: 64)

At Chinnanee, Forster discovers a rapidly flowing stream. He describes it in terms very similar to the above: 'The velocity with which the water was precipitated, its roaring noise, and the narrow shaking bridge, gave full occasion for the use of my eye, and the steadiness of my head'. The Indian sublime also affects Forster in the form of mountains, when he claims that he is 'long . . . disgusted . . . imprisoned by mountain piled on mountain' (1798, 1: 300, 229). Here Forster is describing a rugged, irregular and threatening sublime landscape. John Taylor (1799, 2: 151), George Thomas (1803: 41), William Thomson (1788, 1: 22–23), Thomas Motte (*Asiatic Miscellany* 2 [1786]: 10, 24–25), Jemima Kindersley (1777: 82, 92, 183), William Hickey (1925, 3: 323–25), Edward Moor (1794: 49, 62), John McQueen (1757, Mss. Eur. 675: unpaginated), William Jones (1970, 2: 783), James Lind (1811: 61) and Robert Barker (*PT* 65 [1775]: 206) all describe sublimely frightening overflowing rivers and inundated, markerless lands. The descriptions inevitably detail the destruction of roads and such marks of *human* control over land.[8]

Each of these descriptions functions within a rhetoric of inflation. The sea *spills over*, walls and roofs – both bounding structures – cave in, bodies are strewn everywhere, landscapes alter, and markers are lost. The overrunning of boundaries, the undifferentiated landscape (inundated lands), wide expanses of water and destruction, storms, and the resultant feelings of desolation and horror inform these passages. Overrunning and spillage – characteristics of the sublime (Weiskel 1986: 26; Mishra 1994: 22) – are also causes of the desolation, as the above descriptions suggest. The emphasis is on the unquantifiable and illimitable landscape where travellers are under threat, a threat conveyed through the rhetoric of inflation.

In the case of natural desolation such as the ones described above, travellers cannot attribute causes or meanings. Travellers now enter the second moment of their negotiation with the Indian landscape. In order to end or prevent a mere spectatorial role and/or complete powerless 'annihilation' by the landscape, travellers must assert individual agency. This takes two rhetorical forms in the second moment. One, they invest the boundariless landscape with symbolic meaning. Two, they begin to transform the inflated desolation into a *potential locus amoenus*. In the first mode, the landscape is allegorized and meanings read into the various features of the landscape. In the second, travellers suggest potential uses for the land and methods of 'redeeming' the waste, both vectored along a theme of individual and collective effort.

The attempt to 'understand', ascribe meaning, and *explain* Indian landscape was, however, a difficult task. Sara Suleri (1992: 27–29) notes that Burke employs the rhetoric of difficulty and obscurity – itself a feature of the sublime – to describe India and Indian culture. Her comments apply equally well to Forster and his contemporaries, whose descriptions of Hindu religion are filled with terms such as 'obscurity', 'mystery' or their equivalents. Trying to read the inscriptions on a stone pillar in the Allahabad palace, Forster finds that the letters are 'illegible'. Obscurity inflects even topography when Forster looks for a road near Allahabad. He writes: 'it is supposed that some remains of this road would have yet been visible; but on a careful examination I could not discover its most distant trace' (1798, 1: 69, 70). Anthony MacTier, in his unpublished *Journal of a Voyage* (1797–98) also uses the trope of concealed or clouded reality when he writes:

> The clouds in that quarter had assumed the most romantic shapes . . . [their] lengthened forms reaching from the horizon . . . which was tinctured with a

deeper or lighter purple according to *the thickness of the black cloudy vapour through which the sun's now enfeebled rays could scarcely pierce.*

(MacTier 1797–98: unpaginated, emphasis added)

Shifting emphasis from topography to culture, Forster expresses his opinion that it is very 'difficult' to 'know' Hinduism (1798, 1: 30–31, 52). Alexander Dow (1768: xxii) in *The History of Hindostan* describes the 'impenetrable air of mystery' surrounding Hinduism. In the literature of India, writes a reviewer of James Tod's *Annals and Antiquities of Rajasthan* (1830–32), 'history . . . [is] almost unknown' (*QR* 48 [1832]: 1). A review essay speaks of the 'thickness of smoke of circumstances, and the darkness of the excluding mist, or rather of mystification of Indian trading politics' which had prevented people back in England from taking a sufficient interest in the region (*CaR* 7 [1847]: 228). Such images repeat in: Kindersley (1777: 110), Charles Wilkins (*Asiatic Researches* 1 [1788]: 131), William Chambers (*Asiatic Researches* 1 [1788]: 157), Emma Robert's *Oriental Scenes* (1832: 1–23, 25, 44 and elsewhere) and also in political commentaries (*AR* 7 [1764]: 34), pamphlets such as *A Letter to a Late Popular Director* (1769: 2), and book reviews (*MR* 80 [1789]: 699; *ER* 17 [1811]: 314).

Jemima Kindersley's (1777) description of Indian landscape also uses the trope of obscurity, especially when detailing humans (interestingly, the inhabitants are assembled in a group, a rather uncomfortable situation for the English, as Bernard Cohn (1997: 10) points out). Kindersley, describing the Allahabad fair, writes: 'A *moving landscape of grotesque figures*; for the natives of the Southern parts of India, being unused to cold . . . *cover themselves* with blankets and quilts of various colours, to defend them from the weather' (1777: 262, emphasis added). Kindersley's description of 'massed' and veiled figures – and therefore mysterious and perhaps threatening – is also couched in the aesthetics of the sublime.[9] Incidentally, obscurity and darkness were very real problems for the company's soldiers, especially during battle (as letters about the war with Tipu Sultan reveal: see East India Company, *Copies and Extracts*, 1800: 110). On a different but related note, William Hodges writes: 'all that I saw filled my mind with expectations of *what may yet be unseen*' (1793: 5, emphasis added).[10] Likewise a review of James Tod's *Annals and Antiquities of Rajasthan* (1829) also took recourse to the trope of obscurity and concealment when describing the work's contribution: 'Although our view cannot reach the termination of the storied vista, our imagination can build, from the dense clouds that conceal it, a fabric still more grandly beautiful' (*MR* 12 [NS] [1829]: 393). The images of veiling used to describe things as diverse as Indian landscape, people, and religion suggests a whole discourse of obscurity. Besides desolation, difficulty and obscurity are also (sublime) features of India's landscape that English travellers must negotiate in order to arrive at a certain certitude of the self. Travellers continue to search for a light that may penetrate the darkness of India, and which might help them to feel more confident in the desolation.

The absence of identifiable meaning(s) in the negative sublime is negotiated when a metaphor or allegory is inserted into the chain of signifiers. This 'substitution' or allocation of meaning to an empty landscape of desolation is the traveller's defence strategy that alters two things: the absence of meaning, and the traveller's own passive state as spectator. The landscape is now allegorized, and the individual moves from being a passive spectator terrified by the landscape to an active agent, capable of understanding or even influencing the landscape. The attribution of meaning is an appropriative mechanism that asserts the agency of the observer. Ruins constitute a major mode of this metaphorization of the negative sublime. The desolate ruin enables the traveller to attribute any and every 'actual' or 'imaginative' meaning to it, in a 'metaphorical appropriation' of the landscape (John Berger, quoted in Bohls 1997: 87). In travelogues of the late eighteenth century the English traveller interprets Indian desolation as the effect of three causes: uncontrolled nature (rivers flooding, violent monsoons, drought and famine) that persistently ruins crops, lands and human lives; the indolence of the natives (a theme inaugurated from the earliest English travelogues in the seventeenth century); and despotism and war. Ruins play a central role in this mode of ascription of meaning. The ruin and the antiquary, as the eighteenth-century aesthetician Archibald Alison (Andrews 1999: 299–300) and more contemporary scholars such as Rose Macaulay (1964: 37) suggest, provide a space for imagination to roam.

The Select Committee's report on Bengal mentions Madras city's decline in both 'population and culture' due to the company's trading policies (House of Commons 1783: 56). The ruins of Raj Mahal become an excuse for Forster to muse philosophically: 'the instability of monuments of human grandeur cannot, *in any region of the globe*, I apprehend, be more faithfully, or more grievously exemplified than at Rajah Mahal' (1798, 1: 14, emphasis added). Forster has literally inflated the ruin and its 'meaning', where it appears to speak for ruins the world over and yet surpasses them all in terms of degradation. Viewing other ruins, Forster manages to discover a significant meaning in each of them, and thus alleviates the impact of their desolation on himself. Forster, for example, finds Benares stifling because of its narrow streets and the all-pervasive stench. The 'irregular and compressed' streets that lack all 'symmetry and arrangement' appears tolerable only 'from the top of the minarets' (1798, 1: 32–33). The ruined state of the land is then attributed to a human cause. Forster, viewing the town from a vantage point, writes:

> [Eight miles from Benares] . . . the eye is attracted by the view of two lofty minarets, which were erected by Aurangazebe on the ruins of an ancient Hindoo temple . . . the construction on this sacred ruin . . . would appear to have been prompted to the mind of Aurangazebe, by a bigoted and intemperate desire of insulting their religion . . . the Hindoos consider this monument, as the disgraceful record of a foreign yoke.
>
> (Forster 1798, 1: 31)

This 'metonymic viewing' (Charlesworth 1994: 69–70) – observing ruins from high vantage points – distances Forster from the immediacy of the ruins *and* celebrates ruins as symbols for the collapse of an old order. Forster then goes on to describe several other ruins. He describes Kashmir thus:

> Kashmir, having fallen a conquest to the followers of Mahomet, at an early period of their empire in India, when they furiously *broke down every fence* that barred the progress of their religion, felt the full force of a barbarous zeal.
>
> (Forster 1798, 2: 8, emphasis added)

William Hodges (1793: 62), Quintin Craufurd (1792, 1: 102) and, years later, commentators in the *Calcutta Review* (18 [1852]: 139–40) all describe the storm-like effects of the Muslim invasion of India.

Luteef-Ghar Fort, like all other places in George Forster's India, is described as having fallen into ruin, 'deserted, and the passage approaching to it is almost choked up by brushwood, and the projected branches of trees'. Forster analyses each component of the landscape to convey a picture of absolute horror, a place where disaster is waiting to happen. The air has a certain 'malignant quality' and 'communicates its pernicious influence to all animal bodies'. The water is 'baneful', and the air has a 'pestiferous quality'. The branches and leaves of trees fall into the rivulets and 'increase the noxious effect'. And later, 'a vast mass of ruins interspersed through a wide space, marks the ancient extent and grandeur of Kinnouge [Kanauj], though few distinct vestiges now exist' (Forster 1798, 1: 62–63, 92).

Mhow is in ruins when Forster visits the place. Oudh/Awadh is first described thus: '[it is] immediately distinguished . . . by its barren and desolate prospect'. The Ganges at Allahabad exhibits some grandeur for Forster (1798, 1: 65, 67, 68). The Mausoleum at Allahabad has a garden that Forster describes thus: 'from want of culture they look rugged and barren'. The Khusro tomb 'diffuses around it an air of melancholy', and is now falling into ruins. Northwest of Allahabad, Forster again encounters a landscape that is of 'barren and desolate aspect', with the forts and palaces falling into ruin (Forster 1798, 1: 71–72, 77, 78, 80). The *Edinburgh Review* underscores the Indian ruins described in Burnes' travelogue (60 [1835]: 398, 417). George Thomas (1803: 13, 65) and Jemima Kindersley (1777: 74–75, 91, 106) also report several ruined towns. A later traveller, Katherine Elwood (1830, 1: 362), also describes monsoon vegetation as 'rank, rapid and luxuriant', and finds relief only when she sees flowering shrubs. In each case attributing a human cause negotiates the desolation and lack of visible signs or meanings.[11] In most cases, it is Muslim 'invasion' or the sheer lack of initiative in the native that 'produces' the sublime desolation. The traveller has thus transformed the threat of a non-meaning, non-refuge offering place into a place with *some* meaning. The trope of excessive obscurity and the complete collapse of signification is an intensification of an image: what nature has not already destroyed, human wretchedness does. The 'want of culture' that Forster mentions is precisely the lack that the English would eventually fill. In these examples, the strategy of attributing symbolic meaning (collapse of Indian civilization) and ideo-pathological causes (Aurangzeb's 'intemperate' and 'bigoted' desire, as Forster describes it) to the landscape fills the desolation with select signifieds. The landscape has been allegorized with the conflation of the moral and physical topography.

The third 'meaning' attributed to the desolation of the Indian landscape, and closely linked to the second 'explanation' (native despotism) is that of war. The eighteenth-century narrative's reading of Indian landscape attributes the desolation to a lack of cultivation (human acts of omission), or to war (human acts of commission). These landscapes are sites of suffering (of the English, or even of the natives at the hands of their cruel kings) and evoke a sense of melancholy and loss. The paratactic description of massacres and destruction in these travelogues maps a landscape where desolation is inflated to an unbearable, indescribable extent. Meer Jaffer and his associates, Forster claims – citing François Bernier's 1670 text as evidence – ruined Bengal. Forster describes Mongheer thus: 'The fort is in a decayed condition, as well as the private buildings, which are uninhabited'. Bareily's fortification is now 'covered with jungle' with 'little cultivation'. Saseindy is 'wild' and 'barren' without any cultivation (Forster 1798, 1: 15, 81). Travelling further north, Forster enters Najeb Ghur. The description runs:

> The country from Najeb Ghur to this frontier is chiefly a waste . . . The inhabitants say, that in the time of Najeb-ud-Dowlah, the land now *overgrown with wood*, was a cultivated plain; but such is the precarious state of the native territories of Hindostan, from *the inert disposition* which, with little deviation, pervades the body of the people . . . we are not to wonder at the ruinous state into which many of the most valuable provinces of Hindostan have fallen.
>
> (Forster 1798, 1: 193, emphasis added)

Such 'overrun' landscapes, where the land is just wild, with non-productive, unfriendly vegetation, like the one Forster describes and representing another kind of overflowing sublime, also find mention in other commentators (*ER* 60 [1835]: 399).

Near Plassey, the scene of the historic 1757 battle that decisively altered the role of English presence in India, Forster encounters a deserted village. He describes this landscape of desolation in terms of affect, using the landscape to suggest his change of mental state thus:

> The journey of this evening, solitary and dreary, gave a wrong bent to every spring of the imagination, which sullenly refused to receive one chearful or pleasing idea. If such did begin to shoot forth, the prospect of a deserted village, a desolate country, immediately destroyed it, and introduced in its stead, those pregnant with the horrors and miseries of war.
>
> (Forster 1798, 1: 235–36)

William Hickey, for instance, describes the sense of threat that the Indian landscape offers: 'I had the mortification to hear it was impracticable for a European, particularly a female, to travel by land, the entire country being *covered* with Banditti, called hooties, who lived by plunder' (1925, 3: 82, emphasis added).

When proceeding to his friend's house, Hickey undergoes another disquieting experience:

> I walked to his house through a burning sun, and on my way passed the skirts of a camp of Tippoo's, where a number of ferocious-looking fellows eyed me in such a manner as to create considerable alarm in my mind.
>
> (Hickey 1925, 3: 82)

A review of Alexander Burnes' travelogue appropriates this same image when it describes Indian towns as 'infested with robbers' (*ER* 13 [1808]: 95), and a 'fraternity of murderers' as having 'spread its ramifications over the whole of that vast country, from Cape Comorin to the Himalayas . . . destroying multitudes of victims' (*ER* 64 [1837]: 357). In all these descriptions the threat of war or bandits merges with the inconvenience of the landscape. William Thomson treats the desolation of Gujarat, the Carnatic region, and Madras (1788, 1: 97, 174) as the effect of war. Thomson elaborates the link between war, climate and desolation:

> In Europe the horrors of war are mitigated by the mildness of the climate, and the humanity of the conqueror. In Asia, an inveterate antipathy against Europeans conspires with a dry and parched land, where it is not an easy manner for the sick and wounded to obtain even the comfort of water, and, with the rigours of fervid heat, to press down the load of suffering on the defenceless head of him who has none to help him.
>
> (Thomson 1788, 2: 2–3)

Thomson's description links climate, human or Indian reaction to the English traveller and war in a description that maps the physical topography or condition onto the psychological-moral. The climatic condition and the land are instrumental extensions of the 'vile' psychology of the native.

Richard Owen Cambridge's *An Account of the War in India* (1761: 15) describes a war-ravaged Trichy. William Hickey's most detailed topographical description is that of a war-ravaged landscape. Detailing England's war with Tipu Sultan, Hickey describes the countryside in inflationary terms:

> [Tipu's forces] cut off the foraging parties; preventing the approach of supplies, keeping *large bodies* of his [Tipu's] cavalry *always hovering* round about us, murdering the stragglers . . . [Tipu's freebooters] advanced almost to the gates of Madras, marking their progress by fire and sword, and spreading ruin and desolation in *all directions*, burning *whole villages*, massacring the wretched inhabitants without distinction, violating their wives and daughters . . . *totally destroying* the magnificent cantonments for the Cavalry at Wallajauhbad which had been erected by the Company . . . it was a very beautiful structure . . . of this superb edifice the malignant rascals *scarcely left one brick upon another, so effectively did they demolish it.*
>
> (Hickey 1925, 4: 14–15, emphasis added)

Another commentator mentions the difficulty in 'pursuing these remains [Meer Kasim's army] through so extensive a country' (*AR* 8 [1765]: 9).

War, the landscape, climate and the English traveller's suffering can apparently be conveyed only through a descriptive vocabulary of the sublime. The EIC's *Copies and Extracts*, detailing advice on the war with Tipu, also sees Tipu's threat in sublime terms: 'Tippoo's power on its actual scale . . . the prodigious magnitude of their [Tipu and the French army's] preparations, and the incredible progress of their arms, evidently directed at the destruction of British power in India' (East India Company 1800: 37). Jemima Kindersley describes the war-ravaged state of Pondicherry:

> I cannot help figuring to myself the situation of its inhabitants during the siege, their prosperity destroyed, their houses laid waste, widows bewailing the loss of their husbands, and mothers of their children! But they had this consolation, that . . . they fell into the hands of a merciful enemy; the English, ever merciful as brave, never showed it more than on this occasion. Private property was as much as possible secured.
>
> (Kindersley 1777: 74–75)

Here Kindersley is imaginatively re-creating the war and its effects, in the same manner as Forster and others interpreted a range of meanings into ruins. Edward Moor (1794: 112, 125 and elsewhere), George Thomas (1803: 8, 13), William Moorcroft and George Trebeck (1841, 1: 13, 15), Robert Orme (1974: 261) plus reviews of travelogues in periodicals (*ER* 13 [1808]: 85–86), all detail the *topograph-ical* effects of India's wars and cruel rulers. A crucial element in this inflated description of the landscape of war is the actual suffering of English soldiers in the course of the war. The latter half of the eighteenth century saw the publication of several military memoirs, all of which were extensively reviewed or had extracts published in English periodicals and newspapers.[12] These texts therefore consti-tute an important moment in the discursive construction of Indian landscape as one of desolation, privation and possible death. The moment of the imperial sublime is, interestingly, rooted in a context of concern about the British in India – the soldier's suffering, the condition of life, the safety of women and men, and death. The imperial sublime's efforts to subdue and control the land, at least rhetorically, could be read as a response to this concern.

William Thomson (1788, 2: 14, 29) describes the agonies of prisoners. James Bristow (1793: 71–72, 72–73) describes his own floggings. Detailed description of injuries, suffering and death fill the travelogues of James Capper (1783: 109–10), Henry Oakes (1785: 8–9, 19, 21–22, 25–26), Innes Munro (1789: 91), Robert Beatson (1790, 3: 3), James Bristow (1793: 48–49), Edward Moor (1794: 27, 32), Donald Campbell (1801: 276) and John Shipp (1832, 2: 99–100). In one descrip-tion, the prisoner to whom Donald Campbell is shackled dies of cholera, and he is left shackled to the corpse for some time (1801: 284–86). Others like Henry Oakes and Roderick MacKenzie provide a list of survivors of these campaigns and imprisonment (Oakes 1785: 103–24; R. MacKenzie 1793, Appendix, 1: 107–09).

There were debates about the conditions of prisons in India, especially about how European prisoners would fare in them (House of Commons 1782b: 442–43; William Hickey was one of those who provided evidence regarding the Calcutta prisons). Holwell's narrative of the Black Hole was received as a true and horrifying account of events in India (*MR* 18 [1758]: 183). Emily Brittle, travelling in 1780, writes in her *India Guide* (1785) of the 'Goth-like invader' (Hyder Ali) who kept them 'Penn'd up in a fort, like a scar'd flock of sheep' (Brittle 1785: 87). James Bristow (1793: 72–73) even suggests that he has not provided complete details of the horrors for 'it would, indeed, make too large a register of horrors to enumerate every particular instance in which these unfeeling men treated with inhumanity'. Bristow here has conveyed more through his *suggestion* of censorship than through any rhetoric of inflation. These narratives thus construct India not only as a cruel land, but also as a potentially heroic one, where the English soldiers' troubles make a martyr of him.

During the first and second moments of her/his encounter with the Indian landscape of desolation, the traveller has achieved or experienced diverse effects. The traveller has witnessed an Indian sublime of desolation and emptiness. The rhetoric of inflation that these travelogues employ conveys an intensity of danger, destruction and emptiness. The second moment, building upon the first, fills this desolation with meaning. The ascription of meaning prepares the ground for a rhetorical transformation of desolation into something else, and enables articulation of colonial ideology. The second moment also marks the transition from a state of self-preservation to affirmation for the traveller. The negative sublime has been negotiated by attribution of meaning and allegorization of the landscape to 'create' a hermeneutic sublime. The landscape is now ready to be 'renewed'.

The topography of improvement

The third moment of the traveller's encounter with India's sublime landscape grows out of the second. Having attributed a set of meanings in her/his metaphorical appropriation of the landscape, the traveller now seeks to transform her/his own role from spectator to participant. In a bid to negotiate the vast (inflated) emptiness of India, the traveller has already 'filled' it with certain meanings. This is an affirmative act, or at least, the preliminary to one. In the third moment, the traveller suggests a more active role for the individual and the EIC. In this moment, the traveller seeks a transformation of the Indian landscape from a place of threat to a *locus amoenus*, fit (or fitted out) for habitation by the English. In this moment, with the suggestion of a georgic renewal of the Indian landscape, the traveller seeks a degree of equivalence with the land. This is what Tsang Lap-Chuen (1998: 41–42) identifies as the 'appreciative' mode, where the individual attains a 'plenum of being' through, say, a 'good Samaritan' act. Three elements constitute the third moment, and each of the three is articulated from within a rhetoric of improvement that suggests a whole new role for the English. One, the Indian landscape becomes a site of heroic endeavour. Two, a recognition of the land as a site of future wars, where wars are seen as enabling complete control of

India by the English and/or 'liberation' of the Indians from their own despotic rulers. Three, the creation of a *locus amoenus* effected by English labour within India's desolation. An ur-narrative that begins to emerge here is that of India's 'improvement'. The notion of improvement then begins to expand to take in fields as diverse as religion, architecture, gardening, technology, education and aesthetics. However, it is landscape that comes in for the first focused effort by the traveller.[13]

Memorials constitute an important means of 'repopulating' the Indian desolation in this period. Having rejected Indian idols and icons in the first phase of their stay (as Chapter 1 demonstrates), the travellers of the second phase established a new set of icons, a process that was to culminate in the great imperial constructions of the mid-nineteenth century. Several memorials had been built – some even on demand, even though there was occasional criticism of these burial sites and memorials by the British themselves (*CaR* 9 [1848]: 124–27) – over the years to Englishmen and women who had died in India. From the last decades of the eighteenth century, travellers made these memorials a fixture on their itinerary. It is particularly significant that the interest in memorials to Englishmen and women peaks at a time when English presence in India is rather shaky and uncertain.

From the 1750s there were fairly regular desertions by the English and other European soldiers (Grey 1929: 212; Keay 1991: 374). Letters and documents of the period reveal some anxiety in the EIC regarding the matter (Ingram 1970: 20). The House of Commons' Committee of Secrecy filed a detailed report about the crisis, with reports from Robert Clive and others (*Ninth Report*: House of Commons 1773: 671–715). Fort William's letters from the 1760–63 years (*Fort William* 1968, 3: 423), John Bruce's *Historical View of the Plans, for the Government of British India* (1793: 512), James Bristow (1793: 19, 36, 102) and commentators in the *Monthly Review* (45 [1771]: 504) all refer to desertions and the lack of discipline among European troops. Under such circumstances it was important to instil a sense of purpose and fidelity to a larger cause. This was achieved when memorials of dead English soldiers came in for narrative focus in the travelogues, or English achievements were praised in England.

Travelling through Patna, George Forster undertakes a diversion in order to visit the memorial for English soldiers who died in the war with Kasim Ali. The ruins of Patna, to which Forster (1798, 1: 24–25) has already paid some attention, are now cathected on to this memorial. Forster writes:

> Curiosity, and the desire of the moment to indulge a melancholy idea, led me to the spot, where the English were massacred by the order of Cassum Ali. The former buildings are removed, and a well-proportioned monument has been erected in commemoration of that dreadful event, though without any inscription. Perhaps it had been consistent with sounder policy, that no such memorial had been fixed; but as it was judged expedient to record, thus publicly, an act of treacherous cruelty, the cause, I think, should have been explained.
>
> (Forster 1798, 1: 25)

The landscape of desolation and melancholy has been emptied of its native icons ('former buildings'). In place is a new icon, one that becomes – at least for Forster – a memorial to native 'treachery'. Forster believes that the heinousness of the treachery warrants even more detailing.

The landscape has undergone two significant changes here – of desacralization and emptying, and a 'restoration'. The 'restoration' of icons is achieved through substitution, when English icons replace native ones. These icons remove the sense of threat that the ruin evokes (symbolized by the tearing down of old buildings) and converts the site into heroic space. Forster's reasons for visiting Murshidabad are cast in similar terms: '[I visited it so that] I might view the theatre in which those interesting schemes had been agitated, which, after a series of intrigues and blood-shed, advanced the English to dominion of a wealthy kingdom' (Forster 1798, 1: 9). In a review of a tract titled *The Bengalee*, the author refers to the region as a 'bloody theatre' of 'warlike exploits' (*MR* 13 [NS] [1830]: 322–23). The desolate landscape is now a heroic landscape, a *stage* for courageous (British) acts. As a petition from the Liverpool merchants dated 13 December 1768 and tabled in the House of Commons points out, 'the opulent territories lately added to the British possessions in Asia were acquired by the bravery of the British troops' (*Journal of the House of Commons* 32 [1768]: 102). In addition to this new thematic of a heroic landscape, Forster's comments on 'native treachery' enable him to treat the topographic feature as a physiognomic index of the native's moral and psychological traits (see Metcalf 2005: 152–68).

Numerous travellers document their visits to memorials: Edward Moor (1794: 255), Surgeon Johnson (1806: 31), Viscount Valentia – George Annesley – (1809, 1: 83, 188), Moorcroft and Trebeck (1841, 1: 29) and William Hickey (1925, 3: 138–40). William Milburn (1813, 1: 157) mentions that even 'strangers' visit the 'burial places of the Europeans'. A letter to the editor of the *Asiatic Miscellany* (1785, 1: 313) complains that the memorial to Job Charnock in Calcutta was in ruins, and ran the risk of being 'consigned to oblivion'. The first Anglo-Indian novel, *Hartly House, Calcutta* (1789: 1), *opens* with this line: 'the grave of thousands!'[14] This memorial tourism is a new iconography, whereby the desolation of the landscape is negotiated through the melancholic memorial.[15] Memorials functioned to serve two purposes in these travelogues. Evoking the trauma of English settlements in India, achieved through wars, injuries and losses, memorials served as signifiers of 'violence in the present' (to adapt a phrase from David Bunn (2002: 58) to describe the purpose of graves in colonial Africa). They thus kept alive the deeds of 'faithful' soldiers who had died for a 'national cause' (which was exactly what the EIC's actions in India had become by the last decades of the eighteenth century). Jemima Kindersley (1777: 275), for instance, comments that the Black Hole incident was frequently talked about in England. Hickey was to compare his suffering to the victims of the Black Hole (I shall return to this point), thus suggesting a common denominator of suffering for all English in India. The memorials also glorified the personal actions and lives of the English who had died in India, and served as icons of duty for future generations. The *Monthly Review* described Robert Clive as 'the hero of the grand Oriental drama' (*MR* 36 [1767]: 169). He was also praised in *sublime* terms, for acquiring an 'extent of territory . . . an amount of revenue . . . a multitude of subjects' (*ER* 70 [1840]: 361). Years later, an essay by a Madame Cornu on Arthur Wellesley, 'Wellington and the Mahrattas', stated in a description that links landscape, aesthetics and notions of English heroism: 'A few years before the arrival of Wellington in India, our Asiatic possessions were not sufficiently prized in England; but the achievements of that hero in his early years directed attention to those beautiful regions' (*AM* 22 [1852]: 524). Katherine Elwood (1830, 2: 109) writes: 'if we were driven out of the country tomorrow few vestiges would remain but those places, where the English have settled'. Such a heroic-memorial iconography of the travelogue transforms Indian landscape from a miserable death trap into a *potentially* heroic one. With this step the English repopulate the desolation with their own icons.

Memorials were also frequently direct reminders of England's wars in India. In narratives of the 1750–1820 period, war plays a central role in the transformation of the Indian landscape, both as a 'literary' theme and in terms of actual administration. The travellers frequently treat Indian landscape as the *potential* site of war, and the wars themselves as preliminary to control and profits. War thus becomes the second means of transforming the Indian landscape into a potential *locus amoenus* for the English in India. Having allegorized the land, the traveller now suggests a more active role for the individual. This theme begins when the landscape is evaluated for its future use.

The link between wars, a *locus amoenus*, profit, and the rhetoric of improvement that informs this reading or treatment of the Indian landscape is best illustrated in Robert Clive's 1759 letter to William Pitt. Clive's remarks become the framing statement for our reading of the rhetoric of improvement in eighteenth-century travelogues. Clive writes:

> I flatter myself I have made it pretty clear to you, that there will be little or no difficulty in obtaining the absolute possession of these rich kingdoms . . . I leave you to judge, whether an income yearly of two million pounds sterling, with the possession of three provinces *abounding in the most valuable productions of nature* and of art, be an object deserving of public attention; and whether it be worth the nation's while to take proper measures to *secure* such an acquisition – an acquisition which, under the *management* of so able and disinterested a minister, would prove a source of immense wealth to the kingdom, and might in time be appropriated in part as a fund towards diminishing the heavy load of debt under which we at present labour.
>
> (Malcolm 1836, 2: 122–23, emphasis added)

The shift from the individual to the collective is interesting as Clive shifts responsibility for constructive action from himself to England as a whole. The link between war – suggested by his remarks on the need for English soldiers in India – improvement, and England's needs and profits is very clearly emphasized in Clive.[16] John Sulivan (1780: 27), H.T. Colebrooke (1795: 27–30, 99) and others conflate the aesthetic with economic power and 'improvement'. Here is Colebroke:

European families residing longer in India, and enjoying the affluence there; will adorn the country, and increase its stock, with useful and ornamented buildings. Their taste for the elegant superfluities of life, will give encouragement to the industry of the laborious classes of the native inhabitants. Numbers of the natives sharing in the riches, which will again flow into India, will constitute a class of opulent individuals . . . it is certain that they are sufficiently disposed for gratifications, which tend to encourage ornamental arts.

(Colebrooke 1795: 103–04)

The topography is 'analysed' for its use, fertility and productivity, and role in war. The travellers pay particular attention to those features of the landscape that might hinder or facilitate communications, transport, or actual combat. The landscape is thus treated as not only a potential acquisition or possession and source of profit for the EIC/England, but also a site where the *move* towards possession and acquisition may be launched and carried out. The Board of Agriculture in London, therefore, made elaborate arrangements to acquire what it calls 'useful knowledge' about India's plant life and agriculture. This, argues a report of the Board, would be directed at 'promoting industry, increasing articles of sustenance, or alleviating human misery' (Board of Agriculture 1797, 1: 357).

James Rennell, the man behind India's great mapping project, makes the link between war and geographical knowledge explicit when he writes in his *Memoir of a Map of Hindoostan* (1788: iv): 'the war with Hyder Ally and Tippoo Sultan, his successor, has produced much new geographical knowledge'.[17] George Forster, for instance, maps the navigable rivers in the areas that he travels in, mentioning specific uses for them:

These rivers [in the Awadh region] flow through most of the principal towns, and intersect a large space of the country; most of them being navigable for boats, in all seasons of the year. The English armies may be plentifully supplied with provisions and ammunition, in the event of executing any military operation in that quarter.

(Forster 1798, 1: 85)

Immediately after the above description Forster (1798, 1: 85) writes: 'These rivers also present strong barriers against the Mahrattah, Seick [Sikh], or Moghul cavalry'. Richard Cambridge (1761: 32–33), focusing on the Anglo-French wars of 1750–60, sees Indian landscape entirely in terms of the topography's military advantages or disadvantages, as instanced in the description of Gingee town. Cambridge's work was described as something of 'truly national interest' (*MR* 24 [1761]: 253–56). These measured, evaluated descriptions become a rationalization of otherwise incomprehensible and sublime features, and K.K. Dyson (1978: 124) is accurate in describing Jemima Kindersley's (1777) narrative as exhibiting an 'Enlightenment approach to India'. Such a rationalizing spirit is visible in numerous landscape descriptions of the period. James Bristow (1793: 130–33, 133, 134, 134–35), Alexander Dirom (1793: 22–23, 66–67, 69, 90–91), Edward

Moor (1794: 39–41, 101, 110–11, 137, 147–48, 163) and several other memoirs or travelogues contain chorographies of forts and routes.[18]

There is a close narrative link between the *transformative* discourses of war and that of improvement, as I have argued about the texts of Clive and others. War provides a mode of acquiring the land preliminary to transforming it from a desolate waste into a *locus amoenus*. In the third moment of the English traveller's encounter with Indian desolation, this drive towards a *locus amoenus* is the most important of these transformative discourses. If memorials project and embody a sense of 'nationalist' *and* personal heroism in an age of uncertainty, as I have suggested, they also work in conjunction with actual acts of war to become appropriative mechanisms of mapping Indian 'wastes'. In addition to memorials and war, during the third moment of the encounter, the English traveller's search for a *locus amoenus* takes two distinct forms. First, the traveller may seek a social refuge or place of safety, where the social relationships may be either accidental or the result of a personal effort. The social *locus amoenus* is a veritable oasis, a *socio-topographical refuge*, in the desolation. The threat of the landscape is alleviated when the traveller, who may be lost or in need of assistance, discovers companionship *or* topographical refuge. Frequently, one leads to the other, and the traveller who discovers human company (a social refuge) has attained spatio-topographical refuge too (and vice versa). Second, the traveller seeks to 'improve' the landscape to *make* it a refuge. In both forms, eighteenth-century travelogues present the search for refuge in terms of a colonialist rhetoric of improvement.

The rhetoric of the third moment of an English traveller's encounter with sublime wastes also moves swiftly across and between two 'positions': a personal or individual one, and a collective or English one. The theme of improvement and restoration (of India's productive lands) is intimately linked to the efforts of the English, and the actual labour (either at social relationships or with regard to the land) that creates the *locus amoenus*. The way out of desolation into a *locus amoenus* is through the personal interest and labour not of the Indian, but that of the Englishman (with an emphasis on the male's role). This rhetoric of improvement conflated with the rhetoric of labour enables the traveller to contrast the moral topographies of the English and Indians as a binary opposition: the industrious and serious English traveller versus the indolent native.

The search for socio-topographical refuge

The desolation of the Indian landscape is threatening because of the absence of cultivation, people or refuge. The featurelessness of the landscape is threatening when travellers lose their way or find themselves unable to traverse the terrain. The first emphasis is therefore on *spatio-geographical* refuge. The absence of definite landmarks is a negative sublime of terrifying proportions. A Fort William letter sums up this negative sublime:

> Another point we deem it necessary to mention relates to the limits of Calcutta. *There is great difficulty in tracing the Old Limits of the Town*; the descrip-

tions of them, as given by Individuals, or ascertained by the Records, is subject to doubts which *render the limits uncertain.* We think *it would be advisable to fix the boundaries anew,* so as to comprehend a number of new Edifices which properly form a part of the Town of Calcutta, but concerning which Doubts have of late years been made.

(*Fort William* 1972, 10: 589, emphasis added; see also 3: 27)

A review of Colebrooke's (1795) tract on Bengal complains that the author had 'not given the names adopted by them [native cultivators] for the different species of lands' (*ER* 10 [1807]: 36–37). The process of understanding the geographical boundaries of the country before its computing population, revenue, and agricultural produce undertaken by the English in India was a means of alleviating the threat of boundarilessness (as far back as 1705 the EIC had ordered a survey and measurement of the three villages of Dihi, Calcutta, Govindpur, and Sutanuti: Mukhopadhyay 1987: 19).[19] Such images of uncharted territory, unmarked boundaries, overgrown desolation, all suggesting the absence of safe havens, figure in several travelogues, and are in fact a trope used to describe all Asiatic empires.

George Forster's 'real' and frightening encounter with the desolate and unmarked Indian sublime occurs along similar lines:

The shrubes and high grass had so concealed the path, that I was completely bewildered, and had lost my way, when a small village on an eminence attracted my notice, and held out the prospect of relief: but such is the instability of sublunary pleasure, that this promising mark proved a false beacon. The hamlet was unroofed, and its inhabitants had sought a more friendly land.

(Forster 1798, 1: 98)

The landscape is not only 'inhospitable', but also unmarked. The houses are deserted, and there is no immediate *locus amoenus* for Forster. The illusion of refuge is what renders the desolation impossible to handle. Later, Forster is lost again. He writes:

The ground in front being thickly covered with leaves, no appearance of a road was discernible; and my horse, when I mounted, was so much alarmed, that he would not, but with great reluctance, move in any direction . . . After traversing the forest in various directions without perceiving the appearance of tract or habitation, or the vestige of any creature, except great quantities of elephants dung, I, at length, fell into a narrow path, which leading through a long space of woody desert, brought me to a village; whence the people with much kindness conducted me to our halting place.

(Forster 1798, 1: 195–96)

A narrative of an officer, published in 1835, presents a similar search for a socio-topographical refuge. The officer, along with his friend, wanders through a ravine. There is a 'rural grandeur' to the 'mountain-forest scenery, which seemed to rest in sullen slumber'. They listened to the 'wild and mournful notes of the birds of the night, and the jackal's screaming cry'. Then 'suddenly', in the middle of this 'melancholy but pleasing reverie' they see camels and elephants camping, 'making up their quarters for the night' and a group of Hindoos, and the Englishmen, he writes, remained standing 'gazing upon this picturesque native scene' (*FM* 12 [1835]: 665). Once again the presence of natives renders the desolate and melancholic (sublime) space, a picturesque 'scene'. Later George Forster finds himself in a similar featureless, inhospitable landscape. The sense of gloom is dispelled when he comes across a family, and thus enters a social *locus amoenus*:

> On approaching so large a town as Jumbo [Jammu], I expected to have seen a moderately populous country, but the aspect was altogether the reverse . . . the predicament in which I then stood gave a gloomy cast to my thoughts, which naturally adverted to that long established position, of 'man being a sociable animal'; the truth of which few are more convinced than myself . . . on the side of the road, to my great joy, I at length discovered a family sitting on a narrow green spot.
>
> (Forster 1798, 1: 241–42)

Jumah is also described as 'a thick gloomy forest, tenanted only by the beasts of the field, skirts it on the eastern side; and on the other, an *uncultivated flat*, over-run with low wood' (Forster 1798, 1: 196, emphasis added). The language is again inflationary, where the use of descriptives such as 'no appearance', 'long space', 'many miles', and 'completely bewildered' suggests an overwhelming negativity.

William Hickey undergoes similar trauma when travelling through India. When his palanquin bearers get tired, Hickey bribes them to continue the journey. Eventually even this form of persuasion fails: the bearers set him down and run away. Hickey's description of the incident goes like this:

> They set me down in the middle of an immense plain where not a tree was to be seen in any direction nearer than two miles, the sun being actually like a furnace. My mouth and throat were parched almost to suffocation; not a morsel of victuals or drop of water to allay dreadful thirst, and this in a heat no one can have an idea except those unhappy men who were shut up in the Black Hole in Calcutta in the year 1757.
>
> (Hickey 1925, 3: 281–82)

In the case of Moorcroft, travelling in the Leh region, the *Athenæum* reports his difficulties because of the improper naming of places that prevented him from ascertaining their longitudes (4 June 1831: 361). The featureless desolation is a threatening one, as Hickey's comparison to the Black Hole of Calcutta reveals. Edward Moor, describing whirlwinds, emphasizes the formlessness and immeasurability or uncertainty when he writes: '[Whirlwinds] may be seen at a great distance . . . moving irregularly with considerable rapidity, and with a great noise; clouds of dust, and anything light . . . are whirled up to a height beyond the reach of the eye'. Later, he also mentions the absence of habitations (refuge-spots) along the route (Moor 1794: 49, 308). James Bristow, having escaped from Tipu's prison, struggles through inclemental climate and unfamiliar terrain. Like Forster, he finds a socio-topographical *locus amoenus* just in time when some Hindu women find him and provide food and shelter (Bristow 1793: 167–68).

Several themes that indicate the sublime figure in these descriptions. The emphasis is on the absence of identifiable landmarks in juxtaposition with limit-lessness (Hickey's 'not a tree to be seen', Moor's 'beyond the reach of the eye'). The absence of well-defined boundaries, as David Punter (1994: 220–39) points out, is an 'escape', and a prominent feature of the sublime. In addition to the absence of boundaries and paths, the complete absence of amenities and a *locus amoenus* threatens the sense of self-preservation of the travellers. In each case the threat is of *emptiness* and the absence of details. Hickey's comparison of his 'martyred' situation with those of the English soldiers in the infamous Black Hole is particularly interesting. Hickey links the 'treachery' of the native bearers who abandon him with that of the native ruler or army that had imprisoned the soldiers in the Black Hole. The spatial reversal is, however, ironic: for according to the tale, the English soldiers were in an excessively confined space in the 'Hole', and Hickey here is 'confined' by/in the wide emptiness. The descriptions of limitless-ness take the form of the sublime, since the sublime is characterized by *space* rather than *details* (Bermingham 1994: 81–119). Forster and Hickey seek society, a *locus amoenus* in the empty landscape. Forster's description is also interesting because it refers to certain primary conditions of the *locus amoenus*: a *green spot* in the wilderness and *human society*. In sharp contrast to empty and vast spaces, as described in the two passages quoted above, Forster here finds details. The movement from soli-tude to society, from hazard to refuge and from space to detail is the movement from the uncontrolled sublime to the safety of a (social) refuge (Paulson 1982: 9–12, 77–78; Ferguson 1992: 3).

The traveller seeks, on other occasions, to *create* a *social* refuge in the desolation through personal effort. This inaugurates the interlinked themes of industry–labour–improvement in the narrative. The English traveller is seen performing generous acts to help natives. With these acts the traveller forges social bonds that enable creation of 'pockets' of safety, help and even pleasure in the otherwise threatening sublime. Later, these individual acts themselves undergo a transfor-mation in terms of the narrative's emphasis, as I shall demonstrate. Forster's first such act occurs in Banghur Mow, where he meets a group of wounded soldiers. Forster provides some medical aid to these and has, so to speak, left his mark on the native body. It maps his journey in terms of the effects he has achieved (1798, 1: 91, 243). The motif also occurs in William Moorcroft's narrative (Moorcroft and Trebeck 1841, 1: 86, 135–36).

'Improvement' and the creation of socio-topographical refuge

After mentioning these minor individual acts that enable them to form social rela-tionships (interestingly, these relationships are with natives) in the course of their travel, the traveller *extends* the theme to include actions that have transformed Indian landscape itself. The traveller emphasizes generous acts of English individuals that have enabled creation of safe and prosperous cities, promote prosperity and remove threats, contrasting these with the ruined or unsafe cities or rule of despotic native kings. It is at this point that the culture of improvement, the discourse of native laziness and the cult of personal example or effort conflate to suggest an 'Englished' *locus amoenus* within Indian desolation. It is here that the descriptive vocabulary of colonial discourse envelops the travelogue's theme of improvement.

The travellers negotiate the sublime dangers of the Indian landscape by shifting narrative focus on to sites where some activity, or cultivation or vegetation – signs of control over nature – is visible, or at least, *possible*. Luxuriant vegetation indicates a *locus amoenus* where the village/glen/cave offers shelter and succour to the (English) traveller who is weary of unnavigable, overrun or barren, inhospitable lands. The *locus amoenus* – actual or potential – is a site of 'improvement', of land reclaimed from desolation, of a refuge that allows travellers to rejuvenate themselves. The colonial traveller now suggests that the Indian landscape may still be saved through a certain agricultural 'revolution'.[20] Here the emphasis on the lack of native initiative in the texts of John Fryer, John Ovington and others in the 1600–1750 period becomes the anterior moment for the colonial traveller of the late eighteenth century to discuss a shift from an empty, inhospitable landscape to a *locus amoenus* through cultivation. Historically this is coterminous with the utilitarian 'agrarian patriotism' of the great 'age of improvement' in England. Uncultivated land was seen as a colossal waste of resources.[21] William Godwin in his *An Enquiry Concerning Political Justice* (1793) (quoted in R. Porter 2000: 310), John Dalton (quoted in R. Porter 2000: 430), Thomas Whately (1770: 174, 198) and others criticized uncultivated land as unaesthetic, with Arthur Young (1768: 145) even describing it as a 'public nuisance'.

The English in India portray themselves as restoring the land to either its fertile state, or securing it for future cultivation. Thus while desolation is India's *past*, the luxuriant crops and beautiful landscape are the *future*, mediated by English efforts in the *present*. Jemima Kindersley's (1777) comment on the 'securing' of private property (noted above) is particularly interesting since it appears to be the corrective action to the *traditional* absence of private property in India (noted by travellers of the earlier phase). The Permanent Settlement of Bengal in 1793 was an attempt to give such secure 'never-before' proprietary rights to zamindars. Lord Cornwallis, commenting on the Settlement, links property ownership and improvement:

> In a country where the landlord has a permanent property in the soil it will be worth his while to encourage his tenants who hold his farm in lease to improve that property . . . the landed property should fall into the hands of the most frugal and thrifty class of people, who will improve their lands and protect the ryots, and thereby promote the general prosperity of the country.
>
> (Forrest 1926, 2: 74–75)

Colebrooke (1795: 102), likewise, suggested that granting the English right to possess lands in India would help. (For a counterargument about land ownership, directly responding to Colebrooke's, see *ER* 10 [1807]: 39–40.) This linked theme of improvement and cultivated property in India is visible in every single travelogue of the period. And in each case, the narrative stresses the act of working and the theme of labour. Improvement is always seen as linked to labour, especially English labour, and efforts in changing Indian desolation into a safe and productive landscape.

Toponymy, boundaries and maps become crucial in the English interventionary reading of Indian landscape in this period. Forster mentions that the '*boundaries* of Kishtewer [Kishtawar] are not specified, nor is the amount of revenues' (1798, 1: 306, emphasis added). Here the landscape is imaged in terms of order ('boundaries') and profit (revenues) – both indicating a sense of control over nature – in the space of a single sentence. The absence of these two 'marks' of civilization characterizes the landscape as desolate and essentially useless. Once more Forster's narrative emphasis is on the absence of cultivated land. The images recur later in his descriptions of other towns and villages (1798, 1: 199, 305–06). James Rennell (1788: 168–69) mourns the absence of accurate knowledge of the country, a complaint echoed by another reviewer two years later (*MR* 3 [NS] [1790]: 85). Forster's description of the Muslim 'invasion' of India as 'break[ing] down every fence' is equally interesting (1798, 2: 8). The absence of fenced property or land and Muslim 'conquest' are both images of a negative sublime of broken or absent boundaries. Forster's entire narrative is structured around the binary of fence or boundary, with their absence suggesting a negative sublime, and presence the 'cultivated' or cultured.[22] The breaking down of fences signifies both cultural and agricultural chaos to the English traveller. It is precisely this chaos that the English seek to correct before creating a *locus amoenus*.

An account of Bengal underscores how, when the 'English and Dutch had factores here, it was a place of trade, but when they were removed . . . it was reduced to beggary, there being no inhabitants but fishermen' (*GM* 27 [1757]: 307). Alexander Dirom describes the desolation of Bangalore due to the (Mysore) war, and its subsequent 'renewal' under British benevolence thus:

> It was highly satisfying to see how much of Bangalore had recovered during these last two months; several thousands of the inhabitants had returned to their habitations in this with many of the necessaries of life. The inhabitants of several of the villages had also returned, and the recommencement of cultivation proved that the neighbouring country was recovering rapidly from the desolation occasioned by the inhuman policy of Tippoo, who had laid it waste on the first approach of the British army.
>
> (Dirom 1793: 27–28)

In another instance, Robert Beatson notes how the inhabitants of Pondicherry were troubled by a lack of food or protection during the Anglo-French war, and how, eventually, Colonel Coote 'finding the poor creatures constantly fired on as they attempted to return to their inhabitations, took compassion on them and allowed them to pass into the country' (Beatson 1790, 3: 8). These 'Good Samaritan' acts are moments of retrieval and reconstruction of pockets of refuge in a desolate, empty landscape. Viscount Valentia, travelling in 1802–06, comments on farmers returning to English 'protection' (Valentia 1809, 1: 184). Reviewing his *Voyages and Travels to India* the reviewer also agrees that the Indian landscape now exhibits 'a striking instance of the happy effects of British government' (*QR* 2 [1809]: 97). Forster writes of Shahabad, 'The whole of this chief's country evinces the *beneficial effects arising from the encouragement of husbandry*, and the aid of an *active government*. Populous villages, skirted by extensive fields of corn, are seen on all sides' (1789, 1: 99, emphasis added).[23] Warren Hastings is also clear on this point and, surprisingly, praises the Indian's industriousness in *The Present State of the East Indies* (1786):

> The sources of opulence which it [Bengal] possesses is the fertility of its soil, and the number and industry of its inhabitants will, I think, admit, of its yielding the tribute I have mentioned [one crore rupees annually], which is perhaps greater than any other country in the world.
>
> (Hastings 1786: 21–22)

Here cultivation and agriculture symbolize freedom from despotism (as Forster himself suggests in the line following the above description[24]). As late as the first decades of the nineteenth century, travellers such as William Moorcroft and George Trebeck were reiterating this theme of native laziness, where the indolence was seen entirely in terms of a lack of interest in *cultivation*. For instance, Moorcroft and Trebeck describe the Pinjor fort and gardens thus: 'The effect of the whole *when maintained in order* must have been highly pleasing' (1841, 1: 34, emphasis added; see also 59, 92). Jemima Kindersley (1777: 181), Thomas Motte (*Asiatic Miscellany*, 2[1786]: 13) and Innes Munro (1789: 67) refer to the laziness of the natives. William Mackintosh makes the connection between colonialism and improvement explicit:

> Colonization will prove the best means of recovering and re-cultivating the deserted lands, where opulent cities, populous villages, and high cultivation, once gave life and contentment to millions. The industry of the colonists will drain many of those marshy tracts of country, the richness of which will abundantly compensate that labour, while security will thus be provided to both people and cattle against those fierce destructive animals with which the depopulated parts of Hindostan are at present infested.
>
> (Mackintosh 1782: 284)

The lands being highly conducive to cultivation, it becomes all the more inexplicable and unforgivable that the native does not toil hard enough in the fields. The rhetoric of improvement in these narratives is inseparable from its rhetoric of labour and an ethics of work.

However, not all enthusiasm for improvement was directed at *Indian* agriculture. Part of the interest in Indian agriculture and vegetation was due to the pressure to improve agriculture back in England. For example, a letter addressed to Clive proposed that he (Clive) utilize his newly acquired wealth to generously – i.e. *without the profit motive* – improve parts of England itself (*MR* 38 [1768]: 66). Incidentally, the notion of a benevolent government transforming an unruly, war-ravaged India, is also imaged as a reader's experience of the sublime:

> The English reader has frequently ascended the lofty mountains which support the flat but elevated land of Mysor . . . marking the wide-spreading desolation of war, or pursuing the flying hosts of Indian cavalry, till, stopped by some fortress which nature meant to be impregnable. In retracing these steps, in the suite of a mission suggested solely by benevolent views, our sensations acquire force by contrast, and novelty adds her charm to the illusion.
>
> (*ER* 13 [1808]: 85)

Sir John Sinclair, writing in 1819 (the year Moorcroft and Trebeck began their expedition in the Himalayas), suggests introducing scientific agriculture in India. He also suggested that Englishmen should procure from India 'the seeds of such articles as might be cultivated in this country . . . transferring such East Indian productions to our West Indian colonies, as are likely to thrive there' (quoted in Knorr 1968: 240). Moorcroft and Trebeck reinforce the image of the efficient and hardworking English husbandman when they treat the expedition as a means of acquiring knowledge about agricultural practices in the Himalayan regions. The two seek information about farming methods and collect samples, all with the intention of passing it on to the 'world' (Moorcroft and Trebeck 1841, 1: 269, 291–92, 296).[25] The collection of specimens and acquisition of knowledge for purposes of development in India and/or England, or plain curiosity, becomes more pronounced in this period. William Hickey (1925, 4: 237), for instance, describes the 'menagerie' of animals at an EIC building in Barrackpore. These originary moments of what Bernard Cohn terms the 'museological modality' of colonialism enabled the ordering of Indian space and life forms (Cohn 1997: 9–10).

Forster is careful to exclude English efforts and constructions in India from his landscape of desolation: 'Yet I must exclude from those range of ruins the convenient and hospitable house of Mr. Cleveland, which formed a part of the Subahdar's palace' (1798, 1: 14). A description of Fort William declares: 'the Governor's house . . . is a handsome, regular structure, considering the part of the world in which it stands' (*GM* 27 [1757]: 307), thus separating English constructions from its immediate locale. The landscape of desolation is thus 'redeemed' by the creation and presence of an English *locus amoenus*. In order to contrast the image of a landscape of desolation, Forster presents the prosperous state of the region under the leadership of the Englishman Cleveland.[26] Forster's description goes like this: 'This gentleman [Mr. Cleveland] . . . has by an equitable and judicious management of the Rajah Mhal and Bauglepor districts, considerably increased the number of inhabitants, and improved, as well as facilitated, the collection of the revenue' (1798, 1: 23–24).

Distrust of the hill people and region is a constant theme in numerous travelogues. Forster adds: 'He [Cleveland] hath also made strenuous exertions, in drawing the adjacent mountaineers, from their vastnesses to the plains' (1798, 1: 23–24). In an essay on Ranjit Singh and the Sikh kingdoms, a commentator author notes that the warrior-like, 'fanatick' population occupied the hilly, north-western territories of India (*AM* 7 [1845]: 345). In Forster the people of the hills ('vastnesses') are drawn to the plains, thus literally drawing the mountains into the province of governance. The conclusion of this comment is indicative of the real reasons behind the relocation of the mountain tribes. Forster mentions that 'the depredations of these people had, at former periods, rendered the passage of the roads in that quarter so unsafe' (1798, 1: 24). Like the mountains and the desolation that thwart attempts at control, so also these tribes resist order. The creation of a *locus amoenus* must be based, first, on the elimination of 'wild' spaces and second, on the eradication of nomadism or 'unruly' tribes.[27] Similar sentiments were voiced in letters from the Court of Directors to Fort William (*Fort William* 1959, 13: 96) and James Rennell (1788: 60–61).

It is in the light of such descriptions of Indian hills and woods that Forster's comments about Cleveland's efforts suggest imperial significance. The inscription on the memorial to Augustus Cleveland praises him therefore, for having 'accomplished the entire subjection of the lawless and savage inhabitants of the jungle-territory of Raj Mahal . . . inspired them with a taste for the arts of civilised life, and attached them to the British Government by a conquest over their minds' (quoted in *Fort William* 1959, 13: 540–41). The prosperity of the place under the English rule is in contrast to the earlier ruins, and Forster mentions that large markets have now reappeared in the area. His greatest praise is for Cleveland's efforts in creating an oasis in a desolate and unfriendly landscape (Forster 1798, 1: 23, 24). William Hodges (1793: 28, 89–90) praises Cleveland for his residence and for having 'cultivated' natives.

Here cultivation and improvement of the land is seen as a necessary prelude to improving the native. The nineteenth-century notion of the 'white man's burden', which focused on several areas such as native religion and education, is rooted in this cult of improvement, and finds its inaugural expression in the agricultural and architectural (building) images of Forster and Hodges. The cultivation of the native or land is a transformation of the savage, threatening, limit/boundary-less, overgrown native/landscape. The investment of meaning in the second moment of negotiating the sublime is thus crucial to the rhetoric of transformation that informs later descriptions in these travellers. The 'meaning' of the desolation thus derived or posited becomes a useful rhetorical device through which not only the sublime desolation is handled, but also an *effective*, beneficial English presence in India may be justified. The rhetoric of improvement that informs this third moment of the search for a *socio-topographical locus amoenus* stresses the shift from a desolate Indian *past* to the wonderful ('Englished') *present* presence. As Frances Ferguson (1992: 131) puts it in a different context, the traveller 'use[s] the past as a standard by which to measure subsequent growth . . . to see how much things have changed – specifically, to see how things have improved'. The descriptions of the transformation of the Indian countryside rely on such a comparison of past desolation and present 'improved' state.

Writing around this time – also the period of England's population controversies (Glass 1973) – Arthur Young described the transformation of a countryside in *A Six Weeks Tour through the Southern Counties of England and Wales*:

> Once all the country from Holkam to Houghton was a wild sheep-walk, before the spirit of improvement seized the inhabitants; and this spirit has wrought amazing effects; for instead of boundless wilds, and uncultivated wastes, inhabited by scarcely anything but sheep; the country is all cut in a most husband-like manner, richly manured, well peopled, and yielding an hundred times the produce that it did in its former state . . . By means of inclosing they throw their farms into a regular course of crops, and gain immensely by the improvement.
>
> (Young 1768: 19)

Daniel Defoe, travelling through England (1724–26), had emblematized prosperity in terms of populousness (Defoe 1962, 1: 13, 17, 33, 75 and elsewhere).

There is a distinct overlap of themes among Young, Defoe and the eighteenth-century travelogues on India. The *former* (Indian) desolation, 'boundarilessness', lack of human population, barrenness and the *present* (British-governed) populous state, systematized (ordered) cultivation and luxuriance, and thus the creation of a *locus amoenus* out of the 'wastes' are common to all three.

William Hodges describes the transformation of Calcutta almost exactly in Young's terms:

> Calcutta, from a small and inconsiderable fort . . . was soon raised to a great and opulent city, when the government of the kingdom of Bengal fell into the hands of the English . . . From the apparent state of a country, a just estimate may generally be formed of the happiness or the misery of a people. When there is neatness in the cultivation of the land, and that land is tilled to the utmost of its boundaries, it may reasonably be supposed that the government is the protector and not the oppressor of the people. Throughout the kingdon of Bengal it appears highly flourishing in tilling of every kind, and abounding in cattle, the villages are neat and clean, and filled with swarms of people.
>
> (Hodges 1793: 15–17)

The sense of a populous place is crucial in Hodges' narrative. The link between benevolent governments, cultivation, and populous towns is emphasized through a comparison of these with the despotic governments, desolation and deserted, uninhabited villages *of the past*.

Hodges, like other travellers, pays attention to English additions or modifications to the Indian landscape. He writes of his first view of Madras: 'The English town rising from within Fort St. George, has from the sea a rich and beautiful appearance' (Hodges 1793: 1–2). The prospect is direct, a panoptical view uninterrupted by any native constructions. Later, visiting an English family, he writes:

> The moon shone in its fullest lustre, not a cloud overcast the sky, and every house in the plain was illuminated. Each family, with their friends, were in the open porticoes, enjoying the breeze. Such a scene appears more like a tale of enchantment than a reality, to the imagination of a stranger just arrived.
>
> (Hodges 1793: 10)

Here the socio-topographical *locus amoenus* is a fairy-tale land, a place of pleasure and safety. The English house, with its close camaraderie ('each family, with their friends'), is an oasis in the Indian desert. Similar images of English possessions and *locus amoenus* persist throughout Hodges' narrative. In similar fashion Katharine Elwood (1830, 2: 93) praises the house of Eliza Draper (of Lawrence Sterne fame) as 'magnificent', and William Milburn (1813, 1: 170) praises the 'large well built and handsome houses' in Bombay.[28]

Calcutta, the 'capital of the British dominion in the East', is closely observed. Hodges (1793: 14) writes: '[Calcutta is] marked by a considerable fortress, on . . . which is allowed to be, in strength and corrections of design, superior to any in India'. If in the early travelogues we noted the English sense of revulsion at the 'closed' nature of the native houses, Hodges praises the 'open' nature of *English* constructions in India (1793: 15, 41). As early as 1764 Henry Vansittart (1764, 1: 22) had recommended fortifications. One of the important conditions of Meer Jaffer's treaty with the company in fact states: 'If the French come into the country, I will not allow them to erect any fortifications, maintain forces, or hold lands, zemindaries' (*AR* 7 [1764]: 191).

The improvement of the native town is frequently an attempt to make it a better and safer place for the English. India, as the past decades of war, deaths and native resistance had shown, was not exactly safe or friendly towards the Englishman. Efforts were made to render the landscape safer in terms of not just housing and gardens but also in terms of social life, justice and welfare (all constituents of a *locus amoenus*). Thus a petition to the Court of Directors, *Administration of Justice in Bengal*, asked for a better method of trying European prisoners in India, especially in matters relating to their 'transactions and engagements with natives' (1780: 5). In another case there were moves to set up societies for the protection of orphans of British officers and children of non-commissioned and private Europeans in the East India Company's service (see Anon., *Original Papers Relative to the Setting up of a Society in Bengal*, 1784). It is in this context that spatial and landscape 'improvements' of India must be seen.

Robert Kyd pleaded for a botanical garden in Calcutta (*Fort William* 1959, 13: xxviii) and William Hickey (1925, 4: 236) praises Wellesley's 'improvements' – Hickey's term – of Calcutta. *The Times* (London) mentions the planting of a cinnamon garden near Madras, which 'promises to be extremely advantageous' (28 January 1791: 3). John Taylor emphasizes the importance of communication networks and roads for the English in India (1799: 1: 3, 11–13, 33–45). Jemima Kindersley describes the new fort for EIC 'servants' (1777: 277–78). The construction of this fort will, Kindersley notes, rectify the present situation, where Calcutta has no separate Black Town and which 'makes the roads rather unpleasant' (presumably because of the presence of natives). Kindersley also refers to the 'very pretty houses . . . belonging to the English gentlemen' (1777: 277, 281), thus emphasizing the 'cultivation' or improvement aspect of English life in India. Kindersley is also referring to the creation of safe refuges for the English in the midst of India's crowded towns. Captain Barker's report on a new Fort for Calcutta stresses the need to provide a *locus amoenus* within the dirt and danger of India. He suggests that for the construction of the new fort some houses in the area may have to be demolished. But, he adds, most of these are '*houses of no consequence and black-people's houses*' (Sinha 1973: 119, emphasis added). The English also express fears that the native huts, made of straw, posed great danger to English houses in the vicinity (due to the huts' propensity to catch fire). A letter from the Court of Directors dated 11 June 1800 states the need to regulate use of straw huts in large towns, 'preventing or remedying the mischiefs arising from the erecting of habitation in Calcutta, thatched with straw and constructed of mats and other combustible materials' (*Fort William* 1959, 13: 206–07). Once again the ruins of native icons are improved or transformed into a *locus amoenus* through the efforts of the English.

John Taylor finds Coorg a *potential locus amoenus* for the English in India. He suggests 'clearing the country in the neighbourhood of any ground our troops may occupy, and having them sheltered with comfortable habitations' (Taylor 1799, 2: 165–66) to provide this *locus amoenus*. Since Coorg is a hilly, fog-ridden and densely wooded area, Taylor's suggestion of 'clearing' may easily be seen as a negotiation of the native sublime grandeur of mountainous regions through human intervention in nature in order to create a refuge.[29] William Jones describes his 'pastoral mansion' that provides a safe refuge from the 'noxious air of Calcutta'. He describes Alipur as 'quite pastoral', with his house filled with 'two large English sheep . . . we are literally lulled to sleep by Persian nightingales' (Jones 1970, 2: 778, 648). The pastoral landscape, as Ronald Paulson (1982: 11, 28–52) has shown, is this harmless refuge where, the 'most menacing animals are browsing sheep'. Jones' is such a landscape.

Perhaps the most interesting of these English attempts to renew the Indian landscape and the creation of socio-topographical *locus amoenus* through personal effort and a benevolent paternalism is that of George Thomas. After arriving in the Haryana region, Thomas carefully evaluates those lands that appear fertile and agriculturally productive (1803: 65–66, 142, 163, 176–77). Finally he settles himself as an independent chief in the region. Thomas describes his creation of a *locus amoenus* through an individual effort that transforms the land.

> Here I established my capital, rebuilt the walls of the city long since fallen into decay, and repaired the fortifications. As it had long been deserted, at first I found difficulty in procuring inhabitants, but by degrees and gentle treatment,

I selected between five and six thousand persons, to whom I allowed every lawful indulgence.

(Thomas 1803: 93–94)

The efforts of George Thomas almost exactly parallel that of Cleveland (see Forster's description of the latter above). He is able to exactly quantify the new inhabitants, he has rebuilt bounding structures, and even set up the invisible walls of the law. The approach to the Indian landscape is perfectly clear. A 13 March 1761 directive from the Court of Directors to Fort William states:

> Great care must be taken that the farmers do not injure or oppress the inhab-itants; the people should be assembled in every purgunnah, the terms and conditions published & they be publicly told where they are to apply for redress of all grievances, and by kind and humane Government, *numbers may be encouraged to fix their residence* in these territories & *in time all our waste lands may be occupied and greatly improved.*

(*Fort William* 1968, 3: 83, emphasis added)

The *locus amoenus* is thus accomplished. The British triumph over stormy, desolate landscapes, transforming them into productive idylls. As the *Monthly Review* put it, once more taking recourse to the rhetoric of transformation in the aesthetics of the sublime: 'Great Britain has executed this grand scheme of benevolence, and quelled the raging storms of misrule and turbulence into peace' (*MR* 103 [1824]: 127).[30]

The efforts of a George Thomas or a Cleveland in 'repopulating', cultivating and thus controlling the desolate landmarks the third moment of their negotiation of the Indian sublime. Having been first threatened by the desolation, the traveller describes the desolation and the threat through a rhetoric of inflation. The natural sublime plays a prominent role in this section of the travelogue. The second moment is inaugurated when the traveller, under threat of being overwhelmed by the desolation and emptiness, invests the landscape with meaning. The Indian desolation is ascribed to certain causes: nature, native indolence, despotic rulers, and war. The traveller then proceeds to rhetorically transform the landscape into a *locus amoenus*. The search for the *locus amoenus* is couched in a georgic rhetoric of improvement where Indian desolation is associated with its past, and the 'improved' site with the future, mediated by the English's present or presence. With the creation or discovery of a *locus amoenus* the traveller has reached a level of equivalence with the land. In fact, this equivalence is sublime in itself. For, as the *Edinburgh Review* sees it, the 'subject of the government of India' is 'grand' (*ER* [1812]: 472).

4 The missionary picturesque, 1790–1860

During the first part of your journey to the South, your route will occasionally lie along the sea-shore; and the night scene will be diversified by the soft moonlight playing on the distant waters, or touching the nearer spray with its silvery beams. The croaking of the frogs will be exchanged for the upward dashing or retiring murmur of the waves upon beach: and in the fulness of a rejoicing heart you will be ready to cry, 'O Lord, how manifold are thy works; the earth is full of thy riches, so is the great and wide sea also.'

Sometimes the bearers will run along so deep into the water, for their own refreshment, that, with the sea on either side of you, you would feel alarmed, were you in other hands. But it is extraordinary what unhesitating confidence you, involuntarily as it were, place not only in the dexterity, but in the integrity of purpose among the natives. Nor is this confidence misplaced, for, by the providence of God, the moral influence of Europeans over this people is so great, that you might travel alone from Madras to Cape Comorin, and often find yourself thirty or forty miles from any European, without the slightest danger of any advantage being taken of your defenceless situation.

(Tucker 1842–43, 1: 106–07)

Sarah Tucker here appropriates the standard descriptive vocabulary of British missionary writings on India from the 1790–1860 period, a vocabulary drawn from an aesthetic that I term the 'missionary picturesque'. Tucker's scenic landscape is a space of variety, as terms like 'diversified', 'manifold', 'fullness' and 'wideness' suggest. The Indian landscape, in all its 'Providential' variety, beauty and wild fertility, might have been threatening and unsafe at one point. But now, with the moral influence of the European, it has been *made* safe. The Tucker passage conflates a topographical narrative with moral and theological concerns. The colonial 'project' of evangelical reform, as I demonstrate in this chapter, adapts its own visual vocabulary and aesthetic ideas, specifically that of the picturesque, in order to trope Indian primitivism and colonial improvement.

Tucker's meditation on God corresponds to a feature of the 'latitudinarian picturesque': one observed God by observing nature (Mayhew 2000b). Tucker's shift into the theological mode from a purely picturesque-descriptive one merges the book of nature with the book of God (a feature of the eighteenth-century latitudinarian picturesque). More significantly, the discourse of 'improvement' seen in Tucker's description is inscribed within a 'cultural fable' – I adapt Laura Brown's (2001) formulation – of missionary labour. This 'cultural fable' enables the textual construction of a site of harmonized and ordered variety. Such a harmonized landscape functions as a *moral picturesque* of the civic kind, a *Concordia discors* (Andrews 1989: 17–18, 52–54).[1] Wild, unruly nature could not be truly picturesque in the colonial context: it had to be arranged, harmonized and ordered.

The evangelization of India was initiated in the 1780s and early 1790s. Following the initiative of David Brown and Charles Grant, the 1793 Resolution of the Parliament approved of religious facilities for the East India Company workers. The Resolution of the English Parliament of 14 May 1793 declares:

> It is the peculiar and bounden duty of the Legislature to promote, by all just and prudent means, the interests and happiness of the inhabitants in India: and that for these ends, such measures ought to be adopted as may gradually tend to their advancement in useful knowledge, and to their religious and moral improvement.
>
> (*Journal of the House of Commons* 48 [1793]: 778; see also Kaye 1859, Appendix 3: 510–11)

William Carey in his 1792 tract, *An Enquiry into the Obligations of Christians*, emphasizes the need to spread the gospel in the 'dark' cultures across the world. Responses to such calls for missionary work were tremendous.[2]

The evangelical movement was rooted in an Enlightenment ideology, the colonial enterprise, and the discourse of 'Great Britain' (Colley 1992; Bosch 1999; Thorne 1999; Stanley 2001). It is significant that several of the missionaries were themselves participants in debates about the British empire and its sovereignty over India. Missionaries drew up petitions, and offered suggestions and measures regarding land rights, property ownership (by Europeans) and cultivation in India. The Reverend Joseph Mullens testified before the 1858 Select Committee on Colonization and Settlement (India), where a large part of the discussion involved issues of land ownership, development and European settlement (see *Fourth Report . . . Colonization and Settlement (India)*: House of Commons 1858b: 10–29). Petitions signed by Alexander Duff and several other Protestant missionaries pleaded on behalf of peasantry, thereby directly intervening in public debates about land and development in India (House of Commons 1858a: 419–23; 1858b: 290–93). There is a shared rhetoric of evangelicalism and empire elsewhere too. A review of Bishop Heber's travelogue referred to his 'imperial diocese' (*ER* 48 [1828]: 317). John Wilson, a Church of Scotland missionary in Bombay, delivered a sermon on 'British Sovereignty in India' in 1835 (reprinted in his *The Evangelization of India*: J. Wilson 1844: 180–212).

Multiple versions of the picturesque aesthetic, theorized and implemented in landscaping, by William Gilpin, Richard Payne Knight, Uvedale Price, Humphry Repton and 'Capability' Brown flourished in England (Andrews 1989). It had its own politics of land, class, gender and knowledge. It valorized taste, disinterest and property-ownership (Uvedale Price also recommended that gentlemen farmers arm themselves in order to defend their property better in a 1797 tract), while insidiously gendering the 'art' of landscape appreciation and aesthetic 'taste' (Copley and Garside 1994; Fulford 1996; Bohls 1997). More significantly for our purposes, the representation of the rural poor in the picturesque paintings and writings of the 1790s was linked to the rise of evangelicalism (Andrews 1989: 59). Further, the picturesque called for alteration and modification.

The writings of Bishop Heber and James Tod were described as having captured a 'picturesque' India (*Athenæum* 21 March 1828: 259–60; 28 March 1828: 295–96; 21 October 1829: 654, respectively). Fanny Parkes titled her travelogue *Wanderings of a Pilgrim in Search of the Picturesque* (1850), even as Thomas and William Daniell (1784–94: see Archer 1980), William Hodges (1793) and Emma Roberts (1832) published works on the Indian picturesque. Picturesque descriptions and 'scenes' of various places in the 'Orient', and exhibitions of panoramas circulated in England (advertised, for instance, in *Athenæum* 4 June 1831: 363) with remarkable regularity during the 1760–1870 period, and discussions of picturesque theories or scenery went as late as 1900. Nigel Leask (2002) identifies the 'imperial picturesque' in writers like Bishop Reginald Heber, Lord Valentia and others. Romita Ray (1998: 90), working on the Englishwoman's picturesque argues that 'picturesque views ... represented the colonial landscape as an aesthetically pleasing still-life instead of a politically unstable mass of land'. But the picturesque, at least in the case of the missionary narrative, was not simply an appreciation of landscape, or the expression of curiosity and 'first impressions' (Leask), nor was it a 'scene' of 'still life' (Ray). I believe that Leask (2002) and Ray (1998) pay insufficient attention to the *transformative* function of the picturesque aesthetic. The picturesque aims primarily to 'improve' and 'alter' nature (Andrews 1989; Daniels and Watkins 1994). In the colonial context the picturesque was a very *active* aesthetic, and served a crucial ideological purpose: to provide a design for and effect a rhetorical transformation of primitive, wild, variegated India through British intervention. My reading of the missionary picturesque, following Paul Carter, proposes an *intentionality* of the picturesque (Carter 1987: 243). The visible Indian landscape masks, according to the colonial missionary, the invisible but palpable potential for a 'reformed', Christian landscape – and it is the missionary who discovers this potential. When the *Athenæum* (25 August 1832: 556) argues that India's 'picturesque splendour' was worth admiring despite the fact that it may not be 'in conformity with the canons of academic taste' it was suggesting a picturesque that was *different* from the British one. This difference, I argue, is articulated as the colonizing and colonial picturesque in missionary narratives.

The colonial missionary narrative readily appropriates the discourse of picturesque alteration, improvement and harmonizing. The colonial picturesque in India aligned landscape, religion and culture along an axis, while making them the object and goal of horticultural and civic 'labour'. The aesthetic as deployed by missionary narratives in the 1790–1860 period effects a *rhetorical* transformation of India.[3] The missionary picturesque worked in both the natural and civic or social realms, dealing with the Indian landscape and people, often casting the 'civic picturesque' (Andrews 1994a) in the form of a horticultural process, or more precisely a Christian georgic. It transforms India, through Christian georgic effort, from the poor and the immoral to the *Concordia discors* of the deeply moral, Christian landscape.

By the time the missionaries arrived in large numbers in the first decades of the Victorian era, Britain was a dominant political, military and economic power. It also benefited greatly from the association with India, even though the company's finances were often a source of concern.[4] English people in Britain and Anglo-Indians had the same interest in keeping, controlling and using India. England now controlled large parts of the Indian subcontinent and maintained a standing army. The agenda of reform was central to the English function in India during this period, and the missionary picturesque reflects this agenda.

Missionary accounts clearly state the need for more details and information, arguing that these are necessary to show India's importance for Britain. But what is significant is that in the case of the missionary narrative there is a great deal of interest in the 'soul' beneath the landscape, the 'spirit' beneath the trade interests, and the potential for Christian beauty buried in the pagan wilds. Where the imperial sublime sought to impose order over chaotic, unmapped India, the missionary picturesque worked at the level of the low, the deformed and the particular. If the imperial sublime sought to interpret and control the wild, vast, borderless and dangerous India, the missionary picturesque worked at the level of the local and the detail. While the sublime was a (colonial) aesthetic of sweeping vistas and the panorama, the missionary picturesque was an aesthetic of particulars and the immediate. However, the rhetoric of the missionary picturesque is, like that of the imperial sublime, a transformative one, where the rhetoric works through a 'cultural fable' that responded directly to material conditions of living and working in India. A cultural fable, as Laura Brown (2001) conceptualizes it, is often a 'collective enterprise', an imaginative negotiation with a problematic experience. Most importantly, in Brown's formulation, it exerts tremendous aesthetic power (Brown 2001: 1–4). In the case of the missionary narrative about India, the cultural fable consists of several related moves: a civic picturesque that draws on the aesthetics of (Indian) poverty, a narrative of Christian toil seeking the 'improvement' of Indian physical and moral landscape, with a 'final' goal of a Christian *Concordia discors*. The *Concordia discors* marks a moment of *convergence*, of a diverse, wild India into a unified Christian landscape or site.

The missionary picturesque is organized into multiple, interpenetrating levels and moments. The first moment, which I term the 'primitive picturesque', compiles vast amounts of information about India, isolating aspects that it codes as primitive, idolatrous and backward. It constitutes a narrative of exploration, penetration and discovery of the picturesque if 'primitive' India. In effect, it identifies the potential sites of missionary labour and transformation. The second moment in the missionary narrative is what I call the 'Christian georgic'. The missionary offers a kind of 'benevolent design' for India, Indian landscape and Indian people. Here the missionary's toils take centre-stage as the narrative quickly slips into a husbandry narrative of cultivation, hardship, labour, sacrifice and harvest (themes obviously drawn from the New Testament). In the *Concordia discors*, the final moment of the missionary narrative, the text pleads for a greater level of work and a larger field to work in. The missionary text is by now speaking of a Christian India, where particularities of Indian customs and details of Hinduism are erased. This marks a move towards a moral picturesque where the changes wrought move beyond the detail in favour of a generalization or abstraction, where ever-expanding worlds and varieties (of religious, people and cultures) are harmonized into a Christian globe.[5]

The primitive picturesque

Leask (2002: 166–68) has argued that the picturesque was 'antithetical' to the 'survey' mode and rejected details (see also Bohls 1997: 73). My reading, in contrast, proposes that the survey is *constitutive* of and the *necessary* anterior moment in the missionary picturesque. The missionary picturesque's ideology demands a *rhetoric of detail* in its opening moments because it moves from detail to the abstract, and finally, from the primitive to the Christian. Viewing Indian landscape, Hinduism and rituals as (iconic of a) deformity, the missionary narrative effected a rhetorical modification of the same to achieve a harmonized landscape and culture.

The missionary narrative almost invariably begins with a narrative of distances, locations, travel-modes, times of arrival or departure, scenery and topography and, most significantly, the cultural terrain. The geographical narrative, corresponding to the survey mode, functions as a framing and focalizing device because it defines the 'sites' of missionary endeavour, for both the missionary and the reader of the work. The primitive picturesque, driven by an ideology of civic humanism and a fascination for the poor and the suffering, provides accounts of Indian paganism, poverty, futile and immoral actions and general depravity. Focusing on Indian landscape, rituals and religion in the opening moments enables the narrative to show how these particular areas have been transformed into something beautiful and organized. The primitive picturesque has two central features: the detailing of Indian variety and the 'aesthetics of poverty'.

Picturesque variety

Francis Wayland's introductory essay to Eustace Carey's (1836) memoirs of William Carey opens with an account that recalls numerous travelogues of the eighteenth and nineteenth centuries:

> How many a mountain has been scaled, how many a ravine has been threaded, by the enterprising European, in the search of the cow's mouth, that gap in the Himalaya mountains, from which the sacred river of India rushes forth . . . How many a traveller has perished in the sandy deserts of Africa, in fruitless search for the source of the Nile! . . . The inconsiderable

beginning borrows grandeur from the greatness of the result . . . Thus is it in
moral events.

(E. Carey 1836: ix)[6]

It is from such a moment of the adventure-geographical narrative that he shifts to
moral topography. In the third paragraph, therefore, Wayland suggests that the
'establishment of Christianity throughout the British possessions in Eastern India'
is an enterprise similar to exploration and discovery (E. Carey 1836: x).

Wayland's use of spatial and geographical imagery aligns landscape exploration with 'moral events' and missionary work, a move characteristic of the genre
itself. The survey-geographical narrative allegorizes the land in moral terms and
missionary work in spatio-geographical terms. The missionary narratives compiled
vast amounts of data regarding superstitions, belief systems, rituals, religious
events, before stating their intention to change these aspects of Indian life. In
mapping these features of Indian primitivism the narrative serves a very important
end: it identifies and defines the space of intervention and transformation. Indeed,
such information about India was actually demanded by the readers, as reviews
indicate. A review of the memoirs of Henry Martyn, for instance, expressed disappointment at the absence of information on Indian 'history, literature, science or
philosophy' (*QR* 25 [1821]: 438). Travellers who documented India details were
lavishly praised in reviews (*QR* 29 [1823]: 384; *ER* 48 [1828]: 314). The missionaries were aware of this demand for information, as William Clarkson's (1850)
preface seems to indicate:

It is important that Christians at home should be enabled to trace the path of
their Indian missionaries . . . In order that they may do so, it seems advisable
to represent the vivid scenes of missionary labour, not only in their moral
aspects but even in all their physical appearances.

(Clarkson 1850: iii)

The 'physical representations' of the '"Lake of Galilee", "the Mount of Olives"
and "the Wilderness of Judaea"', Clarkson writes, 'impart a vividness to the grand
moral transactions of the New Testament' (1850: iii–iv, emphasis added). Sarah
Tucker (1842–43, 1: 2) promises to provide only such information as 'affect[s] the
duties or feelings of a Missionary'.

Information in these travelogues was thus clearly intended to influence present
and future missionaries. The moral and topographic maps were sites of potential
labour. In order to provide this kind of detail the missionary narrative often took
recourse to the trope of penetration and the discursive devices of an exploration
narrative. A significant moment in the 'cultural fable' of poverty, labour and
improvement was the troping of diversity, mystery and depth of India. It was, in
fact, deemed necessary that the traveller provide a 'moral picture' of the country
(*EcR* 14 [Series 3] 1835: 414). The missionary narrative is no exception to this
norm. The exploration narrative, especially those that dealt with continental
exploration in the late eighteenth and nineteenth-century period, emphasized

adventure, physical endurance, scientific and technical precision and record-keeping (Cosgrove 2001: 208).

Claudius Buchanan, Vice Provost of the College at Fort William, underscores the need to 'penetrate' into the 'interior' of India to gather information (Buchanan 1813a: xvii–xviii). Alexander Duff's work opens with chapters detailing European attempts to find a 'new passage to India' and details of Hinduism, and a chapter titled 'Practical sketches of some of the leading superstitions and idolatries of Eastern India' (Duff 1839: 9–15, 38–195). It is only *after* these chapters that Duff discusses 'the gospel [as] the only effectual instrument in regenerating India' (Chapter 4). Duff's detailed exposition of Indian systems of thought and Hinduism serves as a manual for future missionaries by providing information about the 'problems' involved. Its use of a functionalist terminology to describe both India and the missionary activity – 'practical sketches' (Chapter 3), 'effectual instrument' (Chapter 4) – suggest a georgic ethics of action with an aim to improvement (or what Duff (1839: 284) terms 'regeneration'). The botanical terminology of 'regeneration' and 'propagation' suggests a horticultural discourse that links moral, theological and the natural worlds. Sarah Tucker (1842–43: 12, 28) begins with a detailed examination of the 'difficult' lives of Indian women before describing the entire country as revealing a 'melancholy picture of the power of Satan'. Claudius Buchanan is described as one who 'had a full opportunity of witnessing the dreadful effects of the moral darkness that pervades the Heathen world' (*CO* 9 [1810]: 579). George Pettit's (1851: 4) narrative opens with the trope of ocular penetration, describing Schwartz's arrival in an Indian town as 'purer light find[ing] entrance into Tinnevelly'. Later writers used the ocular-light image to speak of 'penetrating' the zenana, Hinduism and India itself.[7]

Joseph Mullens (1854: 5–7) opens his discussion of the Madras Presidency's missionary history with statistics about the missionaries and converts in the area and a detailed account of the region's geography. Periodicals conveyed detailed information to readers back in England. Thus they carried news reports about missionary activity *and* a wealth of information about Indian geography, rituals and others (*JMH* 31 [NS] [1857]: 98–100; 35 [NS] [1857]: 162–67; 34 [NS] [1857]: 145–49). Information about 'sati' was deemed necessary to 'keep alive the interest still felt by all thinking persons on the subject of our missions to British India' (*CO* 9 [1810]: 484). The aim here is to present as complete a picture of India as possible: its infinite variety and variations of landscape, religions, people and castes.

One of the central effects of this rhetoric of detail in the missionary narrative is the sense of Indian *variety*. Location of mission houses and schools, the topography of the area, distances and modes of transport, tables of data, accounts of conversions, biographical information of missionaries and converts, financial transactions, lists of donors, petitions and correspondence render the missionary account a kind of ethnographic narrative. Information about local rituals, Hindu philosophy and translations of Hindu religious texts are often described as 'striking' and 'peculiar' or 'curious' – all features that characterize the picturesque.

Variety in the rhetoric of the British missionary narratives takes the form of extended descriptions of rituals, modes of worship, differences among the natives, the differences between Christian Britain and pagan India and, more significantly, the various castes that divide Hinduism. Buchanan begins his discussion on conversions of Hindus by noting the 'dissonance' between Christianity and paganism before elaborating on the 'numerous Casts [*sic*] of Religion, and differences of Religious belief' (Buchanan 1813b: 103, 108). Alexander Duff argues that Hinduism's tenets and beliefs 'mingle and interblend in strange heterogeniousness' resulting in 'inextricable confusion', possessing 'endless variety' (Duff 1839: 121, 151). Such images of the excessive and unmanageable varieties of Hinduism are found elsewhere too (Tucker 1842–43, 1: 52; Buyers 1848: 529, 531, 534; Clarkson 1850: 1). It is precisely this chaos and variety, especially the religious one that gets transformed, at least rhetorically, into a *Concordia discors*. And, as for the landscape, the missionary penetrates the surface beauty of India to discover its underlying wickedness.

The 'aesthetics of poverty'

The primitive, the poor, the 'low' are central to the picturesque. The picturesque ruin worked with associations and rude objects to evoke particular sentiments in the observer (Andrews 1989: 45, 59; Whale 1994: 175–95). Rural and 'low' scenes were singular and excited curiosity by their very difference from the metropole. Thus a review of Uvedale Price's *Essays on the Picturesque* (1810) declares: 'thatched hovels, old barns . . . peasant and woodman' as suitable subjects for 'picturesque work' (*QR* 4 [1810]: 377, 380). Another essay describes the raggedly dressed vagabond as the 'very darling of the picturesque' (*BE* 14 [1823]: 250). In most cases such 'scenes' of suffering embodied what Malcolm Andrews (1994a: 286–90) calls an 'aesthetics of poverty'.

This 'aesthetics of poverty' is clearly visible in the missionary tract on India. The 'cultural fable' of physical and moral improvement is informed by an aesthetic that consistently tropes India as poor, focusing on low life and suffering. What is interesting is that the missionary is 'immersed' in the scene, and there is no desire to view the landscape from a distance or from a height. William Buyers in fact complains that there are no 'vistas', 'elevations' or 'landscapes' in Calcutta. It is, he believes 'a place admirably adapted for near sighted people', suggesting a 'low' visual field (Buyers 1848: 43). In lieu of the prospect view, we have a participatory and 'embedded' picturesque where the missionary is ensconced in rural, poor and heathen India.

The 'aesthetics of poverty' generates a different narrative of India. Two features stand out here. First, since the colonial missionary's civic picturesque is keyed to discourses of control, and the colonial 'project' of reform or transformation, it required an intimacy with the sites of labour. That is, the civic picturesque in the colonial context demands that the missionary be an authoritative observer before becoming an expert labourer in these 'fields'. Unlike the 'traditional' picturesque that espoused an ideology of 'disinterestedness', prospects and distance, the civic picturesque in the colonial context asks for heightened interest, 'embeddedness' and intimacy. Driven by a moral and social conscience it demanded first-hand knowledge of native life (features of the civic picturesque, Andrews 1994a: 290). Second, having identified sites of reform and labour (narrated through the rhetoric of detail), it also produces a narrative where crowds, collections of natives and intimacy were less sources of threat than potential sites of labour.

The missionary narrative emphasized living *among* the natives, on the same grounds, as it were. William Carey's (2000: 7) journal opens with a statement: that he will live in a hut 'like the natives'. In one of his early letters, he declares that missionaries should live like the people 'among whom they labour' (E. Carey 1836: 91). Henry Martyn (1851: 255) describes his wish to 'go amongst' the Indians. Sarah Tucker (1842–43, 1: 51) is distinctly uncomfortable in Madras, being 'surrounded by idolaters' – a situation that sets the scene for ordered native Christian crowds later in the narrative (a point to which I return below). Joseph Mullens, in his 6 July 1858 evidence for the Select Committee on Colonization and Settlement (India), mentions the attempts made by three missionary settlements (at Patna, near the Narmada, and near Chotta Nagpur) to 'make the mission self-supporting' through adapting local agricultural practices (House of Commons 1858b: 12). Periodicals like the *Children of the Church Magazine* and the *Juvenile Missionary Herald* detail life in the native colony and settlements.

George Pettitt in *The Tinnevelly Mission* (1851) describes his sentiments when he sees beggars eating inside the now-ruined great hall of a palace:

> I espied in a corner a kind of rug thrown across as a screen, and, behind it, discovered a party of beggars squatting fearlessly on the ground, and employed in boiling their rice for dinner. It was impossible not to sigh as one's imagination flitted back a thousand years, and pictured to itself the splendour of the gay, the proud, and the glorious personages who then fared sumptuously in that very hall, where beggars now, in unmolested repose, prepared their scanty meal.
>
> (Pettitt 1851: 61)

The anonymously authored *A Letter to John Scott Waring* intervening in the missionary debate describes the problems of the 'lower orders of the people and their wretchedness' (Anon. 1808: 17–18). Sarah Tucker focuses on poor schoolgirls (1842–43, 1: 77–78). Pettitt contrasts the poverty with the now-past affluent times – a process Leask describes as the picturesque's 'temporalization' (Leask 2002: 43–53, 173–75). Pettitt's description is one of many missionary tracts that pay sustained attention to the Indian poor, lower castes, widows and aboriginals. The depiction of 'satis', widows, the poverty-stricken, beggars, victims and *fakirs* in innumerable missionary texts and in debates about missionary work appropriates the 'aesthetics of poverty'.

What is significant is that the natural ruin and the ruined body of the beggar or vagrant seem to go together in this 'aesthetics of poverty'. In Pettitt's description, the ruined palace and the ruined beggars together contribute to a sense of ruined culture. The description is interesting for yet another reason. He begins his description of Madurai thus:

I must not stay to describe the magnificent temples, and their sacred tanks; the stone choultry with a thousand pillars; another far grander choultry of the great king Thirumal Naick, its superb throne of dark marble, and its excellent sculpture; or the truly splendid palace of the ancient kings of Madura.

(Pettitt 1851: 60)

At another moment in his narrative he states: 'I must not detain you with an account of our journey, – with descriptions of heathen places visited' (Pettitt 1851: 401–02). Having begun by stating he will not stop to describe the splendid architecture and buildings, Pettitt goes on to expend considerable space over *ruins*. The focus in Pettitt's narrative is either on Indian ruins or on Christian churches. Descriptions of orphans, famine victims, diseased, disabled or starving Indians and the wretched women figured prominently in such narratives well into the last decades of the nineteenth century (see *CMM* September 1881: 100–01; February 1883: 19, 22; May 1883: 57–58; May 1900: 72–75; June 1900: 92–93; July 1900: 103; October 1900: 153–55).

Visuals of beggars and mendicants, which appeared regularly in missionary periodicals especially in the last decades of the nineteenth century, showcased semi-clad Indians, who function as icons of the ruins of both nature and culture, awaiting rejuvenation and vegetal regeneration.[8] The cultivation images in English writings on India are about not only creating new 'fields', but also rejuvenating old ones.

The civic picturesque's interest in these 'lower' rungs of society is linked to the ideology of moral improvement. Incidentally, the aboriginals represent a version of pure primitivism uncontaminated by either Hinduism or Islam in many missionary tracts. Thus the preface to *The Gospel in Santhalisthan* describes the Santhal tribes as having 'resisted the false religions that have been thrust upon them' (Anon. 1875: vii). William Buyers (1848: 78), describing the aboriginal tribes of the regions beyond Bengal proposes that 'some vigorous effort should be made, to bring those tribes to the knowledge of the gospel, before they come entirely under the influence of the Brahmans'. An essay on Assam highlights the 'improvement' of the tribals, who had been induced to 'form an agricultural settlement' (*Classified Digest, 1701–1892*, 1894: 606–08).[9] Numerous periodicals highlight the transformation or conversion of the tribals.[10] Presumably, absorbing the aboriginal into Christianity was a greater social and moral revolution, for it contrasted with Brahminical Hinduism's failed efforts to bring them into the ambit of Hinduism.

Images of crowds are usually cast in either of two modes: as potential converts or sites of labour, or as passive recipients of the gospel. Henry Martyn again expresses the sentiment that being 'amongst' Indians is good: 'Though the multitudes are so great, that a missionary need not go three miles from his house, without having a congregation of many thousands' (Martyn 1851: 348). Scenes depicting large audiences and crowded churches are very common to the missionary narrative. Broach town, William Clarkson (1850: 12) writes, is 'surrounded by flourishing and populous villages, and is a very eligible sphere for missionary labour' (I will return to this image of the sphere later). Crowded Indian villages affect the missionary deeply: 'How is it possible to convey . . . the solemn feelings induced by the sight of large towns and whole districts unblessed by any means of instruction in the knowledge of Christ?' He then comments: 'oh the blessedness of taking the gospel to a numerous people!' (Clarkson 1850: 12, 14). Joseph Mullens (1854: 78) complains that Madras town is too diffuse and that the native population is 'scattered over a wide surface', in 'numerous separate districts'.

With the primitive picturesque several things are achieved. There is now detailed information about the various rituals, customs and regions of India, thereby identifying areas of labour. Showcasing the destitute, the derelict and the oppressed, the missionary narrative has generated an 'aesthetics of poverty' that calls for sustained action. Finally, the narrative suggests an intimacy of the observer and the potential reformer (the missionary) with the sites of future labour, treating India and Indians as spaces of transformation.

The Christian georgic

The missionary picturesque in the colonial 'project' of reform was resolutely georgic. It tropes India as varied and poor in order to recommend action, cast as a georgic intervention in the moral and physical landscape of India.

The missionary narrative, having first generated an aesthetic of Indian poverty, makes two moves. It first details the missionary's moral responses (central to the picturesque mode, Andrews 1989: 50–56). Second, the narrative provides 'models of piety' for missionary work in India. Together these prepare the ground, literally and figuratively, for the most active component of the missionary picturesque: Christian georgic labour.[11]

Indian primitivism and the moral response

The search for a deeper moral landscape under visible beauty was central to the picturesque aesthetic as late as the 1840s. In an essay suggestively titled 'Monsters of Faith', the author asks rhetorically: 'What is cold, dwarfed European faith when compared with the huge monstrous faith of the barbarous land of the sun?', before proceeding to compare the 'faiths' in terms of *topographical* features: the Surrey Hills with the Himalayas, the Thames with the Ganges and the Brahmaputra (*HW* 5 [1852]: 506–08; for another, similar example see *DUM* 20 [1842]: 213). After living in 'primitive' India, the missionary formulates a moral response to what she/he sees. This requires the missionary to penetrate the visible beauty of India to discover its underlying structures. It is here that missionary labours will have their greatest effect: the outward appearance of peaceful natives gathered in prayer must eventually correspond to and reflect the inner 'reality' of the moral goodness of the Indian soul achieved through Christian piety.

After uncovering the barbarism beneath India's picturesque beauty, the missionary develops a 'plan'. Reading the book of Indian nature with the benefit of Christian knowledge – through the 'educated' Christian eye, to modify Peter de

Bolla's (2003) formulation – the missionary is able to locate a 'design' behind the sights. It is also interesting to note that both 'natural' and built landscapes come in for a similar response in missionary writing.

Henry Martyn describes his *first* sight of Calcutta thus:

> The approach to Calcutta, particularly about Garden Reach, where we lay several hours, is very beautiful. The rich verdure and variety of the trees, and the elegant mansions which they partly hide, conspire to render the same highly agreeable to the eye; but the thought of the diabolical heathenism, amidst these beauties of nature, takes away almost all the pleasure I should otherwise experience.
>
> (Martyn 1851: 328)

Martyn seems to uncover a moral geography, where non-Christian religion takes away the pleasure of the physical landscape. William Clarkson (1850: 14) writing about missionary work in Gujarat asks: 'This country, whose fertile fields, waving with tall luxuriant corn, or the snowy cotton-plant, or oil-plants, contrast deeply with the spiritual barrenness of the people . . . "Oh! Who will occupy this beautiful land?"'.[12] Clarkson finds the physical topos where he preaches 'lovely'. However, man, he notes, is 'vile' in this, the 'drearier wilds of heathenism', a comment echoed almost verbatim in a travel narrative on the Ganges published a few years later, mourning the vile human presence in the midst of such great beauty (Clarkson 1850: 65, 67; *JMH* 31 [NS] [1857]: 98–100). Sarah Tucker (1842–43, 1: 92) mourns that the natives' love of flowers is 'degraded to the service of their idols'. Even pageants and celebrations are translated into moral or immoral terms depending on the purpose they served. Thus a pageant at Amritsar in 1853 is described as 'pleasant' and 'splendid' because it was part of a conclave of English officials and Indian rulers or princes on the possibility of suppressing infanticide (*FM* 49 [1854]: 288–89). In each case the landscape invokes not only beauty but also revulsion because the missionary proceeds beyond the visible landscape *into* the morality of the inhabitants. In each of these examples we see the sentimental response (melancholia, horror, revulsion) closely associated with the moral one (of the landscape's 'soul' being an index of Indian primitivism).

The missionary's eye represents, in Benjamin Colbert's (2005: 7–8) formulation, 'motivated perception' in which 'aesthetic, moral or political judgments are brought to bear on the observations of buildings, scenery, peoples of complex tableaux'. The missionary is a true 'observer', moving beyond the tangible object to something else, and motivated by intentions beyond mere landscape appreciation.

As in all picturesque narratives, only a privileged, informed spectator trained in the art of interpretation can interpret the landscape. In the case of the missionary narrative this 'educated' spectator is one who is aware of the moral issues involved when s/he sees the Indian ritual or landscape.

The moral interpretation of the Indian landscape provides the pre-text to the missionary's formulation of a 'design' or agenda for improvement. This constitutes the 'what-must-be-done' moment: the missionary plan. It is a moment of advocacy, where having witnessed the horrors of India, the English traveller proposes and argues for missionary intervention to 'save' India. This plan can, in terms of the narrative logic of the missionary travelogue, only follow the discovery sections: the discovery moment of the primitive picturesque is followed by the interpretive and design moments. The 'fabulous' geography of the missionary travelogue is the construction of a different world, of the plan to create a 'new', improved India.

'Models of piety', designs on the land

This second moment reveals the missionary's plans to transform India, to integrate non-Christian India into the Christian world. By using examples from history and the lives of saints and reformers – Amy deRogatis (2003: 61–89) argues that early missionary work in the American continent was also driven by 'models of piety' – the narratives provide a history and a model for their work in India. While these figures and narratives are models for the missionaries and their activities, they also serve the purpose of suggesting a continuity of transformation: 'improving' India in the same fashion as *earlier* cases of transformed pagan lands. That is, the design argument serves a twofold purpose: of creating a model of behaviour for the missionary *and* the move towards showing how India can be a part of the Christian world just as other regions have been in the past. William Carey describes Elliott and Brainerd, missionaries into the heart of American Indian tribes, as models, before going on to list Paul, Barnabas, John Mark, the Moravian missionaries and the apostles in his *Enquiry* (W. Carey 1792: 70, 71–72). The *Eclectic Review* also cites the 'apostolic labours' of Brainerd – labours, it argues, that have not been carried forward by later missionaries (*EcR* 12 [NS] 1819: 373).

Information about earlier missionaries was also available through extracts published in periodicals like the *Christian Observer*. For example, this periodical published a series titled 'Extracts from the correspondence of Bartholomew Ziegenbalgh and Henry Plutscho, the First Protestant Missionaries in India' (*CO* 9 [1810]: 329–36). This extract was published with a letter to the editor of the periodical, where it stated 'May their [the letters'] reappearance in your work have the effect of again rousing the dormant zeal of many' (*CO* 9 [1810]: 329). Histories of missionary work (*Edifying and Curious Letters of some Missioners of the Society of Jesus from Foreign Missions*, Anon. 1707; John Gillies' *Historical Collections Relating to Remarkable Periods of the Success of the Gospel*, 1754) highlighted European missionary efforts in various parts of the world, and provided role models for later workers. *The Spirit of the British Missions* asked missionaries to 'walk in the steps of the Apostles and Evangelists' (Anon. [Josiah Pratt?] 1815: 76). A funeral sermon by Bishop Wilson for Bishop Corrie prepared a pantheon of 'model' missionaries: David Brown, Claudius Buchanan and Henry Martyn (in Kaye 1859, Appendix 6: 521). James Hough (1832: 119) refers to the missionaries Ziegenbalg and Swartz as the 'pioneers of the present race of missionaries'. Every missionary was evidently familiar with the work of other, earlier workers in the field, and speaks of continuing or extending their work. In order to do so, they required a design, a plan of their 'project'.

William Carey (1792: 77) speaks of the 'glorious design' for missionary activity in India. The terms 'plan', 'system' and 'design' figure prominently in a tract, *Memorial on the Subject of a Mission to Bengal*, signed by Robert Haldane, David Bogue, William Innes and Greville Ewing (Haldane et al. 1797: 5, 6, 12, 13, 16, 27). Tracts like 'On the Probable Design of Providence in Subjecting India to Great Britain' speculated on how Britain was suited to the task of a civilizational mission (*CO* 8.86 [1809]: 85). Alexander Duff (1839: 33) refers to the 'mysterious dispensation of Providence' that gave India to Britain. John Kaye (1859: 477) describes the process of British conquest of India as having happened 'in spite of themselves', thus suggesting Providence and luck but not conscious conquest (see also *CO* [1808]: 249, 261). What is significant is that these 'designs' and plans for the Christian georgic often take recourse to the language of commerce, regulation and military activity.

David Livingstone, the famous missionary traveller in Africa, was one of the first to popularize the phrase, 'Christianity and commerce' (Stanley 1983; A. Porter 1985). Richard Cobbe (1766: 16) argues that building churches in India (specifically, Bombay) is necessary not only to publicize English presence but also for the 'encouragement of trade'. Charles Grant's 1792 manifesto elaborates the profit motif for an entire paragraph before declaring: 'In every progressive step of this work [propagation of Christian religion], we shall also serve the original design with which we visited India, that design still so important to this country; – the extension of our commerce' (Kaye 1859, Appendix 3: 511). William Carey links the missionary and the business enterprises when he writes:

> Providence seems in a manner to invite us to the trial [of journeying across vast seas], as there are to our knowledge trading companies, whose commerce lies in many of those place where these barbarians dwell . . . In the time of the glorious increase of the church, in the latter days . . . commerce shall subserve the needs of the gospel . . . navigation, especially that which is commercial, shall be one great mean of carrying on the work of god . . . [and] there shall be a very considerable appropriation of wealth to that purpose.
>
> (W. Carey 1792: 67–68)

He concludes by speaking of the 'treasure' and 'harvest' that awaits the missionary's labours (W. Carey 1792: 87). When recounting the mission's work he writes in a letter of 1805: 'This has been the most prosperous year the mission has yet seen; we baptized thirteen natives last month' (E. Carey 1836: 319). Claudius Buchanan (1813b: 10) also lists Britain's 'commerce' as the *first* justification for evangelical enterprise. He adds:

> It is lawful for our nation to enrich herself with its [India's] products, and to make it a source of dignity and power; but if she lose sight of the good of the

people . . . the Christian Civilization of her heathen subjects . . . she loses sight of her character as a Christian nation.

(Buchanan 1813b: 97)

Alexander Duff's very first line in *India, and India Missions* refers to India as 'pouring an uninterrupted stream of opulence upon the Western world', and repeatedly uses images of Indian wealth and the language of profits and gains in the opening sections of his account (Duff 1839: 1–3, 5, 33). However, the missionaries were clear that successful commerce could not occur until India was fully Christian, a sentiment expressed by no less than King George III, who in his letter to William Pitt, dated 14 June 1786, states: 'I own I do not think it possible in that country [India] to carry on business with the same moderation that is suitable to an European civilized nation' (George III 1935: 193). In order to recompense for the barbarity of this very profitable space, it was required to Christianize it. Thus John Wilson (1844: 23) argued that nations that are 'intimately connected with Christian countries' either by 'commerce or political relationship' must be the prime focus of evangelical effort. He asks:

For what purpose . . . has God conferred upon us the sovereignty of this great country? Is it merely that we may consume, or export its wealth, find situations of honour and respectability for a portion of England's youth, and offer protection and security to our private trade?

(J. Wilson 1844: 198)

Wilson implies that though these are crucial factors, they are not the only ones: England needs to 'help' India. India's 'claims as a missionary field', in Wilson's words, are 'paramount', and 'the commerce of India is by far the most advantageous that we have in the East, and destitute of it, many of our manufactories at home would be altogether closed' (J. Wilson 1844: 198, 215, 222).[13] Joseph Mullens (1854: 20, 96) describing Mysore lists the reasons why missionary work is facilitated in the region: 'trade is prosperous: soil is fertile: property is secure'. Samuel Wilberforce, Bishop of Winchester and the son of William Wilberforce, declared in a sermon of 1860:

There is a great connection between them [commerce and Christianity]. In the first place, there is little hope of promoting commerce in Africa, unless Christianity is planted in it; and, in the next place, there is very little ground for hoping that Christianity will be able to make its proper way unless we can establish a lawful commerce in that country.

(S. Wilberforce 1874: 213)

In subsequent missionary narratives this alignment of commerce and missionary work takes on slightly different tones, where the preacher or catechist begins to speak of the 'profits' of missionary labours. Here the design argument links commerce with evangelization, and Christianity with empire. The discourse of profit also emerges in the context of the 'moral renovation' theme. The 'profit' of the missionary enterprise is the response from native converts. The 'native agent' – the term is common to missionary narratives – is taught 'to contribute to the gospel which they have themselves received' (Mullens 1854: 116). The money collected through contributions by native converts are used to further a 'moral renovation' of India. Mullens (1854: 118) writes: 'An immense number of churches have been erected by their aid. They subscribe also to the founding of villages as well as societies, and are now endeavouring to establish endowments both by gifts of money and planting lands'. Mullens goes on to provide details of money collected, all the while emphasizing the native converts' 'liberality' (his term). Mullens, in another context, opined that India offered a 'very wide field' for the employment of European capital (House of Commons 1858b: 18).[14]

In the case of missionary narratives, the emphasis on control of native cultures and the land is seen as the anterior moment to improving India as a whole. For this purpose the missionary narrative often makes use of disciplinarian and/or martial terminology to describe their activities. A review of the William Carcy and Joshua Marshman translation of the Valmiki *Ramayan* declared: 'A part of it [*The Ramayan*] has now become our own, and the giant has shrunk into his just proportion . . . reduced almost to a dwarf' and thus tropes Indian culture as shrinking (*QR* 3 [1810]: 380). Joseph Mullens (1854: 118) argues that the effect of the gospel has been to 'elevate the character, and control the principles of the christian poor'. Images of battles, campaigns and wars abound in the missionary narrative. Charles Grant's manifesto of 1792 describes the spread of Christianity in India as 'the noblest species of conquest' (Kaye 1859, Appendix 3: 511). An essay on human sacrifices in India describes the 'continuous struggle against evil' and the 'moral war of enlightened benevolence and Christian civilization' against Indian superstition (*BE* 52 [1842]: 177), thus linking missionary labour with a military campaign. Alexander Duff (1839: 317–20) uses the analogy of military movement to describe evangelical work. An extract published in *Classified Digest of Records of the Society for the Propagation of the Gospel in Foreign Parts 1701–1892* (Society for the Propagation of the Gospel in Foreign Parts, *Classified Digest*, 4th edition, 1894) states: 'India is becoming more and more Christianized . . . It [Christianity] seems to be taking an unalienable possession of the land . . . those who enrolled [i.e. converted to Christianity] by one or two, shall, when the great summary comes, stand up – a great army' (1894: 594). A review of Anthony Grant's *The Past and Prospective Extension of the Gospel by Missions to the Heathen* (1844) describes Grant as 'an active and intelligent officer in an army partially or materially disorganised' seeking to re-establish order among the missionaries. It went on to state how 'extensive regions are laid open to . . . the conquests of love' (*Christian Remembrancer* 8 [1844]: 27, 32). William Buyers (1848), arguing that it was not required to have very large numbers of European missionaries, uses the martial analogy to emphasize domination:

Such an extension of European agency is not required . . . In occupying any great country by an invading army . . . it is quite enough that all the strongest

> fortresses would be taken possession of . . . while for the general settlement . . . and subjugation . . . whose natives who have yielded to, or joined with, the invaders, are generally found to be successful agents . . . the British government in India does not require an immense European force to hold in subjection its mighty empire.
>
> (Buyers 1848: 538)

The narratives, with their 'cultural fable' of the 'wrongs' of India (in terms of culture, nature and religion), now proceed to provide 'solutions' or a programme of action. Often, it includes advice on planting, the acquisition of native languages, the training of native preachers, and advice to the government on how to support missionary work. Buchanan (1813b) thus details evangelical, political and moral motives for the 'diffusion' of Christianity in India.

The emphasis on utilitarian knowledge *and* moral improvement in the 1793 House of Commons resolution has been quoted earlier in the chapter. Marquis Wellesley's efforts in developing the Fort William College are praised in terms that conflate aesthetic, moral and utilitarian concerns:

> In the College of Fort William, he is supposed to have projected a magnificent repository of European principles and Asiatic erudition; a vast moral treasury, in which the stores of written learning and recorded wisdom might indefinitely accumulate, and in which the sages of the East might find studious solitude still more deeply attractive than the sacred shades of Benares. Nothing is more credible than that such prospects as these might fill up the *distance* of the picture which Lord Wellesley had framed for himself.
>
> (*QR* 17 [1817]: 117, emphasis in original)

With such a discourse of 'design' and plans, military 'action' and horticultural changes, the missionary is all set to achieve a transformation of India.

The Christian georgic

'The idle missionary', declares James Hough (1832: 123) in his handbook for missionaries, is an 'anomaly'. The transformation of India could be attained only through rigorous missionary labour. Missionary 'labour', therefore, occupies centre-stage in the narratives through the late eighteenth and nineteenth centuries.

A petition from 'Protestant Dissenters' seeking to promulgate 'the Christian Religion in India' tabled in the House of Commons put it this way:

> The petitioners . . . are also deeply impressed with a full conviction of its proportionate efficacy, to establish, on the most solid foundations, the fabric of social order, and all the highest and best interests of mankind . . . are anxiously desirous that the light and blessings of the Christianity should be gradually diffused over the immense empire of Great Britain in the East,

which, instead of being thereby endangered, would, as they believe on the
ground of fact and experience, derive additional strength and stability from
the spread of Christian religion.

(*Hansard Parliamentary Debates* 25, 11 March – 10 May 1813: 764–65)

The passage employs the rhetoric common to many missionary writings of the
period: the spatial imagery of building and foundations, the theological, the imperial, moral and disciplinarian. The work of imperial 'stability' and social order
involves 'improving' the native from idolatry and superstition to a knowledgeable
race. It will require tackling myriad problems like infanticide, widow-burning, idol
worship, superstition – in short, a tackling of *details*. In order to do so, it had first
acquired, in the moment of the primitive picturesque, a great deal of information
about India's religions and beliefs. It is these areas that the civic picturesque would
operate to alter and improve, regulate and harmonize.

Treating India as something organic ready for horticultural alterations and
regulation, missionary narratives describe Hinduism and Indian life as placed on
the cusp of a major change.[15] A report on 'widow-burning' praises the 'phenomenon of religious change' among the natives before going on to declare: 'The great
fact it teaches is, that *the Hindoo mind is capable of advance even in the department where its
immobility has been deemed most absolute – traditional faith*' (*QR* 89 [1851]: 257–76,
emphasis in original). William Buyers (1848: 530) writes: 'though the masses of
Indian society are more inert than those of most other countries, they are by no
means immoveable'. The rhetoric gestures at an Indian alteration driven by a
moral justification. Interestingly this emphasis on morally 'improving' India
images religious change in agricultural and horticultural terms. The change, of
course, requires a great deal of labour on the part of the missionary.

Having dwelt upon, in great depth, on the variety of Indian primitivism (idol
worship, infanticide, rituals), the missionary tract begins its second stage with a
rhetoric of labour. This moment portrays the Indian variegated landscape of
paganism as a site where the missionary faces physical hardships and obstacles for
the sake of spiritual gain. This is the moment of the Christian georgic. The rhetoric
of labour that is used to describe missionary work often highlights the difficulties
involved in conversion, of church-building and personal suffering. This rhetoric is
also marked by a great deal of the rhetoric of sacrifice and pain. It becomes, in
Beth Tobin's (2005: 36) terms, a georgic of 'virtuous labour', with the goal of cultivating a moral garden (the cultivation of the 'garden' and souls owes much, of
course, to similar metaphors in the Bible). A review of Mrs Carey's memoirs of
Eustace Carey links vegetation, morality and Christianity when it describes how
the missionaries donated the results of their 'personal exertions' – the 'produce of
their fruit-gardens and fish-ponds' – in the 'most self-denying and conscientious
manner' (*EcR* 1 [Series 6] [1857]: 629). Joseph Mullens, testifying before the Select
Committee on Colonization and Settlement (India) even proposes gardening as a
work ethic for British soldiers (House of Commons 1858b: 12–13).

Details are to be now subsumed into a larger picture – Christian India –
through missionary work. The missionary presents himself or herself as the best

qualified person to comment on the Indian condition, and to propose/effect change. Claudius Buchanan in his *An Apology for Promoting Christianity in India* (1813a) states:

> In every heathen nation, the Missionaries are generally best qualified to delineate the character of the inhabitants . . . The commercial men in the East know, in general, very little of the subject . . . they rarely penetrate into the interior . . . As to the literary men, again, who merely consult books, their advantages of information are confessedly very far inferior to those of the Missionaries . . . Gentlemen who had occupied high official situations in that country [India] betrayed a defect of information respecting the state of the natives.
>
> (Buchanan 1813a: xvii–xviii)

Bishop Reginald Heber – even though he was not a missionary in the full sense of the term – is praised not only for 'possess[ing] the eye of a painter and the pen of a poet', but also for having views that were 'liberal, expansive, worthy of a philosopher and a statesman' (*QR* 37 [1828]: 102), suggesting that he was well suited to observe and record.

Missionary work, William Carey (1792: 72, 75–76) argues, calls upon the missionary to abandon the pleasures of life with 'a readiness to endure the greatest suffering at the hands of his Lord, and Master'. Henry Martyn (1851: 211, 341) on the ship to India in 1805 prepares 'to meet new dangers and trials'. India is occasionally described as a 'scene which could have no charms . . . but as a scene of exertion in the service of Christ' (*QR* 25 [1821]: 441). Whitelaw Ainslie (1835: 104) appropriates the phrase 'scene of exertion' in his account of the progress of Christianity in the eastern nations in the 1830s. A review of Martyn's *Memoirs* (1819) describes his life as an example of 'self-denying heroism' (*EcR* 12 [NS] [1819]: 303). James Hough (1832: 2) in his instruction manual for missionaries, *The Missionary Vade Mecum*, describes it as a 'life of self-denial'. Such images of sacrifice and exertion occur in several other tracts and commentaries on missionary work (J. Wilson 1844: 53; Clarkson 1850: 4; *DR* 32 [1852]: 386). The second level of the missionary text consists almost entirely of the toil narrative. Having 'found' the field and identified the plan, the missionary must set to work.

Cultivation is a central trope in all missionary narratives, and may be linked to the significance of the 'fertilizing' metaphor in the ideology of colonial improvement in English writings on Scotland during the eighteenth century (Womack 1989: 61–65). Land is appropriated for different purposes: to be restructured physically, controlled and 'improved', and also to generate *metaphors* for missionary activity. The missionary picturesque attempts to cultivate the land and the moral landscape of the natives, with the aim at the creation of a Christian garden. This trope often borrowed from prevalent vitalist theories of regeneration, cultivation and botany.[16] Here is Duff on what he calls 'the grand ultimate object' of evangelical work in India: 'the intellectual, moral, and spiritual regeneration of the universal mind; – or, in the speediest and most effectual manner, the reaching and vitally imbuing the entire body of the people with the leaven of Gospel truth' (Duff 1839: 284).

William Carey recommends toil of every kind. He suggests that missionaries who arrive in heathen lands 'should cultivate a little spot of ground' for their own needs. Eventually, the missionary community would be able to, 'upon receiving the first crop, maintain themselves'. The women who attend the missionaries, he advises, should understand 'husbandry, fishing, fowling' (W. Carey 1792: 73, 74). Carey – who, incidentally, edited and published William Roxburgh's *Flora indica; or, Descriptions of Indian Plants* (1832) and was eventually elected to the Horticultural Society of London and made the President of the Agricultural Society of India (E. Carey 1836: 369, 373) – had considered applying for the post of a superintendent to the company's botanical gardens upon arrival in Calcutta. An early journal entry states his intention to 'build a hut or two, and retire to the wilderness' (E. Carey 1836: 92, 94). Greville Ewing in his 1797 sermon before the Edinburgh Missionary Society defends missionary work among the 'heathens' through a horticultural analogy: 'Will the garden of the sluggard be cleared of its weeds by a little more slumber?' (Ewing 1797: 27). John Wilson (1844: 253–54) speaks of 'graft[ing] the best habits and institutions of European nations' onto India for its 'improvement', and goes on to argue that a common faith would create a 'union of minds' of 'sovereign and subject', otherwise the relationship would be merely one of 'juxta-position of inanimate parts'. William Buyers (1848: 540), warning that Hinduism and Islam may not readily yield to Christianity, also takes recourse to the organicist metaphor and writes: 'it is scarcely probable that they will, either of them, expire by a gradual process, without at least some spasmodic, and writhing attempts, to destroy their assailants'.

When Carey describes evangelical preaching as 'a fountain [that] casts forth streams of water', he *naturalizes* his discourse. Carey later requests the Baptist Missionary Society to send him some 'instruments of husbandry . . . seeds'. This husbandry, he adds, 'will be a lasting advantage to this country' (W. Carey 1792: 128–29). Francis Wayland's introduction to Eustace Carey's *Memoirs of William Carey* speaks of the 'moral renovation of India' (E. Carey 1836: xi). A review of Edward Moor's *Hindu Infanticide* calls for a 'moral revolution' (*EcR* 8 [1812]: 345). Sarah Tucker (1842–43, 1: 66) cites a comment that 'Southern India is "like a thirsty land longing for water at every pore, but with no man to water it"'. Converts in mission schools were encouraged to take up cultivation and horticulture:

> The latter [the converts] were directed to occupy their minds by learning in the forenoon; and in the afternoon, their hands and feet, by cultivating the school yards and grounds adjacent with different vegetables, which heretofore were bought at the market . . . The Catechists and Christians in the country were continually encouraged to make the best use possible of the ground granted by the government to the chapels and houses.
>
> (*CO* 8 [1809]: 127)

Here agriculture is linked to virtue in the school children. The cultivation of the ground is seen as a mode of organizing the day and enabling the development of the child.

Images of flowing water – canals and streams were essentially systems of communication – suggest linkage, irrigation and communication. In conjunction with images of vegetation, it suggests landscaping, control over land and anthropocentric domination over nature (Womack 1989: 65). In the case of the missionary narrative the drive towards cultivation, both geographical and moral, proposes a harmony of the social and the natural. Christianity 'cultivates' India and Indian souls to create a paradise-like space. William Carey (1792), as noted, refers to the 'rivers' of missionaries fertilizing many regions. John Owen (1816, 1: 362), commenting on the obstacles laid in the way of missionary work in India, writes of the 'attempts simultaneously made to arrest the stream of divine truth, just as it was issuing from its hallowed source to fertilize the moral deserts of Hindoostan'. Another essay spoke of the 'prospect of the full development of the capacities of the richest soil in the world' (*BE* 52 [1842]: 183). A review of Michael Wilkinson's *Sketches of Christianity in North India* (1844) describes the work as 'a genial shower upon parched ground' (*CR* 3 [1845]: 299). William Buyers writes in an extended passage of missionary husbandry narrative:

> The ground has not only been broken in many places, but much seed has been sown, and has begun to germinate. Though . . . the gospel has not been very extensively propagated, yet it has been actually planted, and has struck root in the soil, though it has still much of the feebleness of the exotic, and for years may require to be watched over and watered, lest its healthful growth be prevented by the ungenial influences to which it is exposed. The more care and labour we can bestow on its cultivation, the more speedily it will expand into a strong and healthy tree, extending its wide-spreading branches in every direction, and producing abundance of fruit.
>
> (Buyers 1848: 537)

Duff calls for 'naturaliz[ing]' Christianity so that it may take 'deep root in the soil', 'flourish and perpetuate itself' (Duff 1839: 306; see also 309, 311, 316).

Duff (1839: 301) complains that the present mission school system does not allow the 'youthful plants . . . to fructify and grow into strength, and shoot out into the heavens their wide-spreading branches'. Joseph Mullens (1854: 80) describing the Madras Presidency areas writes: 'The suburb of Vepery stands next in importance not only in relation to the amount of its population, but also to the missionary labour expended upon it'. James Hough (1832: 53) writes: 'every seed, and blade, and plant, must be watched and cherished with unwearied solicitude, that they may be constantly growing unto perfection', and every minister of the Gospel must be 'ever busied in the cultivation of his own plot'. John Wilson (1844: 24) refers to the missionaries as 'spiritual husbandmen'[17] Landscapes thus begin to be viewed and described in terms of either their potential for missionary work or as the result of missionary labours.

A crucial mode of imposing order on the landscape in missionary narratives is to speak of church-building. As early as the 1710s, Richard Cobbe (1766: vii), the chaplain to the East India Company, had recommended the construction of churches so that 'all the island might see that we had some religion among us'. Cobbe's text, *Bombay Church*, is a replenishment narrative, which proposes a Christian refilling of faith in the colony, but a replenishment that works at two levels: fulfilment of the *potential* of the natives to take to Christianity and the emptying out of native systems. Cobbe (1766: 10) begins by saying that at present, the English are forced to 'pay our public devotions in private' in a 'dark and disuniform chapel'. Cobbe images this distinction between religious faiths and beliefs in terms of landscape and spaces of worship when he writes:

> Shall we then, who profess ourselves Christians, and worshippers of the true God, and in a true manner, thus shun the light, as if ashamed of our profession? When the inhabitants around us are not only not ashamed to acknowledge their false and imaginary deities, in the most public manner they are able; but insult us with their number of Churches and Pagodas, even upon our territories?
>
> (Cobbe 1766: 11)

Churches are thus *visible* markers of Christian ownership for Cobbe. He further argues that the beauty of the Christian faith can be made visible to Indians and retained only through such spatial acts of reordering and rebuilding the landscape: 'How is it possible to keep any form, decency, or order (which is the very beauty of holiness) when we are thus irregularly crowded together?' It is this particular mode of transforming the landscape that is central to the missionary narrative: to locate, build or rebuild churches in India so that orderly worship may be performed for the 'public good' (Cobbe 1766: 11, 27, 34). Claudius Buchanan (1813b: 181) states: 'it is indispensable that Churches be erected at the principal stations'. Whitelaw Ainslie (1835: 70–71) argues that with an increase in the number of churches and chapels in the country the natives know that Christians 'fixed religious officers . . . shrines . . . and altars' which 'testify to our increasing religious zeal' but will also 'elevate' the character of the British in the 'eyes of Europe'.[18] George Pettitt proudly mentions the spire he added to a church, a commentator praises Bishop Middleton for building many churches in India, and yet another describes church-building as 'wonderful' (Pettitt 1851: 84: *BE* 85 [1859]: 475; *DUM* 54 [1859]: 341). In all these cases the emphasis is on the visibility of the English Church.

Occasionally, the metaphor of building and monuments is shifted on to the work of the missionaries themselves. Church-building begins to be seen as an instantiation of missionary labour. It becomes iconic not only of religious faith but also of the obstacles overcome in building the house of God. A review therefore praises the work of 'the Corries and the Careys, the Martyns and the Marshmans, the Thomases and the Thomasons, the Browns and the Buchanans . . . whose labours of love have been instrumental in rearing so many monuments for immortality' (*CaR* 3 [1845]: 322). Claudius Buchanan emphasizes the fact that 'the chief Christian Church in British India, was aided by the Hindoos themselves [in the form of Hindu subscriptions]' (Buchanan 1813b: 182–83; see also Cobbe 1766: 25; Pettitt 1851: 237, 240–41, 247).[19] Descriptions of church-building are scattered throughout Pettitt's narrative (1851: 325, 326–28, 373, 379–80, 419, 454–55). A much later essay also describes the transformation of Indian landscape (specifically, Karachi) almost entirely in terms of church-buildings: 'All that [no churches, mosques or temples] is changed now. Christianity is making itself felt, as there are several churches and other fine stone buildings in Kurrachee' (*CMM* 1 February 1881: 19).

Missionary tracts thus saw 'improvement' in both horticultural and moral terms. George Pettitt (1851: 171) refers to a Tinnevelly district as 'the best and most flourishing in the mission'. 'Flourish' is, of course, a botanical term, and suggests luxuriant and wide-ranging growth. Joseph Mullens (1854) having first framed the details of various regions of southern India proceeds to elaborate on 'all the elements of progress' made by missions in the Travancore area. Mullens' extended description is worth quoting in full:

> At the present time the London Mission in South Travancore contains seven chief stations, and about two hundred and fifty outstations; superintended and instructed by eight missionaries, and 105 catechists. The native Christians so-called number 17,600 persons; . . . the out-stations have their village chapels and school-rooms. The head stations have the houses of resident missionaries; large, well-built chapels; and large school-houses for the boarding schools. In some cases a christian school has sprung up at the station: in others, the christians are still mixed up with the heathen population in general . . . Santapuram . . . lies opposite a noble hill which stretches far into the well-tilled rice plain. Its pretty parsonage; its neat church, already too small for the demands of the Christian population; its flourishing girls' school containing more than a hundred girls; its lace establishment; its almshouses for poor widows; its well-planned village; and huge well; all reflect much credit on the perseverance and energy of Mr Lewis, the missionary by which it was founded . . . [In] Jamestown . . . in addition to the usual buildings the station has been planted with a large number of cocoanut trees . . . I shall never forget the happy faces of the Shánár girls in the school at this station, as they plied their merry spinning-wheels, and sang with glee 'Oh! that will be joyful, when we meet to part no more.'
>
> (Mullens 1854: 106–07)

Moral improvement, industry and horticulture are all tied into evangelical activity. New buildings have come up and churches have been built. The villages are 'well-planned' and ordered. There are coconut trees, and the children are all happy in this Arcadian idyll. Describing the lace-makers of Nagercoil – native converts who have been supplied material and trained by missionaries – he underscores the 'respectability and cleanliness of the employment' that 'react upon the mind and character of those who pursue it'. It reminds him, Mullens (1854: 118) writes, of William Cowper's beautiful lines about the working English cottager pursuing like employment. The reference to employment, character and Cowper's 'English cottager' aligns moral, economic and landscape concerns along a continuum. The English cottage, a central feature of the picturesque (Andrews 1989: 8), is here transplanted into a native Christian context. The parallels are drawn to indicate the visual sense of the employment of the converts, their 'profits' on gainful employment and their general character.

The missionary *Concordia discors*

Discussions of the picturesque in nineteenth-century England often spoke of the harmony between humans and nature. Adapting, perhaps, from theories of vitalism, they spoke of the 'family likeness' between art and nature (*DUM* 29 [1842]: 213). This rhetoric of a harmonious universe is central to the colonial missionary narrative, and includes various components: the expansion of Christian missionary labour and the encirclement of the world, the integration of Hindu details into a Christian 'order', enumerative evidence of missionary work and the topos of carefully cultivated, ordered gardens.

Images of heathen lands thrown 'open' for Christian work, yet delineated and enclosed, abound in narratives from the earliest days of missionary work in India. The vast regions of the globe that remain 'dark' become sites of responsibility and duty in what Alan Lester (2000) identifies as the 'global humanitarian imagination' of nineteenth-century Europe. There arose, Lester demonstrates, a 'moral geography of the globe', where Europeans felt a responsibility for 'distant strangers' (Lester 2000: 278). Such a moral geography also furnishes a range of metaphors and rhetorical devices in the colonial text.

As late as the 1890s, the image of expansion remained central to the missionary narrative (and imagination). Thus Silvester Horne (1894: 2) in his account of the London Missionary Society spoke of the 'forward movement in the expanding circle of British influence'. The conjoined images of 'forward' and 'expanding circle' in Horne's description capture both the activity and the *rhetoric* of British evangelicalism in late-eighteenth- and nineteenth-century India. Images of globes, expansion, circles and fields of activity are closely affiliated with the language of Christian duty, responsibility and belief. Missionary writings from the period often mark as the goal of their labours the unification of the variety of heathen people into a Christian globe, whose boundaries are constantly being enlarged to take in more (varieties of) barbarians and cultures. The humanitarian imagination literally encompasses the globe, while being cast in the language of imperial expansion.

William Carey's *Enquiry*, a founding text of Protestant work in India, begins by stating: 'This commission, was as extensive as possible, and laid them under obligation to disperse themselves into every country of the habitable globe, and preach to all inhabitants, without exception, or limitation' (W. Carey 1792: 7). Carey's image of expanding missionary labour without 'limitation' proposes an ever-widening moral geography that subsumes into itself the corners of the non-Christian world. This image of limitless humanitarianism and Christianizing is not new. Richard Cobbe (1766: 43), as early as 1716–17, was complaining in a letter that the chaplains at Fort St George, Madras, were rather 'degenerate and confined', for 'it did not extend itself beyond the bounds of [their] own territories'.[20] The *Concordia discors* of the last moment of the missionary narrative is characterized by this *rhetoric of expansion* and *encirclement*.

In order to demonstrate the need for Christian expansion, Carey first provides a comprehensive database of the extents of paganism. Carey opens his *Enquiry* with a description of sin's *variety*: 'Sin was introduced amongst the children of men by the fall of Adam . . . By changing its appearances to suit the circumstances of the times, it has grown up in ten thousand forms'. Carey dwells on this theme, describing how 'idolatry spread more and more', the 'world was overrun with ignorance' and how civilizations slipped 'into more abundant and extravagant idolatries' (1792: 4–5). Carey also lists the Christian and non-Christian population of every region of the known world (1792: 39–61; 23 pages of the total 87 in the *Enquiry* carry statistics). This information, in the form of tables of statistics, is meant to indicate the extent of heathenism, but also to demonstrate the *potential* scope of the missionary's work: 'It must undoubtedly strike a very considerate mind what a large proportion of the sons of Adam there are, who yet remain in the most deplorable state of heathen darkness'. And then Carey (1792: 62) writes: 'they appear as capable of knowledge as we are'. Aligning the barbarian alongside the Christian anticipates the rhetorical move of the missionary picturesque: the transformation of the heathen that brings him into the circle of Christian faith, into the circle already occupied by the Englishman. Here Carey has translated the numbers of heathens into the number of possible converts to Christianity.

William Carey inaugurates the trope of encirclement and expansion – an ever-widening circle of the Christian world – to describe missionary work when he writes: 'All these things are loud calls to Christians, and especially to ministers, to exert themselves to the utmost in their several *spheres of actions*, and to try to *enlarge* them as much as possible' (Carey 1792: 66, emphasis added). Images of expansion occur elsewhere in Carey (1792: 13, 67, 73, 82). Similar tropes of distance, enlargement and expansion persist in many missionary documents, and serve to illustrate the potential *Concordia discors* of missionary enterprise. It is also important to note that Carey is speaking of a connection between the heathens and the Christians – a version of the Enlightenment's theme of interconnectedness (Reill 2005: 137). It is the underlying commonality that Carey is speaking of here. A review essay describes the task of English missionaries in India as one of 'vastness . . . variety . . . and difficulty'. The word 'difficulty' occurs four times on the same page of this review (*QR* 138 [1875]: 346). A review of Buchanan's *The Star in the East* (1809b) speaks of the responsibilities of having large numbers of people 'in the sphere of [British missionary] influence' (*CO*: 8 [1809]: 316). Examples of the use of the image could be multiplied from William Wilberforce (1797: 164), Buchanan (1813b: 180), *The Spirit of the British Missions* (Anon. 1815: 76) and Joseph Mullens (1854: 9, 20, 82).

One of the central conditions of the missionary enterprise is, therefore, expansion and the overcoming of restrictions. The *Quarterly Review* opens the review of a tract on the East India College and the Wellesley memoirs with an image of expansion and encirclement: 'England has almost always extended her territorial greatness beyond her own narrow pale. It might seem as if an imprescribable privilege had been conferred on us, of possessing a sort of *outer-court* of dominion' (*QR* 17 [1817]: 107, emphasis in original). Later, in this same review, it describes the link between imperial power and colony in terms of such a circle: 'The mother-country moves in a sort of *exterior circle* of power; while the management of the local administration is left almost wholly to the energies of local wisdom and genius' (*QR* 17 [1817]: 109, emphasis added). In another issue the same periodical argued that the missionary enterprise in India had not been very successful, despite the huge amounts of money being poured into it. The solution was cast in a rhetoric of expansion and encirclement: 'We would submit to them whether their *sphere of usefulness* would not be considerably *enlarged* if they would appropriate a greater proportion of their funds' (*QR* 25 [1821]: 452, emphasis added). Similar images can be found in *The Spirit of the British Missions*, which cites an unnamed evangelist's opinion that '[the aim of the missionary society] is nothing less, than to evangelize, not merely a village, a parish, a town, a city, a kingdom; but, if possible, the whole world' (Anon. 1815: 1, 69; see also Clarkson 1850: 10). James Hough (1832) in his manual for missionaries in India employs the image of expansion, cultivation and the circle while advocating caution in all three matters:

> It is natural for an active mind and a zealous spirit to wish to extend his sphere of action to the wildest possible extent. But he should guard against the feeling of impatience, and, instead of flying over the ground, be content to feel his way . . . To confine your exertions within narrow limits will not present so flattering an appearance as the culture of an extensive surface. But, like a prudent husbandman, you should endeavour to measure your field by your means for its cultivation. Otherwise, your vineyard, though planted in every corner, will be overgrown with weeds . . . But it is comparatively easy, more satisfactory, and of a better report, to *extend* them, when your immediate plot is well cultivated, and you have saplings carefully trained, and ready to be transplanted in a distant soil.
>
> (Hough 1832: 107–08, emphasis in original)

Hough recommends expansion of the circle, but also suggests caution in the botanical-horticultural activity in images that echo nineteenth-century horticultural tracts. Here, for instance, is Thomas Andrew Knight's 1812 prospectus for the Horticultural Society of London: 'An ample and unexplored field for future discovery and improvement lies before us, in which nature does not appear to have formed any limits to the success of our labours, if properly applied' (quoted in Elliott 1994).

The image of the circle automatically calls for a concomitant image of centres. And this the missionary narrative provides with amazing frequency. The image of the 'circle' of missions and centre occurs in William Carey in another context – in a letter defending the conduct of his fellow-missionary, Joshua Marshman. Carey writes:

> My plan relative to spreading the gospel has, for several years past, been, to fix European brethren at the distance of 100 or 150 miles from each other, so that each one should occupy the centre of a circle of 100 miles diameter more or less; and that native brethren should be stationed within that circle as preachers, schoolmasters, readers, &c, at proper distances, as circumstances may make convenient.
>
> (W. Carey 1828: 15)

William Buyers and William Clarkson both locate the European missionary at the centre and the native preachers moving outwards in ever-increasing circles to spread the gospel (Buyers 1848: 537; Clarkson 1850: 4, 16, 25, 53). An appeal for missionary volunteers and funds describes 'new kingdoms opening to our [missionary] energies' (*Missionary Magazine and Chronicle* 1 [1837]: 8). In his introductory remarks on the examination papers of Indian youth in the London Missionary Society's Christian Institution in Calcutta (these answer scripts were made available in published form), Thomas Boaz declares: 'it is one of the great facts of the age, that *India is open to the gospel, is open to Christ*' (Christian Institution 1848: iii, emphasis in original). Boaz goes on to locate the 'transformed', *Christianized* Indian at the centre of such a *Concordia discors*: 'he stands in the midst of the opening and clustering beauties, delighted, bewildered and hopeful; delighted with the dissolving views that encircle him' (Christian Institution 1848: v).

The discourse of 'openness' that these narratives articulate is linked, eventually, to the 'encirclement' of heathenism within the Christian globe. Richard Cobbe in his sermons of 1715–18 in Bombay (published in 1766) was already using the image of encirclement to describe the expansion of Christianity in India: 'May this Blessing, not confined to time or place, diffuse itself beyond the circle of this royal settlement, unto the neighbouring factories around us'. He describes the church as being 'deservedly admired for its strength and beauty, neatness and uniformity', being located 'in the midst of the inhabitants [of Bombay town]' (Cobbe 1766: 17, 58). The sense of a uniform religion and belief system is integral to the *Concordia discors* of the empire, as a contemporary commentator stated:

> The assimilation of the Hindoos with our own subjects, by inducing an uniformity of religious *profession*, might indeed accelerate their march to the heights of knowledge and of power: our fears, however, for the security of our Indian possessions, would not be greatly diminished, unless a cordial reception of the doctrines of the Cross were to accompany the profession of faith in Christ.
>
> (*CO* 7 [1808]: 256, emphasis in original)

Claudius Buchanan (1813b: 119) declares that Christianity would 'supply a useful correspondence with the mother country; and would establish a new ground of attachment' between Britain and India. The emphasis on uniformity is linked to the discourse of a Christian space into which India's variety and disorder can be subsumed.

The *Concordia discors* that seems to underlie the cultural fable of missionary labour and the colonial project of improvement is an encirclement of variety into a quiet place. It works at two levels: the unification of missionary efforts into one harmonious whole and the encirclement of natives into a closed garden without distinctions. Thus the trope of *Concordia discors* treats both the missionary and heathen in similar fashion.

William Carey is enthusiastic about the variety among missionaries. His language is cast in the picturesque's descriptive vocabulary of variety:

> I have lately thought that all the little grudges and collisions of parties, which, in their beginnings, are often the cause of so much distress, resemble the springs from which, on a map, a great number of rivers take their rise: many of these in their beginnings seem so near each other, as almost to reduce the country from which they flow to a morass, and their apparent interferences with each other's courses at first appear rather hurtful than otherwise; but after a time they either fall into each other, so as to form rivers of such magnitude as to enrich a whole district, or, which is not infrequently the case, diverge so much as to fertilize regions lying very remote from each other.
>
> (W. Carey 1828: 18–19)

Diversity among preachers and missionaries thus carries the potential to 'fertilize' large and widely separated lands. When William Carey pleads for active missionary work in India, he images the enterprise in terms that subsumed variety into a smooth uniform dimension. He suggests that, for the sake of missionary work, 'the strictest unanimity ought to prevail' among the various denominations within Christianity, where 'the whole body [is] thus animated by one soul' (W. Carey 1792: 81). Later he would declare that 'harmony . . . subsists between all engaged in the work' (E. Carey 1836: 368). The *Memorial on the Subject of a Mission to Bengal* claims that its plea for a mission to Bengal is supported by 'many hundreds of Clergymen of different denominations' (Haldane et al. 1797: 4). Greville Ewing (1797: 32) dismisses 'differences of opinion in the church of Christ' as being 'by no means so formidable'. Claudius Buchanan (1813b: 14) states: 'it certainly is not a consideration of importance, what church or denomination of Christians may be employed in converting heathen nations'. Similar opinions are to be found in Owen (1816, 1: 276–77), in an appeal for greater missionary work in India published in the *Missionary Magazine and Chronicle* (1 [1837]: 188), John Wilson (1844: 4, 23) and the Christian Institution (1848: iii, iv).

The *Church Missionary Atlas* of 1879 presents a table of Christian schools and clergy before describing the success of the missionary enterprise thus: 'This ingathering into the fold of Christ is chiefly the result of the labours of the last fifty years' (Church Missionary House 1879: 59). Thomas Boaz uses the exact same image to describe missionary work, arguing that a direction to conversion in India will enable 'the ingathering of the millions of the East to the fold of hope' (Christian Institution 1848: viii). A review perusing mission documents, declares: 'the missionary spirit has done much to mitigate both the spirit of division and the spirit of exclusion' (*QR* 138 [1875]: 352). The missionaries, claims the tract, *Memorial on the Subject of a Mission to Bengal*, consider themselves the 'citizens of the world, and the earth as their country' and are 'deeply concerned for the welfare of the people of every land' (Haldane et al. 1797: 16). Children in England are inspired to encourage and 'love' Indian children through articles that emphasize the work being done at these enormous distances. Thus a news item on the work of the Young Men's Association's school at Calcutta says: 'Let this account of these dear children in a far off country encourage our readers to love them and pray for them' (*JMH* 31 [NS] [1857]: 110). This rhetoric of sameness and uniformity is the hallmark of almost every missionary narrative of the nineteenth century, where each has begun from detail and concluded with the abstract and the uniform. It is this sense of sameness and uniformity that the missionary narrative hopes to reach in practice.

Passages such as these present the *Concordia discors* of the missionary narrative. Colonial geographies of humanitarianism develop a *Concordia discors* where even primitive people like the aborigines and Indians would have a well-defined 'place' on the globe, or 'god's earth'. Rooted in an Enlightenment ideology of 'encircle-ment' and universal cartographics (Cosgrove 2001: 195–99), the cultural fable of *Concordia discors* was about bringing various cultures/nations/religions into the Christian circle/globe. Encirclement, linked to the latitudinal arc of the late eigh-teenth and early nineteenth centuries, sought to 'appropriat[e] global space by bringing East and West together within a single imaginative realm' (Cosgrove 2001: 207). Part of the missionary picturesque's *Concordia discors* was to indeed link East and West, but within a Christian realm. It was also, clearly, a rhetoric of empire.

Interestingly, the *Concordia discors* of the missionary picturesque also commodi-fied Indian lands, linking it to not only a Christian globalization but also a universal economic network. It located India within a larger movement of mate-rial gain and economic benefits. This is marked by the rhetoric of material gains for both Britain and India in most of the early missionary tracts. William Carey (1792: 70) argues that making Christians of heathens would 'make them more useful members of society' and aligns evangelization with a utilitarian agenda. A reviewer describes the evangelical activity as 'the moral renovation of an empire' (*CO* 10 [1810]: 579). A similar spatial image is visible in Duff (1839: 33, 151), John Wilson (1844: 208) and William Clarkson (1850: 12). In each of these cases the narrative tropes India as a space of reconstruction.

This *Concordia discors*, the central trope in the nineteenth-century missionary narrative, figures in an incipient form as early as William Carey's *Enquiry* where he speaks of the heathens as possessing 'souls . . . as immortal as ours' (1792: 69). Carey's comment links the barbaric, non-Christian nations and cultures of the world and inaugurates a major theme in missionary writings. A tract on Indian infanticide declares:

> In every quarter of the globe, in the Old World and the New, in countries the most remote from each other, among independent races and people that could have had no mutual intercourse, in every stage, too, of national progress, among the civilized and refined as well as the rude and barbarous, it has been found to exist.
>
> (J.C. Browne 1857: 2)

The rhetoric of *Concordia discors* evidently demands erasure of difference and therefore detail for purposes of harmony. I have argued that the moral picturesque of missionary narratives moves from an India of pagan detail via an 'aesthetics of poverty' into a Christian India of massed uniformity, or at least an ordered diversity, a theme visible as early as the first decades of the nineteenth century. Reviewing Thomas and William Daniell's *Oriental Scenery* (1812–16), the *Eclectic Review* stated:

> There are many huge piles of Mahomedan structures . . . In their forms and arrangements they are indefinitely diverse, defying all models and orders. They are fantastic, elaborate, and decorated to infinity . . . There is considerable symmetry in some of the structures, but it is the kindred and conformity of congregated littlenesses. There is no mighty simplicity and compass of conception; no notion of a grand effect . . . There is device and detail . . . The endless particulars seem as if intended to baffle all attempts at forming a collective idea of the whole. What a change of element, to pass from these measureless masses of detail, these bulks frittered into multitudinous shapes, to the harmonious simplicity, the essences, if we may so express it, of the Grecian structures!
>
> (*EcR* 6 [NS] [1816]: 475)

A review of Eustace Carey's *Memoir* of William Carey attacks the work for being too focused on the 'anatomy' and 'literal details' rather than on the 'general effect' (*EcR* 16 [Series 3] [1836]: 453). The accumulation of Indian detail is annoying, unaesthetic and frightening, as the review points out.

The need to incorporate the low and the rude into Christianity dominates the missionary narrative. In the case of missionary writing, the emphasis is on 'absorbing' those communities who have been marked as 'different' and excluded by Hinduism: the 'lower' castes. William Carey mentions that at 'Moypal', three people 'are under very hopeful concern indeed' (i.e. for conversion) before stating that they are all 'labourers' (E. Carey 1836: 181). Sarah Tucker (1842–43, 1: 74) emphasizes that the 'lower' classes were more anxious for education. Other missionary tracts also underscore the fact that their efforts were directed at the 'lower' castes, and are triumphant in announcing any success in converting these to Christianity (J. Wilson 1844: 43; *CMR* 21 [1850]: 121; Mullens 1854: 84, 85). Pettitt (1851: 478, 480) thus mentions that because of 'the preference given to the poor in the Scriptures', they are happier to take in the lower classes and castes into Christianity.

Central to this harmonized Christian *Concordia discors* is the image of the organized and ordered India/Indians. It is significant that periodicals like *Juvenile
Missionary Herald, Indian Female Evangelist* and others, especially from the 1880s,
carried two principal kinds of visuals. One would invariably be of the semi-clad
Hindu *fakir*, the snake-charmer, a hovel or a native ritual. Another set of visuals
would invariably be of Christian schools (with the English teacher-missionary
surrounded by native students) and native preachers. This second component
always showed native converts in formal attire, well groomed and in positions that
are static. While the Hindu or the Muslim is shown indulging in assorted (barbaric)
activity, the native Christian convert is shown posing with the Bible or just
standing still.[21] An essay 'Christianity in India' published in 1877 mentions 'neatly
dressed orphans . . . happy looking, well fed, well taught, well cared for' (*FM* 16
[NS] [1877]: 312). The rhetoric here suggests, subtly, a movement from ineffective or immoral actions to repose and peace, from hectic actions to the peace of
stillness. Occasionally such an image of the native Christian at repose is seen in the
descriptive vocabulary. Henry Martyn, for instance, describes such a scene:

> My romantic notions are for the first time almost realized, – for, in addition to
> the beauties of sylvan scenery, may be seen the more delightful object of
> multitudes of simple people sitting in the shade, listening to the words of
> eternal life . . . I have seen many discover, by their looks while Marshman was
> preaching, that their hearts were tenderly affected.
>
> (Martyn 1851: 349)

George Pettitt, as seen above, describes in detail the Hindu temples and idols in a
missionary picturesque of deformity. Soon after, Pettitt also describes the transformation of the same site: Pettitt, immediately after the above passage in which he
discusses a native temple, provides a description where such a Christian beauty – a
church – is installed on the landscape:

> I visited the village, for the first time, about two months afterward, and
> received a hearty welcome. As I approached their devil-temple, now become
> a house of prayer – enlarged, and for the first time, enlightened by a window
> formed in one of the walls, I beheld their idols scattered in the sand, with
> broken heads, and arms, and legs; and in the course of the morning, when
> sitting along inside, I saw one of the children of the village, about four years
> old, get astride upon the back of one of the largest, which they had kept for
> me, if I should wish to have it, turning it into a toy, whipping it with a straw.
> Some of the people, too, had clothed themselves in the sacred garments of
> their devil-worship, which in their heathen darkness they would have deemed
> it fatal to put on . . . the whole village, consisting of about 180 persons, were
> in regular attendance upon the means of grace. They crowded into the
> prayer-house with more alacrity than order, and seemed delighted at the
> changes that had taken place.
>
> (Pettitt 1851: 240–41)

Such images of multitudes *converging* into a room, garden or location, and that of the centre of a circle are central to the missionary narrative. Missionary narratives almost always highlight moments when natives, who are otherwise scattered in a wild diffusion, come together to listen to the Gospel. This convergence, which represents the *Concordia discors*, constitutes a major feature of every missionary narrative. In sharp contrast to the early moments when the narrative describes chaotic bazaars, streets or varied religious processes, the final moments of the narrative focus on *ordered* crowds. What is also important is to note that in the *Concordia discors* there is only one *activity*: a Christian prayer, and no variation. That is, we have moved from the details of (Hindu) variety to a more ordered generality: Christian faith.

The missionary narrative opens, as noted before, with the rhetoric of detail, providing information about specific sites of missionary work. Having described rural, pagan populations and landscapes, the account ensures that the reader is made aware of the changes wrought in these areas. For this purpose, missionary accounts take recourse to details of another sort: an enumeration of mission schools, converts, clergymen, arranged, most often, in tabulated form and district-wise. In fact an instruction manual for missionaries, *Instructions for Missionaries to the West-India Islands* (1795) specifies this numerical imperative:

> You must specify, distinctly and clearly, what number of negroes have been baptized, instructed and made real converts; what numbers of children are in your school, and what progress they have made in their reading . . . how many hours are employed each day in teaching the children.
>
> (Anon. 1795: 13)

James Hough (1832: 133), likewise, recommends that all missionaries keep 'journals of their proceedings . . . to possess records of their past trials and successes'. We therefore see missionary narratives carrying detailed numbers of missionaries, catechists, schools and students in India (Pettitt 1851: 8; *DR* 32 [1852]: 397, 399, 400, 403; Mullens 1854: 2–3).

George Pettitt, like other missionaries, visualizes Christianity in India as the topos of an enclosed garden. He first lists the advantages that the natives had obtained as a result of conversion: 'The comparative order, cleanliness and prosperity which some of the congregations had attained in consequence of Christian instruction' (Pettitt 1851: 23). Later, developing this point, he writes:

> A *betel-tope*, or plantation, has often presented itself to my mind, as illustrating reason of that admixture of the evil with the good in the Christian Church, which, though all lament, none can preclude. This *tope* is a spot enclosed by a slight hedge, and filled apparently with nothing but *agatti* plants . . . growing near enough to each other to form, by their intermingled branches, a continuous and pleasant shade; but, on closer inspection you will find interspersed everywhere among them, planted in the same soil, and fed by the same water, another plant, too delicate and tender to bear by itself the scorching rays of

the sun . . . so much more valued is this tender plant, that when it is gathered in, the *agatti* which defended it, is sold for a trifling price . . . May it not be that, in the Church of Christ, merely nominal Christians are allowed to mingle with the genuine child of God, and to partake with him of all the means of grace, in order that he may be screened from a severity of persecution, which would otherwise prove too much for his tender faith to bear?

(Pettitt 1851: 68)

The enclosed garden, the references to variety and denominations, the organized Church that mingles and accommodates others constitute a discourse that merges the moral, horticultural and the theological. A little further into the narrative Pettitt returns to this mode of speaking about India:

The sand [the reference is to the dry landscape of Tinnevelly], however, is unfruitful, only for want of water; for my brother Missionary, the Rev. J. Thomas, by multiplying and using wells in the Meignyanapuram station formed by himself, has turned a portion of one of the most sandy deserts I ever saw into an oasis, where everything grows abundantly.

(Pettitt 1851: 70)

Later, Pettitt returns to this same spot to describe in greater detail the theological and horticultural improvements of the region with terms like 'oasis', 'fruitfulness', 'comfort' and detailed accounts of the fruits and trees (Pettitt 1851: 326–27). David Bogue (1797) speaks of Christianity as enabling a breakdown of differences among Hindus. In a sermon preached at the formation of the London Missionary Society, Bogue states: 'The different casts [*sic*] into which the inhabitants of India have been divided, have been considered by many, as presenting a state of society, which must effectively hinder their conversion'. But this, he suggests, is hardly a problem, for conversion would destroy such barriers (Bogue 1797: 187, 189–90). John Wilson (1844: 253) suggests that Christianity 'marks the boundary which separates the civilized from the barbarous or semi-barbarous parts of the world', and once the boundary is 'extended', the 'country included within its limits may be considered as redeemed'. William Clarkson (1851: 55) declares: '[Indians] separated from each other for ages by human laws, they are brought together by the Divine law of love'. Clarkson paints a truly picturesque 'scene' to describe missionary work:

We [the missionaries and native preachers] met, perhaps in our tent, – or perhaps under a tree. In scenes like these there is an indescribable interest. Blessed were the hours when we sat together, conversing on these subjects, and praying beneath the canopy of heaven, strengthening each other's hearts, and laying down our plans of labour for the following day.

(Clarkson 1851: 66)

Similar images of breaking barriers and unification can be seen in many missionary narratives (Duff 1839: 33; Clarkson 1851: 135; Mullens 1854: 3; *FM* 16 [NS] [1877]: 314).

The missionary's description of a peaceful Christian Indian gathering is an example of the *Concordia discors* where the varied multitudes have been organized through the power of preaching into a quiet mass. The site of native gathering that is described here is achieved through the missionary's labour which brings together multitudes. Mass, service, prayers are all discussed in substantial detail in English missionary tracts. Mullens (1854: 25) describes large numbers of natives in passive postures of acceptance of Christianity: 'congregations of all classes amounting sometimes to five hundred persons, listened to their addresses with solemn stillness'. He concludes his tract with an account of how Christians of various denominations have come together in the cause of evangelizing India. His last two paragraphs are full of references to the 'union' of various Christians in this effort. He concludes with the confident assertion that 'numerous' temple cars, and 'all' people (his terms) will eventually become Christian (Mullens 1854: 189–91). This emphasis on a large group of natives sitting in passive attention before the English preacher is a central image in missionary writing.

Henry Martyn (1851: 330, 336) finds such an attentive audience attractive. An account of a mission school in Benares published for English boys and girls back in England describes the settings in picturesque terms:

> Though situated in the midst of a large city . . . is yet standing in the centre of a little field, covered with grass, well sprinkled over with trees (one or two laden with fruit), and all clothed with the richest foliage. And then, if you came at the right time, you might see what I have often seen – a group of travellers comfortably encamped at the back of the school . . . their oxen . . . a half-dozen camels . . . the rural aspect of the scene.
>
> (*JMH* 29 [NS] [1857]: 69)

A moral picturesque is indicated in this description of the rural idyll that has, at its narrative logos, the mission school. Later the narrator goes on to describe the school's classrooms and teaching in detail (*JMH* 29 [NS] [1857]: 70–73), thus mapping a site of regulated native convergence as a site of benevolence, progress and Christian goodness. George Pettitt (1851: 281) describes how 'all [natives] listened attentively' when he argued a theological point with an unbeliever. Later he describes another 'solemn and impressive' occasion. The room, he mentions, was 'crowded with persons'. These natives, he emphasizes, 'behaved with great decorum' and he had 'never see[n] the people so quite and attentive before'. At his farewell dinner, Pettitt is pleased to observe that the native converts and church workers had seated themselves in order: '[they had] arranged themselves in order upon the mats . . . not according to their *caste*, but according to their *rank in the mission*' (Pettitt 1851: 336, 469, emphasis in original). Pettitt's triumphant description and emphasis suggests a whole new ordering – from the 'chaos' of native rituals and processions to the systematic Christian order within the mission. This emphasis on rank is significant, because handbooks to missionaries underscored the need to follow orders. James Hough (1832: 145) writes: 'subordination is the strength, the vital spirit, of any association of men united together for any definite purpose'. Alexander Duff (1839: 260) uses vitalist imagery to describe the ruins of Hinduism, arguing that it has been 'animated' into 'a mould' that shows 'spontaneous growth'. In the space of one paragraph, Duff (1839: 306–08) uses the terms 'propagate', 'flourish', 'vitality' and their cognates over half-a-dozen times to describe evangelical work, all proposing the intrinsic link between life, botany, evangelicalism and 'improvement'. Instead of divisive Hinduism we now have what a review essay describes as 'the whole and universal nature of man' (*Christian Remembrancer* 8 [1844]: 26). The detail has been smoothed over into a universal Christian organism ('vital', as the *OED* informs us, is a term used to describe the principle manifested by living things, especially of plants or vegetative organisms especially in the nineteenth century; see Reill (2005) for 'vitalism' and the nineteenth century). An extreme example of such a process of universalization and erasure of detail occurs in William Buyers (1848), who complains that Calcutta is the most 'east Indian' of all Indian cities. The reason, according to Buyers (1848: 51), is that all residents 'even of pure decent [*sic*], imitate the Europeans in so many things, either important or trifling, that neither their habits nor sentiments, are entirely Indian'.

The *Concordia discors* is a carefully cultivated landscape, ordered, bounded, and controlled by the missionary. It is beautiful because it is Christian and (therefore) moral. There are no references to any detail, only the constant emphasis on a universal grand truth of Christian faith. Duff (1839: 36) describes this utopian space in horticultural terms: 'gladsome bowers, – the abodes of peace and righteousness'. And here is William Clarkson (1850) describing such a pastoral picturesque:

> In the rural scenes of wells and watercourses, fields and orchards, and amid the rural operations of sowing and reaping, threshing and fanning, there was no lack of apt illustrations of those grand truths which relate to the regeneration of man ... Oh for labourers in that and similar regions! Oh for labourers!
>
> (Clarkson 1850: 85)

The 'grand truth' is, of course, about a 'universal' like Christianity, as opposed to the 'details' of paganism. The 'grand truth' is precisely what the picturesque mode seeks to achieve by subsuming details into one circle. Clarkson (1850: 97) goes on to detail the 'nucleus' (his term) of what he calls 'a beautiful garden' (the running title on the pages of this section of his narrative). The *Concordia discors* is never better described than in Clarkson's narrative. In the section titled 'The Christian Village', he begins by emphasizing the 'high fortified wall'. The village is 'surrounded by a moat ... a thorny cactus forms its hedge' (Clarkson 1850: 98). He then quotes:

We're a garden, wall'd round
Chosen, and made peculiar ground
A little spot, enclosed by grace,
Out of the world's wild wilderness!
(Clarkson 1850: 98)

The image indicates the Christian nature of the garden or settlement. Inside, the church – the 'centre of Gospel light' – causes '"streams" to flow "in the desert"'. The people inside constitute a 'band' (Clarkson 1850: 99). But what makes this a true *Concordia discors* is the presence of Hindu converts within the circle. This section, titled 'Hindu Converts, Dwellers in "The Beautiful Garden"', lists the people living within the commune's walls. Interestingly, these converts are termed 'colonists' by Clarkson (1850: 103–13, 114). This description of the *Concordia discors* of a Christian garden is, incidentally, the *largest* section of Clarkson's narrative, and suggests the crucial role of such a 'structure'. It is also important to read this concluding description against Clarkson's *opening* landscape image (already quoted above): 'in the streets of Surat, in the seventeenth century, were to be seen, in strange confusion, Europeans and Asiatics' (Clarkson 1850: 1). Clarkson's narrative has moved from the chaos of a non-Christian space to a controlled, unified Christian *Concordia discors*. His emphasis on cultivation of the moral garden is a moral picturesque (it is surely no coincidence that William Gilpin (1796), the chief theorist of the picturesque, also emphasizes the horticultural element of the poor in his discussion of fertile, well-groomed and highly productive vegetable gardens of poor houses in his *Account of a New Poor House*, 1796: 5, 6, 13). John Kaye (1859: 469) describes 'native Christianity' as 'patches of greenery'. Sarah Tucker describes the construction of such a Christian *Concordia discors* in another village. The 'Native Philanthropic Society', she writes, had as one of its 'principal objects' the 'purchase of land for Christian villages, where the converts might be sheltered . . . and brought more within the reach of regular instruction and superintendence'. She calls them 'cities of refuge', where 'the whole of the inhabitants are under Christian instruction', and their 'miserable, straggling huts' are pulled down and rebuilt 'in regular order' (Tucker 1842–43, 2: 90–91). In Tucker's description several aspects of the missionary picturesque come together: an aesthetic of poverty where the huts are cause for reconstruction, the creation of special, regulated spaces separated from the rest of the neighbourhood, the emphasis on Christian 'instruction' and the imposition of order. This 'city of refuge' is a Christian *Concordia discors* within heathen India, where the converts are protected from 'the violence and persecution of their heathen neighbours', as Tucker puts it (1842–43, 2: 90). Buyers (1848) concludes his massive tract with a poem praising missionary labour in which he writes:

Then, gladly assembling
The swarthy tribes shall raise
Messiah's glorious standard,
And joyful shout his praise
(Buyers 1848: 548)

The image of an orderly assembly of Indians – as opposed to the chaotic crowds of Jagannath – is a tolerable, even pleasing sight. Whitelaw Ainslie (1835: 128) explains, towards the close of his work, the process of evangelization almost entirely in horticultural images when he stated: 'others . . . brought rapidly into the brightness of day, – all, all for some happy purpose, planned, ordered, and arranged, with as much precision as that by which the bud is expanded into the flower'. A mission school, writes Pettitt (1851: 419), now 'presented a far more pleasant sight than the native bazaar that occupied it before'. Duff (1839: 600) speaks of the 'harvest of redeemed souls' towards the end of his work. A later travel essay on Lucknow links this moral and physical improvement of India:

> The capital itself, once the seat of Eastern misrule and selfish luxury . . . henceforth we trust, if we do our duty, and God's blessing rests upon us, to be gradually leavened by Christian civilization – is almost girt by a belt of park-like country.
>
> (*MM* 4 [1861]: 155)

Sarah Tucker, who had earlier described poor, fainting girls, maps the consequences of missionary labour in the fates of the same girls:

> Miserable indeed is the outward condition of many of these poor girls; and yet, happy are they, if they learn, as we hope some of them do, the way to obtain true riches, gold tried in the fire, and raiment made white in the blood of the lamb.
>
> (Tucker 1842–43, 1: 78)

Following the biblical theme of poverty on earth and subsequent riches in heaven, Tucker suggests that even if no visible change has been wrought in their material conditions, their souls have been redeemed, a curious twist of the civic philanthropic mission. In another instance, she underscores the poverty of an old woman, in 'worn and shabby cloth' but who has, in reality, been transformed: 'whose placid thoughtful countenance is a fit index of the spirit of peace and holiness that dwells within' (Tucker 1842–43, 2: 95). In both these passages Tucker, unable to highlight any transformation in the material conditions of the natives, quickly shifts focus to 'inner' wealth and peace. I have already cited Sarah Tucker's description of the excessive 'number' and 'variety' of Hindu processions, whose crowds appear frightening, disordered and are distinctly unChristian (Tucker 1842–43, 1: 52–54). Immediately after this description of a variegated and pagan India, Tucker focuses on a different 'scene'. Addressing herself in the third person, she writes:

> She heard the sound of the bell from the little Mission chapel at the end of the garden, and turning around, she saw it lighted up . . . Her spirit was comforted and encouraged as she watched a few quietly going in one by

one . . . the service was beginning, and prayer . . . which, had no Missionary ever visited Southern India, would have been shouting in the temple of the idol.

(Tucker 1842–43, 1: 55–56)

Tucker (1842–43, 1: 80) also cites a woman who was similarly impressed by native girls – 'above 500' in number – sitting in rows, presenting a 'striking sight'. In his account of the London Missionary Society, Horne (1894: 284) had written of a 'pastoral superintendence'. In both these cases noisy crowds are transformed into quiet worshippers. The natives go in 'quietly one by one' and sing, where otherwise they would have been 'shouting'. There are no milling crowds, only rows of girls. The missionary has achieved order in variety and quietude in noise. The emphasis on uniformity, cultivation and what Teltscher (1997: 78) identified as 'spiritual control' is clear in these passages.[22] In the case of Pettitt, Mullens and Clarkson, the image of convergence, encirclement and boundedness is central to the idea of a moral picturesque.

The missionary picturesque thus works with a 'cultural fable' that generates several related moves. It explores India's primitivism in terms of its variety and poverty, with both generating a particular aesthetic – of the civic picturesque, while casting it in horticultural and botanist terms. It then generates a husbandry narrative, mapping India as a field of labour, producing 'designs' based on 'models of piety', for the missionary labourer to work with. This Christian georgic works towards a plan of unifying India. In the final 'moment' the 'cultural fable' has achieved its most important effect and transformation: India is now a *Concordia discors* where variations have been elided, uniformity imposed, and a beautiful moral and physical landscape created through Christian rejuvenation.

5 The sporting luxuriant, 1850–1920

Reviewing Lord Valentia's 1809 India and Asia travelogue, the *Eclectic Review* complained that the aristocrat traveller had not looked for dangers and exciting things during his sojourn in the Orient (*EcR* 5 [1809]: 690–92). Such a complaint would not have arisen in the latter half of the nineteenth century, when an entire genre grew up around the adventures of Englishmen and women in India: the sporting or *shikar* (hunting) memoir.

Detailed accounts of wildlife had appeared in the writings of the first English travellers in India. Although there are references to hunting in Sir Thomas Roe's journal of 1615–19, and suggestions as to the uses particular animals could be put to (for instance, the deer in William Hunter's essay, *AR* 15 [1772]: 84–91), the sporting memoir emerges only in the nineteenth century. Two of the most popular works in the genre, Thomas Williamson's *Oriental Field Sports* and Daniel Johnson's *Sketches of Field Sports as followed by the Natives of India*, had appeared as early as 1808 and 1822 respectively. George White writing in the 1830s had described hunting grounds in the Himalayan regions (1838: 33–34, 50–51). Other commentators discovered that 'Indian field sports, with their concomitants of hogs, tigers, and nullahs, have been of late years rendered so familiar to stay-at-home travellers' (*BE* 55 [1844]: 329), suggesting a large corpus of hunting narratives.

The sporting memoir effectively emerges as a major genre in the post-1857, post-'Mutiny' period of the new imperialism. A year before the momentous 'Mutiny', commentators declared that 'the problem of governing aliens in religion, language and blood, has been quietly grappled with and triumphantly solved' in India (*FM* 53 [1856]: 92). Despite the tumult of 1857–58, India continued to remain a significant contributor to England's finances – indeed one reviewer pointed out that the loss of the India trade would be a 'serious national calamity' (*QR* 120 [1866]: 201). Lord Dufferin, speaking at the London Chamber of Commerce, underscores the 'enormous benefits conferred upon the people of England' because of the India trade. India, he pointed out, contributed to the welfare of the English people directly: when Russia was unable to supply corn, India sent 600,000 tons of wheat (*BFCJ* 1.5 [1889]: 11). In response to the events of 1857–58, the British now sought to tighten their grip by reorganizing the army, expanding transport and communication facilities and streamlining administration. It was an age when the British experienced a 'sense of vulnerability' in the wake of the armed resistance exhibited by the natives (Metcalf 1998: 160).

In terms of the Indian landscape, much of the terrain had been mapped. After the reorganization of the geographical department of the India Office in 1868 numerous older maps were revised repeatedly to render them more accurate. The country was 'opened up' by the railways, as a commentator put it (*Scottish Geographical Magazine* 7 [1891]: 361). Another suggests that both the railways and the English language moved unhindered through the Indian landscape (*FM* 54 [1856]: 680–84). Marianne Postans believes that the railways would help the traveller see 'enough of the characteristic beauties of the land' and would be a means of taking travellers on picturesque routes (*Sharpe's London Journal* 11 [1850]: 339– 43).[1] Andrew Adams (1867: 63) notes that travel even in the Himalayan regions had become easier with good accommodation. Katherine Elwood (1830, 2: 317– 18) declared the Nilgiris to be a 'terrestrial paradise' with 'the road up the mountains . . . already practicable for palanquins and loaded bullocks'. It was believed that there was no 'stopping the rapid advance of the great locomotive' (*HW* 8 [1853–54]: 440–42). Another commentator predicts that with increased travel facilities, there might soon be 'Indian tourists not by units but by the dozens' (*FM* 53 [1856]: 97). The Himalayan regions, writes a reviewer, are now better known through some 'trust-worthy accounts' (*CaR* 18 [1852]: 72–115). A review of Joseph Hooker's *Himalayan Journals* (1854) puts it this way: 'these and other observers have attacked different points of the Himalayan boundary' (*DUM* 43 [1854]: 671). 'Development' in colonial India went hand in hand with the decrease of unexplored, exotic territory. Even the formidable Himalayas had been 'penetrated' and explored by military personnel, botanists and others. Trains and steam ships on the Ganges altered travel considerably. Explorers such as Alexander Burnes had navigated rivers to gauge their commercial potential (his narrative of the expedition was published in *CE* 11 [1842]: 178–79). Guidebooks from Thomas Cook and John Murray ensured that travellers had access to the newest information on clothing, places, diseases and transport when they set out for India. Through such guidebooks, Inderpal Grewal (1996: 103) argues, 'even the mysterious would become familiar'.[2]

In such a context of well-explored 'civilized' spaces, why does the English traveller turn to the jungles and the Himalayas? My contention is twofold. The events of 1857–58 revealed the cracks in the imperial facade, resulting in a greater drive by the English to demonstrate control. Even the key centres of colonial power – the cantonments and cities – had 'revolted'. In the period of high imperialism, therefore, the English set out to prove themselves by domesticating not only the cities but also the Indian jungles in order to demonstrate control over the wild and the savage. Their accurate knowledge and bravery when dealing with a landscape, one that I term the 'extreme exotic', enables them to survive. The English *shikari* (hunter) experiences pleasure through danger even as he creates his 'territory' within the wilds of India, as he imposes his power over the cruel, cunning tiger. At the same time, he imposes a similar control over the 'wild' native. The extreme exotic, in fact, relies on establishing an equivalence between the wild animal and the native. Joseph Fayrer (1875: 40) quotes one Captain Rogers, who declared that the tiger was a man-eater 'by nature and instinct'. A narrative of bison-hunting described a member of the Bheel tribe as possessing the face of a chimpanzee (*FM* 47 [1853]: 44). Such descriptions of the savage jungle-animal-native are commonplace in the sporting memoir (see, for other examples. W. Campbell 1853: 5, 85, 88; Cumming 1871: 329).

My second contention is that that the extensive documentation and geographical mapping of India generates what Ali Behdad (1994) has presciently identified as a 'disappearing exotic' among 'belated travellers' and a subsequent commodification of land. Adventure itself, notes Patrick Brantlinger (1988: 239), had become a thing of the past in spaces like Africa, forcing the English to turn to romance, dreams and imagination (see also Barrell 2000).

Extending these arguments one can argue that late-nineteenth-century travellers mourned the absence of authentic experience and exploratory adventure because India had already been explored, studied and mapped. There really was no 'fresh' impression or pioneering travel possible in India. The picturesque of Emma Roberts, Thomas and William Daniell, Maria Graham and others had 'covered' India more or less thoroughly, and now the tourist movement had made all spaces equally 'popular'. The *Eclectic Review*'s complaint against Valentia with which I opened this chapter stems from the commonplace feeling of the period that all travelogues seem to be saying the same thing.[3] Reviewing Isabel Savory's sporting memoir, the *Review of Reviews* asks her readers to visit Kashmir before the railways are introduced, thereby 'tarnish[ing] the freshness of the ancient mountains' (*Review of Reviews* 21 [1900]: 158). Frederic Harrison in 'Regrets of a Veteran Traveller' (1897) mourns the increasing tourism (quoted in Brantlinger 1988: 238). 'F.T.P' in his narrative of a sporting expedition near the river Godavari is thrilled that 'much of it [game country] has never been explored and of course not been shot over' (*OSM* 10 [1877]: 141). Fred Markham (1854: 72–73) is certain that 'it would never do to open up these naturally preserved shooting-grounds to the Himalayan public'. Writing the text to accompany Edward Molyneux's paintings, Francis Younghusband states: 'I have known Kashmir since 1887, and ever since I have known it people have said it is getting spoilt . . . The visitor disposed to solitude more frequently encounters his fellow-countrymen'. Younghusband goes on to add how, at one point, the 'sportsman could shoot to his heart's content' without game laws and game licenses (Molyneux and Younghusband 1924: 39, 41). Colonel Tanner of the Indian Survey Department urges:

> I would say go by all means, very soon, before, in fact, all the beautiful trees in the land shall have been converted into Railway sleepers; visit the country before the beautiful camping grounds shaded by trees 500 years old . . . shall have been improved off the slopes of the Himalayas.
>
> (*IF* 17 [1891]: 348)

There is a sense in these comments that the exotic and the picturesque have been eroded because of over-zealous tourists and unrelenting 'development'.[4] The exotic wilds, and the frontier itself, were fast disappearing.

In order to ensure the persistence of the exotic for readers back home, the British traveller had to push the boundaries of the known India. Mrs Handley (1911: 1) expresses boredom with station life and the routine colonial space: 'I found station life very flat when we returned to it – and entirely devoid of verve or even interest'. If the exotic is the 'realization of the fantastic beyond the horizons of the everyday world', as Rousseau and Porter (1990: 15) defined the Enlightenment exotic, the sporting memoir detailed the discovery of such an out-of-the-known exotic in the jungles of India. Brantlinger (1988: 249) notes that 'just at the moment actual frontiers were vanishing, late Victorian and Edwardian occultist literature is filled with metaphors of exploration, emigration, conquest, colonization'. In the face of vanishing frontiers, I suggest, newer frontier experiences had to be found in the jungles in colonial possession. It demanded an experience of something not already available in routine colonial life. The sporting memoir is not necessarily a narrative of discovering new lands, but is definitely about adventures in controlled spaces.

Stilz (2002: 86) argues that without the increased safety and reliability of roads and travel arrangements, Romantic travellers would not have thought of interpreting their experiences as delightful terror. By the 1850s, admittedly, travel arrangements in India had improved considerably. The English had 'laid low the hills, exalt[ed] the valleys and . . . [made] the crooked paths straight', writes Marianne Postans, suggesting a massive mapping of the landscape (*Sharpe's London Journal* 11 [1850]: 343). What is fascinating is that English travellers chose the wilds, with little of these facilities. The response to this increased technological and cartographic conquest and *familiarity* is the search for the 'extreme exotic' landscape. I use the term to indicate both a representational space – the effect of the aesthetic I identify as the 'sporting luxuriant' – and an actual geographical site. If the fantasy-land of the exotic is often 'signposted by danger lights' (Rousseau and Porter 1990: 15), the extreme exotic in an era of geographical familiarity is no fantasy. Indeed, the extreme exotic is marked by a rhetoric of authenticity and highly subjective experience. The extreme exotic is the quest for thrills and dangers in a landscape that is harsh, threatening and inconvenient. It *represents* the dangers of particular encounters even as it searches the landscape for potential sites of such dangers. It is both an attitude and a strategy of exploration.

The extreme exotic is also an interesting counterpoint to the eighteenth-century colonial sublime's negotiations with the landscape. Where, during the earlier era, English travellers found themselves threatened by the landscape and sought safer spots of refuge, cultivation and comfort (as argued in Chapter 3), by the end of the nineteenth century we have English travellers deliberately leaving cultivated spots behind in search of the untamed and the dangerous. In the age of the imperial sublime, floods, thunderstorms and other Indian natural phenomena had generated terror. English travellers now turn to plant and animal life – overgrown jungles, man-eating tigers – as a source of threat that simultaneously offers opportunities of control and pleasure. Further, if the sublime posited and depicted the human as insignificant in the face of vast landscapes, the luxuriant presents the English 'embedded' in and battling dense growths and harsh mountain peaks, before emerging triumphant.

This resulted in the exploration of the wilds, forested areas of India as never before.[5] It might also be seen as a curious parallel to the increasing emphasis on gardening and horticulture in British India (demonstrated by the dozens of gardening manuals, essays in dedicated journals and horticultural tracts that appeared during the last three decades of the nineteenth century).[6] In both cases the aim, I believe, is to domesticate and control Indian vegetation. If the gardening manual proposed neatly ordered beds of flowers and fences, the sporting memoir depicted modes of conquest of the unmapped and the dangerous. Thus Markham (1854: 148–49, 200) makes it a point to underscore the greater beauty of the wild mountains over that of gardens: 'no flower-enamelled mead . . . was ever painted by poet in flowing rhymes, that could equal the gorgeous beauty of this vale of flowers'.

Contemporaneous with the conservationist and forestry movements of the period, when anxiety was expressed over deforestation and the destructive agricultural practices of nomadic and other tribes, the search for the 'extreme exotic' resulted in tours in the Himalayas and other regions in search of game and a new species of colonial traveller emerged: the sporting English person.[7] In 1871, James Forsyth captured this search for new experiences, tribes and frontiers:

> Our early administrators were too fully occupied with the work of restoring prosperity in the open country to have much time to spare for the Gond and his wildernesses; and thus we find that the interior of their country remained an almost unexplored mystery up to a very recent period.
>
> (Forsyth 1996 [1871]: 12–13)

The sporting memoir captures the hunting, mountaineering, exploratory experiences of Englishmen and women. In order to do so it adapted the conventions of triumphal spectacles of exploration, discovery, conquest and power from the Victorian ethos itself. Brantlinger's (1988) influential account sums up the age's desire for spectacle and adventure thus:

> The great [Victorian] explorers' writings are nonfictional quest romances in which the hero-authors struggle through enchanted, bedeviled lands towards an ostensible goal . . . The humble but heroic authors move from adventure to adventure where there are no other characters of equal stature, only demonic savages.
>
> (Brantlinger 1988: 180–81)

Brantlinger here describes not only the exploration-discovery narrative but also the sporting memoir. The sporting memoir is closely aligned with the exploration narrative in terms of the rhetoric of heroism, suffering, harsh landscapes and triumph. In fact, by 1864, adventure was listed as the primary reason for travel in the Himalayan regions (*BQR* 39 [1864]: 121), with one commentator declaring: 'it would, of course, be quite out of all rule to visit India and not to join in a tiger hunt' (*DUM* 43 [1854]: 673). A reviewer of C.J.C. Davidson's *Diary of Travels and*

Adventures in Upper India (1843) castigates him for focusing less on the hunting of the tigers and more on food, thereby suggesting a demand for adventure narratives (*BE* 55 [1844]: 329). J.H. Stocqueller (1845: 97) in his handbook underscores the attraction of the hunt that India affords: 'The sports and pastimes peculiar to the country (hunting, shooting, racing, & c) are accessible to him upon a scale of magnificence and affluence unknown to the English sportsman'.

Extracts from sporting memoirs, shorter narratives of *shikar* expeditions and reviews of these appeared in specialized journals like *Indian Forester*, and literary-cultural periodicals. Some of these narratives even became the subject of poetry, as illustrated by works like 'Tales of the Tinkers', which uses every single stereo-type and image from the sporting memoir (*OSM* 1, 1–2 [1828]: 13–21, 57–64). Since there were few spaces left for discovery, and a whole new iconography of imperial triumph was needed, the jungles presented an Indian alternative to the Nile, lakes or the mountain peaks of Africa. As in the case of the African explorers, the English hunter toils in the landscape and triumphs. The difference was of course in the structures of exploration and the hunt.

The sporting memoir is a highly personal narrative. It details the hunter's emotional, physical, and mental states during the hunt, the experience of 'roughing it' in the wilds, the encounters with tigers and other animals, the killing of the animals, and the extremely dangerous situations they found themselves in. Thus Donald MacIntyre (1891: 352) advises those who hoped to be 'successful in Himalayan sport' to be prepared for 'a good deal of trouble, toil, and frequent disappointment'. Markham (1854: 69) warns: 'whoever intends to go out burret shooting, determined to follow it up to a successful result, must expect to toil in no trifling degree'. Almost every one of the narratives also carries similar advice on various aspects of sporting life: from the choice of tents and firearms to the partic-ular characteristics of game animals.

The hunt, as critics have demonstrated, played a major role in the imperial 'performances' in the colony. It was, along with sports like polo, a means of domes-ticating the colonial landscape and life forms, and a means of constructing ideals of masculinity and Englishness (J.M. MacKenzie 1987, 1988; Mangan 1992; Emel 1998; McDevitt 2004). Pablo Mukherjee (2005: 925–26), following Eric Hobsbawm, has argued that Victorian literature on hunting – incidentally contemporaneous with accounts of the *shikar* in India – was about inventing tradi-tions. It was also a mechanism of class-differentiation where the right to preserve and hunt game identified the sportsman as belonging to a particular social group (J.M. MacKenzie 1988: 16; McKenzie 2000). Local rajas provided the support and the infrastructure. W.H. Sleeman (1995, 1: 286) thus mentions how he went to shoot in the Raja of Dutiya's 'large preserves'. It thus enabled a linkage between the sporting English person and the native raja.

The sporting memoir appropriated the rhetoric of sportsmanship, courage and discipline (Pandian 2001). The *shikar* often combined the image of the macho white hunter and the benevolent protector of other animals, and merged sport with conservation (Rangarajan 1996). Thus E.P. Stebbing (1920: xii, 241–94), writing in the early decades of the twentieth century, expresses anxieties about the 'ever-increasing diminution in the numbers of game animals', and concluded his work with a detailed section on 'game protection and the provision of sanctuaries for the preservation of the Indian fauna'. Debates in the pages of *Indian Forester* often focused on the commercial importance of the forests, the destruction due to the development and expansion of railways and the climatic problems that may arise if the forest cover is lost.[8] William Schlich (1904) and others produced manuals of forestry in which the utility and utilization of forests were discussed.[9]

Julius Jeffreys (1858: 179) writing about the need for recreation for the English soldier in India advocates games and 'full play', arguing that these activities would 'supply [the British army] with mighty commanders'. Reviewing Arthur Brinckman's *Rifle in Cashmere* (1862), the reviewer compares the hunt with military action:

> All who enjoy a good day's march over mountain and through woodland, relieved every now and then by a clever piece of stalking and a sportsmanlike rifle-shot, and can relish the excitement of outpost warfare . . . will read these pages with intense relish.
>
> (*DUM* 60 [1862]: 349)

Major Dalbiac declared that pig-sticking ensured the development of 'those attributes so necessary for every soldier': 'a firm seat, a light hand, a good eye for the country, a bold heart, and a cool head' (*English Illustrated Magazine*, 22 [1899]: 87–92). 'Hunters of the large game of India's magnificent forests', writes Henry Shakespear (1862: 2), 'keep[s] them [the young British boys serving in India] out of a thousand temptations and injurious pursuits'. Walter Campbell's (1853: 7) description links class, the military role and the hunter: 'aristocratic cast of his features, the proud glance of his eye, and his erect military carriage, declared at once the gentleman, the soldier, and the daring sportsman'. Robert Baden-Powell went so far as to declare in 1920:

> If polo and pig-sticking have not altered the history of British India, they have at any rate altered the lives and careers of many young officers . . . They have complete driven out from the British subaltern the drinking and betting habits of the former generation, and have given him in place of these a healthy exercise which also has its moral attributes in playing the game unselfishly.
>
> (Baden-Powell 1920: 31)

What emerges from these narratives is the intrinsic link between hunting and colonial cultures of masculinity and domination. The hunt helped the creation of soldier-like qualities, as Major Dalbiac's statement suggests. Thus, the battle against the elements and wild animals in India was a preparation for other battles. In the colonial context the hunt was another means of asserting colonial, racial, masculine control. H.Z. Darrah (1898: 412) therefore separates himself from the feminine through a recourse to the hunt: 'leaving my wife to the congenial task of putting up curtains, buying carpets, hangings, etc., I started on the 31st of October . . . to shoot a stag'. Walter Campbell (1853: 296) describes hunting as a 'sport so ill-suited to her sex'. An anecdote about a tiger shoot underscores the age of the *shikaris*: 'my friend 18 and I 14 years', in what is obviously a narrative of empire boys and their masculinity (*OSM* 10 [1877]: 91–92). R.S.S. Baden-Powell was to write in his *Scouting for Boys* (1908):

> The 'trappers' of North America, hunters of Central Africa, the British pioneers, explorers, and missionaries over Asia and all the wild parts of the world, the bushmen and drovers of Australia, the constabulary of North-West Canada and of South Africa – all are peace scouts, real men in every sense of the word, and thoroughly up on scout craft, i.e. they understand living out in the jungles, and they can find their way anywhere, are able to read meaning from the smallest signs and foot-tracks; they know how to look after their health when far away from any doctors, are strong and plucky, and ready to face any danger, and always keen to help each other. They are accustomed to take their lives in their hands, and to fling them down without hesitation if they can help their country by doing so.
>
> (quoted in Emel 1998: 103–04)

Baden-Powell's description links sacrifice, codes of conduct, patriotism, talents and pioneer-masculinity. By arguing that these talents help the country, Baden-Powell explicitly linked the pioneer hunter and the boy scout with the colonial enterprise.[10]

In the *shikar* narratives, the hunter-author's rhetoric generates a discourse of colonial conquest. These rhetorical structures, I shall demonstrate, functioned within an aesthetic mode in their description of Indian landscape, the hunt and the hunter's experiences. It is in this context of a disappearing exotic, excessive tourism, the sense of vulnerability and the desire to reassert colonial control (after 1857) that the picturesque is revived in the latter half of the nineteenth century.[11] The search for picturesque scenes in an era of greater imperial control, mapped terrain and improved transport facilities called for and resulted in a new version of the aesthetic. This aesthetic, which constructed the extreme exotic of jungles, tigers and near-death experiences, constitutes what I term the 'sporting luxuriant'. The luxuriant, as Chloe Chard (1999: 200–01) has pointed out in the case of the Grand Tour, combines the languorously beautiful with the terrifying sublime. Every single sporting narrative from the 1850–1940 period, *without exception*, uses the term 'luxuriant' several times over to describe the vegetation of jungles, hillsides and valleys. I am using the term with an additional spin on it. 'Luxuriant' here refers to not only the sense of wealthy, beautiful vegetation but also the sense of lurking danger that every hunter mentions in conjunction with the scenery.

Danger is as integral to the luxuriant as the passively beautiful. What the English traveller seeks is an escape from the routine of everyday life, and therefore embarks on a quest for difficulty. A colonial officer advises:

when bile and nervousness become too intolerable . . . get leave of absence, and ride into the jungle. A good burst after a bear clears off a year's bile in twenty minutes, and a roaring charge, that leaves you in doubt whether you are standing on your head or your heels, frightens out all the nervousness; and in six weeks you may go home quit of both.

(*FM* 46 [1852]: 385)

The luxuriant is an aesthetic of challenges, dangers and eventual conquest. It appropriates and modifies a particular form of the picturesque visible in the last decades of the nineteenth century. Malcolm Andrews (1999: 192) writing about the 'picturing' techniques of Monet in the 1890s detects a change in landscape representations. In the first instance, the land and its sights are just visual fields to be looked at – it is *landscape*. Later, we have a 'complex of sensations, of light, colour, smell, sounds, tactile experience' – it is now *environment*. It moves between passive beauty and terrifying sublimity even as, in the colonial context of British India, the landscape shifts between beautiful 'scenery' to be viewed and/or painted and a threatening 'environment' to be lived in. The sporting luxuriant is the aesthetic that describes and transforms passive, beautiful landscapes (i.e. artistic subjects) – into life-threatening environments where danger is experienced. It is a picturesque aesthetic that treats the landscape as a site of pain and potential heroism before declaring it a conquered space. In effect, it moves from sights to sites.

The sporting luxuriant serves a *transformative* function. In its inaugural moment it first details a passive picturesque, a landscape of great scenic plenty and beauty. The passive picturesque, the narratives emphasize, conceals wild, dangerous and life-threatening life forms *within* the scenic landscape. Together the picturesque's passivity and potential threat open up the sporting luxuriant's transformative function. In the second moment, the picturesque begins to modulate into a site of danger through the aesthetics of risk. Such a siting of threat or danger then makes it imperative that the Englishman (or, occasionally, woman) encounter the danger and triumph over it. In the final moment of the luxuriant narrative the colonial has acquired a trophy of the threat, achieved a degree of control – physical, epistemological and rhetorical – over the Indian wilds. This personal saga of suffering and success constitutes the sporting narrative. My interest is less in the ethos of masculinity that evolves within the sporting narrative than in the aesthetic aspects of the genre. Like the earlier chapters, this one too demonstrates how aesthetics enabled the colonial narrative's transformation of India.

The passive picturesque

In the sporting memoir details of the actual hunt are always preceded by a narrative about the country that approximates to the picturesque conventions of landscape description.[12] This picturesque description first details a passive, 'harmless' Indian picturesque consisting of villages, people and countryside, which then merges with a narrative of luxuriant vegetation, rugged topography and wildness. 'Scenes' and 'sights' are described in substantial detail. The first moment of this picturesque is characterized by a rhetoric of sensory gratification. The Englishman, armed and accompanied by native beaters and servants, takes in the sights, sounds and smells of Indian wild spaces. James Forsyth (1996: 15) states that his aim is to 'present . . . the lighter and more picturesque aspects of a country'. James Inglis writing in 1892 begins by describing a landscape of multi-sensory pleasures:

> To lie on the river-bank and watch the animation and picturesque grouping in the broad shallow of the troubled stream below, as the great elephants gambol in the cooling pool and splash their heated heaving sides with spurts and dashes of water from the river, is a sight that would gladden an artist's heart.
>
> (Inglis 1892: 3)

Inglis (1892: 3) then goes on to list the various sights to be met in 'the dear old happy hunting-grounds of a good mofussil district in India'. Here Inglis focuses on the visual pleasure that India offers, though the reference to 'heated' sides suggests other senses such as the tactile. The reference to a relaxed mode of *watching* animal life suggests leisure and recreation. When he concludes with a reference to the 'artist's heart', he has transformed the sight into the subject matter of artistic representation – a characteristic mode of the picturesque aesthetic. Preceding his description of a tiger hunt, Inglis paints the picture of 'gaiety and animation', with elephants, native beaters, English hunters all setting forth, presenting a 'fine sight'. It is an extremely visual narrative, with serial descriptions of dew 'glistening', 'pearly drops', 'glittering sparkling showers', 'bobbing' heads of elephants and 'glittering kookries' in the hands of native servants. Inglis underscores the absolute passivity of the picturesque: 'All over the vast plain there is a dew-bespangled mead. All over the vast plain there is a soft diffused radiance – a fresh brightness, an exuberance of life and colour – and the heart of the hunter is glad' (Inglis 1892: 63, 64).

The auditory picturesque is emphasized through details of the 'crowing' of the black partridge, the 'calling' of quails, the 'snatches of songs', 'gay repartee and banter'. And the tactile is also a contributor to the luxuriant's sensory pleasures: '[Elephants] here and there plucking down a succulent bunch of juicy reed tops, swishing it against their might sides, and then slowly crunching it up with evident satisfaction and gout [*sic*]' (Inglis 1892: 64).

In an earlier work, *Sport and Work on the Nepaul Frontier* – which he published under a pseudonym, 'Maori' – Inglis speaks of a land that is the 'perfect picture of orderly thrift, careful management, and neat, scientific, and elaborate farming' (Maori 1878: 9). Another hunter-sportsman, H.Z. Darrah, writes:

> My tent was pitched in a spot very like England in its surroundings. In front a low quick hedge separated the patch of grass on which the tent stood from a field of growing winter wheat. To the left was a green lane between two hedgerows, and all about fine trees were dotted.
>
> (Darrah 1898: 415)

Immediately afterwards Darrah (1898: 416) describes 'pleasant day[s]' and 'lovely panorama[s]'. A review essay of the period described places and people in the Sikkim-Darjeeling regions as 'very picturesque' (*BQR* 39 [1864]: 127). Isabel Savory (1900: 118–19) describes 'the isolation of those magnificent wilds' before going on to state: 'the higher we climbed, the more beautiful was the scenery'. Markham's narrative underscores the beautiful scenery several times before details of the hunt (Markham 1854: 6, 9, 15, 18, 46, 52). Walter Campbell (1853: 6) describes the 'pretty little cottages' 'scattered irregularly' over the hills in Ootacamund. (The 'irregular', one recalls, was a central feature of the eighteenth-century picturesque.) Campbell follows up his description of 'pretty little cottages' with the description of a valley:

> Clothed with the richest herbiage, flanked by stupendous mountains, the sides of which were intersected with numerous and well-wooded ravines. It was a glorious sight, and one to inspire a poet or a painter, independently of the feelings which warmed the blood of the sportsmen . . . The higher hills were still shrouded in mist, whilst the bosom of the valley was flooded with a deluge of light . . . The armed beaters . . . were scattered about in picturesque groups.
>
> (W. Campbell 1853: 11)

Images of Indian villages and the countryside picturesque thickly populate every sporting narrative (W. Campbell 1853: 205; Cumming 1871: 55; Inglis 1892: 62; Stebbing 1920: vii).

The hills and mountains, which constitute the major topographies of nine-teenth-century sporting narratives, acquire very different connotations in the Victorian period. As Elaine Freedgood (2000: 101) has demonstrated, geologists, aestheticians, showmen all represented mountains as useful in their beauty, geological-mineralogical utility, and their challenge as objects of study. Mountaineering memoirs – a genre that peaks in the 1840–1900 period – contrib-uted to this aura around mountains. Hereford Brooke George, writing in the first edition of the *Alpine Journal*, declared that the 'climbing spirit' was

> A form of restless energy, that love of action for its own sake, of exploring the earth and subduing it, which has made England the great colonizer of the world, and has led individual Englishmen to penetrate the wildest resources of every continent.
>
> (quoted in Freedgood 2000: 126)

Mountaineering, conquest and imperialism are clearly linked in George's comment.

In these descriptions picturesque animals, plants and people populate the land-scape of sensory gratification. This is the first moment of the passive picturesque where the English *shikari* perceives a landscape of quiet repose. It is interesting to note that the English traveller suggests the landscape to be worthy of an artist:

everything is picturesque. Further, the emphasis on sensory gratification is very clear: sights, sounds and smells are catalogued as sources of pleasure in each one of the sporting memoirs. The sporting luxuriant, I argue following Malcolm Andrews, moves from 'landscape' to 'environment'. The shift is from the passive picturesque of a visually arresting but distant native 'scene' or 'landscape'. The same 'scene' becomes the setting for a very *intimate* experience – the hunt, where the English hunter engages with the various elements of the scene (the vegetation, the terrain, the animals, the sounds of the prey, and others). In fact the picturesque becomes a luxuriant in this movement when English hunters have to negotiate with the various elements that are now less 'scenes' than immediate settings for their acts. It is also significant to the sporting luxuriant that the visual and auditory pleasure of the passive picturesque merges into the pleasure of gun-smoke and the thrill of bloody killings. The hunt transforms the passive picturesque into something totally different, as we shall see.

This scenic landscape is not what the *shikari* seeks. From the picturesque scenes viewed and/or painted by Thomas and William Daniell or Emma Roberts, we now have the English hunter 'entering' into the picturesque to discover something predatorial and dangerous. Beneath the picturesque lurks danger – which in fact is the destination of the English hunter. All sporting narratives exhibit a combination of passive beauty with terrifying grandeur, the 'scenery' of repose with the potential for dangerous action. With this, the second moment, the passive picturesque begins to modulate into something else entirely. It moves from an object of passive consumption (viewing) to a space of experience.

Crucial to this sporting luxuriant is the element of what Chard (1999: 226) terms 'framed isolation'. English hunters deliberately seek out spots and sights that are radically distinct and distant from their everyday life. Indeed, integral to the sporting memoir is the emphasis on the distance from 'civilization', the barracks, and other humans. Derived from the nineteenth-century tourist register, the English hunter in the Indian wilds sets out to seek isolated areas, undisturbed by human settlements. The extreme exotic is drawn from such a perspective. As early as the 1830s, George White (1838: 50) had described the 'dismal solitudes' of the hill-districts. James Inglis opens his *Sport and Work on the Nepaul Frontier* with an emphasis on his location: 'the villages and jungles on the far off frontiers of Nepaul' (Maori 1878: vi). In his opening chapter he describes a landscape where things are radically different. Difference, difficulty and danger are central to the rhetoric of the extreme exotic, even in the age of high imperialism. Indeed, Stebbing (1920: vii) mourns the fact that the jungles of India were now 'easy of access', thereby suggesting a loss of exclusivity and solitude. A kind of frontier narrative, the sporting memoir seeks to expand the boundaries of the familiar, to exceed it by exploring the unknown. The emphasis on the strange, the new, the isolated and the eerie contribute to this aspect of the sporting memoir.

One territory, writes Inglis, has 'strange tribes', and is populated by 'strange wild animals' that 'dispute with these aborigines the possession of the gloomy jungle solitudes' (Maori 1878: 1). Inglis is clearly painting an unfriendly and difficult land here. In his later work Inglis (1892: 2) once again speaks of 'jungle solitudes'. Another speaks of the peace of the jungle, away from the 'busy haunts of men' (*QSM* 10, 111 [1877]: 71). A narrative about bear hunting in India describes the Deccan as 'little disturbed by man' (*FM* 46 [1852]: 373, 375). Walter Campbell (1853: 288) mentions his sentimental solitudes and rude excitements. Isabel Savory's (1900: 128) description of her feelings when she arrives at the top of a mountain are illustrative: 'The intoxicating air: what a life it was to lead – alone upon the roof-tops of the world!'. S.C. Logan writes in his narrative of a hunt in northern India: 'I inquired what had happened that we were put down like this in such a lonely spot. I felt rather alarmed, for there were fully twenty-five coolies, and I had only one man on whom I could rely' (*Nineteenth Century* 37 [1895]: 105). Stebbing in 1920 wrote of the Indian jungles:

> The jungle is so intangible, and there is probably to be found in each one of us that instinct which still survives, no matter how deeply it may be overlaid by present-day civilization, the instinct which takes us back to the time when the world was young and its inhabitants few; to the days when the greater portion of the land surface of the Globe consists of pathless jungles against which our ancestors waged unremitting war, and amongst which they lived and died.
>
> (Stebbing 1920: x)

Two observations may be made about the emphasis on solitude in these memoirs. First, the image of the jungle as primal, before time and frozen is a temporal picturesque for the English traveller (J.M. MacKenzie 1988: 192; Leask 2002). Stebbing (1920: xi) goes on to add that the Indian jungles were India's 'forgotten history', where 'hidden in these pathless wastes the remains of cities and towns and evidences of a high civilization in a remote past are to be found'. Forsyth (1996: 76) also refers to parts of central India as a mystery, where 'no mortal foot has ever trodden the dark interior'. Valentine Ball (1880: vii) emphasizes that his travelogue describes wild beasts and plants, in 'regions many of which have been seldom visited or described before'. Watching crocodiles, Andrew Adams (1867: 42) is reminded of 'the eons of the world'. Like the guidebook, which often highlights 'premodern sites . . . as visible connections with established and sometimes ancient civilizations' (Gilbert 1999: 281), the sporting memoir seeks to capture the antiquity of the Indian past – but, interestingly, in its wild spaces. Indeed, one commentator declared that though vastness and antiquity can be found in different regions of the world there is 'no other country in which the two elements are so perfectly united' (*Greater Britain* 1 [1890]: 224). In a sense, this construction of the Indian wild space as antiquity was a contrast to the changes in the hunting tradition in England. During the Victorian period and its industrialization, the law prohibited unauthorized slaughter of animals, a move that affected hound hunting (Ritvo 2002: 33–39). In the case of India the construction of the jungle as a site frozen in time generated two prominent features of the space: as a space for sport, and as a primitive site as distinct from industrialized society as imaginable.

Second, the emphasis on solitude in these memoirs is an ironic one. James Duncan (1997: 50), writing about colonial exploration narratives in Africa, has argued that the 'rhetoric of absence' in exploration narratives was clearly racist because it relegated the Africans to something less than human and therefore unworthy of representation. English people do not see anything 'between' themselves and the land: the native is invisible. What is ironic in the case of the sporting memoir's theme of dangerous solitude is that a team of beaters and native assistants accompanied almost every English *shikari*. Despite the presence of so many natives in the same space, the English treat the wilds as 'empty'. The picturesque here is constructed precisely through this process of emptying: the only way of rendering the landscape scenic was to empty it of natives.

This construction of an India of sleepy hamlets, pleasant surroundings and luxuriant vegetation is a necessary opening move for another reason: the later 'action' involving the English appears more dramatic. The passive picturesque corresponds to the 'equanimity' – as Suleri (1992: 103) describes it – of the aesthetic, where life itself is (di)stilled into a picture for consumption. However, in the case of the sporting memoir this passive picturesque has other, less peaceful subtexts. In each of the above passages, we have a pastoral picturesque, even though the 'setting' is the jungle: animals gambolling, people engaged in mundane tasks, all of which are 'recorded' by the English traveller.

Many of the picturesque scenes in such sporting memoirs suggest the *potential* for action and drama. Inglis (1892: 41) writes: 'Besides these we saw and could have shot numerous hog-deer, wild pig, a tiger-cat, a porcupine, innumerable crocodiles, and aquatic birds in endless variety and diversity'. Inglis has here painted a less-threatening, if picturesque, landscape. But, in keeping with the rhetoric of the sporting memoir, he shifts narrative focus onto the potential of threat and danger that even a landscape of smaller animals (as listed above) might carry. In the very next paragraph Inglis writes:

> Nor are these the only denizens of the dense brakes and populous sand banks and waters. At any moment a tiger, a herd of wild buffalo, a hyæna, or wolf, may get up before the elephant, while a rhinocerous is not by any means a rarity.
>
> (Inglis 1892: 41)

Forsyth speaking of a 'marvellous scene of beauty' – the Marble Rocks near Jabalpur – shows how even this scene of dream-like beauty has hidden dangers: bees that attack anybody in the vicinity, rendering the place 'inhospitable'. The river here has 'repulsive crocodiles', which convert the 'fair scene' into something foul. Later, Forsyth adds: 'Stalking the mountain bull among the splendid scenery of these elevated regions, possesses more of the elements of true sport than almost any other pursuit in this part of India' (Forsyth 1996: 33–35, 36, 112).

Stebbing in his *Jungle By-Ways in India* (1911) writes:

> But is it only the memory of the animals killed or the sport enjoyed which grips us so fast as we look back? We think not!
>
> Visions of the beautiful scenery, some of the most beautiful in the world, amongst which it is pursued, have added so much to its zest and enjoyment.
>
> (Stebbing 1911: 5)

Passages that explicitly map the excitement of encountering danger in apparently picturesque settings are found in other narratives. An essay on Indian scenery moves from 'herds of graceful spotted deer' to the 'grim beauty . . . [of] . . . the leopard and the tiger' in the same sentence (*FM* 12 NS [1875]: 790). Forsyth (1996: 112) finds the excitement of 'stalking the mountain bull' heightened because it occurs in the 'splendid scenery of these elevated regions'. Walter Campbell (1853: 255–56) speaks of the combination of romance and danger that one encounters in India's wilds. Campbell's descriptions render the landscape itself a wild one. Markham (1854: 71) states: 'There is a charm in the very hunting amidst scenery of such grandeur and magnificence as is found in the wild regions it inhabits, which far more than compensates for all the toil and fatigue attendant on it'. Another hunter-author declares:

> Beautiful in the extreme, the very *beau idéal* of all one's most romantic ideas of wild outlandish forests, through which the wild buffaloes should come crashing, or beneath whose boughs some beautiful and savage wild beast should lie grinning and snarling.
>
> (*FM* 46 [1852]: 376)

The passive picturesque is the inaugural stage for the brave English hunter to detect and deal with the dangers that lurk within and beneath the 'surface' beauty of the scenery. In all the above cases the passive picturesque opens on a quiet, scenic landscape, full of diverse sights and sensory pleasures. But this same passive picturesque also conceals dangers. The passive picturesque, the anterior moment of the sporting luxuriant, is the depiction of a landscape of beauty that is menacing. The 'scene' is now a setting of trials and tribulations. It is an environment. The passive picturesque thus marks the launch of a transformative aesthetic that calls for descriptions of action that deal with the 'environment' of danger, and to conclude with the narrative of triumph. Like the earlier aesthetics of the marvellous, the sublime and the picturesque, the sporting luxuriant also serves a colonial function of altering and controlling Indian lands. After the prosperous and fertile, the borderless desolation and the pagan, it is the turn of the jungle.

The aesthetics of risk

Describing the route to the source of the Jumna, George White (1838: 53–55) declared that not many would find the wild beauty of the landscape adequate compensation for the risks involved. Henry Shakespear (1862: 1) opens his *Wild Sports of India* with a self-description that goes as follows: 'there are few who have followed the calling [*shikar*] with more zeal and delight, or who can look back with greater pleasure to many hairbreadth escapes and successes'. Shakespear's declaration summarizes the feelings expressed in several sporting memoirs where pleasure is achieved through the conquest of danger and the experience of great personal risk.[13] The aesthetics of risk and pain was a mode of reasserting colonial control.

The English hunter's travel through the Indian jungle in pursuit of game was a journey where pleasure and danger coexisted. As Chard (1999: 213) has pointed out, danger in tourism allows the traveller 'to combine a frisson of excitement and a reminder of risk with a self-congratulatory awareness of having survived'. The hunter sought *regulated* danger and pleasure in the Indian landscape. What is significant about the sporting luxuriant is that the rewards for risk-taking are almost continuous: you gain pleasure in the very midst of danger. The sporting memoir's mapping of the scenery and picturesque landscape now modulates into a description of threat and danger as attention shifts to lands devastated by 'brute' animals, the risk involved in hunting them and the rewards it brings.

Pleasure was derived from the joy of shooting wild animals and birds. Organized hunts, with beaters, native servants, elephants and horses, ensure that the English hunter collected a decent 'bag'. Further, governmental demarcation of shooting territories and regulation of hunts guaranteed a set of trophy heads and skins for the hunter. But pleasure also lay in encountering the wilds in their 'raw' form. In Indian sporting life, notes Inglis (1892: 4), 'truth is often stranger than fiction'. With this one statement in his opening pages, Inglis distances the Indian wilds. On the one hand he affirms that even the unbelievable incidents are true. On the other he is able to construct the sheer difference of the Indian territory: such incidents can happen *only* in India, a strategy that Mary Baine Campbell (1999: 13) has termed the 'exoticisation of distance'.

The extreme exotic is the territory between civilization (the English) and barbarity (the animal world). The risk narrative of the sporting memoir is a narrative of control and conquest of the extreme exotic that is India by the English colonial. The aesthetics of risk in the sporting memoir is, as noted earlier, a crucial component of the sporting luxuriant that constructs a dangerous India to be conquered by the English hunter. The aesthetics of risk locates the English in the midst of life-threatening environments in order to demonstrate not only the completely unsafe exotic that is India, but also the English person's courage in actively seeking such spots. In this, the second moment in the sporting luxuriant preliminary to triumphal landscapes, the aesthetics of risk uses two principal modes. It first details an extreme exotic. Later it produces risk narratives of the English experience in this extreme exotic.

The extreme exotic

Stephen Keck (2004: 396) has pointed out that lush tropical foliage and fauna was integral to the picturesque aesthetic of late-nineteenth-century British representations of Burma. However, what is puzzling is Keck's (2004: 397) conclusion that the 'exotic and monstrous jungle life fits into the Oriental and picturesque qualities of the East'. The wild, with its man-eating tigers and dangerous boars, was less a picturesque image or scene to be viewed than a very real physical threat to even the armed British traveller. What I term the 'extreme exotic' is the active pursuit of danger and authentic experience in such locales as jungles, unmapped terrain (what there was of it by then) and precipices. The picturesque here was not about the appreciation of a beautiful landscape and exotic jungle life. Rather, the picturesque is only a preliminary moment in what turns out to be (expectedly) a very dangerous place. The complete enjoyment of the foreign is made possible by confronting the more dangerous aspects of it. In fact, as we shall see, wild environments are deliberately sought after and 'encountered' so that a heroic self-image is created. If the sea was the site of testing and assertion of British heroism and identity, as Nina Lübbren (2002: 41) argues, following Linda Colley (1992), then the jungle provided a significant site for heroic racial and colonial endeavour.

The fauna and flora are, in the extreme exotic, unique for their characteristics, which include a propensity for human-flesh in the case of the former. They are picturesque because they constitute a magnificent sight, as every hunter-traveller informs us. But the picturesque in these cases does not end with the recognition of the royal Bengal tiger's looks or features. The picturesque is *recast* as the extreme exotic when the traveller perceives the landscape or animal's power (and desire) to harm the *shikari*-onlooker. The landscape, with its tigers and dangerous crocodiles, becomes an allegory for lawless and uncontrollable India, especially in the wake of 1857. One Captain Rogers even compared tigers to thugs and dacoits, advocating a complete elimination of both (quoted in Rangarajan 1996: 150).

Such an extreme exotic is constructed through very specific narrative modes in the *shikar* memoir.

The terror of the terrain

The sporting memoir first underscored the difficulty of the terrain and its differences from 'civilized' towns and habitations. James Inglis writes of his accommodation:

> There was no regular house for the [Planter's] assistant, but a little one-roomed hut, built on the top of the indigo vats, served me for a residence. It had neither doors nor windows, and the rain used to beat through the room, while the eaves were inhabited by countless swarms of bats, who, in the evening flashed backwards and forwards in ghostly rapid flight, and were a most tolerable nuisance.
>
> (Maori 1878: 7)

Inglis' opening topographical description in his later work runs thus:

> To the ordinary reader in an English or Australian town, or to any one indeed who has not lived in India, the bare recital of many of the most common incidents of a day's shooting in that land of glowing colour, teeming life, and romantic associations, seems exaggerated, strained and unnatural. To come suddenly, for instance, on a gaunt, haggard, dishevelled devotee, hollow-eyed and emaciated, his almost nude frame daubed over with barbaric pigments, brandishing curious-looking weapons, shouting uncouth discordant rhymes, or waking the forest echoes with cries like those of the wild beasts, among

whose jungle solitudes he takes up his abode, would rather startle the nerves of the ordinary dweller in cities. And yet these wandering *jogees* or *fakeers* are to be met with in almost every jungle from Cape Comorin to the Spiti.

(Inglis 1892: 2)

Here Inglis sets up an opposition between the (colonial) city and the Indian jungle, between the 'ordinary reader' and the hunter who encounters such a land populated with *fakeers* and *jogees*. The terrain and location are full of hardships and risks. If in the former case it is a site allocated to him, in the second, it is a deliberate choice for sport.

Inglis' (1892) narrative quickly swerves from the passive picturesque to the more threatening luxuriant in the opening pages. Having described peaceful settings of jungle animals, Inglis writes:

To . . . [see] the blue fowl step daintily from one to the other, pressing them for a moment beneath the surface; and then as the lazy *raho* pops his round nose above water to suck in a fly; to see the long ugly serrated nose of the man-eating saurian surge slowly through the yielding element – that is a picture which one can never hope to see equalled, in varied interest in any land.

(Inglis 1892: 3)

Inglis carefully merges his description of a quiet, peaceful Indian landscape into one about lurking danger. The image of the crocodile swimming towards its unsuspecting prey through a 'yielding element' (water) is menacing, and alters the picturesque nature of the same. Inglis also goes on to locate such a mix of the passive picturesque and the threatening luxuriant as a special feature of India, claiming that this is not found in 'any other land'. The rhetoric, by locating danger as a routine feature of the Indian picturesque, creates an extreme exotic. Later Inglis continues this same rhetorical mode of opening the shooting scene with a picturesque narrative before following it up with the extreme exotic. Having described, as noted above, a landscape with 'soft diffused radiance' he proceeds to write: 'It [one of the elephants] had never been charged before by a wounded tiger, and its courage was not equal to such an unexpected strain' (Inglis 1892: 66). Gordon Cumming mentions how he 'made good bags' shooting birds and antelopes in an area which he had just described as having 'picturesque temples', that is, a site of luxuriant wildlife. In another case the luxuriant is also threatening because the land is occupied 'by a wild and turbulent race of Bheels' (Cumming 1871: 55, 57, 69, 329, 334). Two pages after his description of pleasant days and lovely panoramas, Darrah (1898: 420) informs us that he has shot a bear. With this event the topography itself is transformed: 'there was plenty of blood and there was no difficulty in seeing which way the bear had gone'.

The memoir's luxuriant combines the picturesque or the beautiful's passive beauty with the wild, near-terrifying aspects of the sublime. The luxuriant foliage is not the mere flourishing of plant life – it conceals dangers of the sublime variety in the form of tigers and boars. The hills and valleys are not simply picturesque, but possess threatening ravines, precipices and potentially dangerous slopes. George White (1838: 34) describes such dizzying terrain in his account of the Himalayas. The missionary Joseph Mullens, testifying before the Select Committee on Colonization and Settlement (India), spoke of the difficult terrain of the hills in the Darjeeling and 'Cherra Poonjee' areas (House of Commons 1858b: 11–12). Likewise, J.R. Martin testifying before the same committee highlighted the problems of other hilly areas (House of Commons 1858a: 18). Indeed, one of the central features of the sporting memoir is its careful teasing out of the dangerous luxuriant beneath the passive picturesque. The narrative thus underscores the danger that lurks beneath the gently beautiful.

The sporting memoir's descriptive vocabulary merges the passively beautiful with the threatening sublime when it mixes and matches the sleepy hamlet and the green slopes with predator-ridden environments and harsh mountain conditions. It prepares the way for a narrative where the English hunter has to toil against nature in order to win trophies and establish his command.

What is fascinating is that on the one hand the Englishman, in the wake of 1857, sought to secure himself and his family within cantonments and marked-off walled territories, a series of 'boxes' each walled off from the larger Indian world (Metcalf 1998: 177). On the other hand we have the intrepid English hunter deliberately setting out for the wilds, being exposed to harsh climates, rough terrain and dangerous animals. This context of the sporting luxuriant is worth pondering over.

My contention is that the wilds represent, for the English *shikari*, a space that is simultaneously India and not-India. If, as Metcalf (1998: 173) argues, the India of the nineteenth century was marked by threatening dirt and disease (and, after the 1857 'rebellion', mutinous, treacherous natives), the wilds constitute a space that was a part of India and yet was distinct from any of these *other* threats. A commentator in *Fraser's Magazine* (53 [1856]: 93) even declares: 'we forbear to describe the metropolis of India, because it is eminently Anglo-Saxon'. Perhaps, therefore, a truer India exists in the extreme exotic of the jungles. The luxuriant, as troped in and by the sporting memoir, is about a more 'natural' India, devoid of potentially treacherous natives (who have been disarmed). It is about the English setting out to seek danger in what is a part of India but which poses a different order and kind of threat from that of the town. The luxuriant's emphasis on natural threats from vegetation, animal life and climate is in sharp contrast to the mutiny narratives of the time where the controlled environs of the town, cantonment and barracks had concealed the gravest threat (the 'rebel' sepoy). The shift in source of threat is significant for this particular reason: English hunters were *prepared* for the luxuriant's dangers and threats. In fact they sought it. It becomes their source of remaking India by facing danger, experiencing suffering and finally triumphing.

The wilds in the sporting memoirs constitute a geographical locating of risk. Risk is taken in places that appear picturesque and scenic. The geographical locating of risk, argues Freedgood (2000: 121–22), constructed through contrasts, a safe England, where danger and threat was always elsewhere. In the case of the sporting memoir, I argue, the search for areas of danger could be read as a response to 1857, where the danger erupted from within the barracks and canton-ments – sites where the colonial administration had assumed it had greater pres-ence and control. The wilds, on the other hand, were unmapped, out of the regular route. As noted earlier, Inglis (1892) underscores the fact that such risks and life-threatening events happened in Indian wilds alone, where truth is stranger than fiction. This precise plotting of the landscape of risk ensures that the hunt will transform the space into a conquered territory. Inglis' subsequent reference to the 'far-off Indian hunting-grounds' emphasizes this geographical locating of risk preliminary to a deliberate seeking out of the same.

Intimate encounters

Inglis emphasizes the ferocity of the terrain by focusing on the animals, high-lighting their ferociousness and potential threat:

> To meet face to face a surly boar, having tusks that would badly 'rip' an elephant, and who resents your intrusive approach – to note the stealthy slouching gait of some lithe leopard, stalking the peaceful antelope or graceful spotted deer . . . the snarling battle for the fragments of a carrion feed between hissing vultures, or howling wolves, is a revelation of savage animal life that one does not soon forget.
>
> (Inglis 1892: 2–3)

Inglis' narrative emphasizes the *intimacy* of the encounter with danger. The extreme exotic is marked by this intimate engagement with a dangerous land-scape, an experience that is life-threatening, and an immediacy that is not avail-able to an 'ordinary reader in an English or Australian town', as Inglis (1892: 2) puts it. The extreme exotic differs crucially from the 'standard' picturesque in this aspect: there is no 'observing' of the landscape from a distance, rather there is an experience of it from within. This theme of proximity serves to generate a rhetoric of authenticity in the sporting memoir.

There are detailed accounts of victims couched in a rhetoric of authenticity and horrific realism. Inglis (1892: 101) describes victims' bones in order to convey the extent and horror of destruction. Or, in Inglis' earlier narrative, the tiger possesses 'cunning and craftiness'. 'His whole frame', writes Inglis, 'is put together to effect destruction'. Inglis goes on to provide a detailed account of the destructive strength of the tiger. In other cases he describes the wild pig's courage and strength (Maori 1878: 247, 237, 235–46, 89). Gordon Cumming (1871: 17) claims authen-ticity for his narrative thus: 'As I bear the marks of both teeth and claws, I hope my observations may have weight in warning any gentleman . . . of the danger of rashly exposing themselves or their followers when in pursuit of savage beasts'. Savory writes:

> A tiger seen in the Zoo gives no faint idea of what one of his species is, seen under its proper conditions. Beasts in captivity are under-fed, and have no

muscle; but here before us was a specimen who had always 'done himself well', was fit as a prize-fighter, every square inch of him developed to perfection . . . His long, slouching walk, suggestive of such latent strength, betrayed the vast muscle.

(Savory 1900: 265)

Robert Baden-Powell, writing about pig-sticking, emphasized the brutal realism of the hunt: 'blind to all else but the strong and angered foe before you, with your good spear in your hand, you rush for blood with all the ecstasy of a fight to the death' (quoted in J.M. MacKenzie 1988: 189). James Inglis writes:

Anyone who has ever enjoyed a rattle after a pig over good country, will recall the fierce delight, the eager thrill, the wild, mad excitement, that flushed his whole frame, as he met the infuriate charge of a good thirty-inch fighting boar, and drove his spear well home.

(Maori 1878: 84)

Markham (1854: 374) hopes to return one day, 'to face Bruin in his haunts'. Thomas Williamson highlights the fact that in his work *Oriental Field Sports* (1808), the visuals show 'subjects in their natural course':

Thus, the scenery in the series of Hog-hunting is regularly preserved as an open country; such as is best suited to that branch of sporting; while the Tiger series will be found generally to possess that grandeur of situation peculiar to the nature of that animal's haunts.

(Williamson 1808, 1: vi)

Joseph Fayrer's (1875: 1) tract on the Bengal tiger emphasizes the fact that he had encountered the animal in 'his home . . . his native swamps and jungle'.

This rhetoric of authenticity, where the wild animal must be seen and encountered in its 'true' space, is central to the sporting memoir's construction of the extreme exotic.

The hunter is always in close *proximity* to the dangerous animal, close enough to mark features on the face or body. Almost every sporting memoir provides descriptions that reveal the proximity of the hunter to the animal. Savory (1900: 274) notes that one of the tigers she shoots sprang past her, 'so close that I found his blood splashed over my gun-barrels afterwards'. In fact, the rhetoric of proximity and intimacy even results in terms of endearment. Stebbing (1911: 5) writes: 'There is the off-chance of our coming across "stripes" or "spots", as the *shikari* man affectionately designates the two animals he ever most wishes to meet . . . the tiger . . . and the leopard or panther'. Another narrative mentions that there was 'not two inches of space' between the hunter's head – he has been grabbed by a tiger and is being carried off in its jaws – and the point where another hunter shoots (*HW* 6 [1852]: 69).

In other cases the landscape was so devoid of humanity that it almost resembled another world: 'It was an eerie spot, and as the wind moaned and the branches rustled, the imagination conjured up all sorts of sights and sounds in the impenetrable shadows' (Savory 1900: 125). Donald MacIntyre (1891) writes of another place:

> A wild and eerie-looking spot this certainly was, with its frowning precipices, beetling crags, and tall black pines. As the shades of night closed down on our gloomy surroundings, the big owls began their dismal hootings from the dark echoing pine-wood across the torrent, as if deriding our futile attempt on the charmed life of that black old *tahr*.
>
> (MacIntyre 1891: 295)

However difficult the terrain and inhospitable the climate, the dramatic possibilities of encountering, battling and conquering wild beasts surpassed the battle with the terrain or elements. The emphasis on proximity and authenticity transforms the land from the mere 'scene' of the passive picturesque to the 'environment' of the sporting luxuriant. It showed the English hunter embedded in the land, dealing with the danger in close proximity to it. It generated a risk narrative that emphasized pain and danger, a crucial moment in the construction of the English hunter's triumph.

Brute realities

The extreme exotic demanded a rhetoric that emphasized not only the utter difference of the landscape (from anything else in colonial India: the town, the village, the cantonment) but also the brutal, extreme nature of the land. One way of achieving this aesthetic of the extreme exotic was to highlight the brutal nature of India. The luxuriant was in fact a colonial bestiary.

Underscoring the brute nature of the animals is a central feature of the colonial sporting memoir. The tiger represented, for the British in the nineteenth century, all that was lawless about/in India (Rangarajan 2001: 25). It was, therefore, the colonial hunter's task to ensure a disciplining of the lawless, whether they are tribes (like the Santhals) or tigers. What is fascinating about the hyper-animalization of the animals in the extreme exotic is the imposition of moral judgements upon animal behaviour and even looks. For instance, when James Inglis describes the shooting of a python, he mentions that the python had swallowed a whole deer. Two observations are made by Inglis at this point. The python, writes Inglis, 'presented a very curious and uncommon illustration of the evil effects of greed and gluttony'. Soon after he declares that the python's injury – the result of swallowing the deer's horns – had 'rendered the skin perfectly useless as a specimen' (Inglis 1892: 42). The first comment reduces the python to a glutton. The second rejects it as a source of profit (as trophy). Inglis provides graphic accounts of the killing of a buffalo by the tiger, thereby underscoring the latter's ferocity. Here

Inglis highlights the fact that the tiger had 'boldly ventured into the very midst of the enclosed herd', and despite the 'wild stampede of the *bataneas*, or herdsmen, the tiger had managed to stick to his prey and undauntedly carry it off'. He variously describes an injured tiger as a 'monster' and 'devilish' (Inglis 1892: 62, 66, 67). In another case, Inglis devotes a full chapter, titled 'Never trust a tiger', to the tiger. Here he details man-eaters, described as a 'cunning sneaking rogue', 'an old brute', a 'cruel whiskered robber' and others. He is described as possessing 'an unholy appetite for human flesh', and 'know[ing] the habits of the village population as minutely as does the tax-gatherer'. Another is said to pay 'diabolic attentions' to the villages (Inglis 1892: 99, 100, 102). In another text Inglis refers to the tiger as the 'royal robber', the 'striped and whiskered monarch of the jungle' (Maori 1878: 226). Markham (1854: 137–38) provides details of the brutalized bodies of the victims. MacIntyre (1891: 59) refers to a tiger as 'a perfect feline demon'. In another case the tiger is referred to as 'an abject cur' (Stebbing 1911: 225). Wolves in Central India are 'hideous brutes' that steal children (Forsyth 1996: 59–60). Young tigers, writes another hunter, 'are frequently blood-thirsty and cruel beyond their requirements' (*IF* 16 [1890]: 430). Forsyth (1996: 31) speaks of taming a wild camel, where the animal had 'his nose rebored and [was] starved into a peaceful return to the uses of his race'. A review describes the 'extraordinary tenacity of life exhibited by a bear' (*DUM* 60 [1862]: 347). Even a mortally wounded bear, writes another hunter, 'is savage to the last' (*FM* 46 [1852]: 383). Walter Campbell (1853: 212, 250) refers to the malignity of the tiger, describing him as 'an incarnate devil'.

The rhetoric renders the animal into something else entirely.[14] The construction of the tiger or boar as a mean, ferocious creature preying on innocent and helpless natives (or even the hunters' elephants) was central to the extreme exotic's brutalizing mode. The foe had to be worthy of the kill. Clearly these were cultural images of animals that informed the hunters' actions. Thus, when Forsyth (1996: 31) speaks of the camel as returning to 'the uses of his race', he is functioning from within a cultural notion of what the camel race was meant to do. The excessive brutalization of the animals in the sporting memoir was instrumental in the construction of the colonial mastery narrative. The hunters conquered those they considered worthy opponents: man-eating tigers and wild boar.

Central to the extreme exotic's excessive brutalization of the animal was the rhetoric of depopulation. Every sporting memoir describes at least one landscape destroyed by the tiger or another wild animal. Inglis writes: 'I have known whole tracts of fertile country to relapse into untilled jungle, from the presence of a single man-eating tiger. I have seen villages entirely deserted from the same cause'. Children 'seemed to have a scared look, as if a dead weight was on their spirits'. The entire place 'betokened desolation and decay' (Inglis 1892: 101–02, 107). Here Inglis compiles instances of abandoned villages with a dramatic, fictionalized account of a tiger attack in order to paint a luxuriant landscape of danger. In his earlier work Inglis describes how the wild pig destroys crops (Maori 1878: 88, 91). Inglis' narrative shows a remarkable shift from the scenic beauty of the landscape to the signs of destruction:

Whole tracts of fertile fields, reclaimed from the wild luxuriance of matted jungle, and waving with golden grain, have been deserted by the patient husbandmen, and allowed to relapse into tangled thicket and uncultured waste on account of the ravages of this formidable robber. Whole villages depopulated by tigers, the mouldering door-posts, and crumbling rafters, met with at intervals in the heart of the solitary jungle, alone marking the spot where a thriving hamlet once sent up the curling smoke from its humble hearths, until the scourge of the wilderness, the dreaded 'man-eater', took up his station near it, and drove inhabitants in terror from the spot. Whole herds of valuable cattle have been literally destroyed by the tiger.

(Maori 1878: 236)

William Rice (1857: xi) speaks of the 'depredations carried out constantly by these ferocious beasts of prey'. Joseph Fayrer (1875) provides statistics about the extent of destruction caused by tigers: in a period of six years ending in 1866, 4218 persons killed by tigers, 1407 by leopards, 4287 by wolves (Fayrer 1875: 40, 42, 43 and elsewhere). He goes on to quote a government report that recorded how one tigress alone had caused 'the desertion of thirteen villages, and two hundred and fifty square miles of country were thrown out of cultivation' (Fayrer 1875: 42). The depopulation narrative is a moment in the aesthetics of risk because it emphasizes the danger the English are not only about to face, but also to rescue the native from, at great risk to themselves. It marks the extreme exotic because unlike traditional depopulation narratives of war and sickness (as we have seen in the case of the eighteenth-century sublime), we have a landscape that has been ravaged by animal life. Fascinatingly, it is precisely the juxtaposition of the terrifying beauty of the tiger with its potential for destruction that constitutes the extreme exotic's landscape with which the English hunter is about to grapple.

The deliberate seeking of the extreme exotic was a mode of preventing random and therefore uncontrollable risk from other spots. Risk was now locatable in mountains, jungles and other such areas.

Risk narratives

Walter Campbell (1853: 2) opens his account with a mention of the 'tragical fate of poor Monro', an anecdote that must serve, he states, 'to impress . . . readers with a wholesome dread of the tiger's cannibal propensities'. In a sense this captures the tone of the entire sporting narrative: risk, injury, even death will figure as prominent themes. In fact, *difficulty* was central to the sporting ethos, as John MacKenzie (1988: 172) points out.

The extreme exotic prepares the ground for the Englishman or woman to assert their powers. Armed with guns, a team of like-minded hunters, assisted by native 'beaters', often travelling on horse- or elephant-back, the colonials now proceeded to deal with the land in very different ways from their predecessors, who were more keen on providing a painterly picturesque, though the narrative was often supplemented by photographs and sketches of animals, animal heads, trophy bags and the hunter.[15]

The sporting luxuriant's main component is a remaking of the Indian landscape through personal risk, pain and suffering, and conquest over fauna and flora. There is no painterly picturesque or panorama where the landscape is viewed from a distance. The picturesque modulates into something else when nature is treated as a process than a picture. The emphasis shifts from 'landscape' to 'environment' (Andrews 1999: 192–93). This means the 'artist' – in this case the author of the sporting memoir who records sights and action – has a more intimate engagement with the land than the painter. There is a 'mutually affective relationship between the "organism" and its environing "current field of significance"', writes Andrews (1999: 193). In the extreme exotic the word-painter of the landscape is often involved in a struggle with nature and its varied life forms. The sporting luxuriant is marked by this shift of emphasis *within* the picturesque, a shift that signifies not only a search for the completely new but also increasing colonial control over the land.

Reading Victorian mountaineering memoirs Elaine Freedgood (2000) proposes an ethos of 'cultural masochism'. 'Cultural masochism' is a 'collective means of preemptively expressing and relieving anxiety: it is both the enactment and the popular representation of a voluntary and knowing embrace of danger'. This 'voluntary' encounter, suggests Freedgood, 'prevent[s] random encounters with danger'. The embrace of risk in Alpine mountaineering becomes a way of 'colonizing the future', of bringing potential and future danger into the present and 'neutralizing its potential threat' (Freedgood 2000: 104–05). This notion of a 'cultural masochism', where pain and pleasure are inextricably linked, and which actively seeks dangers, is a useful mode of dealing with the risk narrative of the sporting memoir.

James Inglis describes the dangers encountered during hunts. Narrating an incident when the elephant bolted in fear, he writes:

> Soda-water bottles popped; cartridges, tumblers, a water-bottle, cigars, fragments of canework, and splinters of wood, were scattered all around, and with the wreckage of the unfortunate *Howdah* banging against her ribs, the now ten times more maddened elephant tore through the jungle, fully persuaded that the devilish tiger was seated on her rump.
>
> (Inglis 1892: 67)

Isabel Savory describes a bear attack:

> The resurrected bear charged right down upon us! . . . There was absolutely no time to act! – no time to think! Though severely wounded she sprang at M, who was nearest her, was on her hind feet in a second, making for M's face and striking at it with her strong arms. My blood froze! – it was a horrible sight, and so unexpected! Thank Heaven! The *chota shikari* was a plucky man and rose to the occasion.
>
> (Savory 1900: 127, ellipsis in original; see also 267)

Walter Campbell writes:

> Nothing now can save him – every rifle has been discharged – three bounds
> more, and poor Lorimer is a mangled corpse. The tiger has gathered himself
> together for the last spring – Charles can bear it no longer, but burying his
> face in his hands, groans aloud. Ha! He's down – it's all over – No! hark to
> that shot – 'tis Mansfield's rifle – the ragged bullet whistles through the air,
> and the tiger, rearing up to his full height, falls back gasping in the last
> agonies.
>
> (W. Campbell 1853: 49)

The paratactic syntax in these descriptions adds to the sense of the dramatic,
which is precisely the structure of the sporting memoir.

The description of ascents in the sporting memoirs highlights the risks involved.
Isabel Savory writes:

> There was no path of any sort or kind, and we simply clambered up the face
> of the forest . . . The reason it was hard work was on account of the rarefied
> atmosphere; we were climbing between fourteen and fifteen thousand feet
> above sea level, and until you have grown used to this altitude breathing is
> laborious.
>
> (Savory 1900: 120)

On another occasion they 'followed a rugged and ill-defined path up a steep
incline for about four miles' (Savory 1900: 122).

The conquest of Indian wilds is, of course, predicated upon the killing of the
tiger or the boar. The thrill of 'laying low the gallant grey tusker, the indomitable,
unconquerable grisly boar' is unmatched, writes James Inglis (Maori 1878: 84).
Here the visual and auditory pleasure offered by the passive picturesque has been
transformed through the act of hunting and killing. Thus Inglis, who provides a
detailed description of such a passive picturesque, full of sensory pleasures, quickly
swerves into a different mode altogether. He concludes his paragraph – incidentally, the opening pages of his memoir – thus:

> And, most thrilling and memorable of all, to see the convulsive upward leap,
> and hear the throttled gasping roar of a wounded tiger, as the whiff of powder
> smoke from your trusty gun salutes you like grateful incense – that's one of the
> sensations that makes the dull pulses throb and quicken their beat.
>
> (Inglis 1892: 3)

Here Inglis rejects the 'dull' pleasures of a passive picturesque (whose description
has already been quoted above) in favour of the sensory pleasure of the hunt.

The sporting memoir flourishes, it must be noted, after the 1857 'mutiny'. The
'mutiny', which was a radical rupture in the fabric of British rule in India, was a
danger that was foreseen by very few of the colonials. In the wake of the events of
1857–58, the natives were disarmed and the army reorganized. My argument is

that the *shikar* 'movement' in the post-1857 phase was a form of 'cultural masochism' that sought out dangers to neutralize them in the here and now so as to prevent any random dangers in the future. Metcalf (1998: 160) notes that post-1857 memoir and fiction often 'evoked a remembrance of a time … when all Englishmen, and especially English women, were at risk of dishonour and death'. Thus a review essay on 'mutiny' tracts writes of the 'blood of our countrymen not yet dry, and the cries of our countrywomen still ringing in our ears' before warning of greater dangers in the future (*QR* 102 [1857]: 535). Similar essays were being published on the 'dangers in India', dealing with what one writer described as a 'vague sense of coming evil' (*MM* 15 [1866–67]: 412–16). Thus, the future of the empire was discussed in terms of the dangers it was *likely* to face. The temporal frames of these dangers are somehow shifted from the future to the present, and the source of danger from natives to animals and landscape.[16] From the 'vague sense' of danger, the sporting memoir shifts focus to specific situations and sources of danger. This, I believe, is the purpose of the 'cultural masochism' of the sporting memoir.

In the case of the sporting luxuriant, the passive picturesque, as I have demonstrated, encodes a discourse of potential action and violence. Sara Suleri (1992: 103), reading the post-'mutiny' memoir of Harriet Tytler, has shown how the feminine picturesque colludes in the public narrative of the Raj, where the picturesque's 'equanimity transmutes into the discourse of a sentimentality that possesses an inherently violent excess'. The sensory pleasures of the passive picturesque soon become transformed into the pleasures derived from dangerous encounters with wild animals, life-threatening situations and the sights and sounds of killings. The passive picturesque's 'equanimity' here 'transmutes' into narratives where risk-taking even in picturesque settings leads to pleasure. In fact it is the discourse of risk woven into the picturesque that constructs a landscape of pleasure.[17]

Central to the construction of the landscape of risk via the sporting luxuriant is the theme of pain and suffering. In terms of the actual 'process', the hunt in Asian territories was very different from the settings of domestic sport in England. The territories were vast, the animals more ferocious and the terrain more difficult. In short, the dangers of the hunt were far greater in India than in the relatively more controlled system in England (Ritvo 2002). Thus, the deliberate seeking out of the most desolate or dangerous spaces within India is an interesting ethos in itself. As Callum McKenzie puts it:

> overseas hunting was labeled 'real sport' in which the pursuit of wild animals on their own 'primeval and ancestral ground, as yet unannexed and unappropriated in any way by man' assumed a mythical identity heightened by the masculine skills required to conquer.
>
> (McKenzie 2000: 74)

As we have seen, numerous English writers emphasize the radically unruly and untouched nature of the Indian jungles. These serve to underscore the pioneer role of the hunter who, facing very real dangers, manages to penetrate the wilds, extend the frontier and arrive at an exotic when the exotic had all but disappeared.

Sporting memoirs invariably mentioned instances of falling, injury and death. Pain, as Elaine Freedgood (2000) (following Elaine Scarry 1985), has argued, was a mode of un-making and re-making the world. When pain is invoked voluntarily and remains under the control of the 'creator', it remakes the world into a place over which its creators can exercise greater control (Freedgood 2000: 112–14). In the sporting memoir, the world is remade through suffering and pain so that it allows the English colonials to imagine themselves as indomitable, danger is subject to his military, administrative and physical control. Instances of injury, near-death situations and pain are recurrent features of the sporting memoir. Cumming's narrative, for instance, highlights such escapades in considerable detail (Cumming 1871: 53–54, 191–92, 328, and elsewhere). A narrative of tiger-shooting mentions how the author recalls friends who had passed away, 'in death-struggles with the wild denizens of the forest' (*OSM* 10.111 [1877]: 72). Joseph Fayrer (1875: 47) in his tract on the Bengal tiger writes: 'I have seen the severest injuries inflicted by the tiger recovered from rapidly, others after profuse suppuration and sloughing off of the torn and stretched tissues'.

Such narratives served to emphasize the dangers the English hunters voluntarily sought and experienced. The cultural masochism that drove the English into seeking such experiences was a mode of thwarting the unnameable and unidentifiable threat they perceived from the more 'civilized' parts of India. In order to remake India into a more controlled space, the English had to encounter greater dangers, in harsher situations so that they prove themselves master not only of the town but also of the jungle, over man and beast. The aesthetic of risk sets the scene, as it were, for the transformation of the jungle into a landscape of triumph. Suffering was thus integral to a reassertion of nationhood, possession and imperial power.[18]

Triumphal landscapes

James Inglis prefaces the description of a successful hunt with the following statement:

> When we . . . heard that near the village of Pertaubgunj a man-eater had taken up his abode, and was levying his terrible blackmail on the terror-stricken inhabitants, it needed little incentive else, to make us determine to beat him up, and free the neighbourhood from his diabolic attentions.
>
> (Inglis 1892: 102)

Inglis concludes his Introduction in *Tent Life in Tigerland* with a statement of his intention 'to portray . . . a real presentment of the life of a pioneer in the Indian backwoods' (Maori 1878: 5). Together the two statements construct the final moment of the sporting memoir: the triumphal landscape of India. The memoir moves from a passive picturesque that is India through an extreme exotic that tests the English hunter, to a trophy landscape conquered, protected and mapped by the English. For Inglis these people were 'pioneers' and saviours. The extreme exotic that is India is a site where the English sought new relations with difficult environments and triumphs. Several components make up the triumphal landscape of the sporting memoir.

The conquest of the landscape – especially mountainous terrain, jungles and hills – generates a sense of mastery and control. The mobility of the white 'body' – a feature of imperialism, as Radhika Mohanram's (1999) work demonstrates – through unmapped, supposedly impenetrable jungle in each and every sporting memoir shows the luxuriant as providing the source of a heroic landscape. Freedgood (2000: 103), reading mountaineering memoirs from the Victorian age, argues that such a sense of mastery was provided for both – those who had actually climbed and those who read their accounts. Extending this line of argument, I propose that the nineteenth-century *shikar* account which generated a sense of colonial power and racial mastery over the harsh terrain and wild animals may be read as a source of inspiration for the readers back home.

The saviour shikari

One way of emphasizing the triumphal nature of the Indian extreme exotic is to depict the English hunter as a saviour. By saving the natives from man-eating tigers and other predators, the hunters cast themselves in the role of heroic saviours. The narratives provide detailed descriptions of the sufferings of the natives at the maws and paws of tigers and other creatures. James Inglis (1892) goes one step further: he provides an imaginative account of a tiger attack. The narrative details how 'hushed affrighted women hurry on, their hearts thudding with trepidation . . . cast uneasy startled glances into every bush, and start at every rustle in the tall feathery swaying grass'. Later Inglis speculates on how the tiger got the 'wretched loiterer'. He also refers to the 'heroic' lives of Britons in the wilds of India (Inglis 1892: 100, 101, 360). William Rice (1857: 28) informs us that the natives were 'very willing to have the tigers about their villages destroyed' because the predators were killing their cattle. These instances construct the image of vulnerable and brutalized natives, who await a saviour who will protect them from the predators.

Another method of transforming India into a triumphal landscape is to highlight the ineffectual native. Sporting memoirs of the period are full of descriptions of the Indians' fear of the animals, their inability to safeguard their lives and property, and their ineffective modes of hunting. Inglis describes the confusion and terror among natives when an elephant bolts:

> The beaters came pouring out of the jungle by twos and threes, like the frightened inhabitants of some hive or ant-heap. Some in their hurry came tumbling out headlong, others with their faces turned backwards to see if anything was in pursuit of them, got entangled in the reeds, and fell prone on their hands and knees . . . I, who had witnessed the episode, could not help . . . [bursting into] a resounding peal of laughter.
>
> (Maori 1878: 231)

Later Inglis describes native beaters running out from the forest 'like so many rabbits from a warren when the weasel or ferret has entered the burrow' (Maori 1878: 233). Another hunter relates how a native falling down 'looked like the frightful hairy Jack-in-a-box, all mouth, teeth, and bristles, that they sometimes sell in London toy-shops' (*FM* 46 [1852]: 381). Another narrative, about a bear hunt, emphasizes native cowardice throughout (*IF* 26 [1900]: 637–38). Isabel Savory describes how a native comes rushing up to the English in the forest, scared of the bears in the area. The English, writes Savory, 'promised him we would not be eaten up by bears'. On another occasion Savory writes with a great deal of sarcasm about the natives: 'our tiffin coolie . . . who had been valiantly watching our movements from the branches of a tree' (Savory 1900: 121, 127–28). The native is afraid of the animals, whereas the English *woman* is not. In many cases, writes Inglis (1892: 101), the English find that the idolatrous natives worship the tiger to 'propitiate' the 'very incarnation of destruction'. But the English, armed with better knowledge and equipment, conquer the animal. In such descriptions the natives are reduced to ineffectual, scared creatures.

When the English arrive at a village, they are 'hailed as . . . friendly deliverers' (Inglis 1892: 106). Campbell (1853: 224) also uses the 'rescue theme' in his narrative. Savory (1900: 124) mentions how one Jemadar came up to the English and described a bear attack, and pleaded with them to visit the bear cave. A woman traveller, having witnessed a tiger's killing of an antelope, remarks that ever since a reward (of fifty rupees) was announced for the discovery of a tiger, the numbers of these animals have been diminished (*CE* 11 NS [1849]: 106).[19] Cumming (1871: 56) is even called upon to render medical aid on one occasion. The villagers, he writes, 'said that they had great confidence in a white man'. Henry Shakespear adds another dimension to the saviour *shikari* role when he links hunting to evangelical activity:

> To him who has been blessed with the gifts of good nerve, energy, and strength, that he may save the bodies of these same ignorant heathen from the fell destroyer that lives in the forest and preys upon them. Who shall say that the poor idolater saved by the latter from destruction shall not become converted to Christianity by the former?
>
> (Shakespear 1862: 3)

Savory (1900: 122) writes: 'In the [1860s] the country was literally swarming with them, and people were afraid to go from one village to another after dark; they have been shot more of late years, and those palmy days are no more'.

Later she adds: 'Judged by the standard of the greatest good to the greatest number, the laws of humanity justify the working of a tiger-shoot, to my mind'. She comments after they have shot a tiger that had killed a native: 'and so the poor native's death was avenged' (Savory 1900: 259, 275). Kate Martelli is unequivocal in her assessment about the *shikar*: 'Tigers are shot in India, not as game is in England for hunting, to give amusement to men, horses and dogs . . . but to save the lives of natives and their cattle' (quoted in Trollope 1983: 207–08).

The triumphal landscape is one where the English colonial hunter has revenged and/or saved the native. The image of the saviour, however, is not the only element in the make-up of the colonial hunter.

Sportsmanship and the 'ethics' of hunting

The 'ethics' of sportsmanship is crucial to the image of the colonial hunter in the triumphal landscape. As early as 1808, Williamson had declared that the Indian system of hunting, with 'two or three hundred elephants and thirty or forty thousand horse and foot', 'beating' for game was no sport (Williamson 1808, 1: xii). Savory (1900: 279) complains: 'The native village *shikaris* are rapidly ruining the country. These *shikaris* shoot simply for food; and as they kill hinds, does, young. etc., indiscriminately, there are no deer left'. Rice (1857: 24, 28) is also contemptuous of the native modes of hunting in which, he claims, 'skin alone is the desirable object, not the sport which his death in a fair fight gives' and in which a 'tremendous retinue' turned out to hunt the animal. Markham (1854: 16) declares that 'being easily got at, the Himalayan sportsman looks upon the *kakur* somewhat with indifference, except in the absence of larger game'. Such passages glorifying the ethics of the English hunter contrasted with the cruelties of the native hunter are seen in other writers (Sterndale 1877: 55–56; Sleeman 1995 [1893], 1: 286–88).

These narratives map the differences in English and native approaches to hunting, or even between 'sporting' English hunters and other, ordinary ones. Thus Adams (1867: 47) speaks of the destruction of *shikar* grounds due to deforestation. MacIntyre (1891: 46) mourns the 'indiscriminate destruction of game at all seasons . . . which has ruined sport'. Stebbing (1920), outlining a plan for conservation of game animals in India, proposes that 'a certain proportion of the head of a particular species to be shot in an area' may be allotted to the local District Officials. These suggestions, he argues, 'are made only in the interests of that particular quality all Englishmen pride themselves in possessing – Fair Play' (Stebbing 1920: 281). Inglis, Forsyth and other commentators in periodicals spend considerable time describing the native cruelties to animals and the English approach to the hunt (Maori 1878: 71–74; Forsyth 1996: 191; see also *CE* 9 NS [1848]: 303–04; *DUM* 60 [1862]: 347). It was even proposed that native *shikaris* be kept out of reserved forest areas so that the English district officer and his cronies could get better game (*IF* 17 [1891]: 413). In other cases the English even objected to the native modes of cattle-grazing, where their calls spoilt the chances of a good *shikar* (*IF* 26 [1900]: 635).

Inglis (1892) states that for the low-caste native, when it comes to sow's flesh. 'his sporting conscience has no qualms'. Inglis then proceeds to elaborate on English hunting ethics:

> The European ideal of the sport is to give the bird something like a fair chance. Only the tyro, or the sordid pot-hunter, would think of such devices as are in the eyes of the native perfectly legitimate and even praiseworthy. The European sportsman will even at times exercise considerable ingenuity

to 'flush' his birds; to make them 'rise', so that he may 'take them on the wing'. The native *shikaree*, on the contrary, will exhaust every conceivable cunning device to lull his intended quarry into a false security.

(Inglis 1892: 342)

Inglis compares the native's modes of hunting to the 'methods of the old poacher in the old country', and argues that this difference in approaches is because in India, 'arms of precision are . . . unknown' (Inglis 1892: 342). Weaponry and modes of hunting were markers of cultural and racial difference in the sporting memoir. The Indian with his crude matchlocks – and, after 1857, the government had banned the Indians from possessing anything other than the clumsy muzzle-loader guns, a fact noted by Joseph Fayrer (1875: 51) – and his crude and 'cruel' approach to animals was far inferior to the sophisticated English sportsman-hunter.

Sporting advice, colonial knowledge

William Rice (1857), narrating his tiger-hunting experiences in the 1850–54 period, opens his preface with a statement of intentions:

> My object in writing these pages is to give . . . some account of the most exciting and glorious sport this world affords – Tiger-shooting; believing that it is a subject that which excites general interest, and as to which considerable amount of ignorance exists even in India.
>
> (Rice 1857: v)

Years later, Dietrich Brandis, the first chief conservator general writes: 'officers [of the Indian Forest Service] were obtained from the Army and other sources, who in the pursuit of sport and adventure had acquired a love of forest life and an intimate knowledge of the country, the people and their languages' (McDonell 1929: 85–97). Taken together, the two statements link several aspects of the sporting memoir. The adventurer and sportsperson was a source of knowledge, even as they penetrated the forests for the thrill of hunting. Further, there was a martial aspect to the forestry movement. Knowledge, military control, adventure all come together in the person of the English hunter. This intimate link between *shikar* and knowledge informed English colonial assumptions from the 1800s to as late as the 1930s. Williamson (1808, 1: v) in his preface to *Oriental Field Sports* stated that publications such as his own added to the fund of knowledge.

Admittedly, the *shikar* expedition combined English and native modes of the hunt. In fact, prior to the 'mutiny' of 1857 British and native hunters helped each other and went on expeditions together (J.M. MacKenzie 1988: 170, 174–75). Natives also supplied information about animal haunts and movements to the English hunter, in a good example of what Chris Bayly (1999) has identified as the colonial information order. However, the narratives' emphasis on the technological superiority of the English hunter suggests that local knowledge needs to be supplemented with English courage and firearms. This reading is invited by the sporting memoir's repeated recounting of native deaths at the hands of animals, native cowardice and native failures at the hunt. Despite their intimate knowledge of the animals, the memoirs suggest, it often requires an English person to effect a complete conquest.

The sporting memoir, having mapped the landscapes of picturesque scenery, risk and finally colonial triumph, ensures that the British mastery of the land is underscored and maintained through detailed advice. The sporting memoir functioned as a guide to future conquests of the Indian wilds. It served prominently to enthuse the English to hunt. Several aspects of this triumphal landscape of epistemological and technological dominance draw our attention.

A popular way of showing the English hunter's complete control over Indian jungles and animal life was to exhibit familiarity with the ways of both. Sporting memoirs often carried detailed studies of the tiger's habitat or the bear's life. Thus Rice (1857: v) states that he had had 'several splendid opportunities of observing the habits of these animals, and ascertaining how they may be best killed'. Fayrer's *The Royal Tiger of Bengal* described itself as a 'sketch of the natural history and habits' of the animal (1875: 1). Tiger shooting was different in the Madras and Bengal regions because the habitat and terrain were different, and for a successful expedition this *knowledge* was necessary (Fayrer 1875: 29). Others wrote 'natural history notes' on the tiger, its modes of hunting and feeding habits and detailed case studies of game animals (see, for instance, 'Natural History Notes on the Tiger', *IF* 16 [1890]: 427–28, and Lydekker's *The Game Animals of India, Burma, Malaya and Tibet* (1907)).

With such a move of exhibiting knowledge about India's teeming wildlife, the *shikar* memoir enters the final moment of the sporting luxuriant: Indian landscape has been altered from the great, dangerous unknown to the knowable and manageable. The risk narrative that provides the route into the luxuriant highlights the dangers only to show the triumph of the English hunter. The luxuriant is now a heroic landscape, where risk is sought, planned for and conquered.

Working its way from the hunt to the animal (or at times in the reverse order) the English hunter both neutralizes and highlights the threat these animals pose. Thus Inglis states that the tiger is 'beautiful but dreaded', and he describes one G. S. and his brother as 'acquainted with all the haunts and habits of every wild creature' (Maori 1878: 235). In his later work, Inglis mentions that he had 'supreme control' over the land. After narrating an incident when a tiger, presumed dead, attacked one of the elephants, he concludes: 'the moral is – never trust even a dead tiger' (Inglis 1892: 109, 110) – thus offering a lesson to future hunters. Later, recounting the stupidity of a fellow-hunter, he concludes: 'and here lies the moral. NEVER AGAIN ON FOOT!' (Inglis 1892: 334, emphasis in original).

Integral to a triumphal landscape was the construction of a new epistemology itself. Sporting memoirs proceeded, very often, to 'read' the jungle and suggest a coherent vision of an other world, distinct from the cantonment, the city and the barracks. The hunter who seeks out and experiences the Indian extreme exotic then proceeds to provide instructions on the arms to be used, the habits of the animals, the method of hunting, and other subjects. When Inglis (1892: 2) refers to the 'ordinary reader in an Indian or Australian town', he is proposing a distinction between the ignorant reader from the town or city and the hunter who went into the jungle and experiences it. Isabel Savory (1900) writes: 'It cannot be realized by those who have not felt it, and it gives the ordinary Britisher no adequate idea whatever to read that it was 104 in the shade'. No one, writes Savory, 'who has not been in a similar situation could understand the excitement of those moments'. Savory marks out the 'ordinary' Britisher from the seasoned hunter-colonial here. She then goes on to state: 'the sight of a "Miss Sahib" risking her life in such hazardous adventures filled them [natives] with amazement' (Savory 1900: 263–64, 281, 271–72). When Savory concludes her memoir, the triumphalist rhetoric emphasizes all the crucial elements of the sporting luxuriant: risk and danger, heroism and pleasure: 'But, after all, it is worth it, and a high price has to be paid *because* it is worth it' (Savory 1900: 283, emphasis in original). Markham (1854: 79–80), likewise, argues that even though the travel is tough, 'the sport will repay you'. R.L. Kennion (1910: 312) echoes the sentiment: 'Hundreds of *sahibs* had shot thousands of ibex, but no one had yet succeeded in taking a photograph of a wild ibex – a feat that was far more difficult, and therefore more meritorious'. Stebbing (1920: x) declares: 'without a knowledge of their habits and characteristics you may pass months, even years, in the jungles without seeing, save by accident, pelt, horn or hoof'. Stebbing is here emphasizing the need to possess accurate knowledge of the jungle terrain. Others provided detailed descriptions of the most effective methods to capture animals alive (for instance, a narrative by H.B. Bryant on capturing the elephant, *IF* 21 [1895]: 34–36). An 'observer' writing in *Indian Forester* (16 [1890]: 427) suggests that 'if we value the tiger for the sport he affords, it is but fair that we should interest ourselves in his habits'. In his earlier work, Inglis devotes an entire section to the correct mode of shooting leopards and tigers, having first outlined the animals' haunts, feeding habits and general abilities. He then advises future hunters on guns and the curing of animal skins (Maori 1878: 125–31, 227–28, 236–46, 247, 356–61). Cumming (1871: 18–21) devotes a separate section to the curing of animal skins too. The instructional sections in the sporting memoir are 'illustrated' with examples from the *shikari*'s own hunting expeditions, thereby lending the 'guide' a sense of authenticity. In other texts, the older, more experienced hunter advises the 'griffin' on the correct modes of shooting, the right kinds of guns and the precautions that must be exerted to survive the Indian wilds (for instance, in W. Campbell 1853: 91–92). The sporting memoir must also be read as a *guide* to Indian forests, fauna and flora and the best modes of acquiring a 'bag'. The memoir maps habitats, hunting patterns, technological devices (including guns), items to be used for expeditions and health risks.[20] Every single memoir is a detailed account directed at *future* hunters.

David Gilbert (1999: 281) has pointed out that even though travel guidebooks emerged in the age of tourism (the nineteenth century), there was little distinction between the tourist guidebook and popular genres like literary travel writing and topographical writing. While guidebooks on the correct modes of behaviour were being produced for the English officers and civilians in India, the sporting memoir functioned as an etiquette and guidebook for the extreme exotic.[21] We can read the sporting memoirs as marking the creation of a distinct persona: that of the knowledgeable English adventurer and sports person.

To begin with it is directed at a different class of English person: the adventurer. It also proposes a form of education and experience not available to the other English in India: that of risk. Finally, it sets apart the *shikari* as a conquistador of the wilds, as opposed to the administrator or the bureaucrat in the city. This is why Inglis (1892: 3–4) suggests that the 'sneers and stupid imbecilities of the untravelled and inexperienced sceptic' only 'excite his [the English adventurer-sportsman's] good-natured pity'. In another case, he also refers to the ignorant English hunter, who makes mistakes because he is 'quite inexperienced in the ways of Indian woodcraft, and blissfully ignorant of the peculiarities of elephants and tigers' (Inglis 1892: 329). The white *shikari* is a traveller, as opposed to the tourist, because he – it was usually a male – sought the undiscovered and preferred to see travel as a route to self-development rather than being passive consumers of places.[22]

The sporting memoir as guidebook, therefore, rhetorically *prepares* the forests, animal life and the otherwise uninhabited wilds for exploration, study, collection and political and economic exploitation by detailing animal haunts, seasons, suitable weapons and gear. The sporting memoir makes even the dangerous jungle 'available' for consumption by the English. The luxuriant as an aesthetic generated by the sporting memoir first constructs the wilds, then proceeds to demonstrate exactly how the wilds could be controlled and regulated through personal suffering, pain and endeavour.

Spectacle and dominance

'I know not a finer spectacle than a line of elephants beating for a tiger', writes Markham (1854: 7). Markham's comment draws attention to a central purpose and feature of the imperial hunt: spectacle. From the early decades of the nineteenth century an English person's tour through the district itself was a massive spectacle, where the entourage of elephants, bearers and assistants accompanying the English sahib often extended for miles. Emily Eden, for instance, travelling with her brother Governor-General Lord Auckland, just before the 'mutiny', was accompanied by about 12,000 people, presenting a majestic spectacle (Eden 1930: 31). The British in the Victorian age sought to demonstrate the empire's might through rituals and spectacles such as the durbars, losing no opportunity to exhibit imperial authority and majesty (Cannadine 2002; Cohn 2002). The hunt served this same purpose, especially after the 1857 'mutiny' when the need to reassert imperial dignity and power became more pronounced.

The triumphal landscape exhibited symbols of authority, a feature associated with the hunt from Mughal times (J.M. MacKenzie 1988; Pandian 2001). Spectacle was, in any case, central to the Raj because, as Metcalf (1998: 167–71) puts it, the Raj needed a 'ringing show of self-confidence' during this period. Young English civilians setting out to accept posts with the Indian Civil Service were often told that in India 'he lives among a race who are peculiarly sensitive to external pomp and circumstance' (*MM* 4 [1861]: 264). As the hunt became increasingly ceremonial (mainly for the benefit of the natives and the egos of the English, even though they occasionally hunted in small parties), the rhetoric of spectacle is integral to this moment in the sporting memoir. The hunters were extremely conscious of their role as *rulers*. The hunt becomes a means of reiterating racial superiority especially in the wake of 1857. Inglis (1892) draws together the hunt, imperialism and the issue of race when he writes:

> I recently came across an incident of cool heroism and bravery on the part of a few of our own kith and kin, which shows that the good old qualities of our race are not wholly wiped out yet, and which is such a capital illustration of the dangers of tiger shooting I have just been referring to, and the opportunities it affords for individual courage and daring, that it may fitly close this present chapter.
>
> (Inglis 1892: 111)

The individual's courage, for Inglis, expands or merges into a racial characteristic, within the context of the tiger hunt in India. Savory mentions that what follows (the description of a tiger shoot) is narrated 'as it struck a well-known Mem-sahib'. Her description of the expedition demonstrates the dimensions of spectacle: 'Our caravan really formed a most imposing train as we set off from Warungal station' (Savory 1900: 255, 256). Rice (1857: 24) mentions the 'large crowd' of men who accompany him. Inglis (1892: 63) mentions the 'line of elephants' and beaters that set out on the shoot. In another instance, he sets out with no less than 'some dozen of the finest elephants' making an 'imposing procession of stately elephants . . . surrounded by the white-coated sahibs, with their broad, mushroom-looking sun hats' (1892: 324). Walter Campbell (1853: 12) and Gordon Cumming (1871: 13) both mention the attention and services their hunting expedition received from natives.

The spectacle of the sporting memoir also, frequently, encodes the power relations at work between the English hunter and the native assistants. An illustrative example would be Inglis' account of the tracking of a tiger with a large retinue of natives:

> It was truly an Oriental sight, to see nearly thirty huge lumbering elephants toiling heavily over these ridges, plunging into the still bayou-looking lagoons, and, with the picturesque *puggrees*, bronzed naked skins, and polished spears of the natives, who were clinging to the ropes like so many great monkeys, the scene was altogether a striking one.
>
> (Inglis 1892: 103)

Later he refers to them as 'apes'. The reduction of the natives to 'monkeys' and 'apes' in Inglis' narrative emphasizes the difference between rulers and ruled. Earlier he had described the movement of the expedition as 'majestic'. Success, he writes, often depends on being able to procure arms, beaters and 'an array of elephants' (Inglis 1892: 109, 64, 98).

It is such a consciousness of their position and stature that informs Savory's comments on specific incidents on the expedition. When the other woman in Savory's team, 'M', misses a shot, Savory writes: 'It was the easiest shot in the world . . . Great Goodness! – missed him! . . . M looked more like suicide than anything, and the *shikari*'s pity was so many coals of fire' (Savory 1900: 137–38). Here the collapse of the spectacle is completely catastrophic. But what is insufferable is the *native shikari*'s pity for the Memsahib. Savory's writing underscores the fact that the failure was unacceptable because it had been in the presence of the native. The spectacle of the hunt, which serves to emphasize British supremacy, had collapsed in full view of the native it was supposed to impress. In another case, the *Indian Forester* (21 [1895]: 63) reports the 'success' of Miss Ribbentrop, the daughter of an Inspector-General, listing her kills: 'a tiger, a panther, and a fine stag', even specifying the guns and technique she used. The luxuriant's catalogue of trophies – detailed lists of animals killed appeared regularly in the *Oriental Sporting Magazine* (see, as a sample, the issue of 10 February 1877: 51–56), arranged chronologically to show the successes of each day in particular areas – is a catalogue of triumphs over the Indian wilds.

The natives, hired only as assistants to the English hunters, are subordinated to both the English hunters and the land. The Englishman was of course the colonial master. The land alters from being mere 'scenery' (a process that involved treating it as empty through a rhetoric of absence, as noted above) to a heroic 'setting' or 'environment' for the English actions. This process not only renders the land a site of conquest and triumph, but also was alienated from its primary users: the tribals and the natives. The sporting narrative, in short, serves as an exploration narrative, a conquest narrative through its risk narrative: the English hunters who risk their lives in the wilds emerge triumphant rather than the tribal or the natives who have lived there all their lives. The sporting memoir converts the land into a foreign space for the native itself.[23]

Risk itself functions to generate a spectacle in the sporting memoir. It reinvents the trauma and loss of control that the wilds represented, in what was actually a situation of excessive control. *Shikar* granted the English colonial temporary control over even social risk (epitomized in the native) by controlling the 'script' of the risk, as Anne McClintock (1994: 147) has argued in another context.

The sporting luxuriant facilitates the reiteration of identities – of the colonial master who has just remade India through conquest, suffering and pain, of the Indian who is cowardly and weak, of the Indian landscape which is a site of danger but which can be conquered and controlled by the adequately equipped English person. The sporting luxuriant thus shifts from the passive picturesque to a triumphal landscape via the aesthetics of risk in order to show colonial mastery. The luxuriant is an aesthetic of mutual affect: the landscape is transformed and 'domesticated' by the colonial hunter even as hunters themselves have been transformed into heroes.

Notes

Introduction: aesthetic negotiations

1 *London Journal* (17 April 1725, 19 June 1725, 5 June 1725, 31 July 1725, 4 September 1725), *The Englishman* (8–10 October 1713, 29–31 October 1713, 3–5 December 1713), *London Mercury* (16–20 June 1682, 23–27 June 1682, 7–11 July 1682, 11–15 August 1682), *English Post* (31 December 1701–2 January 1702, 5–7 January 1702, 7–9 January 1702, 4–6 February 1702, 16–18 February 1702) and *City Mercury* (4 July 1692 and 13 March 1693).

2 The exceptions are Suleri (1992) and Leask (2002). Despite the absence of aesthetics as a subject of scrutiny, the most detailed exploration of European representations of India (1600–1800) remains Teltscher's (1997) *India Inscribed*. Colonial visual representations of India have been better studied for their aesthetics (Ray 1998; J. Robertson 2002). The standard study of British aesthetic responses to Indian art remains that of Mitter (1977).

3 See Lach and Van Kley (1990) for statistics. An index of the popularity of these travelogues is provided by the statistics of the holdings of England's Royal Library (shifted to the Cambridge University Library in 1737). In the Royal Library catalogue for the eighteenth century, under Class 'O', series I–VI, out of a total of 697 volumes, 106 books were titled 'Voyages' or 'Travels'.

4 Pagden (1993: 21) demonstrates the 'principle of attachment' in European representations of the New World.

5 Youngs (1994: 8) warns us that 'travel writing feeds from and back into other forms of literature'. Borm emphasizes that 'the *literary* is at work in travel writing' (Borm 2004: 13, emphasis in original). For attempts at definition and genre-description, see Fussell (1980), M.B. Campbell (1988) and Martels (1994).

1 Marvellous difficulty, 1600–1720

1 Todorov (2000) argues that even travellers such as missionaries, soldiers and merchants were colonizers, where each represents a specific form of colonialism: spiritual, military and commercial.

2 The scientific gaze sought to record the particular, and narrated the same in a plain, factual style, just as topographical drawings functioned antithetically to 'artistic' renderings of the land (Stafford 1984: xix, 3–7, 31–56, 348–49).

3 In the seventeenth century, travellers who gave up their country's culture for the other's was a 'renegade'. Nathaniel Hardy (1658: 38) in his sermon, *The Pious Votary and Prudent Traveller*, for instance, warned against seduction by other nations (see Warneke 1995: 227–39; Chard 1999: 45–46).

4 On the instructions for travellers, see Batten (1978: 88–89). Most instructions recommended that travellers detail chorographic as well as moral landscapes. It was therefore expected that the traveller would use both a scientific and a moral approach to new lands, a feature of the medieval 'encyclopedic' approach to landscape description (Cahn 1991; Edney 1997: 42).

5 Nicolas Monardes' natural history of the Indies appeared in English in 1577. On natural histories, mapping and power, see Helgerson (1986), Helsinger (1997), Biggs (1999) and M.B. Campbell (1999: 62). On such geographical-cartographic 'dealings' with the New World, see Koch (1998). On regional geographic writing and natural histories, see Butlin (1990).

6 The *Transactions* also printed extracts and reviews of European travelogues (10. 119 [1675]; 11. 130 [1676]; 12. 137 [1677–78]). Travellers frequently used their predecessors' material for their purposes. Teltscher's (1997: 2–3) comparativist work, however, warns, quite correctly, that though these European discourses 'create a network of intersecting and contending discourses about India', they cannot be 'forced to tell a single narrative about colonial expansion'.

7 The *Transactions* regularly published accounts of the plants imported by or gifted to the Royal Society as 'curiosities' for scientific study (2. 264, 267, 271, 274 and 276 [1700–701]; Vol. 23 Nos. 277, 282 and 287 [1702–3]). On the role of the botanic gardens in imperialism, see Brockway (1999) and Tobin (2005).

8 Wonder in the early modern period was a preliminary to investigation. A pamphlet (attributed to Charles Blount in the Cambridge University Library catalogue), *Miracles, No Violation of the Laws of Nature*, describes wonder as a characteristic of the ignorant (Anon. 1683: 3). Rene Descartes distinguished between wonder and astonishment, where the latter was *excessive* wonder on par with sickness (Descartes 1989 [1645–46, 1649], sections: 2.53, 2.71, 2.75–76 and 2.78). The marvellous substituted for the theologically loaded 'miraculous' (Greenblatt 1991: 79). On medieval and early modern wonder, see Daston and Park (1998) and Sell (2006). For eighteenth-century forms of geographical narratives, see Edney (1997) and Cormack (1997). The seventeenth-century English travelogue on India exhibits features of *both* genres, where the aesthetic of the marvellous forged a link between the 'mechanistic' and empiricist geographical form and the personal travel narrative.

9 On the 'explanatory' role of the marvellous, see Todorov (1975).

10 On the 'wonder shift' in early modern Europe, see Platt (1997: 26–27).

11 The French physician-traveller, François Bernier in his 1671 tract, also paints such a picture of paradise in India's Kashmir (Bernier 1979). Incidentally, Bernier's paradise was a cultivated one.

12 The East has, at least since the time of Marco Polo, appeared to the West as abundance (M.B. Campbell 1988: 109).

13 The catalogue and the enumerative modality is not restricted to English travellers in India. The Frenchman Gabriel Dellon, in his *A Voyage to the East-Indies* (English translation, 1698) devotes parts of his narrative to the plant and animal life of India. These he divided into carefully titled sections: 'Of Malabar', 'Of the Two Fruits called the Jacque and the Mango', 'Of Pepper, Cardamon, Cinnamon and Bethel', 'Of the Elephant and some other Animals of Malabar', 'Of the Tiger, and some other Creatures of Malabar', 'Of some other Animals; of the Jaccal; of the Buffler; of the Civet Cat and Ape' (Dellon 1698: 61–91).

14 On the land, garden and women 'enclosed' for profit in seventeenth-century poetry, see Malcolmson (1994).

15 On the ideologies of landscape representation, see Bermingham (1986).

16 And the monstrous was, right into the eighteenth century, associated with the aesthetic of the marvellous (Daston and Park 1998: 210–12).

17 Several descriptions of India's great wealth circulated in Britain in the seventeenth century. Thomas Mun (1621) computed the profits to be obtained from the East India

trade. One hundred years later, the *London Journal* of 31 July 1725 advertised Salmon's *Modern History*, number 13, thus:

> This pamphlet treats of the European settlements and factories on the coasts of Coromandel, Malabar and Bengal, particularly of Fort St. George, Cochin, Goa, Bombay and Surat, and contains *a particular account of the diamond mines of Golconda and Visapoo.*
>
> (*London Journal* 31 July 1725: n.p., emphasis added).

18 Hastings writes in his *The Present State of the East Indies*:

> The sources of opulence which it [Bengal] possesses in the fertility of its soil, and the number and industry of its inhabitants will, I think, admit, of its yielding the tribute I have mentioned [one crore rupees annually], which is perhaps greater than any other country in the world.
>
> (Hastings 1786: 21–22)

A different version of such a rhetoric of incomparability is available in George Forster (1798, 1: 14) who, describing the ruins of a town in north India, writes: 'The instability of monuments of human grandeur cannot, in any region of the globe, I apprehend, be more faithfully, or more grievously exemplified than at Rajah Mahal'.

19 Quadflieg (2004: 29) suggests that, at least in the early modern period, the travellers, in exploring Others, explored themselves. Dyson (1978: 3) also notes that private and public worlds converge in the travel narrative: there is both observation and introspection. Quadflieg's argument serves my purpose here in suggesting that the epistemological ordering of India was as much about India as it was about the Englishman's need to assert his own identity when faced with the Other.

20 Barbour (2003: 41) has rightly argued that this idea of the 'expansive East' 'conjured up in narrow England' enabled the representation of Asia and Africa as a great barbaric spectacle for English consumption. The marvellous aesthetic highlights the vast spectacle even as it suggests modes of (rhetorically) controlling the expanse.

21 Such descriptions anticipate dozens of eighteenth-century travel writings wherein the Indian rivers are constantly spilling over, breaking walls, and inundating man-made structures. See, for instance, Jemima Kindersley (1777: 82, 92, 183); Thomas Motte (*Asiatic Miscellany* 2 [1786]: 10, 24–25); William Thomson (1788, 1: 22–23); Edward Moor (1794: 49, 62); John Taylor (1799, 2: 151); George Thomas (1803: 41); James Lind (1811 [1768]: 61); William Hickey (1925, 3: 323–25); William Jones (1970, 2: 783). All these narratives carry descriptions of frightening overflowing rivers and inundated, markerless lands. For a detailed analysis of this image, see Chapter 3.

22 Cohn (1997: 9–10) points out that the Englishman preferred to view India from a distance.

23 Spencer (1973: 15) identifies the enclosed garden as a *hortus conclusus*, a place of safety and refuge in early modern England. An enclosed garden was also, incidentally, a sign of possession (Seed 1995: 28–29).

24 As late as the eighteenth century, the aesthetics of landscape was shaped by encounters with less familiar and far more frightening 'wildernesses' overseas (Helsinger 1997: 16–17). Cultivated landscapes, gardens and orchards symbolized culture, the spirit of scientific inquiry, and Christian faith. Abraham Cowley in his poem to the Royal Society, contrasted wildernesses with cultivated gardens. Cowley referred to Francis Bacon as having 'passed' the 'barren wilderness' to stand on the border of the 'promised land', and thanked him for having opened the 'orchard' of knowledge (Sprat 1667: unpaginated).

25 Francis Bacon in *The Great Instauration* (1620) declares that he would admit nothing except on the 'faith of [his] eyes' (http://etext.library.adelaide.edu.au/b/bacon/francis/instauration). On visualism in history, see Classen (1993). On the 'problems' with sensate knowledge in early modern Europe, see Spolsky (2001). Sell (2006: 58–59)

argues that the introductory remarks of the early travel narrative were attempts to capture the audience's goodwill (what was called *captatio benevolentiae*), and constitutes the ethos of the narrative itself.

26 On the theme of observation and possessing, see Greenblatt (1991: 122); Pratt (1992: 7, 78); Kamps and Singh (2001: 3–4); Spolsky (2001: 29–30, 66–69).

27 Notice here the parallels with Thomas Hobbes who, in *The Leviathan* (1651), writes:

> Desire, to know why, and how, CURIOSITY; such as is in no living creature but Man; so that Man is distinguished, not only by his Reason; but also by this singular Passion from other animals . . . a Lust of the mind, that by a perseverance of delight in the continual and indefatigable generation of knowledge, exceeds the short vehemence of any carnal pleasure.
>
> (Hobbes 1976 [1651]: 124, emphasis in original)

28 Spolsky (2001: 18–20) distinguishes between the early modern's Pyrrohnist scepticism, which doubted methods of discovery, whether they derived from sense impressions or from reason, and its academic scepticism, a kind of intellectual disbelief that perpetually sought truth.

29 Interestingly, Roe (1990: 283) is disconcerted when he realizes that he is the subject of the native women's gaze. In this case, he is unable to see the women himself, since they are behind the purdah. For a reading of the function, structure and ideology of visuality, visibility and organization of space in Thomas Roe, see Nayar (2002).

30 For the rhetoric of discovery, see Singh (1996).

31 In the seventeenth century natural philosophers referred to themselves as 'curious' or 'ingenious'. To be 'curious' meant to combine 'a thirst to know with an appetite for marvels', paying attention to new, rare and exotic objects/phenomena (Daston and Park 1998: 218). For a study of the 'disinterested' gentleman of science in this period, see Dear (1992).

32 Daniel Carey (1996) has demonstrated out how the travel narratives fed back into the English intellectual milieu.

33 On the mapping of physical differences between English and Indian climate/landscape/disease as the *essential/unchanging* difference between races/cultures, see Harrison (1996, 1999).

34 The *Philosophical Transactions* of 1676 quotes an illuminating incident from Jean-Baptiste Tavernier's travelogue. An English minister sees a group of jugglers performing 'miracles' along the Surat–Agra highway. He is shocked to see that among the audience are some East India Company men. The minister, enraged at such heathenish acts, declares that 'he would never again give communion to any one of those that should stay any longer there to see more of such (by him reputed magical) things' (*PT* 11. 130 [1676]: 752). India as a place of magic was therefore a dangerous influence, as the minister's action suggests

35 See Kindersley (1777: 181); Thomas Motte (*Asiatic Researches* 2 [1786]: 13); Munro (1789: 67), among others.

36 Seed (1995: 18–19) argues that England's central characteristic was the 'peculiar fixity' of its settlements, some of which went back by a thousand years. This fixity suggested a sense of permanence that contrasted with India's ruins. On the antiquity of English villages, see Roberts (1973).

37 In the nineteenth century elephantiasis would become central to the colonial medical, cultural and critical imaginary about the tropics (Stepan 2001).

38 This theme from Ovington will be cited years later in a review essay which brands the early English at Surat as licentious, ungodly, and given to excessively luxurious lives (*CaR* 9 [1848]: 119–21).

39 Thomas Mun (1621: 57) in his *Discourse of Trade* spoke of 'religiously avoid[ing] common excesses of food and raiment'. The discourse against luxury – which contextualizes depictions of Indian excesses – was directed primarily against food, clothing and

material culture (see Sekora 1977). The arrival in England of several Indian (and Asian) products was perceived as a threat to local industry and trade. Shipments of Asian textiles – to mention just one item of the trade – increased from 273,647 pieces in 1664 to 1,760,315 pieces in 1684. Indian products, now mass consumed, apparently threatened the very fabric of English society, and induced a sense of luxury. For studies of the economics of the East India trade, see Chaudhuri (1978) and Robins (2006). For a discussion of debates over the 'corruption' of English society due to the Eastern trade, see Bhattacharya (1998), especially Chapter 4.

40 Enumeration in these travelogues may be linked to the rise of political arithmetic in England. John Graunt, Charles Davenant and William Petty popularized the gathering of 'social information'. For a discussion of the rise and implications of political arithmetic and institutions of information-gathering, see Rusnock (1999) and Higgs (2004). For the early modern belief in the enumerative technique as a sign of Western rationality, see Goody (1996: 49–81).

41 M.B. Campbell (1988: 30, 55) draws parallels between the commercial cataloguing of commodities and the ethnographic 'recording' of racial features. In English writings on India, the conflation of the commercial and the natural is paralleled, also, by a conflation of the natural with the moral. Ordering and categorization into different 'heads' was also an important form of natural history writing.

42 Enargheia was a feature of medieval rhetoric where the evidence of the *senses* was paramount (Barilli 1989: 73).

43 Francis Bacon, for instance, praised Plato for his ability to 'define and to divide' (quoted in Vickers 1968: 30).

44 Interest in the 'curiosities' of the East may be gauged from the fact that during the seventeenth century alone, there were over sixteen major separate accounts of the Mughal Empire and an additional ten reported on it (Lach and Van Kley 1990). The anonymously authored *Directions for a Proper Choice of Authors to form a Library* (Anon. 1766), under 'Travels and Voyages', lists the mandatory Purchas and Hakluyt collections, the Salmon volumes, and the Indian travelogues of John Fryer and Thomas Herbert (Anon. 1766: 20, 22).

45 For a detailed analysis of European views of Indian iconography, see Mitter (1977). By emphasizing the Hindu worship of such monsters, the English traveller presented Hinduism itself as 'illogical and perverted' (Teltscher 1997: 23).

46 As late as 1757, John Grose in *A Voyage to East Indies* undertakes a similar desacralizing when he describes the Elephanta Caves as offering a potential site for picnics (Grose 1757: 62–63).

47 *The Englishman* of 12–13 December 1713 advertised the volume *The Travels of the Jesuits*, emphasizing that it was 'written by the learned missionaries' and contained 'an account of the strange customs, manners, superstitions, & C of several nations not mentioned by other travellers', Advertisements for maps, globes and such travelogues constantly emphasized the epistemological benefits to be obtained from these texts. *The London Mercury* regularly advertised Glanius' *A New Voyage to the East-Indies*, between June and August 1682 (16–20, 20–23, 23–27 June; 30 June – 4 July; 7–11 July; 11–15, 18–22, 25–29 August). *The Postman* advertised a proposal 'for printing a complete collection of "Voyages and Travels" extracted from Hakluyt and Purchas' (8–11 May 1701), travelogues (15–17 July 1701, 4–6 December 1701, 16–18 December 1701, 17–18 January 1702), and maps (5–7 February 1717, 25–27 April 1717).

48 Moorcroft and Trebeck in their *Travels in the Himalayan Provinces of Hindustan and the Panjab* describe the Pinjor fort and gardens thus: 'The effect of the whole when maintained in order must have been highly pleasing' (Moorcroft and Trebeck 1841, 1: 34, also 59 and 92). See also Kindersley (1777: 181); Munro (1789: 67); Thomas Motte (*Asiatic Miscellany* 2 [1786]: 13).

49 The English travelogue on India here intersects with the Grand Tour travelogue in its theme of the Englishman's real or potential corruption in the lands of excess and loose

morals. See Warneke (1995: 74–85); Chard (1999: 59–61). For a statistical account of the destinations and 'sights' on the Grand Tour, see Towner (1996: 96–138).

2   The social monstrous, 1600–1720

1   Ambroise Paré's *On Monsters and Marvels* (1573) was an early attempt to systematize the causes and typology of monsters. Paré (1982: 3) defined monsters as 'things that appear outside nature'. Paré was also the first to inaugurate the idea that the mother's imagination might play an important role in the production of monsters (1982: 38–42). The text that did most to popularize 'monstrous races' was undoubtedly the controversial *The Travels of Sir John Mandeville* (first published 1356–57 in France), included in the first edition of Hakluyt's *Principall Navigations* and of which at least 250 manuscripts survive! (Moseley 1983; Seymour 1993). It may have influenced Christopher Columbus (Moseley 1983: 9). One of the most comprehensive studies of the monstrous in Western thought is J.B. Friedman's *The Monstrous Races in Medieval Art and Thought* (1981). Specific explorations include Huet (1993); Tiffany (1995); Burnett (2002); Crawford (2005), among others.

2   Cotgrave's *Dictionarie* (1611) describes the grotesque as 'pictures wherein (as please the painter) all kinds of odde things are represented without anie peculiar sence, or meaning, but merely to feed the eye', Thomas Blount's *Glossographia* (1670) uses the exact same definition as Cotgrave's but adds a sentence: 'hence taken for any rude misshapen thing' (Blount 1670: 301). M.B. Campbell (1988: 61, n. 9) notes that the question of whether the grotesque inheres in nature or in art has been answered differently in different eras. In other cases thinkers in early modern Europe claimed that monsters were not divine portents but the creation of nature itself, where nature *as artist* ingeniously crafted other forms for admiration (Daston and Park 1998: 200). I follow Campbell here, seeing the grotesque as a means of portraying the alien. On the grotesque as contained in art, see Dorrian (2000).

3   M.B. Campbell (1999: 236), reading John Bulwer's *Anthropometamorphosis* (1650), argues that such tracts tended to posit England as Nature and Asia, Africa and America as Culture (see also Thomson 1972: 14, 21; Dorrian 2000: 310–17).

4   The Indian monstrous in English writings on India approximates more closely to what Park and Daston (1981: 23) identify as the third strain in monster-representations, the anthropological mode. With the noticeable decrease in the religious interpretations of monsters in the seventeenth century, commentators turned to the anthropological mode, discussing monstrous races of men in Africa and Asia (see also M.B. Campbell 1988; Bates 2005).

5   Advice books such as Philip Sidney and William Davison's *Profitable Instructions* (1633: 4) instructed travellers to record what commodities were consumed and exported in the foreign lands.

6   An interesting parallel to this pre-colonial rhetoric of consumption would be that of Thomas Coryate, whose work, *Coryate's Crudities* (1611), had a lengthy title which went thus:

> hastily gobled up in five moneths travells in France, Savoy, Italy, Rhetia commonly called the Grisons country, Helvetia alias Switzerland, some parts of high Germany and the Netherlands; newly digested in the hungry aire of Odcombe in the county of Somerset, and now dispersed to the nourishment of the travelling members of this kingdome . . .

7   Interestingly Thomas Mun in his later tract on the benefits of the East India trade, *England's Treasure by Foreign Trade* (1664, written 1622–23) describes the Prince as a greedy and destructive paunch given to excessive consumption (quoted in Healy 2002: 164–65).

8 The term 'profligate', which, the *OED* informs us, meant 'abandoned to vice or vicious indulgence; recklessly licentious or debauched; dissolute; extremely or shamelessly vicious' is, interestingly, also used to describe self-destruction by Ovington. He describes Indians as 'being profligate of their own lives' (Ovington 1696: 345). This is a curious twist to the rhetoric of consumption where the taking of one's life is also seen as excessive indulgence. On the theme of consuming selves, see Burnett (2002).

9 The full title indicates the target of the attack:

> in dress and apparel: wherein naked breasts and shoulders, antick and fantastick garbs, patches, and painting, long perriwigs, towers, bulls, shades, curlings, and crispings, with an hundred more fooleries of both sexes, are condemned as notoriously unlawful. With pertinent addresses to the court, nobility, gentry, city and country, directed especially to the professors in London.

10 I adapt Crawford's (2005: 33) theorization of 'fashion monsters' here. Crawford notes that infant deformities and monstrous births in early modern England were perceived as resembling human fashion excesses.

11 See, for instance, the tract *England's Vanity* (1683: 16–18). Another commentary, attributed to Alexander Pope, declares that 'amiable simplicity of unadorned nature' was better than the artifice of the times (*The Guardian* 173, 29 September 1713, in Stephens 1982: 562–65).

12 Curiously entanglement is associated with a *non-European* context. In a polemic against Cromwell, the writer complains how 'the whole nation was enchained in a more than .Egyptian bondage' during the Protectorate (*The English Devil* 1660: 3).

13 Incidentally, many tracts of the period described the absence of 'proper' clothing, especially in women, as 'monstrous'. See the anonymously authored pamphlet, *The World's Infection; or a relation of the monstrous and abominable sin of women* (Anon. 1700).

14 It might also be linked to the excessive use and circulation of India and China products in England. There were several petitions by weavers, fan makers and others protesting against the import of Indian goods during this period. The popularity of 'Oriental' products was very high. John Ovington, for instance, published a tract on tea, in which he commented that the 'drinking of it' is now 'universal' in England (Ovington 1699: 2). A petition by 'fann-makers' to the House of Commons, for instance, pleaded that the importation of 'fanns and fan-sticks, as well as silk and callicoes' in order to protect England's manufacturers (Anon. 1695, *The Case of the Fann-makers*: n.p.). For a reading of these tracts, see Bhattacharya (1998).

15 Bhattacharya argues, correctly, that the hoarding of wealth, absence of circulating specie and fashion excesses were seen as symbols of a degenerating body politic. The 'erotic economies' predicated upon the female body that Bhattacharya points to are no doubt central to the pre-colonial imaginary (Bhattacharya 1998: 23–35). What escapes Bhattacharya's otherwise astute analysis is that the language of erotic economy generated its own *aesthetic*, that of the grotesque.

16 Robertson (1996:1) argues that the grotesque functions as a 'mediating principle between order and non-order'.

17 The discourse against luxury was directed at what was perceived as excessive consumption of material goods. In terms of economy, protests at the excessive import of India products circulated through seventeenth and eighteenth-century England, as Bhattacharya (1998: 95–98) demonstrates. The 'beastly' image here ties up closely with tracts like *England's Vanity* which sarcastically dismissed 'the whole frantick herd running about with gilded horns, and platted manes, presenting themselves to the angry deity for sacrifice' (Anon 1683: 31).

18 Earlier Terry (1655: 17–19, 26) had compared Africans unfavourably with animals and described the people of Souldania as 'beasts in the skins of men, rather than men in the skins of beasts'.

19 The Oriental despot and the tyrannical Asiatic king was a common image of the early modern stage as well, exemplified in Christopher Marlowe's *Tamburlaine* and John Dryden's *Aureng-zebe*.

20 Tiffany (1995: 27) notes that human sexual activity is allegorized as a human-beast confrontation in early modern plays; this is what she terms 'erotic beasts'.

21 Terry's description of India as a fleshly paradise is prefigured in his own earlier tract where he warns Englishmen of falling prey to 'loose' behaviour in India: see his *The Merchants and Mariners Preservation and Thanksgiving* (1649: 29–30).

22 The interest in the oriental erotic was not, of course, restricted to India. The sexual lives of the Turkish empire and the Arab world were also subject to this same scrutiny. Thus an advertisement for Salmon's *Modern History* no. 22, emphasizes that the volume carries a wealth of detail about the Turkish emperor's harem, royal concubines and female slaves (*London Journal* 7 May 1726: n.p.).

23 In 1584 Richard Haklyut in 'Discourse of Western Planting' had recommended that the idling vagabonds, being 'very burdensome' on the commonwealth should be sent off to 'Western parts, especially in New Foundland' to clear the landscape and employ themselves usefully (Haklyut 1935, 2: 234–35). Two centuries later, Fort William, Calcutta, recommended in a letter dated 18 May 1793, to the Court of Directors, that it might use male convicts to clear the islands around the Hoogly Harbour (*Fort William* 12 [1793–95]: 245).

24 Abjection, as Julia Kristeva tellingly argues, is a 'border'. It is a 'fragile state' where 'man strays on the territories of animal'. The abject in Kristeva helps delineate a clean and proper body (Kristeva 1982: 9–12). 'Filth' was often associated with moral corruption during the Renaissance and the seventeenth century, as the *OED* points out. Terry uses the term several times to describe moral depravity.

25 See Huet (1993), Friedman (2000), among others.

26 On the wild man and the jungle, see Hayden White (1972).

27 Semler (1996: 70) sees these two features as aspects of the mannerist grotesque.

28 Harpham (1982: 16) defines this sense of emergent comprehension as the 'interval of the grotesque'.

3 The imperial sublime, 1750–1820

1 A document entitled *Some Thoughts on the Present State of our Trade to India* pointed out that the annual losses from the EIC amounted to £666,000 (*MR* 10 [1754]: 369–71). For the comparative economic status of the French, English and Dutch East India companies in this period, see Gupta (1966: 24–47); Chaudhuri (1978: 440); Prakash (1998: 268–80).

2 The first English translation of Longinus, by John Hall, appeared in 1652. But it was Nicholas Boileau's French translation (1674) that really established Longinus' influence. Some of the thinkers of this new aesthetic were Joseph Addison, Mark Akenside, John Baillie, Hugh Blair, Edmund Burke and Lord Kames (Henry Home).

3 The *Eclectic Review* suggests that readers expect different travelogues and information from travellers depending upon the latter's background. Thus, 'public expectation', it states, will be high when a British nobleman produces a travelogue. The review is disappointed in Lord Valentia's travelogue because, contrary to such expectations, and despite his 'high and enviable privilege', his writings do not furnish 'some direct light to moral, political, and philosophical enquiry' (*EcR* 5 [1809]: 689–90). Later, reviewing Emma Roberts' *Scenes and Characteristics of Hindostan* (1835), the magazine describes her as 'uniting feminine tact and minuteness of observation with the masculine tone acquired by travel' (*EcR* [Series 3] [1835]: 415), thus providing a gendered account of travelogues and their narrative conventions. For a detailed study of women's use of narrative conventions and aesthetics, see Bohls (1997).

4 I have adapted this three-stage model from Lap-Chuen's (1998: 41–43) theory of the experience of the sublime.

5 For a study of the influence of the continental artists on English aesthetics, see Manwaring (1965).

6 Travel, exploration and landscape also influenced other areas. The emphasis on the improvement of colonies was so pronounced during this period that even the arts were described using agrarian imagery. Landscape and exploration become common metaphors for writers, especially when speaking of 'discoveries' in the Orient. For instance, book reviews would refer to 'fields' of Oriental knowledge opened up by scholars (*MR* 80 [1789]: 697, 2 [NS] [1790]: 369). *Gentleman's Magazine* in July 1752 published a speech (presumably by William Beckford) in which the speaker described the 'plentiful' potential of the East Indies entirely in agrarian terms (*Gentleman's Magazine* 22 [1752]: 298).

7 The *OED* informs us that while the root of 'paramount' signifies *topographical* position (specifically, 'above'), one of the meanings of the word is 'proprietor'. Forster's term thus suggests both ownership and – aptly, for a study of colonial topography – locational hierarchy. The panoptical position which the term gestures at will be a prominent theme in nineteenth-century English travel writing on India.

8 Stafford (1984: 176) comments about the image of rivers in travelogues: 'quiescence was perceived as essential even within those things most apparently characterized by fluidity'. The Deluge was an important subject of the apocalyptic sublime during the seventeenth century (Paley 1986: 7–19). The poem that won the Seatonian Prize for Poetry in 1789 was, by sheer coincidence, John Roberts' 'The Deluge',

9 Critics like Hildebrand Jacob (1735) considered massed groups to be sublime (cited in Ashfield and de Bolla 1996: 53–54).

10 This anticipation of something-more-to-come is a characteristic feature of eighteenth-century travel writing. Hodges (1793) suggests that the 'big event' of his tour is yet to come. Museologists and collectors in England express similar sentiments about the not-fully known but imaginatively recreated (with meanings/significance *attributed* to them). John Claudius Loudon (1835: 460) in his mammoth *Encyclopaedia of Gardening*, for instance, speculates on what *other* treasures lie concealed in the Orient.

11 Robertson (2002: 110) argues that the work of the Daniells with the focus on decay was a 'Gothic version of India in which visitors would be moved to contemplate their own mutability in the faces of layers of decay that spoke of unimaginable pasts'. I am not sure the English perceived *their* mutability in Indian ruins. Rather, the descriptive vocabulary of eighteenth-century travel writing seems to gesture towards Indian ruins in order to show an *Indian* decay. But the immediate shift of focus to English-improved landscapes suggests a belief in their ability to stem this decay.

12 Narratives of suffering during India voyages or sojourns were not in itself new to eighteenth-century England. As early as 1712, Richard Hall had published *The History of the Barbarous Cruelties and Massacres, committed by the Dutch in the East-Indies*. What is astounding about the 1750–1800 period is the extraordinary proliferation of these narratives. Narratives of the Bengal 'revolution' and the Mysore wars were the most common. James Bristow (1793: vii) mentions William Thomson's *Memoirs*. *The Times* carried a regular report on the war and the atrocities of Tipu Sultan (17 January 1785, 13 May 1785, 25 June 1785, 14 September 1785, 16 September 1785, 27 February 1788, 18 July 1791, 19, 20, 29, 30 August 1791, 7, 8, 15, 16, 27 September 1791, 6, 7, 8, 11, 19 October 1791, 1 December 1791, 15 December 1791, 10 February 1792, 9 April 1792, 10 April 1792, 16 July 1792, and on several other days). Between 7 June and 13 October 1786 – five months – *The Times* carried ten reports of Tipu's death, the rumours, and 'credible' truths about it. Reports and comments about the suffering of the English also appeared in the *Annual Register* (1758: 278–87; 1764: 39–40; 1791: 77–80 and 1792: 89–103). Reviews of such narratives of war and suffering also appeared in the *Monthly Review* (18 [1758]: 183; 72 [1785]: 379; 78 [1788]: 64–65; 7 [NS] [1792]: 231), the *Asiatic Annual Register* (1798–99, 'Supplement to the Chronicle': 254–56, 258–60,

'Characters': 1–6) and the *Critical Review* (8 [1759]: 268–71; 10 [1760]: 454–55; 12 [1761]: 144–45; 15 [1763]: 305; 16 [1763]: 249–58; 17 [1764]: 155–56; 32 [1771]: 382–84). This kind of coverage of events in India would occur decades later – during and after the 1857 'mutiny'.

13 The shift in representation from a sublime and threatening landscape to one of potential improvement in eighteenth-century English travelogues on India is also embedded in the dynamics transforming the English countryside, and an emergent aesthetics of landscape representation (see Rosenthal 1982: 44–71; Cosgrove 1984: 233–34).

14 Nussbaum (1995: 1) identifies the author as Phebe Gibbes. Monica Clough prepared a new edition in 1989.

15 'Melancholy' was, of course, part of the new literary taste in England, best exemplified by the Graveyard School of poetry, most notably in the work of Edward Young, Robert Blair and Thomas Gray. Further, in the mid-eighteenth century ruins were deliberately built/located to evoke melancholy (Hunt and Willis 1975; Thacker 1983).

16 The *OED* lists, among others, the following meanings of 'management': 'the working or cultivation of land, the process of manuring', 'an instance of managing; an administrative act', 'manner of proceeding' and 'the administration of a commercial enterprise'. The term suggests several themes and, in this case, approaches to landscape and India. In England the propertied gentry was being called to defend lands and property during the period of disaffection, bread riots (1794), and such. For example, Uvedale Price (1797: 14–15), landscaping enthusiast and theorist of the picturesque, advised the gentry to arm itself. The conflation of military, agricultural and economic registers in this rhetoric of improvement – in Clive (cited in Malcolm 1836, 2: 122–23) and others, such as Price (1797) or Sulivan (1780) – is fascinating.

17 Interestingly, when the newspaper, the *Evening Post*, was launched in 1709, its stated intention was to provide '*Geographical Description of those Places relating to the Seat of War*, in order to a perfect Understanding of the Transactions' (quoted in Sutherland 1986: 129). For a discussion of the link between landlords, estate management, and 'improvement', see Christopher Clay in Thirsk (1985: 119–251).

18 Travellers viewed these fortifications mainly as obstacles or challenges to be overcome. In the period that these memoirs were written, these fortifications were essentially enemy camps to be defeated by the English. Descriptions of routes and approaches functioned as icons of 'live' dangers. In this sense, mountains were truly sublime because one of the essential components of the sublime was that it was a (masculine) *challenge*.

19 Under James Rennell, British mapping projects turned from maritime charts to mapping of inland waterways – also seen in Forster (1798), as noted – towns and villages, military route plans (Bayly 1999: 49, 145). Bayly (1999: 161) argues that the Great Trigonometrical Survey of the last decades of the eighteenth century acted as a conduit for colonial knowledge because it gathered information for military purposes. There were other kinds of measurement too. Edward Ives (1773: 38–42), for instance, carefully plots weather conditions over several months. A meteorological diary kept at Calcutta (1 February 1784 – 31 December 1785) by Henry Trail was later published in the *Asiatic Researches* (2 [1799]: 421–47). Details of drugs and other East Indian produce for the benefit of the EIC were also being published at this time (see, for instance, the pamphlet *A Short History of Drugs*, 1779).

20 Pratt (1995: 61) suggests that the land in colonial writing is always empty, and therefore looking forward to the colonialist's 'improving eye'.

21 Several individual and institutional efforts went into propagating the ideology of improvement during the long eighteenth century. The forty-six volumes of *Annals of Agriculture* and the establishment of the Board of Agriculture (1793) were influential, as was Arthur Young. One of the 'useful projects' described by the *Annual Register* was usually husbandry. For Arthur Young's influence, see Mingey (1975). On 'agrarian patriotism', see Bayly (1989: 79–80, 121–22). Tracts on husbandry and improvement, however, circulate in England right from the mid-sixteenth century: Blith (1649).

Sharrock (1659) and Hartlib (1659). For the history of agricultural innovations in England in this period, see Thirsk (1985: 533–849).

22 The emphasis on fences and boundaries in the travelogues under consideration is rooted in the context of the great enclosure movement in England (Briggs 1971: 40–42; Hoskins 1992: 78–79).

23 John Claudius Loudon in *Treatise on Farming, Improving and Managing Country Residences* (1806) revived the term 'husbandry' and coined the phrase 'landscape husbandry' (Daniels and Watkins 1994: 13–41). The urge to improve, then, was partly the result of the current English ideology of husbandry, which granted a certain cultural capital to the landowner and agriculturist. The cult of personal effort and benevolent patronage by propertied gentry is rooted in the sense of obligation, duty and responsibility of late-eighteenth-century England. Institutions for the poor, sick and aged mushroomed after 1750. In the colonial context it assumes very different connotations, especially in terms of power, control and subordination. On the sense of a 'moral economy' and the rise of 'civic humanism' in eighteenth-century England, see Williams (1973: 59); Barrell (1986: 1–162). For the link between landscape aesthetics and civic humanism, notions of property and social stratification, see Bohls (1997: 73–82).

24 Incidentally, agrarian reform rarely meant planting *woods* (Bushaway 1982: 65–101; Daniels 1989: 42–82). William Gilpin (1973 [1791], 2: 40–41) distrusted forest dwellers. In India, Robert Orme (1974: 300) and John Taylor (1799, 2: 162) express their suspicion of forest dwellers.

25 Sir Joseph Banks, the botanist on Captain Cook's 1769 expedition to the South Seas, brought back 17,000 new plants to England. By the close of the eighteenth century, 5000 additional exotic plants had been imported (Streatfield 1981: 10). John Loudon (1835: 378) mentions Moorcroft's efforts at collecting 'exotic' plant species from India in his *Encyclopaedia*. Alexander Pope's famous 'grotto' had mineral and plant specimens from all over the world. On Joseph Banks, see R.E.R. Banks et al. (1994).

26 Barrell (1985: 35–88) argues that 'labour' enters the Georgian landscape paintings in contrasts of work and laziness. He suggests that this, in some ways, contrasts the labouring class and the propertied gentry. In the case of colonies, I suggest, the contrast between indolence and labour becomes the contrast between the native and the English. The poor/native who does not work is contrasted with *Cleveland*'s 'efforts' to create if not an ideal landscape, at least a *locus amoenus*.

27 See Nicolson (1963: 215–17, 269–70, 313–16); Paulson (1982: 11); Punter (1994: 22).

28 In a perceptive analysis, Joseph (2004) shows how notions of 'home' in eighteenth- and nineteenth-century English writings on India blurred the borders between public/private, native/foreigner and colonizer/colonized. Joseph (2004: 96) rightly points out how 'the ability to make an English home in India . . . becomes a test for the empire's own future'. Joseph's argument comes very close to my own about the British search for and creation of the *locus amoenus* in India. Where I depart from Joseph is in my reading of the aesthetic categories used to search, locate and isolate such a space.

29 Authorities such as James Lind and others suggested that native labour may be used to clear the forest areas, cut roads and improve the land since their bodies were better suited to the climate (Lind 1811 [1768]: 104–05, 117; see also *Fort William* 12: 245).

30 A few years later, however, the EIC itself was seen as besieged by storms. 'The storm is brooding against the East India Company; and it will not be long before it will burst', writes a commentator (*FM* 1 [1830]: 260). Clearly, the trope could serve different purposes, and the aesthetics of the sublime was not a colonizing one alone.

4 The missionary picturesque, 1790–1860

1 Andrews (1994) suggests that the picturesque, which had been restricted to landscape painting and description in the eighteenth century, is associated with 'the aesthetics of poverty' in the Victorian age, where there appears to be an attraction towards the

grimy, poorer working classes as picturesque. The response to such sights of poverty is, Andrews notes, of a 'higher' picturesque that rebels against the 'surface picturesque' of merely admiring the low. This higher picturesque was linked to a moral conscience (Andrews 1994: 283–90).

2 Tracts like *Observations on the Present State of the East India Company* (1807), and people like Thomas Twining (1807), John Scott (1808a, 1808b) and Scott Waring (1809), for instance, furiously debated the benefits (or lack thereof) of missionary activity in the colonies. Others like William Buyers (1848: 68–71) interrogated particular kinds of missionary work, like the Calcutta missions' work in preparing textbooks for the entire country. These debates were also published in periodicals like the *Christian Observer*. For an account of the debates, see Fisch (1985). In the early stages the East India House was cautious about promoting or even encouraging evangelical work. The Despatch from East India House to the Governor-General in Council, dated 7 September 1808, declares:

> [our] paramount power . . . in India . . . imposes upon us the necessity, as well as strengthening our obligation, to protect the native inhabitants in the free and undisturbed profession of their religious opinions, and to take care that they are neither harassed not irritated by any premature or over-zealous attempts to convert them to Christianity.
>
> (Kaye 1859, Appendix 4: 515)

Kaye (1859: 491) writing in the immediate aftermath of the 1857 'revolt' declared: 'in the neutrality of the Government lies the hope of the missionaries'. Other commentators, mourning the 'lower standard of missionary qualification', asked for a rethinking of the qualifying processes of missionaries to India for the success of the evangelizing mission (*Contemporary Review* 1 [1866]: 123–41). For studies of the evangelical movement in India, see Neill (1985), Alban et al. (2005).

3 Almost every missionary seems to have been familiar with her/his contemporaries' works. Their rhetoric, images and even phrases overlap. Johnston (2003: 4) is surely correct in suggesting that many of these accounts were 'recycled', often plagiarizing from each other.

4 In 1805–06, for instance, the company's expenses exceeded its income by £260,000 in India alone, as *Observations on the Present State of the East India Company* points out (Anon. 1807: 3).

5 Images of a Christian empire, encirclement, expansion and the subsuming of multitudes and varieties into a Christian circle were already making its appearance in 'local' discourses in England. A tract, *Lectures on Ecclesiastical History*, by George Campbell (1800), spoke of the expansion of the church in Europe in imperial terms. Campbell notes that initially there were many towns, villages, and tracts of land, in the province, 'wherein there were no christians at all'. He then describes the progress thus: with conversion, people would 'join themselves to the nearest congregation . . . this was one of the principal causes of the gradual enlargement of the parishes . . . (when Christianity became the religion of the empire . . . by the sudden accession of multitudes of converts from all quarters') (G. Campbell 1800, 1: 233; see also 258, 276 and elsewhere).

6 There is an editorial and textual issue involved here: Eustace Carey (1836: iv) admits that he has taken his uncle, William Carey's, 'original documents' and 'woven them into a tissue of [his] own'.

7 The zenana was the focus of most of women's missionary accounts, especially in the 1850–1900 period. See, for example, Mrs Weitbrecht's *Women of India* (1875); Mary Tuck's *East and West* (1900?); Irene Barnes' *Between Life and Death* (1901) among others. My interest here is less with the gendered nature of missionary accounts about Indian women and the zenana – well studied by Murray (2000), Nair (2000), Semple (2003) – than with the representations of Indian landscape.

8 Numerous examples of such representations exist in late nineteenth-century periodicals. See, for instance, *Children of the Church Magazine*, 4 (1895); 7 (1898): Cover, 60. Examples may also be found in *CMM* (June 1896: 87; August 1896: 121; March 1898: Cover; May 1898: 73, August 1898: 121; January 1900: 10–11; July 1900).

9 Occasionally, commentators back 'home' paid attention to the classes of missionaries themselves, highlighting the work ethic of the lower class of Englishmen. Thus a review of John Clark Marshman's *Life and Times of Carey, Marshman, and Ward* (1859) emphasizes that the Serampore missionaries were 'low-born and low-bred mechanics' apostates' (*DUM* 54 [1859]: 337).

10 For example, *India's Women* 13 [1893]: 505; 14 [1894]: 374–76; 14 [1894]: 393–96; 14 [1894]: 438–41. The interest in the welfare of the lower castes and aborigines is not confined to British territories in India alone. The interest in civilizing the aborigines was a major nineteenth-century project in most of British Settlements. For documents on the subject, see *Report from the Select Committee on Aborigines (British Settlements)* (House of Commons 1836). In other cases, hope was expressed that *tribals* such as the Khonds would lose their superstitions and false beliefs (*Christian Remembrancer* 4 [NS] [1842]: 387–88). The British and Foreign Aborigines Protection Society was praised for its work (*EcR* 4 [Series 4] [1838]: 319–31).

11 For changing notions of labour, ethics and Christian virtue in the English georgic, see Low (1985).

12 An interesting use of the picturesque aesthetic when speaking of Indian flaws is seen years later in the speech of Lord Lepel Griffin at the Royal Colonial Institute. An account of the speech summarized his opinions thus:

> If he were asked to express in a few sentences the virtues and advantages of the Native States [of India], contrasted with their vices, he would observe, in the first place, that they were picturesque. Their brightness and colour, the tawdry splendour of their Courts, the unimaginable inefficiency of their soldiery, their grotesque travesty of justice and administration, made a grateful change from the sober, dull monotony of British rule.
>
> (*BFCJ* 1.3 [1889]: 17)

13 In some cases it was suggested that missionaries who went out to toil did so because there was 'no opportunity for rising into notice at home' (*QR* 25 [1821]: 439). Later tracts also emphasize India's role in providing employment and opportunities to English people (*QR* 120 [1866]: 198–220; *MM* 3 [1860–61]: 417–26).

14 One suggested mode for the improvement of India was to allow English people to acquire land and settle (Colebrooke 1795: 103–04; *A View of the Present State and Future Prospects of the Free Trade and Colonization of India* (Crawfurd 1828); *ER* 48 [1828]: 312–47). 'Planting' – here used metaphorically, but a common agricultural and horticultural term – was, in the case of William Shenstone's (1764) tract on gardening, associated with the picturesque. Shenstone (1764: 218), interestingly, argues that 'the works of a person that builds, begin immediately to decay; while those of him who plants begin directly to improve. In this, planting promises a more lasting pleasure, than building'.

15 Curiously, at least one commentator believes that India is ready for the 'diffusion' of Christianity because, finally, there is a 'great improvement in the general tone of morality among *European* residents' (*CaR* 18 [1852]: 180, emphasis added).

16 On vitalist theories and landscape in the nineteenth century, see Reill (2005).

17 Daniels (1992) argues that during the Enlightenment, the management of smaller plots was construed as a model for managing the country itself.

18 Churches also had other iconic functions. A Garrison Order issued at Madras, dated 3 June 1799, after the conclusion of the war with Tipu Sultan, describes the process of receiving the standard of the dead Indian king:

> The standard and colours having been presented to the Governor General, his Lordship will proceed with them to the Church; and after they have been deposited at the altar, the flank companies will return, and take up their stations at the parade.
>
> (*Asiatic Annual Register* 1798–99: 262)

19   Ironically, some of the pagan or immoral landscape and structures were constructed by their *European* benefactors. William Ward (1863: 179) notes that many of those who 'erect temples in Bengal are principally the head-servants of Europeans, who appropriate part of their gains to these acts of supposed merit'.

20   Such criticism of the absence of strong faith, generosity or the drive to Christianize was common. The *Calcutta Review* (9 [1848]: 117) accuses the early traders in India of the same lack of love for God. Debates about the appropriate behaviour of the church and missionaries extended well into the nineteenth century, and serves to show that the missionary movement itself was never coherent or smooth in its functioning. Edward Storrow, for instance, criticizes Jesuit missionaries for compromising with Hindu rituals, and his criticism was taken up and extracted in periodicals (*Review of Reviews* 3 [1891]: 468).

21   *Children of the Church Magazine* 6 (1895): Cover; 6 (1897): Cover, 60; 6 (1897): 36; 7 (1898): 21; 7 (1898): 4; 7 (1898): Cover. Also *CMM* 1 April 1881: 45.

22   There were two different spatial arrangements too, apparently. Sarah Tucker writes:

> benches used by the European congregation were removed, to leave a clear space in the middle of the chapel, to be occupied by the natives sitting on the floor, or when kneeling, prostrating themselves so low that their foreheads touched the ground.
>
> (S. Tucker 1842–43, 1: 59–60)

5   The sporting luxuriant, 1850–1920

1   One commentator suggests another, interesting, consequence of the introduction of railways in India: 'Along with the railways will come a train of moral consequences to which we cannot shut our eyes . . . we may expect the native, when they become more familiar with us, to cease to regard us as demigods' (*FM* 56 [1857]: 164).

2   For a study of the English guidebook, see Vaughan (1974). On the role of guidebooks in colonization, see Mitchell (1988).

3   The criticism of the lack of authentic adventure narratives might also be related to the sudden growth of panoramas and exhibitions in London. Panoramas staging historical events like 'The Storming of Seringapatam' and 'The Battle of Trafalgar' were hugely popular. The 'spectacular realism' of these shows were often derided by the Romantic poets as being cheap substitutes for the actual experience of travel (Wood 2001: 6–14, 102–04). The panorama generated a familiarity with the object (re)presented (Galperin 1993: 42).

4   In the context of Africa the novelist Rider Haggard mourned: 'where will the romance writers of future generations find a safe and secret place, unknown to the pestilent accuracy of the geographer, in which to lay their plots?' (quoted in Brantlinger 1988: 239).

5   Other kinds of exploration, with more commercial intent, were also taking place during this time. Thus Boverton Redwood triumphantly announced in a paper read out to the Society of Chemical Industry and reprinted in a periodical, a comprehensive database of the oil fields of India, from Balochistan to Assam and Burma (*BFCJ* 2.11 [1890]: 117–21; 2.12 [1890]: 139–40; 2.13 [1890]: 168–69).

6   For instance, Pogson's *Indian Gardening* (1872), Johnstone's *Gardening* (1903) and Mrs. Temple-Wright's *Flowers and Gardens in India* (2nd edition 1893, 8 editions by 1934).

Periodicals like *Garden and Forest* (7 [1894]: 56; 10 [1897]: 26) also carried helpful advice on Indian plants.

7 For studies of the conservation and forestry movement in colonial India, see, among others, Gadgil and Guha (1993).

8 The Forest Act of 1878 was an attempt to control access to game and forest areas. The definition of forest produce was expanded to include hides, horns and tusks. The Act also effectively excluded local land users from the reserved forests – a move that ensured complete domination by the British officials (Rangarajan 1996: 158–59).

9 The more popular ones were William Schlich's *A Manual of Forestry* (1904 [1889–96]) and Berthold Ribbentrop's *Forestry in British India* (1900).

10 For a study of the boy-scout ideal and the empire, see Warren (1986).

11 The nineteenth century was the age of tourism. The first tourist guides appeared from Baedeker's in Germany in 1829. England achieved this milestone with *Murray's Guide* in 1836 (John Murray claimed, however, that it was not Baedeker but the Murray *Handbook* that came first on the scene. See his essay, 'The Origin and History of Murray's Handbooks for Travellers', *Murray's Magazine* 6 [1889]: 623–29). Cook opened the world's first travel agency in 1845. Cook organized the first 'Circular Tour of the Continent' in 1856, and the first tourist trip around the world in 1872. The Great Exhibition (London, 1851) showcased products and commodities from around the world. Panoramas as a form of entertainment that 'familiarized' also evolved during this period. For a brief sketch, see Korte (2000), especially Chapter 5.

12 The conventions of the picturesque continued to inform British and European writings about the Orient even in the 1890s. Thus a travel essay on Benares described it as a 'picturesque native city' (*MM* 3 [1860–61]: 58, 61). Henry Bruce (1909: xx) travelling in the Malabar region in the 1900s described it as 'infinitely picturesque and romantic'.

13 This is also the age when the risk from native diseases and climate begin to be addressed through concrete proposals regarding hygiene, sanitation and the health of the army. Harriet Martineau, for instance, wrote an extended essay on the theme bringing to the attention of the British public the life of the soldier in India (*MM* 8 [1863]: 332–40).

14 What is also interesting is that, occasionally, the Englishman was also likened to one of these animals. Edward Braddon in *Thirty Years of Shikar* (1895), for instance, declares that the boar 'is like an Englishman in that it does not know when it is beaten' (quoted in J.M. MacKenzie 1988: 188).

15 Landau (2002) has convincingly argued that the camera and the gun contributed equally as 'tools of empire' (he adapts the phrase from Daniel Headrick's (1981) influential book of that title). The photographs of slain animals, topographies and trophy bags in the sporting memoir – usually framed beside the gun-toting English *shikari* – clearly functioned as signifiers of imperial control. Landau (2002: 147) demonstrates how the photography of Africa shared some of the personnel, techniques and even technology of the hunt. Sontag (1973) has also shown how the vocabularies of photography and hunting overlap. The *OED* informs us that 'snapping' a shot is the same as 'sniping' – which means to shoot at a moving target (where the latter is of course the central activity of the hunt).

16 Other sources of danger persisted. The health of the English soldier, the diseases likely to be contracted by serving in India, and the enormous numbers of deaths continued to be the subject of narratives that tropes India as a landscape of disease. For instance, Harriet Martineau writing in 1863 declared that the English soldier was 'doomed to know health no more – and either to die early or live in chronic suffering' (*MM* 8 [1863]: 332–40). The cultural masochism of the sporting memoir and the shikar expedition was, I believe, a mode of anticipating and controlling the danger that was imminent in the form of disease and suffering by *seeking* the latter in the form of the hunt.

17 In at least one case the 'mutiny' and shikar came together. One 'A.S'. recounts his experience of encountering a well-built native in the forests. This native, A.S. states,

reached for his sword on seeing the Englishman. A.S. believes the man is a mutineer (*OSM* 10. 110 [February 1877]: 56–60).

18   In a persuasive reading Shaw (2002: 74) has argued that after Waterloo and France writers often used images of pain and suffering to demonstrate 'individual and national resubstantiation'. Pain thus becomes a means of resignifying patriotism, nationalism and national identity. In the context of colonial India, such a saga of suffering was made available after 1857. What is crucial about the sporting memoir, however, is the deliberate seeking of suffering.

19   As early as 1809 commentators back in England made note of the 'war' against Indian tigers, where ten rupees was paid for the head of a full-grown one, five for a leopard or tiger's cub, stating that 'no public money could be better employed' (*QR* 2 [1809]: 93). Depopulation due to predators were themes in periodicals too. For instance, Salsette, writes a commentator, is now merely 'the haunt of the tiger and other beasts of prey' (*OH* April 1827: 130).

20   Separate guidebooks to hunting were also being published, some, like Maurice Tulloch's *The All-In-One Shikar Book*, as late as 1940.

21   See, for instance, United Provinces of Agra and Oudh's *Manual on Indian Etiquette for the Use of European Officers Coming to India* (1910) and S. Iftikhar Husain's *Hints on Indian Etiquette* (1911). Earlier works included essays on 'Anglo-Indian Manners' in the *Oriental Herald* (September 1829: 471–89).

22   The distinctions between tourists and travellers are explored by, among others, Buzard (1993).

23   Dietrich Brandis, writing in 1897, hints at such an alienation of the natives from the forests when he wrote: 'the larger the number of natives employed in responsible positions in the forests, the more forestry will cease to have the character of an exotic plant, or a foreign artificially fostered institution' (*Imperial and Asiatic Quarterly Review, and Oriental and Colonial Record* 3 [Series 3] [1897]: 253). Though Brandis is speaking of institutional forestry the argument, I believe, serves the *shikar* narratives equally well.

Bibliography

Unpublished sources

McQueen, J. 'Remarks in the Brittania East India-man bound for Madras and China, AD 1757', Mss. Euro 675, India Office Records.

MacTier, A. *Journal of a Voyage from Britain to India on Board the Surat Castle*, Mss. 22, Cambridge University Library.

Watson, H. Untitled (1764–77), Mss. Euro D 759, India Office Records.

Government publications

Hansard Parliamentary Debates 25 (1813).

House of Commons (1773) *Ninth Report from the Committee of Secrecy, appointed to Enquire into the State of the East India Company*, ed. Sheila Lambert, *House of Commons Sessional Papers of the Eighteenth Century. Vol. 137. George III. Secret Committee Reports 8 and 9. 1773*, Wilmington, DE: Scholarly Resources, 1975.

House of Commons (1782a) *First Report from the Select Committee, appointed to take into Consideration the State of the Administration of Justice in the Provinces of Bengal, Bahar, and Orissa*, ed. Sheila Lambert, *House of Commons Sessional Papers of the Eighteenth Century. Vol. 138. George III. Reports on Justice in Bengal 1781 and 1782*, Wilmington, DE: Scholarly Resources, 1975.

House of Commons (1782b) *Fourth Report from the Committee of Secrecy, appointed to Enquire into the State of the East India Company*, ed. Sheila Lambert, *House of Commons Sessional Papers of the Eighteenth Century. Vol. 143. George III. Secret Committee Reports 4 and 5. 1782*, Wilmington, DE: Scholarly Resources, 1975.

House of Commons (1782c) *Sixth Report from the Select Committee, appointed to take into Consideration the State of the Administration of Justice in the Provinces of Bengal, Bahar, and Orissa*, ed. Sheila Lambert, *House of Commons Sessional Papers of the Eighteenth Century. Vol. 139. George III. Select Committee Reports, 2–6, 1782*, Wilmington, DE: Scholarly Resources, 1975.

House of Commons (1783) *Ninth Report from the Select Committee, appointed to take into Consideration the State of the Administration of Justice in the Provinces of Bengal, Bahar, and Orissa*, ed. Sheila Lambert, *House of Commons Sessional Papers of the Eighteenth Century. Vol. 140. George III. Select Committee Reports 7–9. 1783*, Wilmington, DE: Scholarly Resources, 1975.

House of Commons (1836) *Report from the Select Committee on Aborigines (British Settlements); with Minutes of Evidence, Appendix and Index. Communicated by the Commons to the Lords.* Shannon: Irish University Press, 1968.

House of Commons (1858a) *First Report from the Select Committee on Colonization and Settlement (India).* London: n.p.

House of Commons (1858b) *Fourth Report from the Select Committee on Colonization and Settlement (India).* London: n.p.

Journal of the House of Commons 32 (1768).

Journal of the House of Commons 48 (1793). New edn 1803.

Fort William – India House correspondence

Vol. 3, 1760–63, R.R. Sethi (ed.) Delhi: National Archives, 1968.

Vol. 10, 1786–88, R. Singh (ed.) Delhi: National Archives, 1972.

Vol. 12, 1793–95, A. Tripathi (ed.) Delhi: National Archives, 1978.

Vol. 13, 1796–1800, P.G. Gupta (ed.) Delhi: National Archives, 1959.

Primary sources

Periodicals and serials

Ainsworth's Magazine (AM)
Annual Register (AR)
Asiatic Annual Register 1798–99
Asiatic Miscellany Vol. 1 (1785), Vol. 2 (1786)
Asiatic Researches Vol. 1 (1788), Vol. 2 (1799)
Blackwood's Edinburgh (BE)
British Foreign and Colonial Journal (BFCJ)
British Quarterly Review (BQR)
Calcutta Monthly Register
Calcutta Review (CaR)
Chambers's Edinburgh Journal (CE)
Children of the Church Magazine
Children's Missionary Magazine of the United Presbyterian Church (CMM)
Christian Observer (CO)
Christian Remembrancer
Church Missionary Record (CMR)
Critical Review (CR)
Dublin Review (DR)
Dublin University Magazine (DUM)
Eclectic Review (EcR)
Edinburgh Review (ER)
English Post
Evening Post
Fraser's Magazine for Town and Country (FM)
Gentleman's Magazine (GM)
Greater Britain
Household Words (HW)
India's Women

Indian Female Evangelist
Indian Forester (IF)
Indian Gardener
Juvenile Missionary Herald (JMH)
London Journal
Macmillan's Magazine (MM)
Missionary Magazine and Chronicle Relating Chiefly to the Missions of the London Missionary Society
Monthly Review (MR)
New Monthly Magazine
Nineteenth Century
North British Review (NBR)
Oriental Herald and Journal of General Literature (OH)
Oriental Sporting Magazine (OSM)
Philosophical Transactions of the Royal Society (PT)
Quarterly Review (QR)
Review of Reviews
Scottish Geographical Magazine
Tait's Edinburgh Magazine (TE)
The Englishman
The London Journal
The Post Man
The Times (London)

Books and pamphlets

Adams, A.L. (1867) *Wanderings of a Naturalist in the Western Himalayas and Cashmere*, Edinburgh: Edmonston & Douglas.

Ainslie, W. (1835) *An Historical Sketch of the Introduction of Christianity into India*, Edinburgh: Oliver & Boyd.

Allingham, W. (1698) *A Short Account of the Nature and Use of Maps*, London: Mount et al.

Anderson, W. (1708) *Four Sermons Preached at Fort William, in Bengal, in the East Indies*, London: printed by E.P. for Tho. Horne.

Anon. (1660) *The English Devil*, London: printed by Robert Wood for George Horton.

Anon. (1683) *England's Vanity*, by a Compassionate Conformist, London: John Dunton.

Anon. [Charles Blount?] (1683) *Miracles, No Violation of the Laws of Nature*, London: Robert Sollers.

Anon. (1695) *The Case of the Fann-makers who have petitioned the honorable House of Commons, against the importation of fanns from the East-Indies*, Broadside, n.p.: n.p.

Anon. (1700) *The World's Infection; or a relation of the monstrous and abominable sin of women*, Edinburgh: n.p.

Anon. (1707) *Edifying and Curious Letters of some Missioners of the Society of Jesus from Foreign Missions*, London: n.p. 2 vols.

Anon. (1766) *Directions for a Proper Choice of Authors to Form a Library*, London: J. Whiston.

Anon. (1769) *A Letter to a Late Popular Director, Relative to India Affairs*, London: G. Kearsly.

Anon. (1779) *A Short History of Drugs & c, Likewise China and Lacquered Ware the Produce of the East Indies*, London: H. Adams.

Anon. (1780) *Administration of Justice in Bengal: the several petitions of the British inhabitants of Bengal*, London: n.p.

Anon. (1784) *Original Papers Relative to the Setting up of a Society in Bengal for the Protection of the Orphans of Officers*, London: J. Cooper.

Anon. (1795) *Instructions for Missionaries to the West-India Islands*, London: n.p.

Anon. (1799) *Plan of an Asiatic Register*, London: n.p.

Anon. (1807) *Observations on the Present State of the East India Company*, London: J. Ridgway.

Anon. (1808) *A Letter to John Scott Waring*, London: printed by Ellerton & Byworth for J. Hatchard.

Anon. [Josiah Pratt?] (1815) *The Spirit of the British Missions*, London: A. M'Intosh.

Anon. (1875) *The Gospel in Santhalisthan*, London: James Nisbet.

Anon. [Phebe Gibbes?] (1989) *Hartly House, Calcutta* (1789), ed. M. Clough, Toronto: Broadview.

Bacon, F. (1620) *The Great Instauration*, online at: http://etext.library.adelaide.edu.au/b/bacon/francis/instauration (accessed on 22 May 2006).

Bacon, F. (1625) 'Of Travel', in J. Spedding et al. (eds) *The Works of Francis Bacon* (1860), Boston, MA: Brown & Taggard. 12: 138.

Bacon, F. (1627) *The New Atlantis*, online at: http://etext.lib.virginia.edu/etcbin (accessed on 23 May 2006).

Baden-Powell, R.S.S. (1908) *Scouting for Boys*, London: n.p.

Baden-Powell, R.S.S. (1920) *Memories of India*, Philadelphia, PA: David McKay.

Ball, V. (1880) *Jungle Life in India; or the Journey and Journals of an Indian Geologist*, London: Thos De La Rue.

Baptist Missionary Society (1896) *One Hundred and Fourth Annual Report of the Committee of the Baptist Missionary Society*, London: Alexander & Shepheard.

Barnes, I. (1901) *Between Life and Death: The Story of C.E.Z.M.S. Medical Missions in India, China, and Ceylon*, London: Marshall Brothers.

Beatson, R. (1790) *Naval and Military Memoirs of Great Britain, from the Year 1727 to the Present Time*, London: printed for J. Strachan.

Bernier, F. (1979) *Travels in the Mogul Empire* (1671), New Delhi: S. Chand.

Best, J.W. (1935) *Forest Life in India*, London: John Murray.

Best, T. (1934) *The Voyage of Thomas Best to the East Indies, 1612–1614*, ed. W. Foster, London: Hakluyt Society. Series II, Vol. 85.

Birdwood, G. (ed.) (1965) *The Register of Letters of the Governor and Company of Merchants of London Trading into the East Indies, 1600–1619*, London: Bernard Quatrich.

Blith, W. (1649) *The English Improver, or a New Survey of Husbandry*, London: T. Wright.

Blount, T. (1670) *Glossographia*, 3rd edn, London: printed by Thomas Newcomb.

Board of Agriculture (1797) *Communications to the Board of Agriculture*, Vol. 1, London: W. Bulwer for Board of Agriculture.

Bogue, D. (1797) *Sermons Preached in London at the Formation of the Missionary Society, September 22, 23, 24 (1795)*, London: Barrett & March.

Bolton, W. (1908) *Travancore*, London: London Missionary Society.

Bolts, W. (1772) *Considerations on Indian Affairs*, London: printed for J. Almon in Piccadilly, P. Elmsley in the Strand and Richardson & Urquhart.

Bowrey, T. (1997) *A Geographical Account of Countries Round the Bay of Bengal 1669 to 1679* (1905), ed. R.C. Temple, New Delhi: Munshiram Manoharlal.

Braddon, E. (1895) *Thirty Years of Shikar*, Edinburgh: William Blackwood.

Brinckman, A. (1862) *Rifle in Cashmere: a narrative of shooting expeditions in Ladak, Cashmere and Punjaub*, London: Smith, Elder.

Bristow, J. (1793) *A Narrative of the Sufferings of James Bristow belonging to the Bengal Artillery during Ten Years Captivity with Hyder Ali and Tippoo Saheb*, London: John Murray.

Brittle, E. (1785) *The India Guide, or Journal of a Voyage to the East Indies in the Year 1780*, ed. J. Dallas, Calcutta: George Gordon.

Browne, J.C. (1857) *Indian Infanticide: its origin, progress, and suppression*, London: W.H. Allen.

Browne, T. (1970) *Religio Medici* (1642), Menston, UK: Scolar Press.

Bruce, H. (1909) *Letters from Malabar, and on the Way*, London: George Routledge.

Bruce, J. (1793) *Historical View of the Plans, for the Government of British India*, London: n.p.

Bruton, W. (1638) *News from the East-Indies, or, a Voyage to Bengalla*, London: J. Oakes.

Buchanan, C. (1809a) *Letter from Tanjore*, New Haven, CT: from Sidney Press, printed for the Connecticut Religious Tract Society.

Buchanan, C. (1809b) *Star in the East*, Walpole, NH: printed by Cheever Felch.

Buchanan, C. (1813a) *An Apology for Promoting Christianity in India*, London: printed for T. Cadell and W. Davies.

Buchanan, C. (1813b) *Colonial Ecclesiastical Establishment*, London: Cadell & Davies.

Buchanan, C. (1817) *Memoirs of the Life and Writings of the Rev. Claudius Buchanan*, ed. H. Pearson, Philadelphia, PA: Benjamin & Thomas Kite.

Burke, E. (1987) *A Philosophical Enquiry into the Origin of our Ideas of the Sublime and Beautiful*, ed. J.T. Boulton, Oxford: Basil Blackwell.

Buyers, W. (1848) *Recollections of Northern India*, London: John Snow.

Cambridge, R.O. (compiled) (1761) *An Account of the War in India*, London: T. Jefferys.

Campbell, D. (1801) *A Narrative of the Extraordinary Adventures and Sufferings by Shipwreck and Imprisonment*, New York: L. Nichols.

Campbell, G. (1800) *Lectures on Ecclesiastical History*, London: printed for J. Johnson and A. Brown. 2 vols.

Campbell, W. (1853) *The Old Forest Ranger, or the Wild Sports of India*, 3rd edn, London: Arthur Hall, Virtue.

Capper, J. (1783) *A Free Enquiry into the Various Causes of the Alarming State of our Affairs in the East Indies*, London: n.p.

Carey, E. (1836) *Memoirs of William Carey*, Boston, MA: Gould, Kendall & Lincoln.

Carey, W. (1792) *An Enquiry into the Obligations of Christians, to use Means for the Conversion of the Heathens*, Leicester, UK: printed and sold by Ann Ireland. Online at: www.wmcarey.edu/carey/enquiry/anenquiry.pdf (accessed on 13 February 2006).

Carey, W. (1828) *Letters, Official and Private*, London: Parbury, Allen.

Carey, W. (2000) *The Journal and Selected Letters of William Carey*, collected and ed. T.G. Carter, Macon, GA: Smyth & Helwys.

Castell, R. (1728) *Villas of the Ancients Illustrated*, London: printed for the author.

Christian Institution (1848) *The Youth of India Speaking for Themselves: being the substance of the examination papers of the students of the London Missionary Society's Christian Institution or College in Calcutta, with a few introductory remarks by Rev. T. Boaz*, London: John Snow.

Church Missionary House (1879) *Church Missionary Atlas*, 6th edn, London: Church Missionary Society, Seeley, Jackson, & Halliday.

Clarkson, W. (1850) *Missionary Encouragements in India: or, the Christian Village in Gujarat*, 9th edn, London: John Snow.

Cobbe, R. (1766) *Bombay Church*, London: printed by J. and W. Oliver.

Colebrooke, H.T. (1795) *Remarks on the Present State of the Husbandry and Commerce of Bengal*, Calcutta: n.p.

Collins, S. (1717) *Paradise Retriev'd: plainly and fully demonstrating the method of managing and improving fruit-trees against walls*, London: printed for John Collins.

Coryate, T. (1611) *Coryate's Crudities*, London: printed by William Stansby.

Cotgrave, R. (1611) *A Dictionarie of the French and English Tongues*, London: Adam Islip.

Craufurd, Q (1792) *Sketches Chiefly Relating to the History, Religion, Learning, and Manners, of the Hindoos*, London: T. Cadell.

Crawfurd, J. (1828) *A View of the Present State and Future Prospects of the Free Trade and Colonization of India*, London: James Ridgway.

Cumming, G. (1871) *Wild Men and Wild Beasts: scenes in camp and jungle*, Edinburgh: Edmonston & Douglas.

Daniell, T. and Daniell, W. (1812–16) *Oriental Scenery: or views of the architecture, antiquities, and landscape scenery of Hindoostan*, London: W. Daniell and Longman.

Darrah, H.Z. (1898) *Sport in the Highlands of Kashmir*, London: Rowland Hall.

Davidson, C.J.C. (1843) *Diary of Travels and Adventures in Upper India*, London: Henry Colburn. 2 vols.

Defoe, D. (1962) *A Tour through the Whole Island of Great Britain*, London: Dent. 2 vols.

Dellon, G. (1698) *A Voyage to the East-Indies*, London: printed for D. Browne, A. Roper and T. Leigh.

Dennis, J. (1693) *Miscellanies in Verse and Prose*, London: printed for James Knapton.

Descartes, R. (1989) *The Passions of the Soul*, trans. S. Voss, Indianapolis, IN: Hackett.

Dirom, A. (1793) *Narrative of the Campaign in India, which terminated the war with Tippoo Sultan, in 1792*, London: W. Bulmer.

Dow, A. (1768) *The History of Hindostan*, London: T. Becket and P.A. De Hondt.

Duff, A. (1839) *India, and India Missions*, Edinburgh: J. Johnstone.

East India Company (1800) *Copies and Extracts of Advices to and from India, Relative to the Cause, Progress, and Successful Termination of the War with the Late Tippoo Sultaun*, London: printed for the use of the proprietors of East India stock.

Eden, E. (1930) *Up the Country: letters written to her sister from the upper provinces of India*. Oxford: Oxford University Press.

Elwood, K. (1830) *Narrative of a Journey Overland from England, by the Continent of Europe, Egypt, and the Red Sea to India in the years 1825, 26, 27 and 28*, London: Henry Colburn and Richard Bentley. 2 vols.

Ewing, G. (1797) *A Defence of Missions from Christian Societies to the Heathen World: a sermon, preached before the Edinburgh Missionary Society*, Edinburgh: J. Ritchie.

Farewell, C. (1633) *An East-India Colation*, London: printed by B.A and T.F.

Fayrer, J. (1875) *The Royal Bengal Tiger: his life and death*, London: J. and A. Churchill.

Forrest, G. (ed.) (1926) *Selections from the State Papers of the Governors-General of India, Lord Cornwallis, Vol. II, Documents*, Oxford: Basil Blackwell.

Forster, G. (1798) *A Journey from Bengal to England through the Northern part of India, Kashmire, Afghanistan, and Persia, and into Russia, by the Caspian Sea*, London: R. Faulder. 2 vols.

Forsyth, J. (1996) *The Highlands of Central India: notes on their forests and wild tribes, natural history and sports* (1871), New Delhi: Asian Educational Services.

Fryer, J. (1698) *A New Account of East-India and Persia*, London: R.I. Chiswell.

George III (1968) *The Letters of King George III*, ed. B. Dobree (1935), New York: Funk & Wagnalls.

Gillies, J. (compiled) (1754) *Historical Collections Relating to Remarkable Periods of the Success of the Gospel*, Glasgow: Robert and Andrew Foulis. 2 vols.

Gilpin, W. (1796) *Account of a New Poor House*, London: printed at the Philanthropic Reform.

Gilpin, W. (1973) *Remarks on Forest Scenery* (1791), Richmond, UK: Richmond Publishing.

Grant, A. (1844) *The Past and Prospective Extension of the Gospel by Missions to the Heathen*, London.

Gray, T. (1935) *Correspondence*, ed. P. Toynbee and L. Whibley, Oxford: Clarendon. 3 vols.

Grey, C. (1929) *European Adventurers of Northern India, 1785 to 1849*, ed. H.L.O. Garrett, Lahore: Government Printing.

Grose, J. (1757) *A Voyage to East Indies*, London: printed for S. Hooper and J. Morley.

Hakluyt, R. (1935) *The Original Writings and Correspondence of the Two Richard Hakluyts*, ed. E.G.R Taylor, London: Hakluyt Society. Vol. 77 of Second Series. 2 vols.

Haldane, R., Bogue, D., Innes, W. and Ewing, G. (1797) *Memorial on the Subject of a Mission to Bengal, Addressed to the Directors of the Honourable the East-India Company*, London: n.p.

Hall, R. (1712) *The History of the Barbarous Cruelties and Massacres Committed by the Dutch in the East-Indies*, London: n.p.

Hamilton, A. (1997) *A New Account of the East-Indies* (1727), New Delhi: Asian Educational Services. 2 vols.

Hamilton, C. (1791) *The Hedàya, or Guide: a commentary on the Mussulman laws*, London: printed by T. Bensley. 4 vols.

Handley, M.A. (1911) *Roughing it in Southern India*, London: Edward Arnold.

Hardy, N. (1658) *The Pious Votary and Prudent Traveler*, London: John Clark.

Hartlib, S. (1659) *The Compleat Husband-man: or, a discourse of the whole art of husbandry; both forraign and domestick*. London: Edward Brewster.

Hastings, W. (1786) *The Present State of the East Indies*, London: John Stockdale.

Herbert, T. (1634) *A Relation of Some Years Travels, begun Anno 1626*, London: William Stansby and Jacob Bloome.

Hickey, W. (1925) *Memoirs*, ed. A. Spencer, London: Hurst & Blackett. 4 vols.

Hobbes, T. (1976) *The Leviathan*, ed. C.B. Macpherson (1651), Harmondsworth: Penguin.

Hodges, W. (1793) *Travels in India, during the Years 1780, 1781, 1782 and 1783*, London: J. Edwards.

Hooke, R. (1665) *Micrographia*, London: Royal Society.

Hooker, J.D. (1854) *Himalayan Journals, or notes of a journalist in Bengal*, London: John Murray.

Horne, S.C. (1894) *The Story of the LMS*, London: Missionary Society.

Hough, J. (1832) *The Missionary Vade Mecum*, London: Hatchard & Son, Nisbet.

Husain, S.I. (1911) *Hints on Indian Etiquette Specially Designed for the Use of Europeans*, Lucknow: M.L. Bhargava at the Newul Kishore Press.

Inglis, J. (1892) *Tent Life in Tigerland*, London: Sampson Low, Marston.

Ingram, E. (ed.) (1970) *Two Views of British India: the private correspondence of Mr. Dundas and Lord Wellesley: 1798–1801*, Bath, UK: Adam & Dart.

Ives, E. (1773) *A Voyage from England to India*, London: printed for Edward and Charles Dilly.

Jeffreys, J. (1858) *The British Army in India*, London: Longman, Brown, Green, Longman, & Roberts.

Johnson [Surgeon] (1806) *An Account of a Voyage to India, China & C. in His Majesty's Ship Caroline, performed in the Years 1803-4-5*, London: Richard Phillips.

Johnson, D. (1822) *Sketches of Field Sports as followed by the Natives of India*, London: published for the author by Longman, Hurst, Rees, Orme & Brown.

Johnson, S. (1995) *Dr. Johnson and Mrs. Thrale's Tour in North Wales, 1774*, Clwyd, UK: Wrexham.

Johnstone, W.W. (1903) *Gardening, A Guide for Amateurs in India*, Mussoorie: Mussoorie Times and Mafasalite.

Jones, W. (1970) *Letters*, ed. G. Cannon, Oxford: Clarendon. 2 vols.

Kaye, J.W. (1859) *Christianity in India: an historical narrative*, London: Smith, Elder.

Kennion, R.L. (1910) *Sport and Life in the Further Himalaya*, Edinburgh: William Blackwood.

Kindersley, J. (1777) *Letters from the Island of Teneriffe, Brazil, the Cape of Good Hope, and the East Indies*, London: J. Nource.

Langley, B. (1728) *New Principles of Gardening*, London: A. Betterworth and J. Bately.

Lettsom, J.C. (1799) *The Naturalist's and Traveller's Companion* (1772), 3rd edn, London: C. Dilly.

Lind, J. (1811) *An Essay on Diseases Incidental to Europeans in Hot Climates* (1768), Philadelphia, PA: William Duane.

Locke, J.C. (1997) *The First Englishmen in India* (1930), Delhi: Munshiram Manoharlal.

Long, J. (1973) *Selections from Unpublished Records of Government for the Years 1748 to 1767 Inclusive*, ed. Mahadevaprasad Sinha, Calcutta: K.L. Mukhopadhyay.

Loudon, J.C. (1835) *Encyclopaedia of Gardening* (1824), 5th edn, London: Longman, Rees, Orme, Brown, Green & Longman.

Lydekker, R. (1924) *The Game Animals of India, Burma, Malaya and Tibet* (1907), revised by J.G. Dollman, London: Rowland Ward.

McDonell, J. (1929) 'Early days of forestry in India', *Empire Forestry Journal* 8: 85–97.

MacIntyre, D. (1891) *Hindu-Koh: wanderings and wild sport on and beyond the Himalayas*, London: William Blackwood.

MacKenzie, R. (1793) *A Sketch of the War with Tippoo Sultaun*, Calcutta: printed for the author. 2 vols.

Mackintosh, W. (1782) *Travels in Europe, Asia and Africa*, London: John Murray. 2 vols.

Malcolm, J. (1836) *The Life of Robert, Lord Clive*, London: John Murray. 3 vols.

Maori [pseud. James Inglis] (1878) *Sport and Work on the Nepaul Frontier*, London: Macmillan.

Markham, F. (1854) *Shooting in the Himalayas*, London: Richard Bentley.

Marshman, J.C. (1859) *Life and Times of Carey, Marshman, and Ward*, London: Longmans. 2 vols.

Martyn, H. (1851) *Journals and Letters*, ed. S. Wilberforce, New York: M.W. Dodd.

Meierius, A. (1589) *Certaine Briefe and Speciall Instructions for Gentlemen, Merchants, Students, Souldiers, Marriners*, London: n.p.

Milburn, W. (1813) *Oriental Commerce*, London: Black, Parry. 2 vols.

Molyneux, E. and Younghusband, F. (1924) *Kashmir*, painted 1909, Edinburgh: R. and R. Clark.

Moor, E. (1794) *A Narrative of the Operation of Captain Little's Detachment, and of the Mahratta Army*, London: George Woodfall.

Moorcroft, W. and Trebeck, G. (1841) *Travels in the Himalayan Provinces of Hindustan and the Panjab; in Ladakh and Kashmir; in Peshawar, Kabul, Kunduz and Bokhara, from 1819 to 1825*, ed. H.H. Wilson, London: John Murray. 2 vols.

Mullens, J. (1854) *Missions in South India*, London: W.H. Dalton.

Mun, T. (1621) *A Discourse of Trade to the East-Indies*, London: printed by Nicholas Okes for Iohn Pyper.

Munro, I. (1789) *A Narrative of the Military Operations, on the Coromandel Coast, against the Combined Forces of the French, Dutch and Hyder Ally Cawn, from the Year 1780 to the Peace in 1784; in a series of letters*, London: for the author by T. Bensley.

Oakes, H. (1785) *An Authentic Narrative of the Treatment of the English who were taken Prisoners on the Reduction of Bednore by Tippoo Saib*, London: G. Kearsley.

Orme, R. (1974) *Historical Fragments of the Mogul Empire, of the Morattoes and of the English* (1782), ed. J.P. Guha, New Delhi: Associated.

Ovington, J. (1696) *A Voyage to Surat, in the Year 1689*, London: Jacob Jonson.

Ovington, J. (1699) *An Essay upon the Nature and Qualities of Tea*, London: R. Roberts.

Owen, J. (1816) *The History of the Origin and First Ten Years of the British and Foreign Bible Society*, London: printed for L.B. Seeley. 2 vols.

Paré, Ambroise (1982) *On Monsters and Marvels* (1573), trans. J.L. Pallister, Chicago, IL: University of Chicago Press.

Parkes, F. (1850) *Wanderings of a Pilgrim in Search of the Picturesque during Four-and-Twenty Years in the East*, London: Pelham Richardson. 2 vols.

Pettitt, G. (1851) *The Tinnevelly Mission: of the Church Missionary Society*, London: Seeleys.

Philanthropic Society. (1795) *Instructions for Missionaries to the West-India Islands*, London: printed at the Philanthropic Reform.

Pogson, F. (1872) *Indian Gardening*, Calcutta: Wyman.

Price, U. (1796) *An Essay on the Picturesque*, London: J. Robson.

Price, U. (1797) *Thoughts on the Defence of Property, Addressed to the County of Hereford*, London: sold by J. Allen and J. Debrett.

Purchas, S. (ed.) (1905) *Hakluyts Posthumous, or, Purchas His Pilgrimes* (1625), Glasgow: James MacLehose. 20 vols.

Ralegh, W. (1971) *The History of the World* (1614), ed. C.A. Patrides, London: Macmillan.

Rennell, J. (1788) *Memoir of a Map of Hindoostan; or the Mogul Empire* (1783), enlarged edn, printed for the author.

Ribbentrop, B. (1900) *Forestry in British India*, Calcutta: Office of the Superintendent of Government Printing.

Rice, W. (1857) *Tiger-Shooting in India*, London: Smith, Elder.

Roberts, E. (1832) *Oriental Scenes, Sketches, and Tales*, London: Edward Bull.

Roberts, E. (1835) *Scenes and Characteristics of Hindostan, with Sketches of Anglo-Indian Society*, London: n.p. 3 vols.

Roberts, J. (1789) *The Deluge: a poem*, Cambridge: Archdeacon.

Roe, T. (1641) *His Speech in Parliament wherein he sheweth the cause of the decay of coine and trade in this land*, London: printed for John Aston.

Roe, T. (1990) *The Embassy of Sir Thomas Roe to India, 1615–19, as Narrated in his Journal and Correspondence* (1926), ed. W. Foster, New Delhi: Munshiram Manoharlal.

Savory, I. (1900) *A Sportswoman in India: personal adventures and experiences of travel in known and unknown India*, London: Hutchinson.

Schlich, W. (1904) *A Manual of Forestry*, London: n.p. 3 vols.

Scott, J. (1808a) *Remarks on the Sermons Preached before the University of Oxford, by Dr. Barrow, and the Rev. Mr. Nares, on the prize dissertations of the Rev. Mr. Pearson, and Mr. Cunningham, read at the Universities of Oxford and Cambridge*, London: J. Ridgway.

Scott, J. (1808b) *A Vindication of the Hindoos*, London: R. and J. Rodwell.

Select Committee of the Court of Directors (1793) *First, Second and Third Reports of the Select Committee of the Court of Directors of the East India Company*, n.p.

Shakespear, H. (1862) *The Wild Sports of India*, London: Smith, Elder.

Sharrock, R. (1659) *The History of the Propagation & Improvement of Vegetables*, Oxford: printed by A. Lichfield for T. Robinson.

Shenstone, W. (1764) 'Unconnected thoughts on gardening', *Annual Register* 7: 214–22.

Shipp, J. (1832) *Memoirs of the Extraordinary Military Career of John Shipp*, 3rd edn, London: Hurst, Chance. 3 vols.

Sidney, P., Robert (Earl of Essex) and Davison, W. (1633) *Profitable Instructions*, London: printed [by John Beale?] for Benjamin Fisher.

Sinha, M. (ed.) (1973) James Long, *Selections from Unpublished Records of Government for the Years 1748 to 1767 Inclusive*, Calcutta: K.L. Mukhopadhyay.

Sleeman, W.H. (1995) *Rambles and Recollections of an Indian Official* (1893), New Delhi: Asian Educational Services. 2 vols.

Society for the Propagation of the Gospel in Foreign Parts (1893) *Classified Digest of Records of the Society for the Propagation of the Gospel in Foreign Parts 1701–1892*, 4th edn, London: Society for the Propagation of the Gospel in Foreign Parts.

Sprat, T. (1667) *The History of the Royal Society of the Royal Society of London*, London: printed by T.R. for J. Martyn at the Bell.

Stebbing, E.P. (1911) *Jungle By-Ways in India*, London: John Lane and The Bodley Head.

Stebbing, E.P. (1920) *The Diary of a Sportsman Naturalist in India*, London: John Lane and The Bodley Head.

Sterndale, R.A. (1877) *Seonee or Camplife in the Satpoora Range*, London: S. Low.

Stock, S.G. (1894) *God's Earth; or, Well Worth: a missionary book for boys and girls*, London: Church Missionary Society.

Stocqueller, J.H. (1845) *The Hand-book of India: a guide to the stranger and traveller, and a companion to the resident*, 2nd edn, London: W.H. Allen.

Sulivan, J. (1780) *Observations Respecting the Circar of Mazulipatam*, n.p.

Switzer, S. (1718) *Directions for the General Distribution of a Country Seat into Rural and Extensive Gardens, Parks, Paddock, & C.*

Switzer, S. (1742) *Ichnographia Rustica: or, the nobelman, gentleman, and gardener's recreation* (1718), London: J. and J. Fox. 3 vols.

Taylor, J. (1799) *Travels from England to India in the Year 1789, by the way of Tyrol, Venice, Scandacoon, Aleppo, and over the Great Desert to Bussora with Instructions for Travellers, and an account of the Expense of Travelling*, London: S. Low. 2 vols.

Temple-Wright, I. (1922) *Flowers and Gardens in India*, revised and ed. by W. Burns, Calcutta: Thacker, Spink.

Terry, E. (1649) *The Merchants and Mariners Preservation and Thanksgiving*, London: printed by Thomas Harper.

Terry, E. (1655) *A Voyage to East-India*, London: T. Martin and T. Allestrye.

Thomas, G. (1803) *The Military Memoirs of Mr. George Thomas*, compiled by W. Francklin, Calcutta: Hurkaru.

Thomson, W. (1788) *Memoirs of the late War in Asia, with a Narrative of the Imprisonment and Sufferings of our Officers and Soldiers, by an Officer of Colonel Baillie's Detachment*, London: John Murray. 2 vols.

Tuck, M. (1900?) *East and West: the story of a missionary band*, London: London Missionary Society.

Tucker, J. (1757) *Instructions for Travellers*, Yorkshire: SR.

Tucker, S. (1842–43) *South Indian Sketches*, London: James Nisbet. 2 vols.

Tulloch, M. (1940) *The All-In-One Shikar Book: an everyday guide to field sports in India*, Bombay: D.B. Taraporewala.

Twining, T. (1807) *A Letter, to the Chairman of the East India Company, on the Danger of Interfering in the Religious Opinions of the Natives of India*, London: J. Ridgway.

United Provinces of Agra and Oudh Miscellaneous Government Publications. (1910) *Manual on Indian Etiquette for the Use of European Officers Coming to India*, Allahabad: Government Press.

Valentia, Viscount [George Annesley] (1809) *Voyages and Travels to India, Ceylon, the Red Sea, Abyssinia, and Egypt, in the Years 1802, 1803, 1804, 1805, and 1806*, London: for William Miller by W. Bulmer. 3 vols.

van Linschoten, J.H. (2003) *Civil and Corrupt Asia: image and text in the 'Itinerario' and the 'Icones' of Jan Huygen van Linschoten* (1598), ed. E. van den Boogaart, Chicago, IL: University of Chicago Press.

Vansittart, H. (1764) *A Narrative of the Transactions in Bengal, from the Year 1760 to the Year 1764*, London: J. Newberry. 3 vols.

Walpole, H. (1948) *The Yale Edition of Horace Walpole's Correspondence*, ed. W.S. Lewis, G.L. Lam and C.H. Bennett, New Haven, CT: Yale University Press.

Ward, W. (1863) *A View of the History, Literature, and Religion of the Hindoos*, 5th edn, Madras: J. Higginbotham.

Waring, S. (1809) *A Letter to the Conductors of the Christian Observer*, London: James Ridgway.

Weitbrecht, M. (1875) *The Women of India and Christian Work in the Zenana*, London: James Nisbet.

Whately, T. (1770) *Observations on Modern Gardening*, London: printed for T. Payne.

White, G.F. (1838) *Views in India, Chiefly among the Himalaya Mountains*, ed. E. Roberts, London: Fisher, Son.

Wilberforce, S. (1874) *Speeches on Missions*, ed. H. Rowley, London: n.p.

Wilberforce, W. (1797) *A Practical View of the Prevailing Religious System of Professed Christians*, London: T. Cadell.

Wilkinson, M. (1844) *Sketches of Christianity in North India*, London: n.p.

Williamson, T. (1808) *Oriental Field Sports*, London: W. Bulmer. 2 vols.

Wilson, C.R. (ed.) (1983) *Early Annals of the English in Bengal*, New Delhi: Bimla. 2 vols.

Wilson, J. (1844) *The Evangelization of India*, Edinburgh: William Whyte.

Young, A. (1768) *A Six Weeks Tour through the Southern Counties of England and Wales*, Dublin: n.p.

Secondary sources

Adas, M. (1990) *Machines as the Measure of Men: science, technology, and ideologies of Western dominance*, Delhi: Oxford University Press.

Alban Jr, D., Woods Jr, R.H. and Daigle-Williamson, M. (2005) 'The writings of William Carey: journalism as mission in a modern age', *Mission Studies*, 22.1: 85–113.

Andrews, M. (1989) *The Search for the Picturesque: landscape aesthetics and tourism in Britain, 1760–1800*, Palo Alto, CA: Stanford University Press.

Andrews, M. (1994a) 'The metropolitan picturesque', in S. Copley and P. Garside (eds) *The Politics of the Picturesque*, Cambridge: Cambridge University Press.

Andrews, M. (ed.) (1994b) *The Picturesque: literary sources and documents*, Mountfield, UK: Helm Information. 3 vols.

Andrews, M. (1999) *Landscape and Western Art*, Oxford: Oxford University Press, 1999.

Archer, M. (1980) *Early Views of India: the picturesque journeys of Thomas and William Daniell, 1786–1794*. London: Thames & Hudson.

Arnold, K. (2000) 'Trade, travel, and treasure: seventeenth-century artificial curiosities', in C. Chard and H. Langdon (eds) *Transports*, New Haven, CT: Yale University Press.

Ashfield, A. and de Bolla, P. (eds) (1996) *The Sublime: a reader in British eighteenth-century aesthetic theory*, Cambridge: Cambridge University Press.

Bailey, A. (2001) '"Monstrous manner": style and the early modern theatre', *Criticism*, 43.3: 249–84.

Banks, R.E.R. et al. (eds) (1994) *Sir Joseph Banks: a global perspective*, Kew, UK: Royal Botanic Gardens.

Bann, S. (1999) *Under the Sign: John Bargrave as collector, traveler, and witness*, Ann Arbor, MI: University of Michigan Press.

Barasch, F.K. (1971) *The Grotesque: a study in meanings*, The Hague: Mouton.

Barbour, R. (2003) *Before Orientalism: London's theatre of the east 1576–1626*, Cambridge: Cambridge University Press.

Barilli, R. (1989) *Rhetoric*, trans. G. Menozzi, Minneapolis, MN: University of Minnesota Press.

Barrell, J. (1983) *The Dark Side of the Landscape: the rural poor in English painting, 1730–1810* (1983), Cambridge: Cambridge University Press.

Barrell, J. (1986) *The Political Theory of Painting from Reynolds to Hazlitt*, New Haven, CT: Yale University Press.

Barrell, J. (2000) 'Death on the Nile: fantasy and the literature of tourism, 1840–60', in C. Hall (ed.) *Cultures of Empire: colonizers in Britain and the empire of the nineteenth and twentieth centuries: a reader*, Manchester, UK: Manchester University Press.

Bates, A.W. (2005) 'Good, common, regular, and orderly: early modern classifications of monstrous births', *Social History of Medicine*, 18.2: 141–58.

Batten Jr, C.L. (1978) *Pleasurable Instruction: form and convention in eighteenth-century travel literature*, Berkeley, CA: University of California Press.

Bayly, C.A. (1989) *Imperial Meridian: the British empire and the world, 1780–1830*, London: Longman.

Bayly, C.A. (1999) *Empire and Information: intelligence gathering and social communication in India, 1780–1870*, Cambridge: Cambridge University Press.

Bearce, G.D. (1961) *British Attitudes towards India, 1784–1858*, Delhi: Oxford University Press.

Behdad, A. (1994) *Belated Travelers: orientalism in the age of colonial dissolution*, Durham, NC: Duke University Press.

Berg, M. (2005) *Luxury and Pleasure in Eighteenth-Century Britain*, Oxford: Oxford University Press.

Bermingham, A. (1986) *Landscape and Ideology: the English rustic tradition, 1740–1860*, Berkeley, CA: University of California Press.

Bermingham, A. (1994) 'The picturesque and ready-to-wear femininity', in S. Copley and P. Garside (eds) *The Politics of the Picturesque: literature, landscape and aesthetics since 1770*, Cambridge: Cambridge University Press.

Bhattacharya, N. (1998) *Reading the Splendid Body: gender and consumerism in eighteenth century British writing on India*, Newark, DE: University of Delaware Press.

Bicknell, P. (1981) *Beauty, Horror and Immensity: picturesque landscape in Britain, 1750–1850*, Cambridge: Fitzwilliam Museum.

Biggs, M. (1999) 'Putting the state on the map: cartography, territory, and European state formation', *Comparative Studies in Society and History*, 41.2: 374–411.

Bohls, E. (1997) *Women Travel Writers and the Language of Aesthetics, 1716–1818* (1995), Cambridge: Cambridge University Press.

Borm, J. (2004) 'Defining travel: on the travel book, travel writing and terminology', in G. Hooper and T. Youngs (eds) *Perspectives on Travel Writing*, Aldershot, UK: Ashgate.

Bosch, D.J. (1999) *Transforming Mission: paradigm shifts in theology of mission*, New York: Orbis.

Brammall, K.M. (1996) 'Monstrous metamorphosis: nature, morality and the rhetoric of monstrosity in Tudor England', *Sixteenth Century Journal*, 27.1: 3–21.

Brantlinger, P. (1988) *Rule of Darkness: British literature and imperialism, 1830–1914*, Ithaca, NY: Cornell University Press.

Briggs, A. (1971) *The Age of Improvement, 1783–1867* (1959), London: Longman.

Brockway, L.H. (1979) *Science and Colonial Expansion: the role of the British Royal Botanic Gardens*, London: Academic.

Brown, L. (2001) *Fables of Modernity: literature and culture in the English eighteenth century*, Ithaca, NY: Cornell University Press.

Bunn, D. (2002) 'The sleep of the brave: graves as sites and signs in the colonial Eastern Cape', in P.S. Landau and D.S. Kaspin (eds) *Images and Empire: visuality in colonial and postcolonial Africa*, Berkeley, CA: University of California Press.

Burke, P. (1999) 'The philosopher as traveler: Bernier's orient', in J. Elsner and J-P. Rubies (eds) *Voyages and Visions: towards a cultural history of travel*, London: Reaktion.

Burnett, M.T. (2002) *Constructing 'Monsters' in Shakespearean Drama and Early Modern Culture*, London: Palgrave-Macmillan.

Burton, A. (1996) 'Contesting the zenana: the mission to make "lady doctors" for India', *Journal of British Studies*, 35.3: 368–97.

Bushaway, R.W. (1982) 'From custom to crime: wood gathering in eighteenth and early nineteenth century England, a focus for conflict in Hampshire, Wiltshire and the South', in J. Rule (ed.) *Outside the Law: studies in crime and order, 1650–1850*, Exeter, UK: University of Exeter Press.

Butlin, R.A. (1990) 'Regions in England and Wales, c. 1600–1914', in R.A. Dodghson and R.A. Butlin (eds) *An Historical Geography of England and Wales* (1978), London: Academic.

Buzard, J. (1993) *The Beaten Track: European tourism, literature, and the ways to culture, 1800–1918*, Oxford: Oxford University Press.

Cahn, W. (1991) 'Medieval landscape and the encyclopedic tradition', *Yale French Studies*, 80: 11–24.

Campbell, M.B. (1988) *The Witness and the Other World: exotic European travel writing, 400–1600*, Ithaca, NY: Cornell University Press.

Campbell, M.B. (1996) '*Anthropometamorphosis*: John Bulwer's monsters of cosmetology and the science of culture', in J.J. Cohen (ed.) *Monster Theory: reading culture*, Minneapolis, MN: University of Minnesota Press.

Campbell, M.B. (1999) *Wonder and Science: imagining worlds in early modern Europe*, Ithaca, NY: Cornell University Press.

Cannadine, D. (2002) 'The context, performance and meaning of ritual: the British monarchy and the "invention of tradition", c 1820–1977', in E. Hobsbawm and T. Ranger (eds) *The Invention of Tradition* (1983), Cambridge: Cambridge University Press.

Canny, N. (ed.) (1998) *The Origins of Empire*, Oxford: Oxford University Press.

Carey, D. (1996) 'Locke, travel literature, and the natural history of man', *The Seventeenth Century*, 11.2: 259–80.

Carlton, C. and Carlton, C. (2004) *The Significance of Gardening in British India*, Lewiston, NY: Edwin Mellen.

Carter, P. (1987) *The Road to Botany Bay: an essay in spatial history*, London: Faber & Faber.

Cassuto, L. (1997) *The Inhuman Race: the racial grotesque in American literature and culture*, New York: Columbia University Press.

Chakravarty, G. (2005) *The Indian Mutiny and the British Imagination*, Cambridge: Cambridge University Press.

Chard, C. (1999) *Pleasure and Guilt on the Grand Tour: travel writing and imaginative geography 1600–1830*, Manchester, UK: Manchester University Press.

Charlesworth, M. (1994) 'The ruined abbey: picturesque and Gothic values', in S. Copley and P. Garside (eds) *The Politics of the Picturesque: literature, landscape and aesthetics since 1770*, Cambridge: Cambridge University Press.

Chaudhuri, K.N. (1978) *The Trading World of Asia and the English East India Company 1660–1760*, Cambridge: Cambridge University Press.

Classen, C. (1993) *Worlds of Sense: exploring the senses in history and across cultures*, London: Routledge.

Clay, C. (1985) 'Landlords and estate management', in J. Thirsk (ed.) *The Agrarian History of England and Wales, Vol. V, 1640–1750, ii: Agrarian Change*, Cambridge: Cambridge University Press.

Cohen, J.J. (1996) 'Monster culture (Seven Theses)', in J.J. Cohen (ed.) *Monster Theory: reading culture*, Minneapolis, MN: University of Minnesota Press.

Cohn, B.S. (1997) *Colonialism and its Forms of Knowledge: the British in India*, New Delhi: Oxford University Press.

Cohn, B.S. (2002) 'Representing authority in Victorian India', in E. Hobsbawm and T. Ranger (eds) *The Invention of Tradition* (1983), Cambridge: Cambridge University Press.

Colbert, B. (2005) *Shelley's Eye: travel writing and aesthetic vision*, Aldershot, UK: Ashgate.

Colley, L. (1992) *Britons: forging the nation, 1701–1837*, New Haven, CT: Yale University Press.

Cormack, L.B. (1997) *Charting an Empire: geography at the English universities, 1580–1620*, Chicago, IL: University of Chicago Press.

Cosgrove, D.E. (1984) *Social Formation and Symbolic Landscape*, London: Croom Helm.

Cosgrove, D.E. (2001) *Apollo's Eye: a cartographic genealogy of the earth in the Western imagination*, Baltimore, MD: Johns Hopkins University Press.

Crawford, J. (2005) *Marvelous Protestantism: monstrous births in post-Reformation England*, Baltimore, MD: Johns Hopkins University Press.

Daniels, S. (1989) 'The political iconography of woodland in later Georgian England', in D. Cosgrove and S. Daniels (eds) *The Iconography of Landscape*, Cambridge: Cambridge University Press.

Daniels, S. (1992) 'Love and death across an English garden: Constable's paintings of his family's flower and kitchen gardens', *Huntington Library Quarterly*, 55.3: 433–58.

Daniels, S. and Watkins, C. (1994) 'Picturesque landscaping and estate management: Uvedale Price and Nathaniel Kent at Foxley', in S. Copley and P. Garside (eds) *The Politics of the Picturesque*, Cambridge: Cambridge University Press.

Daston, L. and Park, K. (1998) *Wonders and the Order of Nature 1150–1750*, New York: Zone.

Davis, I. (2002) 'Consuming the body of the working man in the latter Middle Ages', in L.H. McAvoy and T. Walters (eds) *Consuming Narratives: gender and monstrous appetite in the Middle Ages and the Renaissance*, Cardiff: University of Wales Press.

de Bolla, P. (2003) *The Education of the Eye: painting, landscape, and architecture in eighteenth-century Britain*, Palo Alto, CA: Stanford University Press.

Dear, P. (1992) 'From truth to disinterestedness in the seventeenth century', *Social Studies of Science*, 22: 619–31.

DeRogatis, A. (2003) *Moral Geography: maps, missionaries, and the American frontier*, New York: Columbia University Press.

Dorrian, M. (2000) 'On the monstrous and the grotesque', *Word and Image*, 16.3: 310–17.

Drayton, R. (2000) *Nature's Government: science, imperial Britain, and the 'improvement' of the world*, New Haven, CT: Yale University Press.

Duncan, J. (1997) 'Sites of representation: place, time and the discourse of the other', in J. Duncan and D. Ley (eds) *Place/Culture/Representation*, London: Routledge.

Dyson, K.K. (1978) *A Various Universe: A study of the journals and memoirs of British men and women in the Indian subcontinent, 1765–1856*, Delhi: Oxford University Press.

Edney, M.H. (1997) *Mapping an Empire: the geographical construction of British India, 1765–1843*, Chicago, IL: University of Chicago Press.

Elliott, B. (1994) 'The promotion of horticulture', in R.E.R Banks et al. (eds) *Sir Joseph Banks: a global perspective*, Kew, UK: Royal Botanic Gardens.

Emel, J. (1998) 'Are you man enough, big and bad enough? animal eradication in the US', in J. Wolch and J. Emel (eds) *Animal Geographies: place, politics, and identity in the nature-culture borderlands*, London: Verso.

Farnham, W. (1971) *The Shakespearean Grotesque: its genesis and transformations*, Oxford: Clarendon.

Ferguson, F. (1992) *Solitude and the Sublime: romanticism and the aesthetics of individuation*, New York: Routledge.

Fisch, J. (1985) 'A pamphlet war on Christian missions in India 1807–9', *Journal of Asian History*, 19.1: 22–70.

Fisher, M.H. (ed.) (1996) *The Politics of the British Annexation of India, 1757–1857* (1993), Delhi: Oxford University Press.

Fletcher, A. (1975) *Allegory: the theory of a symbolic mode* (1964), Ithaca, NY: Cornell University Press.

Freedgood, E. (2000) *The Victorian Writing of Risk: imagining a safe England in a dangerous world*, Cambridge: Cambridge University Press.

Friedman, J.B. (2000) *Monstrous Races in Medieval Art and Thought*, (1981), Syracuse, NY: Syracuse University Press.

Fulford, T. (1996) *Landscape, Liberty and Authority: poetry, criticism and politics from Thomson to Wordsworth*, Cambridge: Cambridge University Press.

Fulford, T., Lee, D. and Kitson, P.J. (2004) *Literature, Science and Exploration in the Romantic Era: Bodies of Knowledge*, Cambridge: Cambridge University Press.

Fuller, M.C. (1995) *Voyages in Print: English travel to America 1576–1624*, Cambridge: Cambridge University Press.

Fussell, P. (1980) *Abroad: British literary traveling between the wars*, New York: Oxford University Press.

Gadgil, M. and Guha, R. (1993) *This Fissured Land: an ecological history of India*, New Delhi: Oxford University Press.

Galperin, W.H. (1993) *The Return of the Visible in British Romanticism*, Baltimore, MD: Johns Hopkins University Press.

Ghose, I. (1998) *Women Travellers in Colonial India: the power of the female gaze*. Delhi: Oxford University Press.

Gibson, M.E. (1999) 'Henry Martyn and England's Christian empire: rereading *Jane Eyre* through missionary biography', *Victorian Literature and Culture*, 27: 419–42.

Gilbert, D. (1999) '"London in all its glory – or how to enjoy London": guidebook representations of imperial London', *Journal of Historical Geography*, 25.3: 279–97.

Gilbert, R. (1999) 'Seeing and knowing: science, pornography and early modern hermaphrodites', in E. Fudge, R. Gilbert and S. Wiseman (eds) *At the Borders of the Human: beasts, bodies and natural philosophy in the early modern period*, London: Macmillan.

Gillies, J. (1994) *Shakespeare and the Geographies of Difference*. Cambridge: Cambridge University Press.

Glass, D.V. (1973) *Numbering the People: the eighteenth century population controversy and the development of census and vital statistics in Britain*, Farnborough, UK: D.C. Heath.

Goody, J. (1996) *The East in the West*, Cambridge: Cambridge University Press.

Greenblatt, S. (1991) *Marvelous Possessions: the wonder of the new world*, Oxford: Clarendon.

Greenblatt, S. (ed.) (1993) *New World Encounters*, Berkeley, CA: University of California Press.

Grewal, I. (1996) *Home and Harem: nation, gender, empire, and the cultures of travel*, Durham, NC: Duke University Press.

Grosz, E. (1990) 'The body of signification', in J. Fletcher and A. Benjamin (eds) *Abjection, Melancholia and Love: the work of Julia Kristeva*, London: Routledge.

Gupta, B.K. (1900) *Sirajuddaulah and the East India Company, 1756–1757: background to the foundation of British power in India*, Leiden, Netherlands: E.J. Brill.

Guthke, K.S. (1990) *The Last Frontier: imagining other worlds from the Copernican revolution to modern science fiction*, trans. H. Atkins, Ithaca, NY: Cornell University Press.

Hadfield, A. (1998) *Literature, Travel, and Colonial Writing in the English Renaissance, 1545–1625*, Oxford: Clarendon.

Hall, C. (2002) *Civilising Subjects: colony and metropole in the English imagination, 1830–1867*, Chicago, IL: University of Chicago Press.

Harpham, G.G. (1982) *On the Grotesque: strategies of contradiction in art and literature*, Princeton, NJ: Princeton University Press.

Harris, J.G. (1998) *Foreign Bodies and the Body Politic: discourses of social pathology in early modern England*, Cambridge: Cambridge University Press.

Harris, J.G. (2004) *Sick Economies: drama, mercantilism and disease in Shakespeare's England*, Philadelphia, PA: University of Pennsylvania Press.

Harrison, M. (1996) '"The tender frame of man": disease, climate, and racial difference in India and the West Indies, 1760–1860', *Bulletin of the History of Medicine*, 70.1: 68–93.

Harrison, M. (1999) *Climate and Constitutions: health, race, environment, and British imperialism in India, 1600–1850*, Delhi: Oxford University Press.

Headrick, D.R. (1981) *The Tools of Empire*, Oxford: Oxford University Press.

Healy, M. (1999) 'Bodily regimen and fear of the beast: "plausibility" in Renaissance domestic tragedy', in E. Fudge, R. Gilbert and S. Wiseman (eds) *At the Borders of the Human: beasts, bodies and natural philosophy in the early modern period*, London: Macmillan.

Healy, M. (2002) 'Monstrous tyrannical appetites: "& what wonderful monsters have lately ben borne in Englande"', in L.H. McAvoy and T. Walters (eds) *Consuming Narratives: gender and monstrous appetite in the Middle Ages and the Renaissance*, Cardiff: University of Wales Press.

Helgerson, R. (1986) 'The land speaks: cartography, chorography, and subversion in Renaissance England', *Representations*, 16: 51–84.

Helgerson, R. (1992) *Forms of Nationhood: the Elizabethan writing of England*, Chicago, IL: University of Chicago Press

Helsinger, E.K. (1997) 'Land and national representation in Britain', in M. Rosenthal, C. Payne and S. Wilson (eds) *Prospects for the Nation: recent essays in British landscape, 1750–1880*, New Haven, CT: Yale University Press.

Higgs, E. (2004) *The Information State in England: the central collection of information on citizens since 1500*, London: Palgrave-Macmillan.

Hooper-Greenhill, E. (1992) *Museums and the Shaping of Knowledge*, London: Routledge.

Hoskins, W.G. (1992) *The Making of the English Landscape* (1955), London: Hodder & Stoughton.

Huet, M.H. (1993) *Monstrous Imagination*, Cambridge, MA: Harvard University Press.

Hulme, P. (1992) *Colonial Encounters: Europe and the native Caribbean, 1492–1797* (1986), London: Routledge.

Hulme, P. and Youngs, T. (eds) (2002) *The Cambridge Companion to Travel Writing*, Cambridge: Cambridge University Press.

Hunt, J.D. and Willis, P. (eds) (1975) *The Genius of the Place: the English landscape garden 1620–1820*, London: Paul Elek.

Janowitz, A. (1990) *England's Ruins: poetic purpose and the national landscape*, Oxford: Basil Blackwell.

Johnston, A. (2003) *Missionary Writing and Empire, 1800–1860*, Cambridge: Cambridge University Press.

Jordan, S. (2001) 'From grotesque bodies to useful hands: idleness, industry, and the labouring class', *Eighteenth-Century Life*, 25.3: 62–79.

Joseph, B. (2004) *Reading the East India Company, 1720–1840: colonial currencies of gender*, Chicago, IL: University of Chicago Press.

Kamps, I. and Singh, J.G. (eds) (2001) *Travel Knowledge: European 'discoveries' in the early modern period*, New York: Palgrave.

Keay, J. (1991) *The Honourable Company: a history of the English East India Company*, London: HarperCollins.

Keck, S.L. (2004) 'Picturesque Burma: British travel writing 1890–1914', *Journal of Southeast Asian Studies*, 35.3: 387–414.

Kilgour, M. (1990) *From Communion to Cannibalism: an anatomy of metaphors of incorporation*, Princeton, NJ: Princeton University Press.

Knorr, K.E. (1968) *British Colonial Theories, 1570–1830*, London: Frank Cass.

Koch, M. (1998) 'Ruling the world: the cartographic gaze in Elizabethan accounts of the new world', *Early Modern Literary Studies*, 4.2: 1–39.

Korte, B. (2000) *English Travel Writing from Pilgrimages to Postcolonial Exploration*, trans. C. Mathias, London: Macmillan.

Kristeva, J. (1982) *Powers of Horror: an essay on abjection*, trans. L.S. Roudiez, New York: Columbia University Press.

Lach, D.F. and Van Kley, E.J. (1990) 'Asia in the eyes of Europe: the seventeenth century', *The Seventeenth Century*, 5.1: 93–109.

Landau, P.S. (2002) 'Empires of the visual: photography and colonial administration in Africa', in P.S. Landau and D.S. Kaspin (eds) *Images and Empire: visuality in colonial and postcolonial Africa*, Berkeley, CA: University of California Press.

Lap-Chuen, T. (1998) *The Sublime: groundwork towards a theory*. New York: University of Rochester Press.

Leask, N. (2002) *Curiosity and the Aesthetics of Travel Writing, 1770–1840: 'from an antique land'*, New York: Oxford University Press.

Lester, A. (2000) 'Obtaining the "due observance of justice": the geographies of colonial humanitarianism', *Environment and Planning D*, 20: 277–93.

Lim, W.S.H. (1998) *The Arts of Empire: the poetics of colonialism from Ralegh to Milton*, Newark, DE: University of Delaware Press.

Linton, J.P. (1998) *The Romance of the New World: gender and literary formations of English colonialism*, Cambridge: Cambridge University Press.

Low, A. (1985) *The Georgic Revolution*, Princeton, NJ: Princeton University Press.

Lübbren, N. (2002) '"Toilers of the sea": fisherfolk and the geographies of tourism in England, 1880–1900', in D.P. Corbett, Y. Holt and F. Russell (eds) *The Geographies of Englishness: landscape and the national past, 1880–1940*, New Haven, CT: Yale University Press.

Macaulay, R. (1964) *Pleasure of Ruins*, ed. C.B. Smith, London: Thames & Hudson.

McAvoy, L.H. and Walters, T. (eds) (2002) *Consuming Narratives: gender and monstrous appetite in the middle ages and the Renaissance*, Cardiff: University of Wales Press.

McClintock, A. (1994) *Imperial Leather: race, gender and sexuality in the colonial contest*, London: Routledge.

McDevitt, P. (2004) *May the Best Man Win: sport, masculinity, and nationalism in Great Britain and the Empire, 1880–1935*, London: Palgrave-Macmillan.

McElroy, B. (1989) *Fiction of the Modern Grotesque*, New York: St Martin's.

McKenzie, C. (2000) 'The British big-game hunting tradition, masculinity and fraternalism with particular reference to "the shikar club"', *The Sport Historian*, 20.1: 70–96.

MacKenzie, J.M. (1987) 'The imperial pioneer and hunter and the British masculine stereotype in late Victorian and Edwardian times', in J.A. Mangan and J. Walvin (eds) *Manliness and Morality: masculinity in Britain and America 1800–1940*, New York: St Martin's.

MacKenzie, J.M. (1988) *The Empire of Nature: hunting, conservation and British Imperialism*, Manchester, UK: Manchester University Press.

Malcolmson, C. (1994) 'The garden enclosed/the woman enclosed: Marvell and the Cavalier poets', in R. Burt and J.M. Archer (eds) *Enclosure Acts: sexuality, property, and culture in early modern England*, Ithaca, NY: Cornell University Press.

Mangan, J.A. (ed.) (1992) *The Cultural Bond: sport, empire, society*, London: Frank Cass.

Manwaring, E.W. (1965) *Italian Landscape in Eighteenth Century England: a study chiefly of the influence of Claude Lorrain and Salvator Rosa on English taste, 1700–1800* (1925), London: Frank Cass.

Martels, Z.V. (ed.) (1994) *Travel Fact and Travel Fiction: studies on fiction, literary tradition, scholarly discovery, and observation in travel writing*, Leiden, Netherlands: E.J. Brill.

Mayhew, R.J. (2000a) *Enlightenment Geography: the political languages of British geography, 1650–1850*, London: Macmillan.

Mayhew, R.J. (2000b) 'William Gilpin and the Latitudinarian Picturesque', *Eighteenth-Century Studies* 33: 349–66.

Metcalf, T.R. (1998) *Ideologies of the Raj*, Cambridge: Cambridge University Press.

Metcalf, T.R. (2005) *Forging the Raj: essays on British India in the heyday of the Raj*, Delhi: Oxford University Press.

Mingey, G.E. (ed.) (1975) *Arthur Young and his Times*, London: Macmillan.

Mishra, V. (1994) *The Gothic Sublime*, New York: State University of New York Press.

Mitchell, T. (1988) *Colonizing Egypt*, Cambridge: Cambridge University Press.

Mitter, P. (1977) *Much Maligned Monsters: history of European reactions to Indian Art*, Oxford: Clarendon.

Mohanram, R. (1999) *Black Body: women, colonialism, and space*, Minneapolis, MN: University of Minnesota Press.

Moseley, C.W.R.D. (ed. and trans.) (1983) *The Travels of Sir John Mandeville*, New York: Penguin.

Mukherjee, P. (2005) 'Nimrods: hunting, authority, identity', *Modern Language Review*, 100.4: 923–39.

Mukhopadhyay, S.C. (1987) *The Agrarian Policy of the British in Bengal: the formative period, 1698–1772*, Allahabad: Chugh.

Murdoch, J. (1990) 'The landscape of labour: transformations of the georgic', in K.R. Johnston, K. Hanson and G. Chaitin (eds) *Romantic Revolutions: criticism and theory*, Bloomington, IN: Indiana University Press.

Murray, J. (2000) 'The role of women in the Church Missionary Soceity, 1799–1917', in K. Ward and B. Stanley (eds) *The Church Missionary Society and World Christianity, 1799–1999*, Grand Rapids, MI: William B. Eerdman.

Nair, J. (2000) 'Uncovering the zenana: visions of Indian womanhood in Englishwomen's writings, 1813–1940', in C. Hall (ed.) *Cultures of Empire: colonizers in Britain and the empire of the nineteenth and twentieth centuries: a reader*, Manchester, UK: Manchester University Press.

Nayar, P.K. (2002) 'Colonial proxemics: the embassy of Sir Thomas Roe to India', *Studies in Travel Writing*, 6: 29–53.

Neill, S. (1985) *A History of Christianity in India: 1707–1858*, Cambridge: Cambridge University Press.

Nicolson, M.H. (1963) *Mountain Gloom and Mountain Glory: the development of the aesthetics of the infinite* (1959), New York: W.W. Norton.

Nottingham Castle Museum (1988) *Ruins in British Romantic Art from Wilson to Turner*, Nottingham, UK: Nottingham Castle Museum.

Nussbaum, F. (1995) *Torrid Zones: maternity, sexuality and empire in eighteenth-century English narratives*, Baltimore, MD: Johns Hopkins University Press.

Pagden, A. (1993) *European Encounters with the New World*, New Haven, CT: Yale University Press.

Paley, M.D. (1986) *The Apocalyptic Sublime*, New Haven, CT: Yale University Press.

Pandian, A.S. (2001) 'Predatory care: the imperial hunt in Mughal and British India', *Journal of Historical Sociology*, 14.1: 79–107.

Park, K. and Daston, L.J. (1981) 'Unnatural conceptions: the study of monsters in sixteenth- and seventeenth-century France and England', *Past and Present*, 92: 20–54.

Paulson, R. (1982) *Literary Landscape: Turner and Constable*, New Haven, CT: Yale University Press.

Platt, P.G. (1997) *Reason Diminished: Shakespeare and the marvelous*, Lincoln, NE: University of Nebraska Press.

Porter, A. (1985) '"Commerce and Christianity": the rise and fall of a nineteenth-century missionary slogan', *Historical Journal*, 28.3: 597–621.

Porter, R. (2000) *Enlightenment: Britain and the creation of the modern world*, Harmondsworth: Penguin.

Prakash, O. (1998) *European Commercial Enterprise in Pre-colonial India*, The New Cambridge History of India, II.5, Cambridge: Cambridge University Press.

Pratt, M.L. (1995) *Imperial Eyes: travel writing and transculturation*, London: Routledge.

Punter, D. (1994) 'The Picturesque and the sublime: two worldscapes', in S. Copley and P. Garside (eds) *The Politics of the Picturesque: literature, landscape and aesthetics since 1770*, Cambridge: Cambridge University Press.

Quadflieg, H. (2004) '"As mannerly and civill as any of Europe": early modern travel writing and the exploration of the English self', in G. Hooper and T. Youngs (eds) *Perspectives on Travel Writing*, Aldershot, UK: Ashgate.

Rak, J. (1998) 'The improving eye: eighteenth-century picturesque travel and agricultural change in the Scottish highlands', in J.C. Hayes and T. Erwin (eds) *Studies in Eighteenth-Century Culture*, 27: 343–64.

Raman, S. (2002) *Framing 'India': the colonial imaginary in early modern culture*, Palo Alto, CA: Stanford University Press.

Rangarajan, M. (1996) *Fencing the Forest: conservation and ecological change in India's Central Provinces 1860–1914*, Delhi: Oxford University Press.

Rangarajan, M. (2001) *India's Wildlife History: an introduction*, New Delhi: Permanent Black and Ranthambhore Foundation.

Ray, R. (1998) 'The memsahib's brush: Anglo-Indian women and the art of the picturesque, 1830–80', in J.F. Codell and D. Sachko Macleod (eds) *Orientalism Transposed: the impact of the colonies on British culture*, Aldershot, UK: Ashgate.

Reill, P.R. (2005) *Vitalizing Nature in the Enlightenment*, Berkeley, CA: University of California Press.

Richards, T. (1993) *The Imperial Archive: knowledge and the fantasy of empire*, London: Verso.

Ritvo, H. (2002) 'Destroyers and preservers: big game in Victorian empire', *History Today*, 52.1: 33–39.

Roberts, B. (1973) 'Planned villages from medieval England', in A.R.H. Baker and J.B. Harley (eds) *Man Made the Land: essays in English historical geography*, Newton Abbott, UK: David & Charles.

Robertson, A.K. (1996) *The Grotesque Interface: deformity, debasement, dissolution*, Frankfurt am Main, Germany: Vervuert.

Robertson, J. (2002) 'Anxieties of imperial decay: three journeys in India', in H. Gilbert and A. Johnston (eds) *In Transit: travel, text, empire*, New York: Peter Lang.

Robins, N. (2006) *The Corporation that Changed the World: how the East India Company shaped the modern multinational*, Hyderabad: Orient Longman.

Rosenthal, M. (1982) *British Landscape Painting*, Oxford: Phaidon.

Rousseau, G.S. and Porter, R. (eds) (1990) *Exoticism in the Enlightenment*, Manchester, UK: Manchester University Press.

Rusnock, A.A (1999) 'Biopolitics: political arithmetic in the Enlightenment', in W. Clark, J. Golinski and S. Schaffer (eds) *The Sciences in Enlightenment Europe*, Chicago, IL: University of Chicago Press.

Said, E.W. (1985) *Orientalism* (1978), Harmondsworth: Penguin.

Scanlan, T. (1999) *Colonial Writing and the New World: allegories of desire*, Cambridge: Cambridge University Press.

Scarry, E. (1985) *The Body in Pain: the making and unmaking of the world*, Oxford: Oxford University Press.

Seed, P. (1995) *Ceremonies of Possession in Europe's Conquest of the New World, 1492–1640*, Cambridge: Cambridge University Press.

Sekora, J. (1977) *Luxury: the concept in Western thought, from Eden to Smollett*, Baltimore, MD: Johns Hopkins University Press.

Sell, J.P.A. (2006) *Rhetoric and Wonder in English Travel Writing, 1560–1613*, Aldershot, UK: Ashgate.

Semler, L.E. (1996) 'Richard Lovelace and the mannerist grotesque', *AUMLA (Journal of the Australasian Universities Languages and Literature Association)*, 85: 69–82.

Semple, R.A. (2003) *Missionary Women: gender, professionalism and the Victorian idea of Christian mission*, Woodbridge, UK: Boydell.

Seymour, M.C. (1993) *Sir John Mandeville*, Aldershot, UK: Ashgate.

Shaw, P. (2002) *Waterloo and the Romantic Imagination*, London: Palgrave.

Singh, J.G. (1996) *Colonial Narratives, Cultural Dialogues: 'discoveries' of India in the language of colonialism*, London: Routledge.

Sontag, S. (1973) *On Photography*, New York: Dell.

Spear, P. (1961) *India, A Modern History*, Ann Arbor, MI: University of Michigan Press.

Spencer, J.B. (1973) *Heroic Nature: ideal landscapes in English poetry from Marvell to Thomson*, Evanston, IL: Northwestern University Press.

Spolsky, E. (2001) *Satisfying Skepticism: embodied knowledge in the early modern world*, Aldershot, UK: Ashgate.

Stafford, B.M. (1984) *Voyage into Substance: art, science, nature and the illustrated travel account, 1760–1840*, Cambridge, MA: Massachusetts Institute of Technology.

Stafford, B.M. (1993) 'Voyeur or observer? Enlightenment thoughts on the dilemmas of display', *Configurations*, 1.1: 95–128.

Stanley, B. (1983) '"Commerce and Christianity": providence theory, the missionary movement, and the imperialism of free trade, 1842–60', *Historical Journal*, 26.1: 71–94.

Stanley, B. (ed.) (2001) *Christian Missions and the Enlightenment*, Grand Rapids, MI: William B. Eerdman.

Steintrager, J.A. (2004) *Cruel Delight: Enlightenment culture and the inhuman*, Bloomington, IN: Indiana University Press.

Stepan, N.L. (2001) *Picturing Tropical Nature*, Ithaca, NY: Cornell University Press.

Stephens, J.C. (ed.) (1982) *The Guardian*, Lexington, KY: Kentucky University Press.

Stewart, S. (1984) *On Longing: narratives of the miniature, the gigantic, the souvenir, the collection*, Baltimore, MD: Johns Hopkins University Press.

Stilz, G. (2002) 'Heroic travellers – romantic landscapes: the colonial sublime in Indian, Australian and American art and literature', in H. Berghoff, B. Korte, R. Schneider and C. Harvie (eds) *The Making of Modern Tourism: the cultural history of the British experience, 1600–2000*, New York: Palgrave.

Streatfield, D. (1981) 'Art and nature in the English landscape garden: design theory and practice, 1700–1818', in D. Streatfield and A. Duckworth, *Landscape in the Gardens and the Literature of Eighteenth-century England*, Los Angeles, CA: William Andrews Clark Memorial Library.

Suleri, S. (1992) *The Rhetoric of English India*, Chicago, IL: University of Chicago Press.

Sutherland, J. (1986) *The Restoration Newspaper and its Development*, Cambridge: Cambridge University Press.

Teltscher, K. (1997) *India Inscribed: European and English writing on India, 1600–1800*, Delhi: Oxford University Press.

Thacker, C. (1983) *The Wildness Pleases: the origins of romanticism*, London: Croom Helm.

Thirsk, J. (1985) 'Agricultural innovation and their diffusion', in J. Thirsk (ed.) *The Agrarian History of England and Wales, Vol. V, 1640–1750, ii: Agrarian Change*, Cambridge: Cambridge University Press.

Thomas, N. (1994) *Colonialism's Culture: anthropology, travel and government*, Princeton, NJ: Princeton University Press.

Thomson, P. (1972) *The Grotesque*, London: Methuen.

Thorne, S. (1999) *Congregational Missions and the Making of an Imperial Culture in Nineteenth-Century England*, Palo Alto, CA: Stanford University Press.

Tiffany, G. (1995) *Erotic Beasts and Social Monsters: Shakespeare, Jonson, and comic androgyny*, Newark, DE: University of Delaware Press.

Tobin, B.F. (2005) *Colonizing Nature: the tropics in British arts and letters, 1760–1820*, Philadelphia, PA: University of Pennsylvania Press.

Todorov, T. (1975) *The Fantastic: a structural approach to a literary genre*, trans. R. Howard, Ithaca, NY: Cornell University Press.

Todorov, T. (2000) 'The journey and its narratives', in C. Chard and H. Langdon (eds) *Transports: travel, pleasure and imaginative geography, 1600–1830*, New Haven, CT: Yale University Press.

Towner, J. (1996) *An Historical Geography of Recreation and Tourism in the Western World, 1540–1940*, Chichester, UK: John Wiley & Sons.

Trollope, J. (1983) *Britannia's Daughters: women of the British empire*, London: Hutchinson.

Vaughan, J. (1974) *The English Guide Book c 1780–1870*, Newton Abbot, UK: David & Charles.

Vickers, B. (1968) *Francis Bacon and Renaissance Prose*, Cambridge: Cambridge University Press.

Von Martels, Z. (ed.) (1994) *Travel Fact and Fiction: studies on fiction, literary tradition, scholarly discovery and observation in travel writing*, Leiden, Netherlands: E.J. Brill.

Warneke, S. (1995) *Images of the Educational Traveler in Early Modern England*, Leiden, Netherlands: E.J. Brill.

Warren, A. (1986) 'Citizens of empire: Baden-Powell, scouts and guides and an imperial ideal, 1900–1940', in J.M. Mackenzie (ed.) *Imperialism and Popular Culture*, Manchester, UK: Manchester University Press.

Watson, B. (1998) 'Fortifications and the "idea" of force in early English East India Company relations with India', in P. Tuck (ed.) *The East India Company: 1600–1858, Trade and Power, Vol. 4*, London: Routledge.

Watson, N. (2002) 'The monstrosity of the moral pig and other unnatural ruminations', in L.H. McAvoy and T. Walters (eds) *Consuming Narratives: gender and monstrous appetite in the Middle Ages and the Renaissance*, Cardiff: University of Wales Press.

Weiskel, T. (1986) *The Romantic Sublime: studies in the structure and psychology of transcendence* (1976), Baltimore, MD: Johns Hopkins University Press.

Whale, J. (1994) 'Sacred objects and the sublime ruins of art', in J. Whale and S. Copley (eds) *Beyond Romanticism: new approaches to texts and contexts 1780–1832*, New York: Routledge.

White, H. (1972) 'The forms of wildness: the archeology of an idea', in E. Dudley and M.E. Novak (eds) *The Wild Man Within: an image in Western thought from the Renaissance to Romanticism*, Pittsburgh, PA: University of Pittsburgh Press.

White, H. (1978) *Tropics of Discourse: essays in cultural criticism*, Baltimore, MD: Johns Hopkins University Press.

Williams, R. (1973) *The Country and the City*, New York: Oxford University Press.

Womack, P. (1989) *Improvement and Romance: constructing the myth of the Highlands*, London: Macmillan.

Wood, G.D. (2001) *The Shock of the Real: romanticism and visual culture, 1760–1860*, New York: Palgrave.

Youngquist, P. (2003) *Monstrosities: bodies and British romanticism*, Minneapolis, MN: University of Minnesota Press.

Youngs, T. (1994) *Travellers in Africa: British travelogues, 1850–1900*, Manchester, UK: Manchester University Press.

Index

Related titles from Routledge

Literary Radicalism in India
Gender, Nation and the Transition to Independence
Priyamvada Gopal

While most readers of contemporary Indian Literature in English and in translation are familiar with the idea of 'freedom at midnight', much less is known about the turbulent period of artistic and cultural transformation that characterised the years leading up to and following Independence in 1947. This study examines one of the most influential – and yet relatively unexamined – literary movements in the twentieth century on the Indian subcontinent. Focusing on writers who were affiliated to the Progressive Writers Association during India's transition from colony to nation, *Literary Radicalism in India* examines in detail some of the most important and controversial works of Indian literature.

Featuring historicised readings of the fiction, essays and films of such prominent figures as Rashid Jahan, Sajjad Zaheer, Ismat Chughtai, Saadat Hasan Manto and Khwaja Ahmad Abbas, the book examines the connections between aesthetics and politics in the context of nation-formation in India and Pakistan. It argues that gender, in this context, was not reducible to questions of 'representing women' but that it was a constitutive point of *contestation* in the struggle to define 'India'.

This thoroughly researched study is a must for all those interested in the impact of nationalism, feminism and social movements on literature, and provides a timely intervention into current debates about Marxism, nationalism and modernity.

ISBN13: 978-0-415-32904-0 (hbk)
ISBN10: 0-415-32904-3 (hbk)

Available at all good bookshops
For further information on our literature series, please visit
www.routledge.com/literature/series.asp
For ordering and further information please visit:
www.routledge.com

Related titles from Routledge

Postcolonial Studies:
a materialist critique
Benita Parry

'There are many signs that the style of postcolonial studies practised in the 1980s and 1990s is evolving towards more materialist, historically circumstanced sorts of inquiry – a kind of enquiry to which Benita Parry has consistently drawn our attention. This collection is certain to play a key role in the transformation of the field.' – *Timothy Brennan, University of Minnesota*

This volume presents a powerful selection of reprinted and new essays by one of the most important critics in postcolonial studies. This text offers an outline of the historical and personal contexts from which Parry's work has emerged, a series of essays that vigorously challenge colonial discourse theory and postcolonialism as we have known them and details a series of readings of well-known texts by authors including Kipling, Conrad, Wells and Forster.

Questioning the future of postcolonial theory, Parry concludes with the compelling argument that theoretical work must strive to join remembrance of the material past with a critique of the contemporary condition, remaining unreconciled to the past and unconsoled by the present. *Postcolonial Studies* offers an invaluable framework on which to build such a future.

ISBN10: 0-415-33599-X (hb)
ISBN10: 0-415-33600-7 (pb)

ISBN13: 978-0-415-33599-7 (hb)
ISBN13: 978-0-415-33600-0 (pb)

Available at all good bookshops
For ordering and further information please visit:
www.routledge.com

Related titles from Routledge

The Post-Colonial Studies Reader
Second edition
Edited by Bill Ashcroft, Gareth Griffiths
& Helen Tiffin

The Post-Colonial Studies Reader is the essential introduction to the most important texts in post-colonial theory and criticism. Updating and expanding the coverage of the highly successful first edition, this second edition now offers 121 extracts from key works in the field, arranged in clearly introduced sections on:

Issues and Debates, Universality and Difference, Representation and Resistance, Nationalism, Hybridity, Indigeneity, Ethnicity, Race, Feminism, Language, The Body and Performance, History, Place, Education, Production and Consumption, Diaspora, Globalization, Environment, The Sacred.

Leading figures in the areas of post-colonial writing, theory and criticism are represented, as are critics who are as yet less well known. As in the first edition, the Reader ranges as widely as possible in order to reflect the remarkable diversity of work in the discipline and the vibrancy of anti-imperialist writing both within and without the metropolitan centres. Covering more debates, topics and critics than any comparable book in its field, *The Postcolonial Studies Reader* provides the ideal starting point for students and issues a potent challenge to the ways in which we think and write about literature and culture.

ISBN10: 0-415-34564-2 (hb)
ISBN10: 0-415-34565-0 (pb)

ISBN13: 978-0-415-34564-4 (hb)
ISBN13: 978-0-415-34565-1 (pb)

Available at all good bookshops
For ordering and further information please visit:
www.routledge.com